An Anthology of African Cultural Studies, Vol. II

This volume focuses on the directions that African cultural studies has taken over the years and covers the following central themes: contemporary issues in African cultural studies; gender and the making of identity; the dual discourses of Afropessimism and Afrofuturism; problematizing the African diaspora and methodology and African cultural studies.

The second of two volumes, the book predominantly pulls together a rich reservoir of previously published articles from *Critical Arts: South-North Cultural and Media Studies*. Taken together the two volumes re-expose for international readers sets of theories, methodologies, and studies that not only have been influenced by global trends, but which themselves have contributed to shaping those trends. While the first volume addressed foundational themes and issues in African cultural studies, this second volume focuses on the directions that African cultural studies is taking; the complex ways in which gender can be seen at work in the making of identity; the juxtaposition of two relatively new themes in African cultural studies, namely Afropessimism and Afrofuturism; the ways in which the presence of continental Africans in the diaspora problematize taken-for-granted conceptions of diaspora and diasporic identity; identifying some of the methodological issues and approaches that have been taken up in African cultural studies work.

This book will be a key resource for academics, researchers, and advanced students of African cultural studies, media and cultural studies, African studies, history, politics, sociology, and social and cultural anthropology, while also being of interest to those interested in the making of global cultural studies and those seeking an introduction to the sub-field of African cultural studies.

Handel Kashope Wright is Senior Advisor to the President on Anti-racism and Inclusive Excellence, Director of the Centre for Culture, Identity and Education, and Professor of Education, University of British Columbia and Senior Research Associate, University of Johannesburg. He is also Associate Editor of *Critical Arts*.

Keyan G. Tomaselli is Distinguished Professor, Dean's Office, Faculty of Humanities, University of Johannesburg and Professor Emeritus and Fellow, University of KwaZulu-Natal. He is founder and now co-editor of *Critical Arts*.

An Anthology of African Cultural Studies, Vol. II

Directions

Edited by
**Handel Kashope Wright
and Keyan G. Tomaselli**

LONDON AND NEW YORK

First published 2025
by Routledge
4 Park Square, Milton Park, Abingdon, Oxon OX14 4RN

and by Routledge
605 Third Avenue, New York, NY 10158

Routledge is an imprint of the Taylor & Francis Group, an informa business

Chapters 1, 3, 5, 7–9, 13 © 2025 Critical Arts Projects & Unisa Press.
Chapters 6, 17 © 2025 Unisa Press.
Chapter 4 © 2025 JLS/TLW.
Chapter 2 © 2025 National Communication Association.
Chapters 10, 11, 19 © 2025 Taylor & Francis.
Chapters 12, 14, 15, 16, 18, 20 © 2025 Critical Arts.
Introduction © 2025 Handel Kashope Wright and Keyan G. Tomaselli.

All rights reserved. No part of this book may be reprinted or reproduced or utilised in any form or by any electronic, mechanical, or other means, now known or hereafter invented, including photocopying and recording, or in any information storage or retrieval system, without permission in writing from the publishers.

Trademark notice: Product or corporate names may be trademarks or registered trademarks, and are used only for identification and explanation without intent to infringe.

British Library Cataloguing in Publication Data
A catalogue record for this book is available from the British Library

ISBN13: 978-1-032-60197-7 (hbk)
ISBN13: 978-1-032-60198-4 (pbk)
ISBN13: 978-1-003-45803-6 (ebk)

DOI: 10.4324/9781003458036

Typeset in Myriad Pro
by Newgen Publishing UK

Publisher's Note
The publisher accepts responsibility for any inconsistencies that may have arisen during the conversion of this book from journal articles to book chapters, namely the inclusion of journal terminology.

Disclaimer
Every effort has been made to contact copyright holders for their permission to reprint material in this book. The publishers would be grateful to hear from any copyright holder who is not here acknowledged and will undertake to rectify any errors or omissions in future editions of this book.

Contents

Citation Information viii
Notes on Contributors xii

Directions: Introduction to *An Anthology of African Cultural Studies, Volume II* 1
Handel Kashope Wright and Keyan G. Tomaselli

PART I
African Cultural Studies: Directions

1 Contemporary Orientations in African Cultural Studies 11
   Jesse Arseneault, Sarah D'Adamo, Helene Strauss and Handel Kashope Wright

2 Cultural Studies and the African Global South 21
   Keyan G. Tomaselli

3 What Has African Cultural Studies Done for You Lately? Autobiographical and Global Considerations of a Floating Signifier 32
   Handel Kashope Wright

PART II
Putting African Gender to Work

4 (West) African Feminisms and Their Challenges 47
   Naomi Nkealah

5 The Female Body in Audiovisual Political Propaganda Jingles: The Mbare Chimurenga Choir in Zimbabwe's Contested Political Terrain 58
   Hazel Tafadzwa Ngoshi and Anias Mutekwa

6 Stylin': The Great Masculine Enunciation and the (Re)Fashioning of African Diasporic Identities 69
   Christine Checinska

PART III
Afropessimism/Afrofuturism

7 Afropessimism: A Genealogy of Discourse 87
   Boulou Ebanda de B'béri and P. Eric Louw

8 The Roots of Afropessimism: The British Invention of the 'Dark Continent' 96
   Noah R. Bassil

9 Rainbow Worriers: South African Afropessimism Online 112
   Martha Evans

10 'Did He Freeze?': Afrofuturism, Africana Womanism, and Black Panther's Portrayal of the Women of Wakanda 132
   Tiffany Thames Copeland

11 Fashioning Africanfuturism: African Comics, Afrofuturism, and Nnedi Okorafor's *Shuri* 150
   James Hodapp

PART IV
Troubling the African Diaspora

12 Random Thoughts Provoked by the Conference "Identities, Democracy, Culture and Communication in Southern Africa" 167
   Stuart Hall

13 Marcus Garvey: The Remapping of Africa and Its Diaspora 179
   Rupert Lewis

14 Whose Diaspora Is This Anyway? Continental Africans Trying on and Troubling Diasporic Identity 188
   Handel Kashope Wright

15 Marking the Unmarked: Hip-Hop, the Gaze & the African Body in North America 200
   Awad Ibrahim

16 Constructing Consciousness: Diasporic Remembrances and Imagining Africa in Late Modernity 215
   Jacinta K. Muteshi

PART V
Methodology and African Cultural Studies

17 Cultural Studies as 'Psycho-babble' 229
   Keyan G. Tomaselli

18 South Africa in the Global Neighbourhood: Towards a Method
   of Cultural Analysis 251
   Michael Chapman

19 Cultural Studies as Praxis: (Making) an Autobiographical Case 259
   Handel Kashope Wright

20 Navigating the African Archive – A Conversation between Tamar Garb
   and Hlonipha Mokoena 274
   Tamar Garb and Hlonipha Mokoena

   Index 284

Citation Information

The chapters in this book were originally published in various volumes and issues of *Critical Arts: South-North Cultural and Media Studies*, except Chapter 4, which was published in *Review of Education, Pedagogy, and Cultural Studies*, volume 17, issue 2 (1995). When citing this material, please use the original page numbering for each article, as follows:

Chapter 1
Contemporary orientations in African Cultural Studies
Jesse Arseneault, Sarah D'Adamo, Helene Strauss and Handel Kashope Wright
Critical Arts: South-North Cultural and Media Studies, volume 30, issue 4 (2016), pp. 465–477

Chapter 2
Cultural studies and the African Global South
Keyan G. Tomaselli
Communication and Critical/Cultural Studies, volume 16, issue 3 (2019), pp. 257–267

Chapter 3
What has African Cultural Studies done for you lately? Autobiographical and global considerations of a floating signifier
Handel Kashope Wright
Critical Arts: South-North Cultural and Media Studies, volume 30, issue 4 (2016), pp. 478–494

Chapter 4
(West) African Feminisms and Their Challenges
Naomi Nkealah
Journal of Literary Studies, volume 32, issue 2 (2016), pp. 61–74

Chapter 5
The female body and voice in audiovisual political propaganda jingles: the Mbare Chimurenga Choir women in Zimbabwe's contested political terrain
Hazel Tafadzwa Ngoshi and Anias Mutekwa
Critical Arts: South-North Cultural and Media Studies, volume 27, issue 2 (2013), pp. 235–248

Chapter 6
Stylin': The great masculine enunciation and the (re)fashioning of African diasporic identities
Christine Checinska
Critical Arts: South-North Cultural and Media Studies, volume 31, issue 3 (2017), pp. 53–71

Chapter 7
Afropessimism: a genealogy of discourse
Boulou Ebanda de B'béri and P. Eric Louw
Critical Arts: South-North Cultural and Media Studies, volume 25, issue 3 (2011), pp. 335–346

Chapter 8
The roots of Afropessimism: the British invention of the 'dark continent'
Noah R. Bassil
Critical Arts: South-North Cultural and Media Studies, volume 25, issue 3 (2011), pp. 377–396

Chapter 9
Rainbow worriers: South African Afropessimism online
Martha Evans
Critical Arts: South-North Cultural and Media Studies, volume 25, issue 3 (2011), pp. 397–422

Chapter 10
'Did He Freeze?': Afrofuturism, Africana Womanism, and Black Panther's Portrayal of the Women of Wakanda
Tiffany Thames Copeland
African Identities, volume 22, issue 1 (2024), pp. 147–165

Chapter 11
Fashioning Africanfuturism: African comics, Afrofuturism, and Nnedi Okorafor's Shuri
James Hodapp
Journal of Graphic Novels and Comics, volume 13, issue 4 (2022), pp. 606–619

Chapter 12
Random Thoughts Provoked by the Conference "Identities, Democracy, Culture and Communication in Southern Africa"
Stuart Hall
Critical Arts: South-North Cultural and Media Studies, volume 11, issue 1–2 (1997), pp. 1–16

Chapter 13
Marcus Garvey: the remapping of Africa and its diaspora
Rupert Lewis
Critical Arts: South-North Cultural and Media Studies, volume 25, issue 4 (2011), pp. 473–483

Chapter 14
Whose Diaspora is This Anyway? Continental Africans Trying On and Troubling Diasporic Identity
Handel Kashope Wright
Critical Arts: South-North Cultural and Media Studies, volume 17, issue 1–2 (2003), pp. 1–16

Chapter 15
Marking the Unmarked: Hip-Hop, the Gaze & the African Body in North America
Awad Ibrahim
Critical Arts: South-North Cultural and Media Studies, volume 17, issue 1–2 (2003), pp. 52–70

Chapter 16
Constructing consciousness: Diasporic remembrances and imagining Africa in late modernity
Jacinta K. Muteshi
Critical Arts: South-North Cultural and Media Studies, volume 17, issue 1–2 (2003), pp. 36–51

Chapter 17
Cultural Studies as 'Psycho-babble'. Post-LitCrit, methodology and dynamic justice
Keyan G Tomaselli
Communicatio, volume 27, issue 1 (2001), pp. 44–57

Chapter 18
South Africa in the Global Neighbourhood: Towards a Method of Cultural Analysis
Michael Chapman
Critical Arts: South-North Cultural and Media Studies, volume 11, issue 1–2 (1997), pp. 17–27

Chapter 19
Cultural studies as praxis: (making) an autobiographical case
Handel Kashope Wright
Cultural Studies, volume 17, issue 6 (2003), pp. 805–822

Chapter 20
Navigating the African archive – A conversation between Tamar Garb and Hlonipha Mokoena
Tamar Garb and Hlonipha Mokoena
Critical Arts: South-North Cultural and Media Studies, volume 33, issue 6 (2019), pp. 40–51

For any permission-related enquiries please visit:
www.tandfonline.com/page/help/permissions

Notes on Contributors

Sarah D'Adamo, Baltimore Green Space, Baltimore, MD, USA.

Jesse Arseneault, Department of English, Concordia University, Montreal, Quebec, Canada.

Noah R. Bassil, Macquarie School of Social Sciences, Macquarie University, Sydney, Australia.

Michael Chapman, University of KwaZulu-Natal, Berea, Durban, South Africa.

Christine Checinska, Visual Identities in Art and Design Research Centre, University of Johannesburg, Johannesburg, South Africa; Curator of African and African Diaspora Fashion, Victoria and Albert Museum, London, UK.

Tiffany Thames Copeland, Montgomery College, Rockville, MD, USA.

Boulou Ebanda de B'béri, University of Ottawa, Ottawa, Canada.

Martha Evans, Centre for Film and Media Studies, University of Cape Town, Cape Town, Western Cape, South Africa.

Tamar Garb, Durning Lawrence Professor of History of Art, and Director, Institute of Advanced Studies, University College, London, London, UK.

Stuart Hall, Sociology Department, Open University, UK.

James Hodapp, Liberal Arts Program, Northwestern University in Qatar, Ar-Rayyan, Qatar.

Awad Ibrahim, Faculty of Education, University of Ottawa, Ottawa, Canada.

Rupert Lewis, Department of Government, University of the West Indies, Mona, Jamaica.

P. Eric Louw, School of Communication and Arts, The University of Queensland, Queensland, Australia.

Hlonipha Mokoena, Wits Institute for Social & Economic Research, University of the Witwatersrand, Johannesburg, South Africa.

Anias Mutekwa, Midlands State University, Gweru, Midlands Province, Zimbabwe.

Jacinta K. Muteshi, The Girl Generation, Nairobi, Kenya.

Hazel Tafadzwa Ngoshi, Midlands State University, Gweru, Midlands Province, Zimbabwe.

Naomi Nkealah, University of the Witwatersrand, Johannesburg, South Africa.

Helene Strauss, Department of English, University of the Free State, South Africa.

Keyan G. Tomaselli, Faculty of Humanities, University of Johannesburg, South Africa; University of KwaZulu-Natal, Berea, Durban, South Africa.

Handel Kashope Wright, Centre for Culture, Identity and Education, University of British Columbia, Vancouver, Canada; University of Johannesburg, Johannesburg, South Africa.

Directions: Introduction to *An Anthology of African Cultural Studies, Volume II*

Handel Kashope Wright and Keyan G. Tomaselli

This collection, *An Anthology of African Cultural Studies*, is composed of two interrelated volumes which together provide one example of the articulation (in both senses) of African cultural studies and some of its principal themes. The essays in both volumes are drawn principally from *Critical Arts*, one of the earliest established journals of cultural studies on the African continent.

The first volume of this anthology, titled Groundings, addresses the inception of *Critical Arts* at the University of the Witwatersrand in 1980, where its founder, Keyan Tomaselli, was then employed. As it is put in Groundings, the "early issue publications of *Critical Arts* (1980–1985) were of a cottage industry IBM golf ball-typed A5 format." Groundings provides a narrative of the contributions *Critical Arts* has made to the articulation of African cultural studies and hence something of an argument for its appropriateness as principal source of essays included in the two volumes of the anthology. Whilst the early focus of the journal was on cultural studies and media studies in Africa, with a strong emphasis on South Africa, *Critical Arts* evolved and after 2005 pursued a much more global scope (Tomaselli and Shepperson, 2000). In that sense, *Critical Arts* is something of a parallel to other long-established journals such as *Cultural Studies* and *Continuum* and more recently established ones such as the *International Journal of Cultural Studies*. However, *Critical Arts* has maintained an emphasis on publishing work on African cultural studies and in that sense is more closely akin to the albeit more recently established *European Journal of Cultural Studies* which started off in 1998 with a focus on Europe, but which has extended its scope globally while maintaining an emphasis on publishing work on European cultural studies.

Critical Arts is a particularly apt source to draw upon since it offers the longest, most consistent and comprehensive set of essays on, and articulation of, African cultural studies. Other cultural studies journals have published on African cultural studies but this has tended to be isolated essays, with few exceptions such as the special issue of *Cultural Studies* on "cultural studies in Africa / African cultural studies" (Tomaselli and Wright, 2008). A second choice might have been the *Journal of African Cultural Studies*, which as its name implies, has African cultural studies as its primary focus. However, this publication was established in 1988 as *African Languages and Culture*, a journal that dealt with African cultures in a loose sense; it only focused on what might be considered cultural studies proper when it was renamed the *Journal of African Cultural Studies* in 1998. A third choice could have been the *Journal of Cultural Studies*, established by the Nigerian Group for the Study of African Cultures in 1999. However, even though it generated some 16 numbers, it ceased publishing in 2010 and its strong corpus is limited to about a decade.

The first volume of this anthology, titled Groundings, laid out the dual instrumentalist and ideological framework of the anthology and identified the following themes as foundational: the case made for African cultural studies; the relationship between continental and diasporic Africa and Africans; the identification and salience of the primary sociocultural identity categories of race, social class and gender; and the relationship between media studies and cultural studies in the African context.

This second volume, titled Directions, operates as a continuation of the first in the sense that it draws on and extends some of the themes addressed in Volume I. However, this second volume also serves to introduce additional themes and, in that sense, stands on its own. Directions, therefore, operates in a dual sense – both as indication of where some foundational themes can be said to be traveling from those foundations of the Groundings volume and also what additional themes can be said to have emerged as significant in African cultural studies. The two volumes are very much interrelated as indicated by the fact that the opening essay in the Groundings volume (Wright and Xiao, 2020) provides an overview of African cultural studies that is inclusive of the themes covered in both volumes of the anthology.

Briefly, the essays in Directions have been organized in five sections representing the following central themes: an overview of contemporary issues or, if you will, some indication of the new directions in African cultural studies; putting African gender to work; the dual discourses of Afropessimism and Afrofuturism; troubling the African diaspora and methodology and African cultural studies.

The first section is titled **African Cultural Studies: Directions** (a title that is reflective of the entire volume). After the Introduction, the first volume, Groundings, opens with an essay that provides an overview of African cultural studies. This second volume, Directions, opens similarly, such that the reader is provided with an overview, whether they read one or the other volume, or both. The volumes differ in the sense that in its first section Groundings goes on to address what constitutes African cultural studies, drawing a distinction between African cultural studies and cultural studies in Africa, etc. In the present volume the entire first section is given over to overviews, providing for what is hopefully a detailed, nuanced and multiple perspective account. More specifically, the essays address the orientation and major themes of African cultural studies, with an emphasis on the most recent of these; an examination of the presence and work of cultural studies in Africa considered as part of the Global South and a reconsideration of African cultural studies as a floating signifier and its utility both to the study of Africa and Africans and contribution to the globalization of cultural studies.

The first volume takes up race, class and gender as broad foundational social identity categories addressed in African cultural studies and does so with some nuance (e.g., taking up albino identity, whiteness as "white tribe" of Africa, social class and its imbrication with race). In this second volume, Directions, the focus is on one identity category, namely gender, which is taken up in terms of its complexities and utility in African cultural studies; in short, the second section is about **Putting African Gender to Work**. The field of African gender studies has tended to focus on women and feminism and faces considerable difficulty challenging the taken-for-grantedness of western, colonial-derived male/female gender binary and heteronormativity. Work which troubles such inherited but ingrained notions are particularly important, including identifying ongoing traditional and contemporary identities and relationships (e.g., Ifi Amadiume's (1987) *Male Daughters, Female Husbands* and

Stephen Murray and Will Roscoe's (2021) discussion of *Boy-Wives and Female Husbands*). In this section masculinity is addressed in terms of the specific function of "stylin'" in shaping contemporary African diasporic identities. The female body is considered in terms of its utility in the specific project of audiovisual political propaganda jingles. Issues of gender equity and women's empowerment are perennial concerns of African cultural studies and far from being taken for granted, feminism has been variously multiplied, eschewed, rearticulated with African approaches (Ebunoluwa, 2009), and replaced with more Africentric conceptions such as Molara Ogundipe-Leslie's (1994) STIWANISM (i.e. Social Transformation Including Women of Africa), Catherine Acholonlu's (1995) motherism and Mary Kolawole's (1997) and Chikwenye Ogunyemi's (1985) African womanism. The section reflects those politics and positions in a consideration of the specificities of West African "feminisms" and their challenges.

The third section of Directions addresses two contrasting and competing theoretical frameworks for understanding Africans' philosophical outlook on Blackness, namely **Afropessimism/Afrofuturism**. The term "afro-pessimism" (lower case "a") has been used since the 1980s as a concept to describe Africa as a continent plagued by wars, failed states, and sustained underdevelopment, with little prospect for positive political and economic change (Kaplan, 1994). Some have defended the term as an accurate description of Africa's status quo (Rieff, 1998/1999), while others, afro-optimists, have resisted the discourse or identified it with Africa's past rather than its present, let alone its future (e.g. Gordon and Wolpe, 1998; Onwudiwe and Ibelema, 2003). Afropessimism (capital "A") was articulated by Frank Wilderson (2020) as another notion; a conception of Blacks, not only in the United States but around the world, as particularly subjected to racism such that they are perennially enslaved, their very humanity questioned globally; anti-blackness as necessary for others to thrive and be fully human. Although the two discourses have mostly operated differently and separately, there has been important work that has brought the two together (Mbembe, 2019; Okoth, 2020), addressing the need to see a complex relationship between continental and diasporic Blackness, (re)introducing the absented role of colonialism and neo-colonialism in Africa's underdevelopment and instability (Rodney, 1973/2018; Nkrumah, 1965; Langan, 2018) as well as the racism that undergirds both A/afropessimisms. With roots in earlier work like Mark Dery's (1994) "Black to the Future," Afrofuturuism is a theory-turned-movement incorporating technology and science fiction in artistic work that envisions and portrays a liberated, empowered Black future. Although it sometimes depicts continental Africa and Africans, it is a diasporic movement that some continental African creatives have embraced (Frearson, 2018). However, some African scholars and artists have resisted having their work readily incorporated into what they identify as the decidedly diasporic discourse of Afrofuturism that is by and positions African-America(ns) as central. Some, like Mohale Mashigo (2018) have rejected Afrofuturism outright as not being relevant to nor appropriate for Africans living in Africa. Alternatively, Nnedi Okorafor (2018) has proposed the related but continental Africa grounded and visioned concept, Africanfuturism, which has been taken up by others (Talabi, 2020; Kiunguyu, 2022). The essays in this section address Afropessimism from an African perspective and cover a genealogy of the concept, its roots in the context of the continent and how it plays out online as a specific contemporary example. The juxtaposing of two discourses, Afropessimism/ Afrofuturism (Africanfuturism), one a fatalist discourse based on post-independence negativity and the afterlife of slavery and the other based on optimistic, futuristic vision and the tension between them, invites a nuanced consideration of Black existence/flourishing, both on the continent and in Africa's diasporas.

The issues of what constitutes the African diaspora and interrelatedly diasporic African cultural studies are both complex and central and are therefore covered in both volumes of this anthology. The ethnoracial diversity of continental Africa has been taken up in the anthology but Blackness and Black Africa are dominant. To help mitigate the complexity of attempting to take up the ethnoracial diversity of both Africa and its diasporas, the conception of continental and diasporic Africans covered in the volume has been restricted to what St. Clair Drake (1986/2014) has referred to as *Black Folk Here and There*. There is a multiplicity of discursive conceptions of the Black Africa and diaspora relationship including African cultural continuity (Clarke, 1976; Shujaa and Shujaa, 2015) and Afrocentrism (Asante, 1988, 1989; Dei, 1994, 1995) which see the diaspora as a cultural extension of Africa to Pan-Africanism (James, 1938; Nkrumah, 1963; Adi, 2003) which forges the links between the two, the Black Atlantic which maps the movements that produced the (intellectual, Atlantic related) diaspora (Gilroy, 1993) to Fanonian thought which sees similarities and links between them but cautions against homogenization (Fanon, 1967). Groundings addresses the need to conceptualize the diaspora in terms of its multiplicity and diversity, Rastafari and Pan-Africanism as examples of conceptual frames of the diaspora and the ideological options and conceptual positions open to the African intellectual, newly arrived in the diaspora when it comes to addressing issues related to Africa. In the fourth section of this volume the diaspora is taken up again, this time with a turn to **Troubling the African Diaspora**. The essays cover such themes as the utility of Garveyism as a means of reconceptualizing both Africa and its diasporas; the discomfiting (self)positioning of the migrant academic as never quite diasporic and no longer quite continental; hip-hop culture and its utility in migrant youth from Africa trying on diasporic Blackness as default identity; continental Africans' ambivalence about diasporic subjects appropriating Africa and African identity and diasporic theorists' caution about diasporic subjects homogenizing, romanticizing and claiming belonging to continental Africa.

The fifth and final section of Directions considers issues of methodology and African cultural studies. Stuart Hall (1992) made clear that early cultural studies at the Centre for Contemporary Cultural Studies (CCCS) was characterized by wide ranging theoretical and methodological foundations and as it has continued as an interdisciplinary, indeed postdisciplinary field concerned with a wide range of issues and projects, cultural studies has remained open methodologically. Although open in terms of empirical research to quantitative, qualitative and mixed-methods approaches, most cultural studies scholars likely fall within feminist, critical and/or poststructuralist research paradigms (Denzin and Lincoln, 2000). It is an indication of the disciplining of cultural studies that despite its methodological openness, there are now textbooks on cultural studies methodology (McGuigan, 1998; Saukko, 2003; Pickering, 2008). Also, it is worth noting that the journal *Cultural Studies ↔ Critical Methodologies* has emerged as a particularly generative site for producing and sharing innovations in critical methodology in general and especially in relation to the interdisciplinary field of cultural studies. Some Afrocentrics have developed African-centred methodology (characterized by being relational, participatory, collaborative, decolonial, holistic, humane) based on Afrikology (e.g., Reviere, 2001; Bangura, 2011; Chilisa, 2019; Royster, 2020). The essays in this section address the importance of and what is involved in navigating the African archive; how the autobiographical (and autoethnographic) can be utilized in articulating cultural studies as praxis; the development of a form of analysis that enables the situation of a national form of cultural studies in the global frame; and a critique of the cultural studies turn to post-litcrit as methodology in South Africa.

It might be useful to conclude not just this text but the two volume *Anthology of African Cultural Studies* by taking up African cultural studies in the context and in terms of its explicit and incidental contributions to cultural studies' global and historical evolution. Cultural studies is notoriously self-reflexive for a number of reasons, from its relative newness and contestations over its origin to the complexity of its relationship with disciplinarity (During, 2006), from reflections on its need to be utilitarian to its ambivalence about its own evolution in national terms to the arcs of its future(s). Although not usually acknowledged, African cultural studies has explicitly or implicitly contributed to these debates. For example, Handel Kashope Wright's (1998) proposal of a praxis-based, Ngugi wa Thiong'o-led (1986), Kenyan origin has challenged and hopefully mitigated the irony of a singular Eurocentric, hegemonic origin story of British founding fathers and English initial naming and institutionalization of cultural studies. From its early, heady radical days of being not merely multidisciplinary and interdisciplinary but indeed anti-disciplinary, cultural studies has mellowed and has been disciplined: initially and with ambivalence in some quarters, becoming what Tony Bennett (1998) has identified as a "reluctant discipline," or what Paul McEwan (2002) calls a "hidden discipline" and now, though some would still resist the designation, simply another discipline. It is quite the statement of the taken-for-grantedness of Africa's marginalization in the world of knowledge production that Valentin Mudimbe has had to contribute to making the explicit case that Africa and Africans have made substantial contributions to the social sciences and humanities (Bates, Mudimbe, and O'Barr, 1993). On the other hand, Mudimbe has been at the forefront of asserting ambivalence about western disciplinarity as the way of organizing knowledge in general and has critiqued anthropology in particular as a discipline that is irredeemable as a field explicitly designed to study non-western cultures as exotic "other" (Mudimbe, 1988), work which opens the way for cultural studies as the postdisciplinary study of Africa and Africans.

Richard Johnson's (1986–1987) early, crucial question, "What is cultural studies anyway?" threatened to become perennial, even as other important questions have emerged such as "why is cultural studies important?" "where is cultural studies?" (answered for example in Meaghan Morris' contributions variously to Australian cultural studies, Hong Kong cultural studies and transnational cultural studies (Frow and Morris, 1993; Morris, 2017; Wright and Morris, 2012); "how does one do cultural studies?" (e.g., Angela McRobbie (2005) asks and provides some concrete answers to both of these questions in *The Uses of Cultural Studies*) and "what does cultural studies do" (a question about the utilitarian nature of cultural studies that Meaghan Morris (1997) poses). African cultural studies has addressed similar and related questions from "what is African cultural studies and how might it be different from cultural studies in Africa?" (a distinction strongly made by Ntongela Masilela, 1988) to "what does it mean to do African cultural studies" (to which Keyan Tomaselli and Nyasha Mboti (2023) provide one answer). Some have wondered aloud, "should we be doing cultural studies in Africa (e.g. Falkof, 2023)?" and others have asked "where is African cultural studies?" a question answered not only in terms of South Africa being an initial (and still dominant) location (Tomaselli, 1988) but by teasing out African cultural studies' not so obvious locations such as its representation in Arab cultural studies (Hamam, 2012). Questions from "what is and what ought to be the place of African cultural studies in global cultural studies" to "what is the relationship between cultural studies and communication studies in Africa or indeed, should there be a relationship between the two? (e.g., Tomaselli, 2012)," are questions answered differently by a journal like the South African journal, *Communicare* which takes up communication studies as a distinct scientific discipline on the one hand (Tomaselli, 2018) and the social theory-based *Critical Arts* on the other, which is subtitled "South-North Media and Cultural Studies" and hence has always juxtaposed and sometimes imbricated media and communication studies and cultural studies.

The two volumes of *An Anthology of African Cultural Studies* invite a consideration of African cultural studies as an object and ongoing project on its own, as well as an albeit not well acknowledged contribution to global cultural studies.

References

Acholonlu, C. O. 1995. *Motherism: An Afro-centric Alternative to Feminism*. Oweri: Afa Publications.
Adi, H. 2003. *Pan-African History: Political Figures from Africa and the Diaspora since 1787*. New York: Routledge.
Amadiume, I. 1987. *Male Daughters, Female Husbands: Gender and Sex in African Society*. London: Zed Books.
Asante, M. K. 1988. *Afrocentricity*. Africa Research and Publications.
Asante, M. K. 1989. *The Afrocentric Idea*. Philadelphia: Temple University Press.
Bangura, A. K. 2011. *African-centred Research Methodologies: From Ancient Times to the Present*. San Diego, CA: Cognella.
Bates, R. H., Mudimbe, V. Y. and O'Barr, J. (Eds.). 1993. *Africa and the Disciplines: The Contributions of Research in Africa to the Social Sciences and Humanities*. Oxford: Blackwell Publishing.
Bennett, T. 1998. "Cultural Studies: A Reluctant Discipline." *Cultural Studies* 12 (4), 528–545.
Clarke, J. H. 1976. "African Cultural Continuity and Slave Revolts in the New World." *The BlackScholar* 8 (1), 41–49.
Chilisa, B. 2019. *Indigenous Research Methodologies*. London: Sage.
Dei, G. 1994. "Afrocentricity: A Cornerstone of Pedagogy." *Anthropology & Education Quarterly* 25 (1), 3–28.
Dei, G. 1995. "African studies in Canada: Problems and Challenges." *Journal of Black Studies* 26(2), 153–171.
Denzin, N. K. and Lincoln, Y. S. (Eds.). 2000. *Handbook of Qualitative Research*. Thousand Oaks, CA: SAGE.
Dery, M. 1994. "Black to the Future: Interviews with Samuel R. Delany, Greg Tate, and Tricia Rose". In *Flame Wars: The Discourse of Cyberculture*, 179–222, edited by M. Dery. Durham, NC: Duke University Press.
Drake, St. Clair. 2014. *Black Folk Here and There*. New York: Diasporic Africa Press.
During, S. 2006. "Is Cultural Studies a Discipline?: And Does It Make Any Political Difference? *Cultural Politics* 2 (3), 265–280.
Ebunoluwa, S. M. 2009. "Feminism: The Quest for an African Variant. *Journal of Pan-African Studies* 3 (1), 227–134.
Falkof, N. 2023. "Cultural Studies in South Africa, or Not." *International Journal of Cultural Studies* 26 (1), 16–21.
Fanon, F. 1967. *Black Skin, White Masks: The Experiences of a Black Man in a White World*. New York: Grove Press.
Frearson, A. 2018. "Afrofuturism is 'creating a different narrative for Africa' say creatives." *dezeen*. www.dezeen.com/2018/04/06/afrofuturism-different-narrative-architecture-design-fashion-africa/
Frow, J. and Morris, M. (Eds.). 1993. *Australian Cultural Studies: A Reader*. St. Leonards, NSW: Allen and Unwin.
Gilroy, P. 1993. *The Black Atlantic: Modernity and Double Consciousness*. New York: Verso Press.
Gordon, D. and Wolpe, H. 1998. "The Other Africa: An End of Afro-pessimism." *World Policy Journal* 15 (1), 49–59.

Hall, S. 1992. "Cultural Studies and its Theoretical Legacies." In *Cultural Studies*, 277–286, edited by L. Grossberg, C. Nelson and P. Treichler. New York: Routledge.
Hamam, I. 2012. "Disarticulating Arab Popular Culture: The Case of Egyptian Comedies." In *Arab Cultural Studies: Mapping the Field*, 186–213, edited by T. Sabry. London: Bloomsbury Publishing.
James, C. L. R. 1938. *A History of Pan-African Revolt*. Washington, DC: Drum and Spear Press.
Johnson, R. 1986–1987. "What is Cultural Studies Anyway?" *Social Text* 16, 33–80.
Kaplan, R. Feb., 1994. "The Coming Anarchy." *Atlantic Monthly* 273 (2), 44–76.
Kiunguyu, K. 2022. "Afrofuturism or Africanfuturism: Is the difference important?" *This is Africa* https://thisisafrica.me/arts-and-culture/afrofuturism-or-africanfuturism-is-the-difference-important/
Kolawole, M. 1997. *Womanism and African Consciousness*. Trenton, NJ: Africa World Press.
Langan, M. 2018. *Neo-colonialism and the Poverty of 'Development' in Africa*. Cham, Switzerland: Palgrave Macmillan.
Mashigo, M. 2018. *Intruders: Short Stories*. Johannesburg: Picador Africa.
Masilela, N. 1988. Preface: "Establishing an Intellectual Bridgehead." In *Rethinking Culture*, 1–4, edited by K .G Tomaselli. Bellville. Anthropos Publishers.
Mbembe, A. 2019. *Necro-politics*. Durham, NC: Duke University Press.
McEwan, P. 2002." Cultural Studies as a Hidden Discipline." *International Journal of Cultural Studies* 5 (4), 427–437.
McGuigan, J. (Ed.). 1998. *Cultural Methodologies*. London: Sage.
McRobbie, A. 2005. *The Uses of Cultural Studies: A Textbook*. London: Sage.
Morris, M. 1997. "A Question of Cultural Studies". In *Back to Reality? Social Experience and Cultural Studies*, 36–57, edited by A. McRobbie. Manchester: Manchester University Press.
Morris, M. 2017. "Hong Kong Liminal: Situation as Method." In *Hong Kong Culture and Society in the New Millennium: Hong Kong as Method*, 3–32, edited by Yiu-Wai Chu. Singapore: Springer.
Mudimbe, V. Y. 1988. *The Invention of Africa: Gnosis, Philosophy and the Order of Knowledge*. Bloomington: Indiana University Press.
Murray, S. and Roscoe, W. 2021. *Boy-wives and Female Husbands: Studies in African Homosexualities*. Albany: SUNY Press.
Ngugi, w. T. 1986. *Decolonising the Mind: The Politics of Language in African Literature.* Nairobi: East African Educational Publishers.
Nkrumah, K. 1963. *Africa Must Unite*. New York: Frederick Praeger.
Nkrumah, K. 1965. *Neo-colonialism: The Last Stage of Imperialism*. London: Thomas Nelson & Sons.
Ogundipe-Leslie, M. 1994. *Recreating Ourselves*. Trenton: Africa World Press.
Ogunyemi, C. O. 1985. "Womanism: The Dynamics of the Contemporary Black Female Novel in English." *Signs* 11 (1), 63–80.
Okorafor, N. Oct. 19, 2018. "Africanfuturism defined." In *Nnedi's Wahala Zone Blog: The Adventures of writer Nnedi Okorafor and her daughter Anyau*. nnedi.blogspot.com
Okoth, K. O. 2020. "The flatness of Blackness: Afro-pessimism and the erasure of anti-colonial thought." *Salvage #7: Towards the Proletarocence*. https://salvage.zone/the-flatness-of-blackness-afro-pessimism-and-the-erasure-of-anti-colonial-thought/
Onwudiwe, E. and Ibelema, M. (Eds.). 2006. *Afro-optimism: Perspectives on Africa's Advances*. New York: Cambridge University Press.
Pickering, M. 2008. *Research Methods for Cultural Studies*. Edinburgh: Edinburgh University Press.
Reviere, R. 2001. "Toward an Afrocentric Research Methodology." *Journal of Black Studies* 31 (6), 709–727.
Rieff, D. 1998/1999. "In Defense of Afro-pessimism." *World Policy Journal* 15 (4), 10–22.
Rodney, W. 1973/2018. *How Europe Underdeveloped Africa*. London: Verso Press.
Royster, P. 2020. *Decolonizing Arts-based Methodologies: Researching the African Diaspora*. Boston, MA: Brill.
Saukko, P. 2003. *Doing Cultural Studies: An Introduction to Classical and New Methodological Approaches*. London: Sage.
Shujaa, M. and Shujaa, K. (Eds.). 2015. *The SAGE Encyclopedia of African Cultural Heritage in North America*. London: Sage.

Talabi, W. (Ed.). 2020. *Africanfuturism: An Anthology*. Brittle Paper. https://brittlepaper.com/wp-content/uploads/2020/10/Africanfuturism-An-Anthology-edited-by-Wole-Talabi.pdf

Tomaselli, K. G. (Ed.) 1988. *Rethinking Culture*. Anthropos Publishers.

Tomaselli, K. G. 2012. "Alter-egos: Cultural and Media Studies." *Critical Arts* 26 (1), 14–38.

Tomaselli, K. G. 2018. "A Self-reflexive Analysis of *Communicare*." *Communicare: Journal for Communication Sciences in Africa* 27(2), 17–30.

Tomaselli, K. G. and Mboti, N. 2013. Doing Cultural Studies: What Is Literacy in the Age of the Post? *International Journal of Cultural Studies* 16 (5), 521–537.

Tomaselli, K. G. and Wright, H. K. 2008. "Editorial Statement: African Cultural Studies." *Cultural Studies* 22(2), 173–186.

Tomaselli, K. G. and Shepperson, A. 2000. "South African Cultural Studies: A Journal's Journey from Apartheid to the Worlds of the Post". *Cultural Studies: A Research Annual*, 5, 3–23.

Wilderson, F. 2020. *Afropessimism*. New York: Liveright Publishing.

Wright, H. K. 1998. "Dare We De-Centre Birmingham? Troubling the Origin and Trajectories of Cultural Studies." *European Journal of Cultural Studies* 1(1), 33–56.

Wright, H. K. and Morris, M. (Eds.). 2012. *Transnationalism and Cultural Studies*. London & New York: Routledge

Wright, H. K. and Xiao, Y. 2020. "African Cultural Studies: An Overview." *Critical Arts* 34 (4), 1–31.

Part I
African Cultural Studies: Directions

Contemporary Orientations in African Cultural Studies

Jesse Arseneault, Sarah D'Adamo, Helene Strauss
and Handel Kashope Wright

ABSTRACT

This paper offers a glimpse of work generated by the 2014 John Douglas Taylor conference on 'Contemporary Orientations in African Cultural Studies'. The conference generated a number of inquiries into the time and place of contemporary African cultural work, many of which theorised beyond the frameworks that postcolonial and globalisation studies frequently offer. Within the shifting paradigms of Cultural Studies, the work of this conference (as well as the current project) moves away from reading the African everyday as exclusively a construction out of a series of colonial histories and relationalities, or global cultural flows. In line with Jean and John Comaroff's Theory from the South (2011), this issue is instead dedicated to relocating the global centres from which Cultural Studies emanates and to positing African work's challenge to normative zones of cultural critique. 'Contemporary orientations' attempts to relocate the time and space of critique in African studies, but it resists the gesture to posit a stable trajectory through which time moves. Rather, the terms of the contemporary and the orientation depend on how they are read in relation to a multitude of other temporalities, orientations, and objects.

Snapshots

That this issue of *Critical Arts* is one of many conversations on African Cultural Studies currently underway both on and beyond the African continent speaks to the robustness of a field that has gained increasing prominence in recent years. That the mapping and documenting of its critical genealogies is not our primary concern in this introduction is a testament to this reality. Handel Kashope Wright's essay in this issue traces some of those historical lineages, paying attention in particular to how the origin-stories of the global field of Cultural Studies might be rerouted and multiplied. While Wright's work is positioned explicitly as an engagement with the definitional questions that have animated the post-Birmingham global Cultural Studies imagination, much scholarship that might be said to fit the category of African Cultural Studies takes different routes into the field, in effect supporting Wright's point that there may well be many originary moments and epistemic genealogies for what we now call Cultural Studies.

A quick survey yields a remarkable range of critical conversations presently unfolding in the field, including work published in journals such as *Critical Arts*, *Journal of African Cultural Studies*, and the recently founded *Eastern African Literary and Cultural Studies*. Other influential and important recent volumes include: *Popular Culture in Africa: The Episteme of the Everyday*, in which editors Stephanie Newell and Onookome Okome bring together some of the most generative contemporary work on popular cultural forms and genres across a range of African sites; the special issue of the journal *Cultural Studies* on 'Private Lives and Public Cultures in South Africa', edited by Kerry Bystrom and Sarah Nuttall (see their 'Introduction'); a 2013 special issue of the journal *Postcolonial Text* on 'Contemporary Youth Cultures in Africa', edited by Paul Ugor, and the book *African Youth Cultures in a Globalized World*, co-edited by Paul Ugor and Lord Mawuko-Yevugah; a number of editions of the journal *Research in African Literatures*, most recently on 'Queer Valences in African Literatures and Films', edited by Neville Hoad and Taiwo Adetunji Osinubi; work in journals such as *Social Dynamics* on the littoral and Indian Ocean as key sites for the production of African Cultural Studies; and a growing body of scholarship engaging environmental justice in the age of the Anthropocene from the perspective of African Cultural Studies.[1] Many of the questions explored on these platforms were taken up by participants in the 2014 John Douglas Taylor conference on the theme of 'Contemporary Orientations in African Cultural Studies' from which this special issue grew, and which also yielded a special issue of the journal *Safundi* on 'Contemporary African Mediations of Affect and Access' (co-edited by Jessie Forsyth, Sarah Olutola and Helene Strauss).[2]

Our current project draws inspiration from the many foundational conversations that have brought us to this juncture to address the expanding sets of concerns that African Cultural Studies might take on under the rubrics of the political, the imaginative, the activist, the popular and the everyday, particularly as they intersect with diasporic, postcolonial, critical race, queer, and feminist theoretical approaches. What we offer is a glimpse of work generated by the 2014 Taylor conference. The idea of a snapshot seems a suggestive metaphor for our work here. Signalling a moment in time represented informally by way of a photograph or a summary, the term conveys some of the impossibilities of fully capturing the range of critical encounters prompted by the conference. More substantively, the term points to some of the risks of framing, documenting, periodising and archiving that have historically attended knowledge production in and about African contexts. If snapshots offer only a truncated, fleeting view of a much larger scene, our use of the term is meant to turn us towards the kinds of political projects that come into view when our conventional frames fail. Paying attention to these failures, we suggest, is key to approaching a field engaged in mapping alternatives to Euromodernity's violently imposed and limiting regimes of spatial and temporal organization.

We open this issue with Gabeba Baderoon's poem 'Learning to love failure' in part to take up Keguro Macharia's provocation in this issue to move beyond the statistical, taxonomic and documentary routes through which scholarly attention to African lives so frequently gets channelled, and to signal our collective commitment to African queer and feminist scholarship's refusal to accept the hierarchical divide between academic theorisation and imaginative, local, and everyday forms of cultural production (Gqola 2001: 11–12; Lewis 2001: 7). Given the extent to which cultural production about Africa has been mired in questions of authenticity (Wainaina 2005; Adichie 2009; Anyaduba, this issue), we seek in this issue to attend to the creative possibilities, histories, archives, pleasures and problems that might emerge when we acknowledge the incompleteness of our frames. To do so is not simply to discard that which preceded our present inquiry; we are, instead, concerned in part with what one might call the chronopolitics of framing, that is, the temporal dimensions of appraising a field at a particular moment in time, and the ways in which one's conceptual orientations are shaped as a result. Attentive to the time it takes 'to plot out alternative lines of inquiry alongside and across well-trodden questions, to read between the lines of received readings, to locate the points of entry that put pressure on disciplinary habits' (Attewell and Trimble 2016: 8), we hope to advance a mode of cultural theorising that is 'self-reflexive not only about the political stances it takes and projects it chooses to undertake but also about its own worldliness, the effects it has upon the world by its very existence' (Wright, this issue).

The conference generated a number of inquiries into the time and place of contemporary African cultural work, many of which theorised beyond the frameworks that postcolonial and globalisation studies frequently offer. Under the shifting paradigms of Cultural Studies, the work of this conference (as well as the current project) moves away from reading the African everyday as exclusively a construction out of a series of colonial histories and relationalities, or global cultural flows. In line with Jean and John Comaroffs' *Theory From the South* (2011), this issue is instead dedicated to relocating the global centres from which Cultural Studies emanates and positing African work's challenge to normative zones of cultural critique.

'Contemporary orientations' attempts to relocate the time and space of critique in African studies, but it resists the gesture to posit a stable trajectory through which time moves. Rather, the terms of the contemporary and the orientation depend on how they are read in relation to a multitude of other temporalities, orientations, and objects. If, for example, the time of modernity gestures toward 'a strong normative teleology, a unilinear trajectory toward the future' (Comaroff and Comaroff 2011: 9), papers collected in this issue attempt to unfix the stability of meanings generated out of such singular conceptions of time. Karin Barber's early work on the African popular has already cautioned against the persistence of the reductive and binaristic temporalities sketched out by terms such as 'tradition' and 'modernity', instead positing the democratic and negotiatory category of the 'popular'. Many of the papers in this collection are cognisant of how specific frameworks for reading time have too readily fixed African cultural meanings to a set of recognisable parameters generated from the telos of Euromodernity's historical and epistemic lineage.

Macharia's statement that '[i]t matters how one slices time' (this issue) resonates with many of the writers in this issue. For Macharia, the hold of time, particularly in the signification practices that articulate identity in African 'precolonial' art, refuses African art coevalness, and relegates it to a bygone cultural past. His attention to contemporary institutions and practices that intersect with African queer and trans bodies provides alternative frames for African Studies praxis and communicates the urgency of historicising African 'culture' outside the traditional periodisations generated by Europe's colonial apparatus.

A number of our other contributors likewise respond to the task of reconceptualising various framings of time within African Studies. Helene Strauss, for example, identifies the politics of securitisation and crisis management deployed in relation to the 2012 Marikana massacre in South Africa as being characterised by strategies of temporal compression typical in contexts of neoliberal governance across the globe. By way of a reading of Rehad Desai's documentary *Miners Shot Down* (2014), she outlines possibilities for contesting the timelines of fast capitalism and in so doing for creating 'better conditions for the work of mourning' (this issue). Conradie and Brokensha, in turn, examine discourses of race and racism among the so-called Born Free generation of South Africa. Their findings, generated out of an online discussion amongst university students born after 1993, suggest that – while apartheid regimes of racial classification remain evident for this generation – the conversations in which contemporary youth are engaging also require an updated critical toolset to account for the changes that the last 20 years have brought. Central to their analysis is the question of how students negotiated with ideologies of race and racism in the contemporary everyday as opposed to relegating racism to a national past. Adwoa Afful's paper, also sceptical of how time is wielded to promulgate progressivist notions of history, provides a reading of Octavia Butler's *Wild Seed*. This paper draws on Afrofuturism to resist the tendency plaguing the legacy of Middle Passage epistemology to chart 'racial formations across a progressivist linear trajectory in the United States especially' (this issue), which also fails to account for the composite temporalities that shape Black women's experiences in relation to the histories of slavery and colonialism in continental African contexts, and to the Black diasporas resulting from both transatlantic slavery and more recent migrations. Resonating with Jennifer Wenzel's attention to multiple timelines in 'Remembering the past's future' (2006), Afful's work generates a reading of time that grounds it in the present's implication in alternative pasts and futures.

If time is an unstable category, so are the spatial determinants of what constitutes the 'orientation' in this issue. If 'orientation is a matter of how we reside in space', as Sara Ahmed (2006: 543) suggests, this issue is cognisant of the movements that shape how African work comes to occupy specific orientations. As Keyan Tomaselli and Handel Kashope Wright (2011:8) insist, '[t]heories and paradigms travel, and as they travel they mutate and change, reconstitute initial emphases, and even forget their origins'. Indeed, if terms such as space and place have been important to postcolonial and globalised accounts of Africa so far – particularly in emphases on local sovereignties and autonomies – this issue is also devoted to unpacking how such terms risk generating too stable an account of African cultural space. Turning to those 'movements' that shape everyday life in contemporary African cultures, many of the works in this issue are interested in how meaning occurs not in fixed locations or self-directed, situated knowledges but in Africa's intra and inter-continental movements. For example, Chigbo Anyaduba's paper posits the primacy of movement within Africa in his consideration of diaspora. Resisting the scholarly trend of reading African diaspora exclusively in terms of external forces (the Middle Passage and European colonialism), his work focuses on Africans' generation of intracontinental and even intranational diasporas, contesting the monolithic status Africa occupies in many accounts of diaspora. Moreover, in its attention to movement, Anyaduba's paper tackles the 'myth that African humanity was something of a fixed cultural essence' (this issue) that is often perpetuated by the racial ontologies deployed in Afrodiasporic studies. The movements on which authors in this issue focus emphasise not so much what African Cultural Studies *is* so much as the process of how it comes to be, where it might go, and what it might do.

The critical processes that make up this field undergird Handel Kashope Wright's genealogy of the field, found in the first essay of this issue. Wright not only exhorts us to continually ask 'What can African Cultural Studies *do*?', but to do so reflexively, recognising its awkwardness alongside its necessity for cultural production on the continent as well as for and against a global, transnational Cultural Studies. Evidence of this reflexivity abounds in the essays collected here. We might summarise what emerges in this set of writings with a secondary question: 'What kinds of gates must African Cultural Studies walk through?', an echo of its original, more urgent formulation by Macharia in 'Trans* & Taxonomy', who asks: 'What kind of gate must the black African queer walk through?' Among others, this question raises the problem of the representivity of African cultural production vis-a-vis 'Africa' or African identities in our shared global context of a knowledge capitalism that has been institutionally and epistemologically shaped by the norms and structures of whiteness. This is a proprietary problem of the archive as well as a practical problem of study: who is African Cultural Studies for, who participates in its worldliness, and how can its projects of knowledge be accessed? Both problems persist in the theoretical and curatorial work of *doing* African Cultural Studies, which is often situated administratively in the Global North and projected in diasporic or transnational terms or by diasporic or transnational representatives, with the primary exception of the established arena for South African Cultural Studies and even the city-specific Cultural Studies (per McKenzie Wark's (1994) formulation cited by Wright in this issue) of Johannesburg.

It is important for us to note that these features manifest in our own editorial work here, organised largely in Canada and South Africa through transnational and transcontinental networks. The titular 2014 conference out of which this special issue has emerged was hosted at McMaster University in Ontario, Canada, yet nevertheless sought to be as transnational as possible through virtual presentations and funding sponsorship for under-resourced scholars based in Africa.[3] We also invited dialogue around the challenges associated with hosting our discussions in North America, with attention to the transcontextual dynamics of settler colonialism for African Cultural Studies projects. Convening fora for African Cultural Studies in these sites, then, necessarily carries the labour of ambivalence that Wright outlines for the status quo of the field: 'distinct (however ambivalently) and yet engaged with and imbricated in global transnational Cultural Studies', wherein it is 'at once relatively diffuse and marginalised and integral and contributory' (this issue).

These lopsided forces that shape inquiry, representation and orientations in the field frame many of the issue's contributions to ongoing thought on political problems of race and relationality. Stated directly in Fanonian thought as: 'For not only must the black man be black; he must be black in relation to the white man' (Fanon 1967: 78), and echoed in the more recent thought of Fred Moten (2008: 178), who writes '[t]his strife between normativity and the deconstruction of norms is essential not only to contemporary black academic discourse but also to the discourses of the barbershop, the beauty shop, and the bookstore', the gravity of Afropessimism remains present. Contra a public and historical discourse that reads Africa in terms of poverty and lack, and a theoretical tradition that documents how the relations produced by slavery, European colonialism and apartheid continue to structure black existence, much of this issue returns us to the performance of the body and the social and institutional framing of its African or Afrodiasporic positioning, so potentially recapitulating its marking 'as an ontological *absence*, posited as sentient object and devoid of any positive relationality, in contradistinction to the human subject's presence' (R.L. 2013). Perhaps most proximate to this structure, Julie Cairnie's study of postcolonial running traces how the transnational running tourism industry, particularly centred on Kenya, makes visible the continuation of the colonial tradition of imposing sport as a site of social and infrastructural control. The texts that form her archive (and her call for its expansion) reify the exotic and primitive body of the colonial gaze by inscribing Kenyan runners with an originary status for running as a human tradition. Through this reinscription, black African excellence becomes an archive of black African excess that registers the ongoingness of nineteenth-century imperial forms of philanthropy and plunder. In her analysis, the

Kenyan body is registered for its performance according to the logics of resource extraction, touristic consumption and cosmopolitan spectacle, which directs us to the need to account for the forms of cultural misrecognition and exploitation (including the ongoing production of gendered and racialised bodies) enacted by the sport of running's expanding transnational industry and its literatures.

However, in other contributions the performative body is more resistant, ambivalent, and contradictory, in gestures or modes perhaps proceeding from Sarah Nuttall and Cheryl-Ann Michael's claim (2001: 1) that an academic 'overdetermination of the political' has elided complex cultural formations that emerge from popular youth cultures, creolizations, and migrations occurring on and off the continent.[4] The efflorescence of Afrofuturism and Afropolitanism in recent African scholarly and cultural production manifests the 'construction of purpose-driven, labile, place-defying identities – identities-on-the-move, in every sense of the term, that remake received geographies and their relationship to subjectivities' that John Comaroff (Claudio 2015: 35) sees as commonplace on the continent in the context of our 'planetary electronic commons'. The politics of these frames and their address of popular and diasporic cultures is contested, such as in the online and academic debates as to whether contemporary Africa is 'ready for' Afrofuturism's science fiction imaginaries and their cultural products or has always been shaped by them.[5]

Additionally contested is Afropolitanism's affordance, per Achille Mbembe's interpretation, of the 'promise of vacating the seduction of pernicious racialised thinking, its recognition of African identities as fluid, and the notion that the African past is characterised by mixing, blending and superimposing' (Dabiri 2014). Critics such as Amatoritsero Ede (2016: 88) argue that identification with Afropolitanism simply marks the symbolic capital of a 'metropolitan instrument of self-affirmation' through the performance of style, design, and a selective (often gender-focused) politics available to those with social and class mobility.[6] Grace Musila, likewise, laments both the failures of Afropolitanism to live up to its promises and the troubling anti-African associations contained in these very promises. As she puts it (2016: 110), '[l]ike Coke Lite or a lite beer, Afropolitanism seems to promise Africa lite: Africa *sans* the 'unhealthy' or 'intoxicating' baggage of Africa'. Central to these critiques are the dynamics of commodification and global cultural consumption, marking the cosmopolitan African with a capitalist identification perhaps exemplarily expressed by the metropolitan phenomenon of a 'spectacular 'hyper-feminine' style' presented by Simidele Dosekun at our 2014 conference, through which young and class-privileged Nigerian women in the city of Lagos see themselves as cosmopolitan consumer citizens and 'postfeminist' subjects.[7]

These debates themselves have been welcomed for their injection of complexity into the discursive terrain of reading African cultural production – an echo evidencing Handel Kashope Wright's exhortation for African Cultural Studies as a 'floating signifier' with a 'multiple and contested' signified. Writers Teju Cole and Aaron Bady have noted how Afropolitanism in particular has enabled questions of class to come to the fore of discourse on contemporary Africa, a necessary corrective to a long history of its analytic displacement onto race ('Africa' as the Euro-American world's 'racial proletariat par excellence' (Bady 2014)), such that the term makes clear that the time has passed in which 'African culture-work was thought to be, as such, a revolutionary act, when simply to exist, and to speak, was to resist imperial hegemony' (ibid). Accordingly, discursive terrains that imagine abjection in Africa become newly charged, such as the radical futurities for Black African women migrants in Adwoa Afful's feminist Afrofuturist reading of Octavia Butler's novel *Wild Seed*. Her analysis replaces the now deterministic archive of Middle Passage epistemology with an 'abjected' and 'migratory subjectivity', which instead centres the protagonist's agency as a gender- and shape-shifter through her auto-reproductivity and homemaking. By reading the body of Butler's Anywanu as itself the home contra diaspora's (in this case violent) lack, Afful extends the often linear tradition of countermemory bound up in the transatlantic slave trade by 'reorienting the intercultural vectors of Black Atlantic temporality towards the proleptic as much as the retrospective' (Eshun 2003: 289). The politics of Afrofuturist representation here can direct our gaze to other states and temporalities, positioning the performative body not against its registration as a lack or overdetermination in negativity, but somewhere in the gap between the speculative record of what will have been and the future memoir in which the subject might opt out of representing itself in these terms. It marks one response of many which are called for in Macharia's naming of 'the problem of representation, which is a problem of the imagination'. His mode of questioning the legibility of both pre-colonial and contemporary archives of the sexualities and genders of African bodies interrogates the future of African Cultural Studies more generally: 'How do Africans imagine? What's the relationship between African imagination and African lives? Why frame acts of representation within documentary terms? Why claim there is a one-to-one relation between what is represented on a cave wall, that is, between what is imagined, and how lives are lived?' (this issue)

One mode African Cultural Studies might employ in concert with this prompt is 'entanglement', which Sarah Nuttall's keynote presentation at our 2014 conference suggested as a project of reading beyond the subject and inadequate old categories, and no longer presuming that our work is the demystification of Africanity in order to expose the facts of complexity, self-mastery, or human agency. Its aptness is clear in the analyses by both Thabisani Ndlovu and co-authors Marthinus Conradie and Susan Brokensha of race and performance in the South African context. In his portrait of begging in Johannesburg, Ndlovu reads the public contestation of 'race' in South Africa through the 'face work' of embodied performances of poverty at traffic stops, wherein modes of begging by diverse bodies generate a communicative language with potential donors. While these public performances of race are never explicitly articulated as 'race talk', the entrenched institutional dynamics of white respectability/fragility are re-enacted by racial encounters in these settings by reifying stereotypes of the black body in the begging postures of servitude, abjection, and cheerfulness. In a different valence, the study of the co-production of race talk in online fora by South African university students conducted by Conradie and Brokensha reveals the strategic avoidance sought by performative digital identities in a persistent landscape of structural racism. Shaped by the institutional and historical frames of transformation for the so-called Born Free generation, the students demonstrated an internalised raced consciousness that casts structural racism as historical and its present-day realities as merely interpersonal or overly binaristic in their politics, a kind of discursive negotiation of race that flatters the pseudo-meritocratic project of 'colour-blindness' in their university setting. One cannot help but trace the encumbrances generated by such a post-political ideology to the uneven application of violent state response to the #RhodesMustFall and #FeesMustFall movements (and the transcolonial solidarity registered by their offshoots globally), which erupted since the time the study was conducted; the suppression of their counter-discourse and its demands makes the need for anti-racist education and institutional decolonization once again clearly present and not past. Both register entanglement, we might say, in the public life of South African politics between precarity's old and new forms and the public demands of living in what Keguro Macharia calls 'a post-taxonomic age, an identity-demanding age' as a lasting feature of the white supremacist world imaginary.

We might also locate the affordances of reading via entanglement in Chigbo Anyaduba's intervention in the discursive terrain of contemporary Afrodiasporic studies, which has largely read 'Africa' as an essentialised racial, historical or cultural origin in relation to the dispersion of its peoples. Anyaduba instead deprivileges dispersion to consider diasporic consciousness as an equally widespread phenomenon for those settled upon or bereft of indigenous sovereignty due to shifting power relations and the imposition of borders in the post/colonial state. Thinking with an African condition of 'disarticulation' extends the question of orientation to political dynamics over what is understood as home in ongoing conflicts on the continent. 'Diaspora space', as theorised by Avtar Brah (1996: 16), is precisely an orientation inhabited by both diasporic subjects and those rendered 'indigenous' by a settler population, so foregrounding 'the entanglement of genealogies of dispersion with those of "staying put"'. This expansionary analytical project hinges on the problem theorised elsewhere by Macharia of 'political vernaculars', through which attachments and detachments from the political are made legible. This framing traces the entanglement between possibility and impossibility, the prospects of Africans assembling themselves alongside the diachronic impediments to those formations. Channelling Ngugi wa Thiong'o, he reminds that vernaculars have been understood as '"home" languages", sites for building anti-oppressive communities, and 'ways of claiming and shaping space' (Macharia 2016). Yet political vernaculars also provide intractable frames for what is politically thinkable and imaginable, especially given their life inside state processes. It is this ambivalence that orients the work of African Cultural Studies here, an ambivalent space inhabited by regenerative, deconstructive and lyrical performances.

Acknowledgements

The editors of this issue owe thanks to many others without whom the work presented here would not have been possible. In particular, we thank the organisers of the 2014 conference, 'Contemporary Orientations in African Cultural Studies' from which many of the papers in this issue derive. These organisers include Jessie Forsyth, Sarah Olutola, and Paul Ugor. This issue is the second of two published following the conference, and we extend our special thanks to the editors, with Helene Strauss, of the other special issue – recently released by the journal *Safundi*— namely Jessie Forsyth and Sarah Olutola. We also thank the keynote speakers of the conference, Tsitsi Dangarembga, Sarah Nuttall, Pumla Dineo Gqola, and Handel Kashope Wright, for giving direction to many of the concerns that coalesce in this special issue. We are also grateful to Gabeba Baderoon for permission to reproduce her poem 'Learning to love failure'. The conference would not have been possible without the generous financial support from the John Douglas Taylor conference fund and the office of the President at McMaster University. We are grateful in particular to Peter Walmsley, Antoinette Somo, as well as a number of students and faculty members at McMaster for their contributions to the conference.

On his part, Handel Kashope Wright wishes to acknowledge the Department of Communications Studies, University of Johannesburg, South Africa, which provided support for him as Senior Research Associate to undertake this work

Notes

1 These include, most recently, a number of panels at the Bayreuth meeting of the 2015 African Literature Association that explored themes such as 'The futures of environmental representation and environmental justice', and the 'Environmental Humanities'; the 2012 session of the Johannesburg Workshop in Theory and Criticism on 'Futures of Nature'; work done by cultural critics such as Jennifer Wenzel and Philip Aghoghovwia on petro-cultures; a workshop held in November 2015 at the Wits Institute for Social and Economic Research on 'Literature in the Age of the Anthropocene'; and, at the 2014 conference on 'Contemporary Orientations in African Cultural Studies', a panel devoted specifically to animality and environmental justice in African contexts (including speakers Jesse Arseneault, Dana Mount, Jordan Sheridan and Nandini Thiyagarajan). The steadily growing body of work on Afrofuturist cultural production and the environment constitutes a particularly exciting area of contemporary Africa-oriented cultural analysis.
2 The conference, held from May 30 to June 1, 2014 at McMaster University in Canada, gathered scholars from around the globe to consider 'Contemporary orientations in African Cultural Studies', and was co-organised by Jesse Arseneault, Sarah D'Adamo, Jessie Forsyth, Sarah Olutola, Helene Strauss and Paul Ugor. Early versions of all but two of the papers included here were presented at the conference. Handel Kashope Wright, who presented a keynote address at the conference, agreed to serve in the additional role of co-editor of this special issue.
3 For the programme of the McMaster conference, see: https://africanculturalstudies.wordpress.com.
4 This notion of the political requires some qualification. Rather than a rejection of the political realities and practices that undergird African cultural praxis, our reference to Nuttall and Michael instead offers a challenge to the authenticity of the political. In that this special issue is partially inspired by feminist and queer work that examines political narratives in those contexts frequently imagined to be apolitical, its aim is to multiply rather than foreclose meanings of the political.
5 See Nnedi Wahala's blog post 'Is Africa ready for science fiction', in dialogue with Nollywood director Tchidi Chikere, here http://nnedi.blogspot.com/2009/08/is-africa-ready-for-science-fiction.html; contra this discussion, see Namwali Serpell's response accounting for how 'Africa has always been sci-fi' http://lithub.com/africa-has-always-been-sci-fi/.
6 See also Alpha Abebe's post 'Afropolitanism: Global citizenship with African routes' on the social identity and practice of Afropolitans: http://blog.qeh.ox.ac.uk/?p=910
7 For more on this research and its recent iterations in publication form, see Simidele Dosekun's webpage https://simidosekun.com

References

Adichie, C. N. 2009. TED lecture: The danger of a single story. *TED Conferences*. http://www.ted.com/talks/chimamanda_adichie_the_danger_of_a_single_story/transcript?language=en (accessed March 12, 2013).
Ahmed, S. 2006. Orientations: toward a queer phenomenology. *GLQ* 12 (4): 543–574.
Attewell, N. and S. Trimble. 2016. The work of return. *Topia: Canadian Journal of Cultural Studies* 35: 7–25.
Baderoon, G. 2006. *A hundred silences*. Cape Town: Kwela Books.
Bady, A. 2014. Afropolitan. *ACLA: State of the Discipline*. http://stateofthediscipline.acla.org/entry/afropolitan (accessed June 8, 2016).
Barber, K. 1987. Popular arts in Africa. *African Studies Review* 30(3): 1–78.
Brah, A. 1996. *Cartographies of diaspora: contesting identities*. London: Routledge.

Bystrom, K. and S. Nuttall. 2013. Introduction: private lives and public cultures in South Africa. *Cultural Studies* 27 (3): 307–332.

Claudio, L. 2015. Thoughts on theorizing from the South: an interview with John Comaroff. *The Johannesburg Salon* 10: 30–37.

Comaroff, J. and J. Comaroff. 2011. *Theory from the South: or, how Euro-America is evolving toward Africa*. Boulder, CO: Paradigm Publishers.

Dabiri, E. 2014. Why I am not an Afropolitan. *Africa is a country*. http://africasacountry.com/2014/01/why-im-not-an-afropolitan/ (accessed 30 May 2016).

Ede, A. 2016. The politics of Afropolitanism. *Journal of African Cultural Studies* 28(1): 88–100.

Eshun, K. 2003. Further considerations of Afrofuturism. *CR: The New Centennial Review*, 3(2): 287–302.

Fanon, Frantz. 1967. *Black skin, white masks*. Translated by Charles Lam. Markmann. London: Picador.

Gqola, P. 2001. Ufanele uqavile: Blackwomen, feminisms and postcoloniality in Africa. *Agenda: Empowering Women for Gender Equity* 50(16): 11–22.

Lewis, D. 2001. African feminisms. *Agenda: Empowering Women for Gender Equity* 50(16): 4–10.

Macharia, K. 2016. Political vernaculars: freedom or love. *The New Inquiry*. http://thenewinquiry.com/essays/political-vernaculars-freedom-and-love/ (accessed May 30, 2016).

Moten, Fred. 2008. The case of blackness. *Criticism* 50(2): 177–218.

Musila, G. 2016 Part-time Africans, Europolitans and 'Africa lite'. *Journal of African Cultural Studies* 28(1): 109–113.

Nuttall, S. and C. Michael. 2000. *Senses of culture*. Oxford: Oxford University Press.

R.L. 2013. Wanderings of the slave: black life and social death. *Mute*. http://www.metamute.org/editorial/articles/wanderings-slave-black-life-and-social-death (accessed June 8, 2016).

Tomaselli, K.G. and H.K. Wright. eds. 2011. *Africa, Cultural Studies and Difference*. New York: Routledge.

Wainaina, B. 2005. How to write about Africa. *Granta: The Magazine of New Writing* 92: 92–95.

Wark, M. 1994. *Virtual geography: living with global media events*. Bloomington: Indiana University Press.

Wenzel, J. 2006. Remembering the past's future: anti-imperialist nostalgia and some versions of the Third World. *Cultural Critique* 62: 1–32.

Cultural Studies and the African Global South

Keyan G. Tomaselli

ABSTRACT

Cultural studies exhibits multiple derivations from different historical conjunctures and places. This essay examines three instances of cultural studies emanating from within Africa, in relation to the field in the North Atlantic. What a "Southern" lens offers the North are different ways of making sense and a transnational framework that enables peer-to-peer conversations. This transe/trance quality is explained via a discussion of the scientifically unexplainable, superstition, and the noumenal. The immateriality of money and its associated human performances as reified by New York stock exchanges is the example through which transnational theoretical hybridity is examined.

While cultural studies is transnational, applications of it tend to be narrowly national. As cultural studies traveled beyond their institutionalized North Atlantic borders from the 1960s, local examples would be sometimes inserted into these North Atlantic theories without assessing whether or not the contexts of transfer were appropriate. Thus was American intercultural studies during apartheid applied to prove the need for racial separation in South Africa.[1] This is a stark example, but even cultural studies, whose *raison d'être* is to unmask beguiling "insider" codes, often carries Western epistemological traces. These traces assume the inherited hegemony of the Northern hereditary epistemological centers that relegate African cultural studies to "area studies," as not therefore being of theoretical interest. For example, at international conferences my presentations tend to be understood as offering "African" examples rather than also engagements of transnational theory. I am "fixed" geographically in terms of my place of residence rather than my international trajectories of theoretical mobility. Or, I am categorized as an activist rather than also a theorist.

This article briefly identifies key initiatives within Africa when cultural studies emerged in different places at different times to do the same democratizing work as elsewhere. The first example is from Kenya and the second and third from Southern Africa. My analysis implicitly draws on the circuit of culture model that explains the exercise of power relations within institutions and, overlaid on these, how people make meaning of texts produced from within the circuit.[2] Stuart Hall's encoding/decoding model had earlier opened the door to wider debates about what is cultural studies and how messages and meanings are shaped by social and economic institutions on the one hand, and audiences on the other.[3] Working in Africa, moreover, requires recognition of meaning making with regard to the nonmaterial, religious, and virtual realms, which have been blind spots in much global cultural studies until recently. This is discussed in the final section.

In defining the Global South, this essay draws on Ruth Teer-Tomaselli's statement that brought the 2012 International Association for Media and Communication Research to Durban on South Africa's East Coast. The contours she maps apply equally to cultural studies as she highlights the need to reassess enduring relations, perceptions, and conceptual dichotomies:

> The theme, "South–North Conversations", reflects the asymmetry of communication flows but without implying the negatives that accompany discussions of the "digital divide"… South–North indicates disparities but not necessarily in negative or passive ways; while "conversations" indicates peer-to-peer equality; a more optimistic vision of global engagement. Old truths concerning "developed-underdeveloped" and "core-periphery" regions and nations are being reassessed … seen in terms of value and meaning systems, historical trajectories, monetary and technological transfers—can[not] be regarded in the same way as previously.[4]

This reframing of what interhemispherical conversational dialogue should be is geospatial, politico-economic, and interhemispherical. The postmillennium world has witnessed the rise of new power blocs, reconfiguring the original North–South linear dichotomy to include China and other parts of Asia. The interpenetration of capital between the blocs replaces dichotomies, and divides with multiplicities and questions the previously assumed intrinsic relevance of Northern theory in Southern contexts. The term, "Global South," has replaced earlier categories like the Third World or developing countries as relations of wealth and inequality transgress national borders and are to be found everywhere. The term also rearticulates the early framing of dependency between First and Third Worlds and invites scholars now to think of the relations of capital as global rather than just being regionally and nationally bounded.

This essay thus aims to reveal the geneses of cultural studies within African conditions and to argue why they should be admitted also into the field's origins.

African variants of cultural studies

The initial application of cultural studies within South Africa via the journal *Critical Arts: North–South Cultural and Media Studies* (1980ff) developed an approach that examined the relationship between texts (representations/interpretivism) and contexts (history, political economy, social practices) and how people and audiences make sense of, and cope (reception), within structures not of their own making. The journal was intended as a political intervention within a performing arts school whose head had hooked its *raison d'être* on a technical reading of Arnoldian conceptions of high art and culture as a civilizing framework.[5] The dissenting *Critical Arts* took the Marxist view that individuals act as active agents within inherited structurations and conditions that they have to ordinarily negotiate, while also often contesting them. The journal thereby opened the way to analysis of black popular performance and cultural resistance strategies by recognizing such theater for the first time as worthy of semiotic study.

Activist cultural studies

Activist cultural studies operates within an interventionist action research framework that implements theoretically derived strategies in alliance with communities of struggle such as unions, faith-based and civic, social justice, and human rights organizations. An example is the use of popular theater in conscientizing ordinary people to the nature of oppression and to identify and narrate their daily experiences as means of creating working class solidarity. In South Africa, such theater produced in conjunction with labor sociologists, for example, explored, in a metonymic vein, issues of the workplace, apartheid repression, and ways of coping with, and resisting racial capitalist oppression. These plays were enacted at union meetings where the entire community would get involved in call and response in asking and answering questions triggered by the interactive performances. As such, these performances underpinned a process of conscientization from the bottom up experiences of workers and the nature of their imprisoning social chains.[6]

One strand of 1980s activist cultural and media studies drawing also on political economy and labor sociology developed alongside mass movements of resistance to apartheid. The 1990s saw the overthrow of apartheid and cultural studies responded to the ensuing policy moment heralded by the postapartheid transition to democracy. South African Cultural studies, thus, found itself positioned on the "right" (liberationist) side of history during the Mandela years (1990–98).

The Mass Democratic Movement (MDM) of the 1980s, which integrated academics, some universities, unions, churches, and local communities in antiapartheid struggle, generated its own organic cultural and media theories and associated practices. This national multiracial popular movement had anticipated the power of cultural mobilization within the black trade unions and prefigured an action-based cultural studies in analyzing and mobilizing alliances between the unions and academics. The MDM thereby provided the ground that enabled a reconstitution of Northern cultural studies into sometimes unique Southern African political, economic, and cultural conditions. From this conjuncture emerged: (a) worker theater that addressed everyday conditions and how to deal with them as discussed above; and (b) black consciousness theater that examined broader questions of identity in the vein of Steve Biko's philosophy of affirmative blackness.[7]

Three African examples of activist cultural studies

Different regions in the world have generated their own organic cultural studies trajectories, sometimes connected to the UK variants. Handel Wright, now in Canada, but originally hailing from Sierra Leone, identified the first instance of cultural studies in Africa.[8] This was the 1970s Kenyan Kamiriithu theater project led by Ngugi wa Thiong'o and Ngugi wa Miiri. This was a short-lived grassroots intervention that eschewed transmission communication models. Dialogical in nature, their theater drew on popular African performance dramaturgy that elaborated rural villagers' quotidian concerns about the failure of independence to deliver people's liberation. The plays and theater group were banned, wa Thiong'o was imprisoned, and the open air theater was destroyed by the army.[9] The events that it generated resulted in the exile of both wa Thiong'o and wa Miiri, with wa Miiri later implementing their popular mobilizing performative strategies in Zimbabwe and Zambia. It was wa Thiong'o who first posed the question of how to decolonize the mind.[10] In contrast, in apartheid South Africa in the 1980s, worker theater and Black Consciousness theater troupes were protected by union and university venues in which to perform, attract audiences, and debate pressing issues via storytelling.

Wright's second reference to the genesis of African cultural studies was to the Birmingham-influenced Contemporary Cultural Studies Unit (CCSU, 1985ff) at the University of KwaZulu-Natal. CCSU drew on each of the debates mentioned above, including the performative strategies generated by the Ngugis, read through social theories, such as Paulo Freire's critical pedagogy,[11] African philosophies and visual anthropology.[12] This moment of resistance to apartheid was theorized and mobilized via communities of struggle that included activist projects with black township cultural groups, media collectives, and popular social movements. The resistance phase was followed by Centre for Communication Media and Society (CCMS) working with the transitional multiparty political agencies like the Convention for a Democratic South Africa in developing cultural, film, and broadcasting policies for the immediate postapartheid era after 1990.[13]

Third was Wright's challenge to Northern Cultural Studies, "Dare we De-centre Birmingham?"[14] This intervention, first presented as a keynote address at the inaugural meeting in Finland of what was later to be formalized as the Association for Cultural Studies, was not developed within the pages of *European Journal of Cultural Studies* where it appeared, except as an unrequited milestone identifying "Africa." On its twentieth birthday, this journal's editors did recall Wright's argument for recognition of cultural studies from Africa.[15] However, the ring-fencing by the editors of *European Journal of Cultural Studies* of the field to just three publications produced from the UK but edited by academics spread across the North Atlantic delimited the preferred geographical terrain of the field to this region. Omitting mention of other journals published and/or edited from other hemispheres also occurred in the face of Wright's life's work that has focused on ensuring the recognition of cultural studies' African originations. *Critical Arts*, established under conditions of political siege 10 years before the first appearance of *European Journal of Cultural Studies*, and others such as *Continuum* edited from Australia, were absent in the *European Journal of Cultural Studies* editorial.

The Birmingham initiative however remains crucial in that it offered strategies for opposing oppression—as in the UK, Zimbabwe, and South Africa. CCMS, for example, worked directly with communities of struggle, at their invitation, in devising strategies to enable alternative media to function as fulcrums of emergent public spheres and democratic organization, and in advising legal teams in preparing briefs to defend their clients in court cases.[16] The subsequent shift at CCSU, later renamed as the CCMS, from resistance to policy drew on the Australian cultural policy moment that had emerged in the early 1990s in that country. Where UK cultural studies offered a critique of both Thatcherism and Stalinism,[17] in Australia, this critique was recalibrated through a Foucauldian analysis of "governmentality" into cultural policy studies in this much less class conflicted society.[18] This rearticulation from resistance to policy revealed that cultural studies did not just have to remain as oppositional as it was and remains in the UK. The Australian rearticulation demonstrated that, when cultural studies intersected with less conflictual class relations, it could be repurposed to affirmatively contribute policy work to, and project implementation within, prevailing governmental institutions in spreading social access via state infrastructures. Where resistance was the principle of cultural studies in the UK and apartheid South Africa, during the 1990s in Australia and South Africa, the field was actually freed up to work with state institutions.

As with the Australian approach, following Ngugi wa Thiong'o, Wright asks the question, "What is cultural studies for?"[19] How can it address social repression through action (such as via cultural policy studies) rather than just critique and explain the relationship between resistance and oppression? As van der Smit observes:

> In appropriating the traditional cultural forms in their indigenous languages Ngugi ensured that the whole community participated so that the theatre became a communication ... that grass-roots theatre has power and a significant impact when a community is actively involved.[20]

Such was the case also of worker theater during apartheid and state policy generation during the transition from apartheid during the 1990s when academics joined with unions, professionals, state bureaucrats, and politicians in devising new policies across all cultural and media sectors.

The fourth cultural studies moment impacting Africa has been the indigenization of some trajectories of cultural and media studies as read through Southern African conditions.[21] These initiatives try to mesh the local with the global, but from the perspectives of the locals themselves. For example, the University of Oslo introduced cultural and media studies to the postgraduate Diploma in Media Studies hosted by the English Department at the University of Zimbabwe. This collaborative trajectory drew on British cultural studies, Jürgen Habermas' theory of the public sphere,[22] and the approaches informed by CCMS.[23] However, at the time of the Oslo–Zimbabwe collaboration, from the mid-1990s, the autocratic tendencies and genocidal behavior of the Zimbabwe government were becoming evident. Where in South Africa, cultural studies was now being incorporated into postapartheid policy making in the form of visions and missions and the restructuring of the state and private enterprise into racially inclusive democratically led operations,[24] in Zimbabwe, the Norwegians and cultural studies-as-critique framework stood helplessly by as the government engaged in postcolonial dismantling and the destruction of the state, agriculture, and even of capital. This process involved the suppression of currency itself, as a bartering economy now operated alongside US dollars and South African rands. The departure of many of the first generation of Zimbabwean cultural and media studies scholars after 2000 resulted in their employment in South Africa, the UK, America, and Scandinavia.[25]

Into the unknown: beyond the material

While the above examples deal with the materialities of resistance, popular empowerment, and democratization in Africa through cultural studies frames, the hidden transcripts of cosmologies, the realm of the immaterial, are always close to the surface in the ways that people make sense, no matter their levels of education. Now, let's expand the discussion of cultural studies into the immaterial that the West categorizes as superstition, which is usually associated with uncivilized barbarians inhabiting the Global South. Superstition is often removed from academic analysis in the industrial world s it is unexplainable except as it is observed in patterns of behavior. Working in African conditions involving ordinary people is a constant reminder that they rarely separate Subject from Object, the spiritual from the nonspiritual, and the natural from the supernatural. However, when one casts an eye on the North and how its people behave within financial institutions, as one example, it becomes clear that their superstitions are no less evident. But, often these superstitions are masked behind rituals that exclude acknowledgment of deeper belief systems that often come across as bizarre to those living in the Global South.

While cultural studies does not necessarily exclude the immaterial, the scientifically unexplainable and unthinkable, and things that exist independently of human senses, it does not explicitly include them either. These "things in themselves," the noumenal experiences, to use Immanuel Kant's term, occur everywhere.[26] Religion and the paranormal are everyday phenomena found in contemporary expressions, films and TV, beliefs, and practices. Even in the age of the European Enlightenment, and despite Cartesian thinking, many cultures, no matter where located or how educated, people continue to live within the noumenal realm, whether discursive or believed, such as within inner cities, refugee populations, faith-based institutions, the economy, and in the ontologies of ISIS, Al Qaeda, and evangelicals. In African ontologies the ancestors (the deceased) are assumed to be ever present, in communion with living people and shaping their corporeal behavior. Usually confined to the discipline of religious studies, or anthropology, such beliefs actually permeate life in general.[27]

European researchers often experience disorientation when they engage ordinary Africans, for what they encounter (the unintelligible) may bear little similarity to that which their disciplines teach them. For example, Jean Rouch had worked among the Dogon and Songhay in Mali and Niger in the 1940s. He was followed by anthropologist Paul Stoller 30 years later.[28] Stoller was initiated into the indigenous practices and rituals of the lives of Rouch's subjects' descendants through mysterious experiences of spiritual and ontological inclusion. It took Stoller a while to work this out. He then jettisoned his Western theories in coming to terms with his West African hosts. Stoller argues that radically empirical anthropologists participate *fully* in the lives of their subjects, but he does not suggest ways of explaining what was experienced.

Cartesian derived analysis cannot explain the scientifically unthinkable. Where industrial societies have analytically separated the Subject from the Object, oral cultures (even if literate) retain this ontological integration. Surrealists take the expression beyond observational representation into a kind of dream world of irreducible images that defy categorization.[29] Surrealist signs are capable of revealing other levels of reality— "surreality"— understood at the level of the unconscious mind rather than any logical thought process.[30]

Once the researcher has experienced "the inside" or "the place where logic bites its own tail," realist science is no longer adequate.[31] When working among ordinary Africans, Western assumptions about the world are uprooted from their foundation on the plain of Western metaphysics. As Stoller further explains:

> Having crossed the threshold into the Songhay world of magic, and having felt the texture of fear and the exaltation of repelling the force of a sorcerer, my view of Songhay culture could no longer be one of a structuralist, a symbolist or a Marxist. Given my intense experience—and all field experiences are intense whether they involve trance, sorcery or kinship—I will need in future works to seek a different mode of expression, a mode in which the event becomes the author of the text and the writer becomes the interpreter of the event who serves as an intermediary between the event (author) and the readers.[32]

There is no "law" in terms of which to "explain" paranormal occurrences and no canon guiding interpretation. Interpretations cannot be solely reduced to the three stage transparent, negotiated, or contested decodings delineated in Hall's encoding/decoding model. Something else is occurring during the encounter.

In the context of the immaterial, the encoding/decoding model is not rendered irrelevant, but merely incomplete. The Peirceian three stage semiotics (icon, index, symbol), through which "all that is present to the mind" is constituted can account for fictions, apparitions, and the immaterial.[33] These are the sense dimensions present in Stoller's anthropology, but which are largely lacking from cultural studies. The inability of contemporary science to explain such events other than labeling them as literary and/or visual genres of magic, the marvelous, the uncanny, or the occult, does not render science or indigenous knowledge bereft. Neither Cartesian nor cultural studies derived methods can explain the paranormal, but they can describe manifestations of them. Rouch never crossed into the immaterial even if he acknowledged this realm. But, he could bodily participate in it via the cine-trance method of representation via his movie camera. This supraconceptual dimension beyond Descartes is where Peirce's notion of the "interpretant"—interpretation/making sense—can signify frameworks beyond the material or phenomenological dimensions such as the uncanny, the marvelous, and the fantastic.[34] Where literate industrialized societies separate Subject from Object, oral cultures tend to retain something (or all) of this sometimes totemistic, integration. What is irrational for Western science is often rational for Africans. When Subject and Object are not separated for the purpose of analysis, essentialism becomes the new rationality—"I know what I know, but I don't know how I came to that knowing." The known and the knowing are located in the subjective existence of the knower. What is known is the phenomenon, what knows is the understanding within the mind of an interpreter, and the source of the phenomenon is *unknowable*: that is, the noumenon, visually represented by cine trance as in Rouch's work. That is why the immaterial needs to be studied—where appropriate—in conjunction with the material realm in order to get a holistic view of how people make sense and why they act as they do. Yet, sacred discourses, suppressed from the bulk of Western positivist and historical materialist analysis, are evident everywhere.[35]

In the spiritual world, and the electronic gaming environment that includes the player as both encoder and decoder, the interpreter is simultaneously actor/participant/encoder/decoder—participating fully, as Stoller observes. Description is the prime scientific option. As Jean Rouch concludes, he had no idea after making 50 films on Songhay possession, "what the techniques of possession are."[36] So he participated in possessions via "cine trance," where the camera becomes part of the performance taking viewers inside the rhythm of events rather than offering explanation.

Let me explain this via the proposition that money is magic whose representation is managed through American financial stock market rituals. The strangeness to Africans of what is taken for granted in New York should become clear. The American stock markets opening and closing ceremonies, as screened on *CNN*, similarly to some African behaviors, are ritualistic forms of possession and worship celebrating the magic of money and its manipulation as a surrealistic life force driven by "markets". Think of *CNN*'s Richard Quest's messianic exhortation in his program, *Quest means business*, "What a profitable hour"—even as the stock exchange may be crashing. For the stockbrokers, such performative rituals such as occur during the daily opening and closing ceremonies are normal and natural, even liminal, but for outsiders, they might be read as bizarre manifestations of possession, greed, and class celebration of global exploitation. The financial traders clapping and cheering from the podiums, engaging in the revelries of profit and the worship of wealth, do not find performative equivalence in the stock markets of other countries. Capital becomes savior, even as it is ephemeral, and the gospel of wealth is what is being celebrated. As Jean and John Comaroffs observe:

> We seek, instead, to draw attention to, to interrogate, the distinctly pragmatic qualities of the messianic, millennial capitalism of the moment: a capitalism that presents itself as a gospel of

salvation; a capitalism that, if rightly harnessed, is invested with the capacity to transform the universe of the marginalized and disempowered.[37]

For us in the Global South, the Nasdaq rituals also signify imperialism, neo-colonial insanity, and capitalistic superstition. The "markets" that are ascribed Godly powers are ascribed transcendent ontological qualities in the US (such as in "market sentiment," and claiming that "the markets" will "decide" or "have spoken," or will "punish," etc.). Commodities and the markets that abound in metaphysical subtleties and theological niceties become authors of events, and stockbrokers are cast as the interpreters of what is "written" in these seemingly disembodied events.[38] As such, the markets are communally constructed illusions that take on the character of the id. They manage virtual currencies whose flows and regulation of exchange relations is represented by mediatized rituals, opening and closing bells, and celebratory behavior enacted for the camera. Materialist in the extreme, they are nevertheless spiritual in nature as they require supernatural belief systems enabled by the (im-)materiality of a stereographic capitalism to function properly. For example, most currency is imaginary—it does not exist on paper or in coins but is projected, stored as electrons on hard drives and recorded on balance sheets. When the transactional use-value of real tangible currency in-the-hand is now cast as a commodity, money is treated as a tradable object in itself, irrespective of the labor expended to produce it. Cryptocurrencies are the ultimate illusion as their values are based on scarcity rather than productivity. They require belief and commodity fetishism rather than measures of baseline measurable asset-based wealth.

The interpenetration of conscious and unconscious dimensions within the capitalist occult makes it difficult for stockbrokers to distinguish the real from the imaginary, since currency is a creature of network effects as it requires a community of shared belief to "work," to exist as something recognizable as money.[39] This occurred with the derivatives and speculative behavior that caused the 2008 housing market collapse. Stock exchanges create existential relations that locate their subjects within both material and immaterial discourses, made intelligible via virtual currencies, bodily and verbal rituals, social performance, and cultural representations. American stockbrokers' belief systems and performances of possession are thus arguably little different to the possession ceremonies of supposedly superstitious Africans.

The appeal of stock exchanges is because they enable such audiences (and brokers, traders, investors) to move out of their material existence and into the liminal surreal world that promises a salvation that financial institutions have created. Individuals maneuver between these often superstitious institutions and their regulatory structures like FICA in their daily lives. While our Western identities are fixed by surveillance mechanisms (e.g., ID cards, driver's licenses, passports and utility bills), our belief in, and relation to, monetary systems positions us as citizens, consumers, and investors. Socialism is equated by Trump with the devil, while for the South, it is actually a mode of production. This rearticulation of the material into the immaterial and of the Subject into the Object provides subjects of financial social practices a firm sense of grounded reality, even as it is imaginary, largely unknowable, and transcendent.

Financial instruments can only be understood in terms of "pasts remembered, futures anticipated, and time measured."[40] Money is accepted because the expectation is that it will retain its transactional character in the future. In Southern Africa, from where I am writing, the financial example would be that the past is experienced via the ancestors (the deceased) in the present, and the present is financially secured by siring many children to look after their parents in the future (the insurance). And, since the ancestors from the past interact with folks in the present, all three dimensions are assumed to coexist simultaneously by ordinary African people.[41] In this context of the ancestors, the late Zambian journalism professor, Francis Kasoma, generated a theory of Afriethics that attempts to explore ways of appropriating a spiritually responsive cultural studies within the epistemological and ontological framework of social theory, social justice, and positionality. He argues for a decentering of money and power-centered journalism in favor of a society-centered journalism grounded on traditional communal values. Kasoma suggests that

> the basis of morality in African society is the fulfilment of obligations to kins-people, both living and dead. It is believed that some of the departed and the spirits keep watch over people to make sure that they observe the moral laws and are punished when they break them.[42]

Such ontologies have different relations to capital, the rituals of capital and its relations to culture.

The noumenal world is experienced as real no matter the ontology of the perceiving individual and no matter where they live or what they think. That is, if the markets are conferred ontological significance and assumed to make decisions, then the noumenal is at play. But, because it is nonmental, it is unknowable. People make judgments on matters as they are relevant to these, or they express opinion: the former is to be seen as a truth-claim, the latter being of a lower order.

Simultaneously, the brutal realities of ISIS's one-dimensional ideology that denies the value of corporeal existence but which uses the tangible weaponry of modernity in its genocidal anti-Enlightenment quest are increasingly evident.[43] In contrast, the role of African ancestors who can be heard but not seen in the present is much more benign. Cultural studies, unlike anthropology, has yet to engage these kinds of practices and their associated belief systems, or to see them in global, rather than just ethnic contexts.

Conclusion

As for interhemispherical peer-to-peer conversations, these are always difficult because of our different contexts, definitions, languages, and epistemological assumptions. Cultural Studies from the South are indeed area studies, but they should not be ring-fenced as such because their analytical frameworks can, indeed, be transnational and transcultural when applied with due contextual sensitivity. Activist cultural studies applies theory in practice and often the practice informs the theory as in the case of Kamiriithu. Doing cultural studies and activist research in repressive states can endanger scholars and practitioners. How to effectively negotiate these conditions becomes part of cultural studies praxis. However, we should not assume that the subjects of industrial and postindustrial societies are themselves living only within materiality. My example of money, magic, and meaning questions any such positivistic claims.

Notes

1. Keyan G. Tomaselli, "Misappropriating Discourses: Intercultural Communication Theory in South Africa, 1980–1995," *Communal/Plural: Journal of Transnational and Crosscultural Studies* 17, no. 2 (1999): 137–58. https://www.researchgate.net/publication/306287047_Misappropriating_Discourse-_Intercultural_Communication_Theory_in_South_Africa_1980-1995.
2. Paul Du Gay, *Production of Culture/Cultures of Production* (London: Sage, 1997).
3. Stuart Hall, "Encoding/Decoding," in *Culture, Media and Language*, eds. Stuart Hall, Dorothy Hobson, Andy Lowe, and Paul Willis (London: Hutchinson, 1981), 128–38.
4. Ruth Teer-Tomaselli, IAMCR bid document, South–North Conversations IAMCR Conference, July 2012. SACOMM-UKZN, 7 June 2011, p. 1, https://iamcr.org/iamcr-2012programme-online.
5. Matthew Arnold, *Culture and Anarchy* (Cambridge, UK: Cambridge University Press, 1869).
6. Astrid Von Kotze, *Organise & Act: The Natal Workers Theatre Movement 1983–1987* (Durban: Culture and Working Life Publications, 1988).
7. See Aelred Stubbs, ed., *Steve Biko 1946–1977: I Write What I Like* (London: Bowerdean Press, 1978).
8. Handel K Wright, *A Prescience of African Cultural Studies: The Future of Literature in Africa is Not What It Was* (New York: Peter Lang, 2004).
9. S.A. Van der Smit, "Ngugi Wa Thiong'o and Kenyan Theatre in Focus" (master's Thesis, University of Namibia, 2007), http://repository.unam.edu.na/bitstream/handle/11070/388/vandersmit2007.pdf?sequence=1&isAllowed=y.
10. Ngugi wa Thiong'o, *Decolonising the Mind: The Politics of Language in African Language* (London: James Currey, 1986).
11. Paolo Freire, *Pedagogy of the Oppressed*, 30th anniversary ed. (New York: Continuum, 2005). See also Emma Durden and Keyan G. Tomaselli, "Theory Meets Theatre Practice: Making a Difference to Public Health Programmes in Southern Africa—Professor Lynn Dalrymple: South African Scholar, Activist, Educator," *Curriculum Inquiry* 42, no. 1 (2012): 80–102.
12. Keyan G. Tomaselli, *Appropriating Images: The Semiotics of Visual Representation* (Højberg: Intervention Press, 1996).
13. Keyan G. Tomaselli, "Alter-Egos: Cultural and Media Studies," *Critical Arts* 26, no. 1 (2012): 14–38.
14. Handel K. Wright, "Dare We De-Centre Birmingham? Troubling the 'Origin' and Trajectories of Cultural Studies," *European Journal of Cultural Studies* 1, no. 1 (1998): 33–56.
15. Joke Hermes et al., "On the Move: Twentieth Anniversary Edition of the *European Journal of Cultural Studies*," *European Journal of Cultural Studies* 20, no. 6 (2017): 595–605.
16. Eric P. Louw, "Rethinking the Leftist Struggle in South Africa," *Critical Arts* 6, no. 1 (1992): 1–25. See also: Keyan G. Tomaselli, "Encoding/decoding, The Transmission Model and a Court of Law," *International Journal of Cultural Studies* 19, no. 1 (2015): 59–70.
17. Stuart Hall, "Life and Times of the First New Left," *New Left Review* 61 (January–February 2010), https://newleftreview.org/II/61/stuart-hall-life-and-times-of-the-first-new-left.
18. Tony Bennett, "Putting Policy into Cultural Studies," in *Cultural Studies*, eds. Larry Grossberg, Cary. Nelson, and Paula A. Treichler (New York: Routledge, 1992), 23–38.
19. Handel K. Wright, "What has African Cultural Studies Done for You Lately? Autobiographical and Global Considerations of a Floating Signifier," *Critical Arts* 30, no. 4 (2016): 478–95.
20. Van der Smit, "Ngugi Wa Thiong'o and Kenyan Theatre in Focus," cccxi–cccxi.
21. Keyan G. Tomaselli and Nyasha Mboti, "'Doing' Cultural Studies: What is Literacy in the Age of the Post?" *International Journal of Cultural Studies* 16, no. 5 (2013): 521–37. See also Keyan Tomaselli, Nyasha Mboti and Helge Rønning, "South–North Perspectives: The Development of Cultural and Media Studies in Southern Africa," *Media, Culture and Society* 35, no. 1 (2013): 36–43.
22. Jürgen Habermas, *The Structural Transformation of the Public Sphere* (Cambridge, MA: MIT Press, 1991).
23. Ragnar Waldhal, ed., *Perspectives on Media, Culture and Democracy in Zimbabwe* (Oslo: University of Oslo, Department of Media and Communication, 1998).

24 Ruth E. Teer-Tomaselli, "Transforming State-Owned Enterprises in the Global Age: Lessons from Broadcasting and Telecommunications in South Africa," in *Political Economy of Media Transformation in South Africa*, eds. Anthony Olorunnisola and Keyan G. Tomaselli (Cresskill, NJ: Hampton Press, 2011), 133–66.
25 Nhamo Mhiriphiri, "This Hard Place and that Hard Terrain: Emerging Perspectives on Media and Cultural Studies on or in Zimbabwe," in *The Palgrave Handbook of Media and Communication Research in Africa*, ed. Bruce Mutsvairo (London: Palgrave, 2018), 427–50.
26 T.I. Oizerman, "Kant's Doctrine of the 'Things in Themselves' and Noumena," *Philosophy and Phenomenological Research* 41, no. 3 (1981): 333–50.
27 Jean Comaroff and John Comaroff, eds., *Millennial Capitalism and the Culture of Neoliberalism* (Durham, NC: Duke University Press, 2001).
28 Paul Stoller, "Eye, Mind and Word in Anthropology," *L'Homme* 24, no. 3–4 (1984): 91–114. Paul Stoller, *The Cinematic Griot: the Ethnography of Jean Rouch* (Chicago: Chicago University Press, 1992).
29 Stoller, *The Cinematic Griot*, 205.
30 Jeannette DeBouzek, "The 'Ethnographic Surrealism' of Jean Rouch," *Visual Anthropology* 2, no. 3–4 (1989): 304.
31 Paul Stoller, *The Taste of Ethnographic Things: The Senses in Anthropology* (Philadelphia: University of Pennsylvania Press, 1989): 54.
32 Stoller, "Eye, Mind and Word in Anthropology," 110.
33 Charles Sanders Peirce, Adirondack Lectures, *The Collected Papers of Charles Sanders Peirce Vol. 1*, in eds. Hartshorne Charles and Weiss Paul (Cambridge, MA: Harvard University Press, 1931), paragraph 284.
34 Tzvetan Todorov, *The Fantastic: A Structural Approach to a Literary Genre*, trans. Richard Howard (New York: Ithaca, 1973).
35 Keyan G Tomaselli, "Virtual Religion, the Fantastic, and Electronic Ontology," *Visual Anthropology* 28, no. 2 (2015): 109–26.
36 Enrico Fulchignoni, "Conversation Between Jean Rouch and Professor Enrico Fulchignoni," *Visual Anthropology* 2, no. 3–4 (1989): 265–300.
37 Jean Comaroff and John Comaroff, "Millennial Capitalism: First Thoughts on a Second Coming," *Public Culture* 12, no. 2 (2000): 292.
38 See, e.g., Karl Marx, *Capital: A Critique of Political Economy*, trans. Ben Fowkes, vol. 1 (New York: Penguin, 1990): 163–4.
39 Lana Swartz, "What was Bitcoin? The Techno-Economic Imaginaries of a New Money Technology," *Cultural Studies* 32, no. 4 (2018): 623–50.
40 Bill Maurer, *Mutual Life, Limited: Islamic Banking, Alternative Currencies, Lateral Reasoning* (Princeton, NJ: Princeton University Press, 2005): 85.
41 Francis P. Kasoma, "The Foundations of African Ethics (Afriethics) and the Professional Practice of Journalism: The Case of Society-Centered Media Morality," *Africa Media Review* 10, no. 2 (1996): 93–116.
42 Kasoma, "The Foundations of African Ethics," 107–8.
43 Chetan Bhatt, "The Virtues of Violence and Arts of Terror: The Salafi-Jihadist Political Universe," *Theory, Culture and Society* 3, no. 1 (2014): 25–48.

What Has African Cultural Studies Done for You Lately? Autobiographical and Global Considerations of a Floating Signifier

Handel Kashope Wright

ABSTRACT

This essay poses and attempts to answer the central question: 'What does African Cultural Studies do?' It takes an autobiographical approach to address the genealogy, status quo and the potential future of the floating signifier that is African Cultural Studies. It unpacks and multiplies African Cultural Studies and contextualises it as a form of African studies and as both interventionist in and contributory to transnational cultural studies. African Cultural Studies' marginality in the global discourse is rearticulated as both a positioning of disempowerment on the one hand and one of generative and insurgent politics on the other. Stressing the need for continental and diasporic Africans to self-identify issues to be addressed (in place of Eurocentric, imposed preoccupations), the essay identifies as examples the always already complex nature of identity and belonging (and the irony of emergent xenophobia); continental and diasporic relations that trouble the taken-for-grantedness of what constitutes Africa(ns), and queer Africa in the face of institutionalised homophobia. Whether local nativist or globally engaged approaches are taken, the essay concludes that African Cultural Studies ought to be self-reflexively dedicated not only to doing Cultural Studies but to what the doing of African Cultural Studies does for Africa(ns) and for Transnational Cultural Studies.

Addressing the status quo and future of 'African Cultural Studies' is a seriously daunting task, but that is what we are gathered here to undertake.[1] The programme promises a truly exciting variety of topics and issues that are to be addressed in the first conference on African Cultural Studies in Canada. But this assumes that there is such a thing as African Cultural Studies and that it is readily recognised. My title troubles this idea by describing African Cultural Studies as a floating signifier. My autobiographical approach will address some global and intellectual considerations. I resist taking up the notion and texts of African Cultural Studies as given and circumscribed, as examples of what Edward Said (1983) decries as an impossibility: texts that exist in a hermetically sealed cosmos. Instead I want to trouble the taken-for-granted meaning of the very category we will be working with at this conference, to unfix and multiply its meaning, to speak to its inherent political nature and relatedness to what Foucault (1980) calls power-knowledge and to emphasize what Said would call its worldliness.

Explaining my title is hopefully a productive way to both introduce and contribute to addressing my topic. I want to follow Stuart Hall's (1992) lead and absolve myself of what he described as 'the many burdens of representation which people carry around'; of an African version of what Hall termed 'the black man's burden' (Hall 1992: 277).[2] In my case and especially as a keynote speaker, the expectation might be that I will speak not only experientially but authentically and authoritatively about continental African identity, Africa and its issues, the African diaspora, Black lives on the continent and in the diaspora and indeed all things Black and African. After all, I am Black and thus have the phenotypical credentials for it; I am a Sierra Leonean, born and bred on the continent and so have the deep historical, spatial and cultural roots for it; I am an African working in the Canadian academy and thus am what Spivak (1999) has called 'the native informant at hand' who can be relied upon to translate Africa and Africans to academics in the audience who are not African. And I am even dressed for the role – in 'African robes', surely about to perform or indeed perhaps already performing authentic Africanness and Blackness or at least the Black African academic at hand.

Taking an autobiographical approach comes with the danger of positioning oneself as unassailably correct in one's authority and authenticity, as narcissistic or as given over to navel-gazing. My intention here is quite the opposite: as Hall (1992: 277) points out, paradoxically, 'in order not to be authoritative, I've got to speak autobiographically'. And to borrow again from Hall's modest intellectualism, more specifically his generative notion 'without guarantees' (Hall 1986; Gilroy, Grossberg and McRobbie 2000; Andrews and Giardina 2008; Wright 2016a), I regard what I am attempting here as 'African Cultural Studies without guarantees', a designation that signals both the high importance of the overall project of articulating (in both senses) African Cultural Studies on the one hand and on the other the caveat that the justness of the overall project is no guarantee that my specific approach and this particular work is effective, correct, and justified. Yes, I will touch on the contours, history and potential future of African Cultural Studies not definitively and authoritatively but rather under the restraint of the personal – decidedly subjectively, even, hopefully, modestly, with necessary caveats and nods to other ways of seeing things and within the limits of my own takes on the issues. I take up African Cultural Studies as actually or potentially utilitarian, not only in the sense of contributions it might make to exploring aspects of African culture and addressing African problems but also and especially in the sense of contributions it is making and could make to our conceptualisation of the origin and history (or more accurately, the origins and histories) of Global Cultural Studies and to the work of representation within it.

Unpacking and Multiplying African Cultural Studies

So, what of our object of study, African Cultural Studies? It is all too easy to take it for granted that the object is identifiable and universally recognised. I have deliberately described it as a floating signifier to trouble this idea. I don't mean to suggest African Cultural Studies is a floating signifier in Claude Levi-Strauss' (1987) original literal sense (i.e. a signifier without a referent or without a signified) but rather in Ernesto Laclau's (1996) overtly politicised sense of the floating signifier having a signified which is in fact the result of a hegemonic process that has appropriated (and obfuscated) various unsatisfied demands. An empty signifier in Laclau's sense is necessarily open to contestation, with claims made upon it by various differing, opposing or allied political stances and causes. In this sense, then, though it might appear to be known, what we are calling African Cultural Studies should more accurately be identified as multiple (reflective of various positions on Africa, African Studies and Cultural Studies) and should be contested over in the struggle for what it can and should become.

Consider, for example, the spatiality of African Cultural Studies: are we speaking strictly about continental Africa or does the concept spill over beyond the continent into its globally dispersed diaspora? Jacinta Muteshi (2003) considers the distinction between continent and diaspora to be substantial and meaningful and is quite wary of the altogether too comfortable appropriations of African dress, names, culture and identity by some in the diaspora (Blacks in New York in her specific example). On the other hand, Molefi Asante (1990: 7), drawing on Wole Soyinka's (1990) criticism of a limited and limiting 'saline consciousness' vision of Africa, has asserted somewhat poetically that 'Africa does not end where salt water licks the shores of the continent'.

And if we are to extend our identities, necessarily uncomfortably beyond what Hall (1996) has rightly called our 'minimal selves', how about Africans and African culture and identity? Do they refer, in strategically essentialised terms (à la Gayatri Spivak) to a homogenous Black Africa or to a notion that acknowledges a complexity of multiple Black ethnicities and cultures? Or, even more complexly, do they refer to the juxtaposition and intermingling of (the always already contested categories) Arabs, Asians, Blacks and whites of various ethnicities and individual and hybridised material cultures and practices on the continent? In the diaspora especially and even on the continent, we can stick with cultural nationalism, which Paul Gilroy (1995: 2) describes as 'conceptions of culture which present immutable, ethnic differences as an absolute break in the histories and experiences of "Black" and "white" people' or we can conceptualise African identity as always already constituted by what Gilroy identifies as the more difficult theoretical/conceptual frames of 'creolization, metissage, mestizaje and hybridity' (ibid).

In disciplinary (and indeed multidisciplinary) terms, African Cultural Studies can be conceptualised in various ways. I'll speak to two of these: first, in relation to area studies as a form of African Studies and second, in relation to the field of Cultural Studies as a distinctive discursive frame within and contributor to Global Cultural Studies. V.Y. Mudimbe (1988) makes the sustained and persuasive argument that African Studies is always already a historical and political construction, one in which the historical and global politics of knowledge construction (what Foucault (1980) cogently calls 'power-knowledge') is inextricably imbricated. More specifically, Mudimbe illustrates that from philosophy to ethnology to anthropology, African Studies is imbricated in the racial/racist, colonial/imperialist, ideological/Eurocentrist relations between Europe as epistemological centre and arbiter and Africa as knowledge object, with even African and Africanist scholars working within Eurocentric frames as imitators of Eurocentric disciplinarity and scholarship. Mudimbe asserts that in fact from explorations to religious conversions to disciplinary examinations, African Studies is actually not about Africa and its peoples and cultures but ultimately about Europe and whiteness. Ethnographies of contemporary 'traditional' African peoples for example are in reality a way of vicariously witnessing and capturing the lived reality of Europe's primitive past and the study of African art is about articulating through Eurocentric criteria-based description and evaluation of the primitive expression of Africans the binary opposite, namely the aesthetic superiority of European art.

What of the 'Cultural Studies" in African Cultural Studies? Are we speaking of applying to the study of Africa the received discursive formation which originated at the University of Birmingham, UK, in the 1960s, originally as a radical, neo-Marxist project and praxis focused on multi-, inter- and, yes, even anti-disciplinary discourse and which has since been tamed and disciplined over time and through its global spread?[3] Or are we speaking of the unfortunately little-known alternative advocated by Ntongela Masilela (1989) in his critique of one of the earliest African Cultural Studies texts, *Rethinking Culture* (Tomaselli 1989), namely an organic discursive formation derived from local African cultures and ways of knowing and drawing on progressive African theorists who engage indigenous knowledge?[4] Or even more complexly, are we speaking, as I advocate and undertake in my own work (e.g. Wright 2004), of the need to hold those two in hopefully productive tension, the result of which is a discursive formation that draws on both African ways of knowing and theorists on the one hand and the discourse of supposedly Global Cultural Studies on the other, and which necessarily exists in dialogue with Global Cultural Studies?

Finally, is there something beyond an awkward, superficial reference to a 1980s Janet Jackson song to my question, 'What has African Cultural Studies done for you lately'?[5] I would like to think so. Beyond the meaning of African Cultural Studies, I want to touch on the function and effects, real and potential, of African Cultural Studies. In other words, I am not only interested in historicizing and addressing the meaning of African Cultural Studies but also in exploring what it has done and can do for the study of Africa and Africans and for the history and future development of the field of Global Cultural Studies. In Cultural Studies terms, I move from Richard Johnson's (1986) famous, generative question, 'What is cultural studies anyway?', to the more recent and potentially equally generative questions by Steven Connor (2003), who asks, 'What can cultural studies do?', and even more substantially, Meaghan Morris (1997: 38) who exhorts that we 'ask in a mundane and unrepentantly academic spirit, not what cultural studies "is" but what it does, and does not, claim *to do* as a working project in the Humanities'. And we can extend Morris' question beyond the Humanities, indeed beyond the disciplines, to ask simply, 'What does Cultural Studies do?', a truncation I have employed elsewhere (Wright 2016a) which expands Morris' question to be about Cultural Studies (and for our purposes here, African Cultural Studies) as an academic field and intellectual project.

The Origin(s) and Global Spread of Cultural Studies: An African Intervention

Cultural Studies emerged in England in 1964 with the establishment of the Centre for Contemporary Cultural Studies (CCCS) at the University of Birmingham, England. It was a neo-Marxist, project-oriented inter/antidisciplinary response to an international series of crises in the Social Sciences and Humanities and its founding fathers were E.P. Thompson, Raymond Williams and Richard Hoggart. This single and singular originary narrative is oft repeated, including in most introductory texts (Bratlinger 1990; Turner 1990; Gray and McGuigan 1993) and is a taken-for- granted history that has passed into common sense. From quite humble institutional beginnings – the CCCS was literally a few offices at the end of a hallway (Hall 1980) – Cultural Studies caught on and spread throughout Britain and on to North America (Grossberg 1993; Morrow 1995), Australia (Frow and Morris 1993), the rest of Europe (Eskola and Vanikkala 1994), on to Asia (Chen 1998) and even trickled into parts of Africa (Tomaselli 1989).

As a graduate student, I was excited about the prospects of a Cultural Studies approach to addressing issues in African Literary Studies (my eventual PhD topic became an argument for making a transition from Literary to a more utilitarian Cultural Studies approach to texts in the African context). Some twenty years later, I continue to be excited about what Cultural Studies makes possible in terms of African Studies, namely an interdisciplinary, representation-sensitive, popular-culture inclusive, overtly social justice-oriented project alternative to traditional, supposedly apolitical, single-discipline or even multidisciplinary approaches to African Studies. However, I have also always been uncomfortable with the received, common-sense origin narrative of Cultural Studies. Even as a (Black, Sierra Leonean) graduate student at a Canadian university, it struck me as deeply ironic that a field and approach to knowledge that was global in scope and which made identity, difference and the politics of representation central and was overtly social justice- oriented had such a definitively single and singular white, male, British origin and only existed elsewhere as a received discourse.

While it is clear that it is at the CCCS that named, institutionalised, academy-based Cultural Studies emerged, the various characteristics of Cultural Studies (project-driven rather than discipline-circumscribed; critique of historical and especially contemporary sociocultural and political arrangements; serious engagement of the popular; overtly social justice oriented; etc.) were all characteristics that could be found in other places and times. What this suggested to me was that we could recognise, indeed ought to recognise, a number of 'origins' of Cultural Studies. I therefore have identified the Kamiriithu Education and Cultural Centre, established in 1977 in the slum village of Limuru, Kenya as the 'true' origin of Cultural Studies, with writer and intellectual, Ngugi wa Thiong'o and the mostly female members of the Centre as the constructors of what we now call Cultural Studies. Kamiriithu surpasses Birmingham in epitomising the characteristics and ideals of Cultural Studies.[6] Finally, I pointed to several other potential originary moments for cultural studies: culturology in Russia in the 1920s, the Harlem Rennaisance in the US in the 1920s and 1930s, the Négritude Movement in France, francophone Africa and the French West Indies in the 1930s (Wright 2004: 65).

I put forward Kamiriithu and other origins with tongue partly in cheek. I did not mean to suggest that the received narrative of a Birmingham origin was wrong, nor was I seriously offering Kamiriithu as a correction of a historical error. Rather, my purpose was to put forward Kamiriithu (and other viable origin narratives) in order to, variously, multiply origins of a now global discourse, draw attention to the fact that Birmingham has been thoroughly 'fetishised', and contribute to alleviating the spectres of an almost colonial history and definite centre-margin trajectories of Global Cultural Studies.

My arguments and those of others from Cultural Studies' margins have had some effect. For example, both Richard Maxwell (2000) and Toby Miller (2006) have produced a multiple, global narrative of the origin and history of Cultural Studies. They include Stuart Hall (Black intellectual from the former British colony of Jamaica) as a founding father and identify origins and trajectories from Britain, France and Italy, Africa, the United States and Latin America. Thus, well beyond contributing to the globalisation of Cultural Studies, some arguments and interventions from African Cultural Studies are also contributing to rethinking the very origins and trajectories of the field and thus to democratising Global Cultural Studies.

National, Regional, Transnational Cultural Studies

The principal way Cultural Studies is being instituted is in distinct national and regional forms (British, American, Canadian, Australian, Nordic, Latin American, etc.). While national and regional varieties of Cultural Studies are a common–sense development, they are also somewhat awkward, if not problematic, for various reasons, including the fact that they homogenise specific local projects into a larger totality on the one hand and get in the way of the cross-fertilization of ideas and projects across national and regional boundaries and hence the development of Transnational Cultural Studies on the other. It is not surprising, therefore, that Hall (1992: 277) once referred to British Cultural Studies as 'a pretty awkward signifier', while Larry Grossberg (quoted in Wright 2001: 155) has critiqued national traditions as 'generally wrongheaded'.

African nation states are, of course, always already awkward in my view, since the vast majority of them are the direct result of European imperialism, more specifically, the Partitioning of Africa and the naming of colonies, sometimes simply after exploitable resources (e.g. the Ivory Coast, the Gold Coast, Cameroon). Post-independence African states and nation-state-based nationalism are therefore inherently ironic as a legacy of European colonialism, and this deepens the irony and awkwardness of the development of national traditions on the African continent. For example, it is indisputable that South Africa has the longest history of established Cultural Studies (see Tomaselli 2012) and while some of the most exciting developments are emerging from that country, the evolution of a distinct South African Cultural Studies adds to the awkwardness of proliferating national forms. Fortunately, the South African example is rare and moreover is rather porous (with the presence, input, interventions and outernational expansions of non-national faculty and graduate students in the South African academy). Cultural Studies is relatively new and quite diffuse in the rest of the continent and, even more importantly, there is a tendency among African Cultural Studies scholars to conceptualise their work and framework on a continental, even pan-African continent-diaspora scale.[7]

What does all of this mean for African Cultural Studies? On the one hand, the category is a formation that avoids some of the pitfalls of national conceptions of cultural studies – extending as it does beyond individual national borders and actually or potentially involving politics that smooths out differences and promotes empowering cohesion. This very conference has drawn a disparate set of scholars together because they identify with and their work fits into the broad category, African cultural studies. And since the 1980s, the journal *Critical Arts*, published out of what was then the University of Natal (now KwaZulu-Natal), with its essays on issues in Media and Cultural Studies of South Africa and other African countries, has made concrete contributions to the establishment of African Cultural Studies. On the other hand, a continental category, let alone continental plus diasporic category, is an overly broad frame that is near-useless when it comes to examining culture concretely – it misses the specificity of discrete local material and other forms of culture. And there is a price to pay for transitioning from the national and continental to the transnational. To continue with the example of *Critical Arts*, the journal is now decidedly global and transnational in scope and while this has meant the inclusion of African Cultural Studies in a global frame, the cost has been the loss of the exclusive focus on Africa and Africans, a void other journals (e.g. the *Journal of African Cultural Studies*)[8] have emerged to fill. It is an awareness of the importance of addressing the complexity and specificity of the local that led McKenzie Wark (1994) to espouse a city–specific Cultural Studies, namely Sydney Cultural Studies, and it is a similar awareness of the need to address the specificity of the local that led the CCCS's successor, the now defunct Department of Cultural Studies and Sociology to make the city of Birmingham the primary locus for students' and even various faculty members' research and praxis projects. It would be interesting to see, in contrast with or in addition to African Cultural Studies, the Cultural Studies of Freetown, Cairo, Lagos, Kumasi, Nairobi and Johannesburg.

My own preference is for African Cultural Studies that is at once distinct (however ambivalently) and yet engaged with and imbricated in Global Transnational Cultural Studies[9] (as in the current scope of *Critical Arts*). As a recent example, in a special issue of the *International Journal of Cultural Studies* I edited on 'The worldliness of Stuart Hall', (Wright 2016a), among essays from Britain, Wales, Argentina, Australia and Finland, I made sure to invite an essay from and on Cultural Studies in the South African context (Tomaselli 2016) and in my own contribution to the collection (Wright 2016b) addressed Stuart Hall's relevance for the study of continental African Blackness. It would be naïve to think of the articulation of African and Transnational Cultural Studies as the mere seamless insertion of African Cultural Studies into an existing Transnational Cultural Studies. In fact, despite the exhortation of Chen (1992) and others, there isn't a thriving Transnational Cultural Studies per se for African Cultural Studies to incorporate itself into and it is unclear whether African Cultural Studies could be sustained as a discrete discourse if it did. Furthermore, the articulation of Transnational Cultural Studies that includes African Cultural Studies necessarily means challenges and changes to both African and especially non-African national and global formations of Cultural Studies. I'd like to flesh out this last point somewhat with a concrete example. Since we've used him before and he serves well as a figure that could represent Ntongela's organic African knowledge, let us turn again to Ngugi wa Thiong'o and tease out a bit what it might mean to appropriate him for Transnational Cultural Studies.

Appropriating Ngugi for transnationalism would involve considering his work as simultaneously Kenyan (national, nationalist), African (continental, African nationalist), Black Atlantic (global, pan-Africanist), postcolonial (global, anti-imperialist), universalist (since he once identified himself as an 'unrepentant universalist' (Ngugi 1993: xvii), and since he has resided and has been writing and teaching in the US for the past while, even American. Thus Ngugi's work would both parallel and encapsulate the struggle over the spatiality of Cultural Studies.

Transnationalism also means having to acknowledge and work with Ngugi's Marxism, his anti-imperialism, his repudiation of the English language in favour of Kikuyu, his Kenyan nationalism and frequent revisiting of Kenya's past, and his (too infrequently acknowledged) universalism and comprehensive pan-African relations and work, however alien, uncomfortable and inconvenient some of these aspects of his work might prove, especially within US Cultural Studies. The range of politics of Transnational Cultural Studies and especially National Cultural Studies is therefore challenged by a figure like Ngugi. It means taking up Ngugi as important not simply as an individual writer and sociocultural critic but also and perhaps more importantly as part of the articulation of national and outernational, indeed transnational discourses of cultural studies. Ngugi's work on Kamiriithu and his decision to reject English and employ Kikuyu in his writings and his proposal of Swahili as the appropriate language of African literature would not only parallel but contribute to the perennial problematic, indeed problem, of the language of cultural studies, a field dominated by

English to the chagrin of figures like Chantal Cornut-Gentille D'arcy (2009) and Daniel Mato (2016), both Spanish speakers who hold that the hegemony of English as the language of Cultural Studies is partly responsible for the failure of Cultural Studies to blossom in Latin America and Spain.

Current Issues and/in Utilitarian African Cultural Studies

One of the issues African Cultural Studies needs to continue to address is its positioning within Global Cultural Studies and the mutual effect the two have on each other. John Hartley has made two comments in passing about Global Cultural Studies that are of considerable import for African Cultural Studies particularly. In his preface to the 'Dismantle Fremantle' special issue of *Cultural Studies* he co-edited with Ien Ang, Hartley initially pointed out that academic Cultural Studies is hedged about by dominant disciplines but then goes on to add that, in spite of this, '[t]here are those for whom cultural studies is not hedged but hegemonic' (Hartley 1992). I believe that observation to be particularly true of African Cultural Studies, not only at the time (the early 1990s) but even today. Looking outward from within African Cultural Studies, one cannot help but feel that despite its spread around the globe, Cultural Studies has never become truly globally representative but rather remains a mostly Eurocentric, indeed Anglocentric (predominantly British-American-Australian) tradition passing itself off as a global intellectual field. In the second instance, Hartley (2003: 9), in his *Short history of cultural studies*, asserts that '[b]y refusing disciplinary orthodoxy, cultural studies kept the door open to innovation from the margins, in line with its longstanding interest in difference and marginality'. That longstanding interest in difference and marginality does or at least should include representation of Africa, Africans and African Cultural Studies. In this sense, the fact that African Cultural Studies remains marginal within Global Cultural Studies is not completely negative, since there is considerable productive potential in marginality. bell hooks (1990) has asserted that the margin is not only a place of disempowerment but also a site of generative and insurgent politics, and what this means is that African Cultural Studies can make significant contributions to the evolution of a truly representative and reinvigorated Transnational Cultural Studies.

There is considerable pressure on African Studies to address pressing, practical issues on the continent. African Cultural Studies could also benefit from a strong (though I would hasten to add not exclusive) utilitarian approach. However, we would need to avoid the western–interest-centred approach which is often reflected in utilitarian African Studies. Altogether too much of the scholarship on Africa is about the political in a traditional sense and altogether too much of that is taken up from a Eurocentric perspective and altogether too much of it is negative, giving rise to the homogenized text of Africa as a political and economic basket case, punctuated by stories and images of religious and ethnic conflict, wars and child soldiers, disease, drought, famine and malnourished babies, corruption and exploitative politicians (Wright 2012). There has been interest in Somalia and Zimbabwe as failed states mainly after a rise in piracy of international shipping by Somalis and attacks on white farmers in Zimbabwe. There is western interest in supposedly Islamic terrorism in Africa only after attacks on the US Embassy in Kenya and when a Nigerian Islamist militant group named 'western education is forbidden' (Boko Haram) pledges allegiance to the Islamic State of Iraq and the Levant (ISIL). And there is interest in Liberia, Guinea and Sierra

Leone only because of quite irrational fear of the threat that the ebola epidemic in West Africa might pose to western countries in these overly connected times (Wright 2016b).

In my view, a utilitarian Cultural Studies demands some attention to other issues and other perspectives, including the need for nuanced, in-depth and social–justice and equity–directed examinations of current issues on the continent and its relationship with the diaspora. For example, even as the discourse of Afropessimism has gained traction (Mbembe 2003; Wilderson 2010; Sexton 2011), it now competes with the idea that we are entering what has been identified as the African era (Comaroff and Comaroff 2012). What does this mean for the potential alleviation of what Samir Amin (1992) in the early 1990s presciently called the Fourthworldization of Africa? From historical 'Ghana must go' in Nigeria and its current reverberations to the demonisation of regular and irregular migrant workers from other African countries in South Africa, to the underreported brutal attacks on and mistreatment of African migrant workers in Libya during the Arab Spring, xenophobia is clearly on the rise on the continent. The silver lining is that this is evidence of movement of Africans within the continent – emigration, immigration, migration – that also makes for what Zygmunt Bauman (2007) calls 'mixophilia', interethnic and even interracial unions and rich cultural mixing, especially in major African cities.

Homophobia has raised its ugly head recently as part of official policy and discourse in countries from Nigeria to Cameroon to Uganda with draconian laws passed that criminalise same sex intercourse and elements of the fifth estate that have endorsed these moves, including by releasing names of real or suspected gay men and lesbians. The silver lining to this is that the very existence of these laws and suppressive measures give the lie to the idea that homosexuality and queerness are completely un-African, a western phenomenon and imposition. Additionally, there are several African countries that are codifying tolerance toward the LGBT[10] community and emergent anti-homophobia activism. Cultural Studies can act not only to document and support queer activists in African countries but to explore the complexity of queer life, including emergent queer lifestyles, the operation and limits of the codification of LGBT rights, and the involvement of western evangelist churches in promoting homophobia, etc. which illustrates not only that queerness is not un-African but rather that it is rabid religion-based homophobia that is the western import.

What constitutes Africa and African identity, especially in terms of the Africa-diaspora continuum, should in my view continue to engage African Cultural Studies. Explorations of the relationship between continental Africa and Africans in the diasporas have focussed on whether those who are diasporic, including those who are doubly diasporic, can and ought to claim an African identity. There has been considerable migration of continental Africans to the West for various reasons (including immediate and later vestigial postcolonial migration from the African margin to European centres, especially of Britain and France; economic migration to North America, Europe and to a lesser extent, Asia). Yet little intellectual attention, including in the field of Cultural Studies, has been paid to this other side of things. Of course sociologists and anthropologists have addressed the presence of African diasporas but this literature has tended to take up a traditional notion of diaspora (members of specific African ethnic or national groups transplanted outside of the continent and maintaining their continental culture elsewhere). What Cultural Studies can contribute is an interdisciplinary exploration of when and to what extent continental Africans in the diaspora can and should claim diasporic identification, and even identity (Wright 2016b).

Conclusion: What Has (African) Cultural Studies Done for You Lately?

I've tried in this brief essay to trouble the taken-for-grantedness of African Cultural Studies and to a lesser extent, Global Cultural Studies. With some specifics, including from my own work and perspectives, I have pointed to some of what Cultural Studies has offered to African Studies on the one hand and what African Cultural Studies has contributed to Global Cultural Studies on the other. In keeping with my efforts to contribute to complicating and multiplying the origins and history of Global Cultural Studies, I have eschewed taking African Cultural Studies as given and singular in favour of considering it as multiple and contested. I have pointed to the ambivalent position African Cultural Studies occupies in Global Cultural Studies – at once relatively diffuse and marginalised and integral and contributory. I have outlined some of the issues that are and should be the focus of contemporary and future African Cultural Studies from the politics of difference (including queer identities, politics and culture on the one hand and social and official homophobia on the other) to intracontinental migration and the ensuing responses of xenophobia and mixophobia, from the relationship between the continent and its diasporas to the place of African Cultural Studies within Global Cultural Studies.

While it is fine to keep doing African Cultural Studies, I think we ought to step back once in a while to consider not just our work in Cultural Studies but what our doing of that work does. As Foucault once declared, '[w]e know what we do and we know, up to a point, why we do it: what we don't know is what what we do does' (in Connor 2003: 209). Cultural Studies has never pretended to be neutral, and African Cultural Studies also should be self-reflexive not only about the political stances it takes and projects it chooses to undertake but also about its own worldliness, the effects it has upon the world by its very existence. The worldliness of African Cultural Studies includes the fact that it is a viable and to my mind preferable alternative to single-discipline and even supposedly politically neutral multidisciplinary area studies of Africa. It also includes the fact that its existence serves (or ought to serve) to have supposedly Global Cultural Studies face what Foucault would call the history of its present – the ironies of its hegemonic whiteness, Eurocentrism and linguistic parochialism.

Whether one wants to take it as given or put it under erasure or consider it a floating signifier, insist on essentialising and romanticising or multiplying and troubling it, there is an existing African Cultural Studies and many, including scholars at this conference, are busy undertaking important work under its rubric, including work based on the national frame (especially South African Cultural Studies). This reality makes interventions and contributions by progressive African and Africanist scholars to African Cultural Studies and Cultural Studies frames for addressing African issues all the more urgent. Despite the caveat that my arguments represent, we cannot not do African Cultural Studies. My plea is that we eschew a coherent, unitary, fixed and in sum, innocent and romanticised African Cultural Studies. Instead, I advocate that we undertake African Cultural Studies reflexively (as Hall would say, 'without guarantees'); that like the mythical Sankofa bird we make progress by heading forward but with our heads turned backwards to capture precious knowledge from the past in the form of the egg that will shape the fragile, precious future we seek; that we revive and utilise the neglected organic, localist frame advocated by Masilela; that we refuse to be the exotic addition and insist on being a robust contribution to Global, Transnational Cultural Studies and that we utilise a Cultural Studies frame to address the pressing and interesting issues facing Africa and its diaspora.

Acknowledgement

I wish to acknowledge the Department of Communication Studies, University of Johannesburg, South Africa, which provided support to me as Senior Research Associate to undertake this work.

Notes

1. This paper was initially presented as the opening keynote address at the John Douglas Taylor Conference: Contemporary Orientations in African Cultural Studies, May 30–June, 2014. I have made some changes (including deleting some sections, writing some new ones and updating some examples), but I have kept the presentation format and flow of the original and produced much of the talk verbatim here.
2. Throughout this essay I employ the overtly politicised, capitalised spelling of 'Black' (with the exception of references to others work where the word is not capitalized (e.g. the quote here from Stuart Hall).
3. For example, Alan O'Connor (1989) pointed in the 1980s to the myriad aspects that collectively constitute 'the problem of American cultural studies', including the downplaying of the (neo) Marxist foundations and connection with concrete Leftist intellectual projects that characterised early British Cultural Studies.
4. More specifically, Masilela addresses the need to develop South African Cultural Studies (as distinct from Cultural Studies in South Africa) but his arguments can be applied to and imbricate African Cultural Studies more generally. His principal call is for the Africanisation of Cultural Studies in South Africa through nativisation.
5. The title quip, 'what have you done for me lately?' in Jackson's (1986) song expresses the artist's frustration with her lover who used to do everything to prove himself her ideal man and who now does few of those things and has fallen sharply in her estimation. Finding Cultural Studies in general and especially African Cultural Studies in particular as a graduate student was for me the discovery of the ideal discourse, nothing short of an academic, intellectual and political home. What I want to channel here is not disappointment with, let alone dismissal of Cultural Studies (Jackson's song is reputedly about her ex-husband, James DeBarge whom she divorced a year earlier) but rather the implied challenge to recover (or more realistically to work on re-making) the magic of those early years.
6. For background on the Kamiriithu Community Education Cultural Centre, including its artistic and cultural work projects and activities, see Kidd (1985) and Ngugi (1997) and for the elaborated version of my arguments for recognition of Kamiriithu as an additional origin of cultural studies and comparison of Kamiriithu and Birmingham see Wright (1998; 2004).
7. The continental, pan-African scope is reflected not only in the overall frame of collections such as Wright and Tomaselli (2008) but in the politics of the individual contributors and hence the essays within such collections.
8. As indicated in the Aims and Scope statement, 'The Journal of African Cultural Studies is an international journal providing a forum for perceptions of African culture from inside and outside Africa, with a special commitment to African scholarship'.
9. For an example of the argument for a Transnational Cultural Studies, see Chen (1992).
10. I employ 'LGBT' (the acronym which stands in for lesbian, gay, bisexual and transgendered) as a practical shorthand for diversity beyond heteronormativity and the straight-gay binary and also to move beyond the impossible politics of specific naming of categories which, in the Canadian context, now has us at 'LGBTTIQQ2SA' (lesbian, gay, bisexual, transsexual, transgendered, intersex, queer, questioning and 2 Spirited Aboriginal). I realise 'LGBT' is too often misused as an already exhaustive 'list' but following Smith and Jaffer (2012), I wish to undertake a politics that moves 'beyond the queer alphabet'.

References

Amin, S. 1992. New world order/systems/disorder. Paper presented to the Department of Political Science and International Relations, University of Toronto, May.

Andrews, D. and M. Giardina. 2008. Sport without guarantees: toward a cultural studies that matters. *Cultural Studies □ □ Critical Methodologies* 8(4): 395–422.

Asante, M.K. 1990. Afrocentricity and culture. In *African culture: The rhythms of unity,* ed. M.K. Asante and W.K. Asante, 3–13. Trenton: Africa World Press.

Bauman, Z. 2007. *Liquid times: living in an age of uncertainty.* Cambridge: Polity Press.

Bratlinger, P. 1990. *Crusoe's footprints: Cultural studies in Britain and America.* London: Routledge.

Chen, H-K. 1992. Voices from the outside: toward a new internationalist localism. *Cultural Studies* 6(3): 476–84.

Chen, K-H. 1998. *Trajectories: Inter-Asia cultural studies.* London: Routledge.

Comaroff, J. and J. Comaroff. 2012. Theory from the South: or, how Euro-America is evolving toward Africa. *Anthropological Forum* 22(2): 113–131.

Connor, S. 2003. What can Cultural Studies do? In *Interrogating cultural studies: Theory, politics and practice*, ed. B. Bowman, 207–220. London: Pluto Press.

Cornut-Gentille D'arcy, C. 2009. A room of one's own? *Cultural Studies* 23 (5–6): 855–872.

Eskola, K. and E. Vainikkala. 1994. Nordic cultural studies: an introduction. *Cultural Studies* 8(2): 191–197.

Foucault, M. 1980. *Power/knowledge: selected interviews and other writings 1972–1977.* Trans. C. Gordon. New York: Pantheon Books.

Frow, J. and M. Morris. 1993. *Australian cultural studies: a reader.* Sydney: Allen and Unwin.

Gilroy, P. 1995. *The Black Atlantic: modernity and double consciousness.* Cambridge, MA: Harvard University Press.

Gilroy, P, Grossberg, L. and A. McRobbie. eds. 2000. *Without guarantees: in honour of Stuart Hall.* London: Verso.

Gray, A. and J. McGuigan. eds. 1993. *Studying culture: an introductory reader.* London: Edward Arnold.

Grossberg, L. 1993. The formations of cultural studies: an American in Birmingham. In *Relocating cultural studies: developments in theory and research*, ed. V. Blundell, J. Shepherd and I. Taylor, 21–66. London: Routledge.

Hall, S. 1980. Cultural studies and the centre: Some problematics and the problems. In *Culture, media, language: working papers in cultural studies, 1972–1979*, ed. S. Hall, D. Hobson, A. Love, and P. Willis, 2–35. London: Hutchinson.

Hall, S. 1986. The problem of ideology: Marxism without guarantees. *Journal of Communication Inquiry* 10(2): 28–43.

Hall, S. 1992. Cultural studies and its theoretical legacies. In *Cultural studies*, ed. L. Grossberg, C. Nelson and P. Trecichler, 277–294. New York: Routledge.

Hall, S. 1996. Minimal selves. In *Black British cultural studies: a reader*, ed. H.A. Baker, M. Diawara and R.H. Lindeborg, 114–119. Chicago: University of Chicago Press.

Hartley, J. 1992. Preface: 'Dismantling' Fremantle? *Cultural Studies* 6(3): 307–310.

Hartley, J. 2003. *A short history of cultural studies.* London: Sage.

hooks, b. 1990. Choosing the margin as a space of radical openness. In *Yearning: Race, gender and cultural politics*, by b. hooks, 203–209. Boston, MA: South End Express.

Johnson, R. 1986. What is cultural studies anyway? *Social Text* 16: 38–80.

Kidd, R. 1985. Popular theatre and popular struggle in Kenya. In *Cultures in contention*, ed. D. Khan and D. Neumaier, 51–62. Seattle, WA: Real Comet Press.

Laclau, E. 1996. Why do empty signifiers matter to politics? In *Emancipation(s)*, by E. Laclau, 36–46. London: Verso.

Levi-Strauss, C. 1987. *Introduction to Marcel Mauss.* London: Routledge.

Masilela, N. 1989. Preface: Establishing an intellectual bridgehead. In *Rethinking culture*, ed. K. Tomaselli, 1–5. Bellville, South Africa: Anthropos Publishers.

Mato, D. 2016. Stuart Hall from/in Latin America. *International Journal of Cultural Studies* 19(1): 43–57.

Maxwell, R. 2000. Cultural studies. In *Understanding contemporary society: Theories of the present*, ed. G. Browning, A. Halcli, and F. Webster, 281–295. London: Sage Publications.

Mbembe, A. 2003. Trans. L. Meintjes. Necropolitics. *Public Culture* 15(1): 11–40.
Miller, T. 2006. What it is and what it isn't: introducing cultural studies. In *A companion to cultural studies*, ed. T. Miller, 1–19. Hoboken, NJ: Wiley-Blackwell.
Morris, M. 1997. A question of cultural studies. In *Back to reality? Social experience and cultural studies*, ed. A. McRobbie, 26–57. Manchester: Manchester University Press.
Morrow, R.A. 1995. The challenge of cultural studies. *Canadian Review of Comparative Literature* 22(1): 1–20.
Mudimbe, V.Y. 1988. *The invention of Africa: gnosis, philosophy, and the order of knowledge*. London: James Currey.
Muteshi, J. 2003. Constructing consciousness: diasporic remembrances and imagining Africa in late modernity. *Critical Arts* 17(1–2): 36–51.
Ngugi wa Thiong'o 1993. *Moving the centre: The struggle for cultural freedoms*. London: James Currey.
Ngugi wa Thiong'o 1997. Women in cultural work: The fate of the Kamiriithu People's Theatre in Kenya. In *Readings in African popular culture*, ed. K. Barber, 131–138. Bloomington: Indiana University Press.
O'Connor, A. 1989. The problem of American cultural studies. *Critical Studies in Mass Communications* 6: 405–413.
Said, E. 1983. *The world, the text and the critic*. Cambridge, MA: Harvard University Press.
Sexton, J. 2011. The social life of social death: on Afro-pessimism and Black optimism. *InTensions* 5: 1–47.
Smith, M. and F. Jaffer. eds. 2012. *Beyond the queer alphabet: conversations on gender, sexuality and intersectionality*. Edmonton, AB: Teaching Equity Matters E-Book Series.
Soyinka, W. 1990. The African world and the ethnocultural debate. In *African culture: the rhythms of unity*, ed. M.K. Asante and W.K. Asante, 13–39. Trenton: Africa World Press.
Spivak, G.C. 1999. *A critique of postcolonial reason: toward a history of the vanishing present*. Cambridge, MA: Harvard University Press.
Tomaselli, K. ed. 1989. *Rethinking culture*. Bellville: Anthropos Publishers.
Tomaselli, K.G. 2012. Alter-egos: cultural and media studies. *Critical Arts* 26(1): 14–38
Tomaselli, K.G. 2016. Encoding/decoding: the transmission model and a court of law. *International Journal of Cultural Studies* 19(1): 59–70.
Turner, G. 1990. *British cultural studies: an introduction*. Boston: Unwin Hyman.
Wark, M. 1994. *Virtual geography: living with global media events*. Bloomington: Indiana University Press.
Wilderson, F.B. 2010. *Red, white and black: Cinema and the structures of U.S. antagonisms*. Durham, NC: Duke University Press.
Wright, H.K. 1998. Dare we de-Centre Birmingham? Troubling the origin and trajectories of cultural studies. *European Journal of Cultural Studies* 1 (1): 33–56.
Wright, H.K. 2001. 'What's going on?' Larry Grossberg on the status quo of theory and theorizing in cultural studies. *Cultural Values* 5(2): 133–162.
Wright, H.K. 2004. *A prescience of African cultural studies: literature studies in Africa is not what it was*. New York: Peter Lang.
Wright, H.K. 2012. Is this an African I see before me? Black/African identity and the politics of western, academic knowledge. In *The dialectics of African education and western discourses: appropriation, ambivalence and alternatives*, ed. H.K Wright and A. Abdi, 182–192. New York: Peter Lang.
Wright, H.K. 2016a. Introduction: the worldliness of Stuart Hall. *International Journal of Cultural Studies* 19(1): 3–10.
Wright, H.K. 2016b. Stuart Hall's relevance for the study of African blackness. *International Journal of Cultural Studies* 19(1): 85–99.
Wright, H.K, and Tomaselli, K. eds. 2008. African cultural studies. Special issue. *Cultural Studies* 22(2).

Part II
Putting African Gender to Work

(West) African Feminisms and Their Challenges

Naomi Nkealah

Summary

This article highlights some challenges facing a set of African feminisms built on indigenous models. These feminisms are: Motherism – Catherine Acholonu; Womanism/Woman palavering – Chikwenye Okonjo Ogunyemi; Nego-feminism – Obioma Nnaemeka; Snail-sense feminism – Akachi Ezeigbo; Stiwanism – Molara Ogundipe-Leslie; African womanism – Mary Modupe Kolawole; and Femalism – Chioma Opara. The challenges under discussion have been grouped into two categories: (1) inclusion vs exclusion; and (2) conceptualisation and target. This article discusses these challenges by posing a series of questions intended to provoke a critical re-assessment of African feminist theorisation. The article then proceeds to analyse a selection of work from *Women Writing Africa: West Africa and the Sahel* (2005) to see what the creative imagination offers as possible resolutions to these challenges. Two songs in the volume are analysed as part of the endeavour to redefine and prune (West) African feminisms.

Opsomming

Hierdie artikel vestig die aandag op enkele uitdagings wat 'n stel Afrika-feminismes wat op inheemse modelle geskoei is, in die gesig staar. Dié feminismes is: Moederisme – Catherine Acholonu; Vrouïsme/Vrouegepratery – Chikwenye Okonjo Ogunyemi; Nego-feminisme – Obioma Nnaemeka; Slakkesin-feminisme – Akachi Ezeigbo; Stiwanisme – Molara Ogundipe-Leslie; Afrikavrouïsme – Mary Modupe Kolawole; en Vroueverheerliking (*Femalism*) – Chioma Opara. Die uitdagings wat bespreek word, word in twee kategorieë ingedeel: (1) insluiting vs uitsluiting; en (2) konseptualisering en teiken. Die artikel bespreek hierdie uitdagings aan die hand van 'n reeks vrae wat daarop gemik is om 'n kritiese her-assessering van Afrika-feminismeteorieë te ontlok. Daarná word 'n keur uit *Women Writing Africa: West Africa and the Sahel* (2005) ontleed om vas te stel watter moontlike oplossings die kreatiewe verbeelding bied om hierdie uitdagings te bowe te kom. Twee liedere in die volume word ontleed as deel van die poging om (Wes-)Afrika-feminismes te herdefinieer en te verfyn.

Introduction

Over the past three decades, African feminisms have increasingly emphasised the need to resist cultural imperialism by which the West undermines the philosophical ideologies and belief systems of African peoples. While problematising aspects of culture that denigrate women, scholars have also argued for the retention of African values favourable to "social cohesion" (Nhlapo, quoted in Steyn 1998: 44). Thus, they embrace feminist models that aim to "revise and retain African traditions" (Chigwedere 2010: 24).

In their engagements with feminism, African scholars have likewise condemned the exclusionary practices of white Western feminisms. These exclusionary practices exist at two levels: on the basis of gender where men are necessarily expunged from feminist spaces and dubbed "the enemy"; and on the basis of race where African women are classified as "women of colour" and their historical trajectories are conveniently repressed in feminist theorising (Lâm 1994; Nnaemeka 2013).

African women's responses to the inequities of Western feminisms have resulted in theorisations of indigenous feminist models that aim to *speak* feminism from (1) an African cultural perspective; (2) an African geo-political location; (3) and an African ideological viewpoint. Emanating from West Africa, and from Nigeria in particular, is a set of indigenous feminisms which have redefined the aims and objectives of feminism in Africa and have reshuffled the feminist agenda for Nigerian women. These feminisms, named and conceptualised with cultural specificity as a guiding framework, provide evidence to the dynamism of African women's engagements with gender relations (Arndt 2002).

Womanism, the most widely applied theory in literary criticism and simultaneously the most controversial, situates the feminist vision within black women's confrontation with culture, colonialism and many other forms of domination that condition African women's lives (Ogunyemi 1985; Kolawole 1997). Sidestepping the controversies around womanism's privileging of "black women", who could be anywhere in the world, stiwanism positions itself as "feminism in an African context" (Ogundipe-Leslie 1994: 207), meaning that it is firmly rooted in the experiences and realities of women in Africa (as opposed to African women in the diaspora). Motherism expands the focus on women in Africa by entrusting the rural woman with the task of nurturing society (Acholonu 1995), while femalism and its central concept of transcendence "stresses the female body in the raw" (Opara 2005: 192) as a site of feminist discourse. Both nego-feminism (Nnaemeka 2003) and snail-sense feminism (Ezeigbo 2012) are firmly hinged on a tripod of gender inclusion, complementarity and collaboration, thereby expanding the tenets of womanism. The sensitivity of these feminisms to African women's diverse experiences of patriarchy, colonialism, neocolonialism, modernisation and globalisation attests to "the growing orientation of women to contextual specificities" (Obiora 1997: 367) and to the maturation of African feminist intellectualism.

These feminisms have several things in common. First, they resist the label "feminism" in its Western definition. Second, they are theorised on indigenous models, which means the theorists take a look into their histories and cultures to draw from them appropriate tools for empowering women and enlightening men. Third, they are underpinned by an ideology of gender inclusion, collaboration and accommodation to ensure that both women and men contribute (even if not equally) to improving the material conditions of women. The validity of these feminisms in articulating African women's concerns and goals notwithstanding, some pertinent challenges arise that prompt engagement with them. I have grouped these challenges into two categories: (1) inclusion vs exclusion; and (2) conceptualisation and target. This article discusses these challenges by posing a series of questions intended to provoke a critical re-assessment of African feminist theorisation.

Beyond outlining challenges, it is important to propose possibilities for resolving them. The book *Women Write Africa: West Africa and the Sahel* (2005) presents itself as a valuable tool in this endeavour. On the one hand, it illuminates the profoundness of the challenges facing (West) African feminisms, and on the other hand it presents oral narratives whose philosophical and ideological worldviews offer possible resolutions to these challenges. This article draws on the experiences of the women scholars involved in the Women Write Africa project to illustrate some of its arguments. It then proceeds to analyse a selection of work from *Women Write Africa* (henceforth referenced as WWA 2005) to see what the creative imagination offers as possible resolutions to these challenges. Two songs in the volume are analysed as part of the endeavour to refine (West) African feminisms.

Before discussing the challenges, however, it is important to state that my use of the phrase "(West) African feminisms" is cautious. Although all the theorists are of Nigerian descent (without necessarily being in possession of Nigerian citizenship), it would be wrong to refer to these feminisms as "Nigerian feminisms", for several reasons. First, the country known as "Nigeria" is a colonial construct. Colonialism lumped together different ethnic groups that were autonomous until subdued by European conquest. To date, Nigerians privilege ethnic identities over a so-called national one. Second, except for Ogundipe-Leslie and Kolawole, these feminists are mainly from the eastern region where the Igbo culture is dominant. They therefore cannot speak *for all* Nigerian women under the banner of "Nigerian feminism". Research has shown that the western and northern regions dominated by the Yoruba and Hausa respectively, have produced their own feminist models that work according to the demands of their cultures, religions and histories (see Bádéjo 1998; Whitsitt 2002). Third, and most significantly, most of these feminisms are conceptualised with African women in mind, acknowledging their diverse cultural experiences but also embracing the commonalities in their encounters with patriarchy (see Kolawole 2004; Nkealah 2006). For this particular reason, I consider them legitimately *African feminisms*.[1] But I also acknowledge their insurgence from a specific region – West Africa – which accounts for the specificity of their cultural ideological slants. The preference for "(West) African feminisms" essentially endorses "a movement to give multivalent representation to the voices of African women" (Sutherland-Addy & Diaw 2005: xxxi).

Challenges

Inclusion vs Exclusion

That the theorisation of feminisms has always been marked by exclusionary practices is attested to by Ibrahim (1997: 147) who notes that "any attempt at naming/renaming [feminism] is inclusive of some and exclusive of other experiences". One of the contradictions of African feminisms is that each brand is conceptualised for a particular segment of the gender-conscious human population to the exclusion of other segments. Motherism elevates the rural woman to the position of a "saviour" in her role as a farm worker and food producer. This rural woman is "the answer to the ever-increasing demand for food", making her the "economic, agricultural, political, commercial and labour base of every nation" (Acholonu 1995: 118). At the same time, the rural woman gives and nurtures life, provides it with spiritual nourishment, and imparts to it the ancient wisdom it needs to survive. She is "the living personification of the earth and all her rich blessings of love, patience, knowledge, strength, abundance, life and spirituality" (Acholonu 1995: 119).

This romanticised rural woman stands on a pedestal of virtue as an iconic example for the modern urban woman who is bereft of virtue. Motherism's construction of the rural woman expunges the urban woman from feminist politics. Although motherism advocates partnerships between women and men in alleviating the devastating effects of colonialism on African peoples, it sidelines the urban woman by allocating to the rural woman the "indispensable role" of "ensuring a future for humanity" (Acholonu 1995: 126). Does this mean that the urban woman has no contribution to make? Or is she so adulterated by the poison called modernity and its accompanying stench of urbanisation that her contribution would be detrimental rather than beneficial? In the meantime, contemporary Nigerian women's writing projects modern, educated, economically independent, and assertive urban women, suggesting that "female experience is … being authentically recreated and female reality is probed and revealed as it is, not as it ought to be, or as it is manipulated to be" (Usman 2012: 251).

Sexual orientation also forms the basis of exclusion in (West) African feminist theorisation. This is both overt and subtle. African womanism overtly rejects lesbianism, while stiwanism subtly dismisses lesbian politics. These feminisms place heterosexual women at the centre of their feminist politics with their emphasis on negotiation with and accommodation of (heterosexual) men – husbands, fathers, brothers and sons. Lesbian, bisexual and transsexual women tend to be completely effaced. Kolawole (1997: 15) claims that "to the majority of ordinary Africans, lesbianism is a non-existent issue because it is a mode of self-expression that is completely strange to their world-view". Does this mean that the minority of women for whom lesbianism is a political act, both to counter heteronormativity and to affirm new sexual identities, cannot be accommodated in African womanism? I think if womanism, or any other brand of feminism for that matter, is to be presented as "a valid African ideology" (Kolawole 1997: 24), it should be constructed as inclusive of all African women irrespective of their sexual orientation.

In describing what she thinks feminism is not, Ogundipe-Leslie (1994: 219) states the following: "Feminism is not a cry for any one kind of sexual orientation and I am not homophobic or heterosexist. Sexual practice in Africa tends to *be* private and *considered* private" (italics in the original). There is a subtle suggestion in this statement that the politics of sexuality is not the business of African feminisms; that sexual orientation is a peripheral matter in the design and execution of African feminisms. Sexuality is cast aside as a "private" matter, and the private is not political in this context.

In the 21st century, where lesbians are being stigmatised and victimised in many African states, it is gravely problematic to subscribe to a feminism that sweeps sexuality issues under the carpet. If African feminisms aim to expose and condemn the manifold forms of oppression African women are subjected to, shouldn't the challenges faced by lesbian women be part of their core priorities? Does not the fact that lesbian women are more vulnerable to ("corrective") rape, social insecurity, physical assault, psychological torture, emotional exile, alienation, and ostracism (all by virtue of not having a male "protector") than straight women demand a revisionist stiwanist framework that puts the needs of these women on the same scale as those of straight women? Interestingly, Ogundipe-Leslie (1994: 223) acknowledges that "feminisms have to be theorized around the junctures of race, class, caste and gender; nation, culture and ethnicity; age, status, role and sexual orientation". (West) African feminisms take all these variables into consideration, but sexual orientation tends to be suppressed. What are the implications of this for African feminist scholar-ship? Even in South Africa, lesbian politics is still marginalised in mainstream feminist discourse. Mainstream feminism in South Africa has always centred on race, gender and class while questions around sexuality remain largely repressed in literary criticisms, with lesbianism being subject to "silencing" (Murray 2011: 52).

A third thorny issue is whether (West) African feminisms are theorised for continental Africans or diasporic Africans. When these feminists speak of "African women", who exactly do they mean? Do they mean continental African women or diasporic African women or both? Is the term "African feminism" itself prejudiced towards diasporic women of African descent? It may seem a trivial matter, but in feminist politics practices of inclusion and exclusion are significant. Hudson-Weems (1998: 149), for example, uses the term "Africanans" in postulating her Africana womanism and she states in her very first sentence that Africanans in the context of her work refer to "continental Africans and Africans in the diaspora". Do (West) African feminisms espouse the same transcontinental framework? Whose interests do they prioritise – women resident in Africa or those living in Europe and America? The experiences of the women participating in the WWA project highlight similar tensions. The editors of the West African volume report:

> The diverse group of people shaping this project did not always share the same vision of Africa or of the project. African-born women and women of African descent, living in exile in the diaspora among other émigrés and exiles and teaching in the academies of the West, were eager to voice their concerns. The largest group, West African scholars and feminists residing in the region, desired to shape a volume that addressed issues internal to the area's history and needs. A third group, made up of Euro-American scholars, some of whom were Africanists, was aware of the lacunae in knowledge about Africa and the needs of U.S. publishing market.
> (Sutherland-Addy & Diaw 2005: xxvii)

This honest report illuminates the extent to which varying interests and visions can create dangerous fault lines in African feminist engagement. Theorising that focuses on the interests of one group of women can easily alienate another group. Moreover, it creates and/or deepens dichotomies (continental/diasporic, black/white, young/old, educated/illiterate, etc.) that breed fragmentation rather than collective action. On the other hand, an all-inclusive theory becomes handicapped by lack of a definitive constituency to put its principles into practice within the delineated context.

Then there is the question of language. Does the highly intellectual language of the theorists take into consideration the linguistic constraints of ordinary literate but not intellectualised women of Africa? While African feminisms are cooked in an African pot (named as such by the cooks) and spiced with indigenous condiments (folklore, traditions, etc.) to satisfy an imagined African palate, the plate on which they are served is anything but indigenous, for the English language remains a foreign language to many women in both rural and urban Africa. Ogunyemi (1996: 102) problematises this issue when she poses the question: "Who does the [African] woman writer write for, since most of her prime subjects, especially rural women, can neither read nor understand the foreign tongue in which the text is presented?" Similarly, I pose the questions: to what class of African women are stiwanism, nego-feminism and femalism directed, couched as they are in developmentalist lingo, academic jargon, and a highly complex philosophical language? If these theories are expressed in a language that only scholars and graduates of universities (and I mean "polished" graduates, not your average passer) can understand, what are the chances of high school teachers using these texts to educate young learners both on the need for gender transformation and the value of theory in scholarship? Is theory meant for only the elite, or can the fruit-and-vegetable seller on the streets, who is an entrepreneur in her own right, also engage with and learn from it? Documenting their theories using the orthography of a language that is embedded with colonial frames of domination poses a challenge to African feminists.

Conceptualisation and Target

The notion of cultural specificity implies that the particularities and/or specifics of women's cultural experiences should inform and modulate feminist theorisation. Thus, African women looked into their indigenous cultures to draw on practices, philosophies and worldviews that they felt impact their lives as women and propounded feminist models based on these cultural symbols. As Nnaemeka (2003: 380) states, "African women working for social change build on the indigenous by defining and modulating their feminist struggle in deference to cultural and local imperatives." The aim was to better navigate the harsh cultural terrain using its own roadmaps and landmarks.

In introducing nego-feminism, Nnaemeka (2003: 376) cites an Igbo proverb ("When something stands, something stands *beside* it"), a Sotho proverb ("A person is a person because of other people"), an Ashanti proverb ("One head cannot go into counsel"), and a Yoruba proverb ("The sky is vast enough for all birds to fly without colliding"). These proverbs underscore the idea of people – irrespective of gender, race or class – working together, and in the process supporting, educating and learning from one another. Nnaemeka (2003: 376) draws on this "knowledge of the African worldview as inscribed in proverbs" to formulate nego-feminism. Building on this indigenous model, nego-feminism is framed as a feminism of "negotiation, give and take, compromise, and balance" (Nnaemeka 2003: 378). Many African women who have grown up in societies that uphold similar values will easily embrace nego-feminism, because it speaks to their cultural understandings of the world. Because nego-feminism resonates with the South African concept of *ubuntu*, it makes itself accessible to South African women who are also involved in feminist projects in both scholarship and activism.[2]

Snail-sense feminism, by contrast, is likely to alienate South African feminists, because it is packaged specifically for Nigerian women. It uses the snail as a model, a creature whose antics and survival strategies are familiar to Nigerian and West African women.[3] Like a snail that traverses harsh terrain with caution, flexibility, foresight, alertness to danger, and the sensibility to bypass obstacles, a snail-sense feminist negotiates her way around patriarchy, tolerates sexist men, collaborates with non-sexist ones, avoids confrontation with patriarchs, and applies diplomacy in her dealings with society at large. As Ezeigbo (2012: 27) states, "it is this tendency to *accommodate or tolerate the male* and *cooperate with men* that informs this theory which I call snail-sense feminism" (my emphasis). Ezeigbo further draws on proverbs in different Nigerian languages – Igbo, Fulfulde and Yoruba – to buttress her argument on the need for women to adopt a conciliatory rather than a confrontational approach to gender-based oppression. I do not know how many women, including Nigerian women, are comfortable in applying this kind of "avoidance" technique in combating sexism and its many attendant manifestations. Snail-sense feminism seems to be envisioned on the hypothesis that Nigerian women are too conscious of *their place* in society to want to upset the social order, when reality tells a contrary tale. Moreover, it engenders a culture of reactive, rather than proactive, resistance.

Femalism presents its own challenges. It projects the female body as a sign by linking "the freedom of woman to that of the African nation", and woman thus becomes "Mother Africa susceptible to various manipulations and intrigues" (Opara 2005: 193). This image of the African woman, which is also extolled by motherism, has been found to be problematic by other feminist scholars as it constructs woman purely in symbolic terms, thereby robbing her of subjectivity and agency (Driver 1988; Boehmer 1992). Woman becomes what Stratton (1994: 48) calls an "index of the state of the nation", a trope she affiliates to a male literary tradition hinged on a Manichean allegory. Larrier (2000: 35) exposes the flaws of this tradition in its "representation of woman as the romanticized African past or the corrupt present", a dichotomy that is clearly masculinist in vision.

Femalism is not grounded in any particular African culture. Rather, Opara (2005: 190) evokes the Western philosophy of existentialism and draws on phenomenology and hermeneutics to explain an "African philosophy of transcendence". To what extent, then, can femalism be described as a theory that offers "realistic, practical and functional" (Ezeigbo 2012: 26) mechanisms for African women to deal with their everyday challenges? Or is theory completely divorced from practice?

A factor that complicates matters for (West) African feminisms is the question of whether to focus on local imperatives or to extend the scope of the theories to meet global challenges. Ogunyemi (1996: 104) speaks specifically about Nigerian women when she states that "women's politics has emphasized the interdependence of the sexes as a womanist ideal … in addressing the multi-faceted Nigerian predicament". Ogunyemi moves from the premise of global womanism (incorporating both African and African-American versions of womanism) in her 1985 article to that of Nigerian womanism in 1996. This shift from a global feminist perspective to a more culturally/nationally defined agenda signifies unresolved tensions in (West) African feminisms. On the one hand, a global perspective privileges the needs of African women globally, with less focus on the specific needs of continental Africans. On the other hand, a localised perspective means that Nigerian womanism is so narrowly defined as to alienate women from outside Nigeria whose feminist politics are moulded by political environments just as repressive as the Nigerian one.

The paradox of African feminist theorisation is that its emphasis on cultural specificity inadvertently results in cultural alienation for women from other cultures who feel marginalised – consciously and unconsciously – by the dominant culture on whose artifacts and symbols the feminist model is built. Personally, I have often felt alienated from the Igbo culture and worldview on which femalism, motherism and snail-sense feminism are modelled, this notwithstanding the fact that I am married to an Igbo man and grew up in a society greatly influenced by Igbo cosmopolitanism. Lâm (1994: 868) captures this feeling of alienation and distance in her angry retort to a white American (feminist) woman: "Goddamn it! Your feminism is not mine, OK? So buzz off!" Her fury stemmed from sensing that a white woman was imposing on her a feminism she did not associate with. This experience of a Third World woman's confrontation with white American feminism in practice illustrates an inherent resistance to embrace a feminism for which one feels a cultural distance, or worse, a complete disconnection bordering on apathy.

Resolutions

Just as (West) African feminisms have looked to oral literature for theoretical inspiration, so can we look into these forms for possible resolutions to some of the challenges facing them. The WWA book contains a number of fascinating oral songs that are instructive. The oral song of the Wolof in Senegal, sung to welcome a new bride, is a good example. The *"Xaxar"* is performed to the accompaniment of drumming and it constitutes "a time of great creativity for women" (WWA 2005: 103). In the song, the first wife welcomes the new wife with satirical greetings, mocking her through innuendos and overt insults of physical ugliness and sexual undesirability. Her friends echo her sentiments by throwing similar insults at the new bride. The following lines illustrate this:

> First Wife:
> My greetings to you, new bride, like one greets a donkey.
> My respects and honor to you, but you're worse than a bitch.
>
> Chorus of Her Friends:
> We greet you, new bride, as we would greet a donkey.
> We respect and honor you, but you're worse than a bitch.
> We greet you, new bride, as we would greet a donkey.
> We respect and honor you, but you're worse than a bitch.
>
> First Wife:
> Will she stay, the new bride, will she stay?
> Will she stay, the new bride, will she stay?
> Look at her, this new bride, her skin's dull and ugly
> she is snotty and dirty, and lousy in bed,
> Will she stay, the new bride, will she stay?
>
> Chorus of Her Friends:
> Will she stay, the new bride, will she stay?
> Will she stay, the new bride, will she stay?
>
> (WWA 2005: 103–104)

The words of the first wife convey resentment and undisguised anxiety, because the arrival of the new bride symbolises her displacement in the husband's affections. Yet, it is in the welcome act itself that her acceptance of the new bride can be situated; it is in the very act of greeting and acknowledgement that she relinquishes space for her co-wife. Thus, this song epitomises the notion of inclusivity – making room for another while simultaneously asserting one's authority and ideological stance. (West) African feminisms can apply this principle by acknowledging the varied orientations of African women's sexuality and accommodating lesbian, gay, bisexual, transgender and intersex (LGBTI) women in their feminist praxis.

Another song to welcome a new bride is that of the Songhai-Zarma of Niger. It is as follows:

Group of First Wives:
> The second wife is worthless.
> May God curse the woman who is worthless.
> The second wife is a stork of misfortune.
> Who heralds winter but cannot stay.

Group of Wives in Second Position:
> Have they gone mad,
> These first wives with their empty heads?
> You were brought here.
> We were brought here.
> Stop the assault.

(WWA 2005: 105)

This song is "an oratorical contest" in which "two groups of antagonists, one supporting the first wife, the other supporting the new bride, confront each other, raising the level of verbal violence" (WWA 2005: 103). It reveals that the second wives resist domination by the first wives by asserting their own voice and authority as legitimate wives. Their command to the first wives to "stop the assault" suggests a heightened consciousness of the politics of space and a profound desire to resist marginalisation. Like these second wives (and this is not an endorsement of polygamy!), African women are sensitive to feminisms that alienate them. And they will, like Lâm cited earlier, stage a vicious resistance to such feminisms. Yet, they can develop a sense of ownership of these feminisms, if they so wish, by subjecting them to scholarly refinement. Formulating new theories is innovative, but it is not the ultimate solution, as new theories breed new challenges.

Conclusion

Speaking about the role of Nigerian drama in making moral statements, Charity Angya (quoted in Nyitse 2012: 188–189) states that "solutions can be proffered but … all of life's issues cannot be resolved by straight clinical solutions". Such is the case with the challenges facing (West) African feminisms. Some of them can "only be resolved through painful compromise" (Sutherland-Addy & Diaw 2005: xxvii), and others not at all. The scholarly efforts of Acholonu, Ogunyemi, Ogundipe-Leslie, Kolawole, Nnaemeka, Opara and Ezeigbo to chart a feminist course for Nigerian women in particular and African women in general is laudable, but the challenges raised in this article suggest that continuous scholarly efforts need to be invested in refining and reaffirming the feminist vision for (West) African women. Engaging with the oral narratives of women in West Africa, as recorded in *Women Write Africa*, is a starting point.

Notes

1. The term "African feminisms" is used here for linguistic convenience only, acknowledging that the theories under discussion have resisted the feminist label by encoding their own renamed labels.
2. Gaylard (2004: 265) has noted the resilience of the concept of *ubuntu* in black South African writing, describing *ubuntu* as "transcultural and transhistorical". That *ubuntu*, loosely translated as African humanism, is also a cherished value in other Nigerian cultures besides the Igbo is evident in Nyitse

(2012) who employs Tiv cosmology to situate the feminist-humanism of Nigerian dramatist Charity Angya.

3 The type of snails being referred to here are land snails (as opposed to sea snails or freshwater snails) with hard shells. These snails are bred in tropical Africa and they grow quite big. They are edible and usually constitute the source of protein in a delicious pot of soup.

References

Acholonu, and Catherine Obianuju. 1995. *Motherism: The Afrocentric Alternative to Feminism*. Owerri: Afa Publications.

Arndt, and Susan. 2002. *The Dynamics of African Feminism: Defining and Classifying African Feminist Literatures*. Trenton, NJ: Africa World Press.

Bádéjo, and Deirdre. 1998. African Feminism: Mythical and Social Power of Women of African Descent. *Research in African Literatures* 29(2): 94–111.Online: <http://www.jstor.org/stable/3820724>. 28 May 2015.

Boehmer, and Elleke. 1992. Stories of Women and Mothers: Gender and Nationalism in the Early Fiction of Flora Nwapa. In: Nasta, Susheila (ed.) *Motherlands: Black Women's Writing from Africa, the Caribbean and South Asia*. New Brunswick, NJ: Rutgers University Press, pp. 3–23.

Chigwedere, and Yuleth. 2010. The African Womanist Vision in Vera's Works. *Journal of Literary Studies* 26(1): 20–44.

Driver, and Dorothy. 1988. Woman as Sign in the South African Colonial Enterprise. *Journal of Literary Studies* 4(1): 3–20.

Ezeigbo, and Akachi. 2012. *Snail-sense Feminism: Building on an Indigenous Model*. Lagos: University of Lagos.

Gaylard, and Rob. 2004. "Welcome to the World of our Humanity": (African) Humanism, Ubuntu and Black South African Writing. *Journal of Literary Studies* 20(3/4): 265–282.

Hudson-Weems, and Clenora. 1998. Africana Womanism. In: Nnaemeka, Obioma (ed.) *Sisterhood, Feminisms and Power: From Africa to the Diaspora*. Trenton, NJ: Africa World Press, pp. 149–162.

Ibrahim, and Huma. 1997. Ontological Victimhood: "Other" Bodies in Madness and Exile – Toward a Third World Feminist Epistemology. In: Nnaemeka, Obioma (ed.) *The Politics of (M)othering: Womanhood, Identity, and Resistance in African Literature*. London: Routledge, pp. 147–161.

Kolawole, and Mary Modupe. 1997. *Womanism and African Consciousness*. Eritrea: Africa World Press.

—— 2004 Re-conceptualizing African Gender Theory: Feminism, Womanism, and the *Arere* Metaphor In: Arnfred, Signe (ed.) *Re-thinking Sexualities in Africa*. Uppsala: The Nordic Africa Institute, pp. 251–268.

Lâm, and Maivân Clech. 1994. Feeling Foreign in Feminism. *Signs: Journal of Women in Culture and Society* 19(4): 865–893.

Larrier, and Renée. 2000. *Francophone Women Writers of Africa and the Caribbean*. Gainesville: University Press of Florida.

Murray, and Jessica. 2011. Daring to Speak its Name: The Representation of a Lesbian Relationship in the Work of Rozena Maart. *English Academy Review* 28(2): 52–61.

Nkealah, and Naomi. 2006. Conceptualizing Feminism(s) in Africa: The Challenges Facing African Women Writers and Critics. *English Academy Review* 23(1): 133–141.

Nnaemeka, and Obioma. 2003. Nego-feminism: Theorizing, Practicing and Pruning Africa's Way. *Signs: Journal of Women in Culture and Society* 29(2): 357–385.

—— 2013. Foreword: Locating Feminisms/Feminists. In: McCann, Carole and Kim, Seung-Kyung (eds) *Feminist Local and Global Theory Perspectives Reader*. New York: Routledge, pp. 317–320.

Nyitse, and Leticia Mbaiver. 2012. From Feminism to Humanism: Exploring the "Difficult Dialogues" in Charity Angya's *The Cycle of the Moon*. In: Doki, Gowon Ama and Ayakoroma, Barclays Foubiri (eds) *Difficult Dialogues in Development*. Ibadan: Kraft Books, pp. 183–192.

Obiora, and Amede 1997 Feminism, Globalization and Culture: After Beijing. *Indiana Journal of Global Legal Studies* 4(2): 355–406. Online: < http://www.jstor.org/stable/20644657 >. 21 May 2015.

Ogundipe-Leslie, and Molara. 1994. *Re-creating Ourselves: African Women & Critical Transformations*. Trenton, NJ: Africa World Press.

Ogunyemi, and Chikwenye Okonjo. 1985. Womanism: The Dynamics of the Contemporary Black Female Novel in English. *Signs: Journal of Women in Culture and Society* 11(1): 63–80.

—— 1996 *Africa Wo/Man Palava*. Chicago: The University of Chicago Press.

Opara, and Chioma. 2005. On the African Concept of Transcendence: Conflating Nature, Nurture and Creativity. *International Journal of Philosophy and Religion* 21(2): 189–200.

Steyn, and Melissa. 1998. A New Agenda: Restructuring Feminism in South Africa. *Women's Studies International Forum* 21(1): 41–52.

Stratton, and Florence. 1994. *Contemporary African Literature and the Politics of Gender*. London: Routledge.

Sutherland-Addy, Esi & Diaw, and Aminata. 2005 Preface. In: Sutherland-Addy, Esi and Diaw, Aminata (eds) *Women Writing Africa: West Africa and the Sahel*. New York: The Feminist Press at the City University of New York, pp. xxiii–xxxi.

Sutherland-Addy, Esi & Diaw, and Aminata (eds) 2005. *Women Writing Africa: West Africa and the Sahel*. New York: The Feminist Press at the City University of New York.

Usman, and Asabe Kabir. 2012. Positive Radicalism and the Representation of Assertive Womanism in Zainab Alkali's *The Descendants*. In: Doki, Gowon Ama and Ayakoroma, Barclays Foubiri (eds) *Difficult Dialogues in Development*. Ibadan: Kraft Books, pp. 243–253.

Whitsitt, and Novian. 2002. Islamic-Hausa Feminism and Kano Market Literature: Qur'anic Reinterpretation in the Novels of Balaraba Yakubu. *Research in African Literatures* 33(2): 119–136.

The Female Body in Audiovisual Political Propaganda Jingles: The Mbare Chimurenga Choir in Zimbabwe's Contested Political Terrain

Hazel Tafadzwa Ngoshi and Anias Mutekwa

ABSTRACT

Zimbabwe's post-2000 political terrain has been highly polarised and contested; a minefield requiring political resourcefulness to negotiate. Political actors in this terrain have employed an array of political and cultural tools, ranging from discourses of black empowerment and democratisation, to written texts and performances of political propaganda to garner support from the electorate and gain political mileage. This article explores the literal and symbolic implications of the entry of the female body into public and political spaces through performance in propaganda jingles in the electronic media, represented here by the Mbare Chimurenga Choir's album 'Nyatsoteerera' [Listen carefully]. Using the Bakhtinian carnivalesque theoretical framework, the article analyses the audiovisual and thematic aspects of the Mbare women's performance, exploring how the female body is cast in the visuals as both object and metaphor in the articulation of a largely masculinist nationalist project. The authors of this article suggest that the choreography exalts the female body as a metaphor for the authoritarian creed, and the gyrating bodies make tangible the objectification and metaphorisation of women in political discourses, while thematically, the lyrics suggest that the Zimbabwean nation cannot be construed outside ZANU-PF's terms, thereby foreclosing any alternative discourse on Zimbabwe.

Introduction

The aim of this article is to discuss the complex and unstable relationship between women performing political music and the notions of the nationalist project in Zimbabwe. The Mbare Chimurenga Choir (henceforth: choir) musical performances, which are the subject of this article, are located within the discourse of popular culture. Discussing song, story and nation in relation to female musicians in Zimbabwe, Moreblessings Chitauro, Caleb Dube and Liz Gunner (1994: 170) assert that 'the messages and images communicated through forms of popular culture have enormous influence in shaping the real language of gender and power relations in a culture'. Through the choir singing, the women express their relationship to the nationalist narrative. The question in this analysis is whether the women, by inserting their voices in the master narrative of the national project, are able to subvert and/or offer alternative versions of this narrative, because singing and dancing offer the opportunity to do so.

The choir is one among a number of nationalist musician groups to grace the Zimbabwean cultural and political stage in recent times. The choir has several albums to its name. The focus of this analysis will be its debut, *'Nyatsoteerera'* [Listen carefully]. Nationalist musicians in Zimbabwe emerged at the same time as nationalism as a phenomenon emerged in colonial Rhodesia. The proliferation of nationalist musicians to serve the nationalist narrative is therefore not unique to the era connoting Zimbabwe's descent into political and economic crisis. Soon after independence, the Ministry of Education and Culture put together the National Dance Company, which toured China, India, North Korea, Germany, France, Bulgaria and Switzerland (Chitauro, Dube & Gunner 1994). The play which the company worked on was entitled *'Mbuya Nehanda'*, which

> charted the history of the liberation struggles of the new Zimbabwe, the first war of 1896 and the second war of independence from which the country had just emerged. It was in a very direct way a nationalist narrative and also one that was meant to identify the new nation of Zimbabwe through its history of struggle and through its culture, all encapsulated in the play. (ibid: 195)

Other musicians who lent their services to the nationalist narrative were the likes of Chinx Chingaira and Thomas Mapfumo. Their singing was inspired by the euphoria characteristic of the period soon after independence. These singers gave voice to the mood of 'national ecstasy' (ibid: 194).

The ideological context of the rise of nationalist musicians of this era was that of cultural nationalism, which often makes its mark when people grapple with issues of national identity. It often accompanies, but is not limited to, political forms of nationalism. Reviewing Thomas Turino's *Nationalists, cosmopolitans and popular music in Zimbabwe* (2000), Ezra Chitando (2002: 84) argues that Turino 'succeeds in showing the centrality of music, dance and other "traditional" practices to the nationalist parties in Zimbabwe'. He goes on to explain how Turino 'succeeds in locating the significance of Chimurenga songs in ZANU's propaganda efforts', and how he traces 'the nationalist efforts to exploit the emotion generated by music in the early 1960s and the Chimurenga songs of the 1970s' (ibid: 85). These observations, in view of current trends as epitomised by the music of the choir, help illuminate the continued significance of Chimurenga music and its potential as a site of propaganda.

The authors submit that the same ideological tool seems to underwrite the emergence of nationalist musicians, performers and their sponsors at a time when Zimbabwe is experiencing an economic and political crisis of governance, induced by contestations for the control of the nation state between the Zimbabwe African National Union-Patriotic Front (ZANU-PF) and the Movement for Democratic Change (MDC).

The entry of female singers and performers into the public domain makes a contribution to the narratives of nation and gender. In a way, it shapes the discourses of the nation while validating the gendered nature of nations and nationalism, as articulated by Anne McClintock (1993: 61), who postulates that 'all nationalisms are gendered, all are invented, and all are dangerous'. The dangerous nature of nationalisms is, perhaps, in the context of Zimbabwe, more pronounced in nationalist music, in which sponsors seek to control the content. Chitauro, Dube and Gunner (1994: 196) recognise the dangers and potential power of song when they argue that 'song, and the way in which it [has] the power to challenge and dislocate official authority, [is] seen as dangerous'. Their observation becomes all the more relevant to this article when the question is raised whether the female singers of the choir are able to subvert the grand narrative of nationalism, or whether there is any trace of agency in their seeming support of a singular version of nationalism. The masculine nationalist grand narrative is imbued with a masculine culture that expresses itself through violence, corruption, greed and intolerance, as manifested in various ways in Zimbabwe. The authors of this article posit that the choir, through their music, can help infuse elements from feminine culture to help temper the masculine discourse that has been at the centre of the Zimbabwean crisis. Any critique of the women's musical performance is done with an acute awareness of the political economy of the production of their music – a political economy which may deter them from exercising their own agency in this regard, bearing in mind that the composition of their music is done under the auspices of their party's ideologues.

This article interrogates the literal and symbolic implications of the entry of the female body and voice, into public and political spaces, through the performance of propagandist political songs. While there have been several entrants into this cultural nationalist project, the analysis is based on the choir, which is largely female in composition – a point which resonates with the aims of this article, namely to explore and critique how the female voice and body are used in the articulation of a largely masculinist nationalist project. According to Chitauro, Dube and Gunner (1994: 176), 'the idea of music and music-making [can be seen] as a means of reclamation of social space'.

This investigation commences by interrogating what can be termed 'the objectification and metaphorisation of the female body' in male political projects. Women's mediational importance in the nationalist project, as symbolic reproducers of the nation, is theorised. The authors employ the Bakhtinian concept of the carnivalesque to show how, for instance, the dances accompanying the propaganda music exploit the hyperbolic and subversive nature of carnival. Mikhail Bakhtin (1984) celebrates the liberatory potential of the carnivalesque, yet, as shown in this article, the carnivalesque is manipulated and harnessed by the powers-that-be for a non-liberatory agenda. The choir's songs, which have been turned into jingles through repeated airplay, are here analysed in terms of their lyrical content, to show how, through their celebratory nature, women continue to applaud male achievements, while appropriating the feminine iconography of motherhood to bolster their image as handmaidens of the nationalist project. They mother the nationalist narrative. These songs-turned-jingles are originally composed as ordinary songs, before being appropriated, modified and played frequently on radio and television by stations which broadcast nationally, in service of ZANU-PF's propaganda drive. The songs are inserted between programmes in the same way advertisements are positioned in programming. Therefore, in Zimbabwe's empirical understanding, these songs function as jingles. This article concludes with the view that while their singing may point to the women's political agency, such agency is undercut by their seeming failure to derive political capital from their efforts, and by the missed opportunity to articulate alternative versions of Zimbabwe for the benefit of women.

The Third Chimurenga jingles, the choir, and mothering the Zimbabwean nation

The music of the choir can be located along the continuum of ZANU-PF propaganda jingles pioneered by Jonathan Moyo – then Minister of Information and Publicity in the ZANU-PF government – during the land reform process in Zimbabwe. The jingles were crafted to bolster the perception that the process of land-redistribution was a continuation of Zimbabwe's struggle for national liberation, which has always been cast as 'phased' (hence the First, Second and Third Chimurenga). In terms of lyrical content, the singers sang of the need to work hard at tilling the land, despite lacking adequate resources. Thus, such jingles as '*Mombe mbiri nemadhongi mashanu sevenza nhamo ichauya*' (loosely translated: 'given your two cows and five donkeys, work very hard as difficult times are ahead of us') were meant to galvanise beneficiaries of the land reform process to work hard, but at another level, the exercise was a subtle admission that the process was found wanting in terms of the farm mechanisation normally associated with commercial agriculture. Another jingle, '*Dai kuri kwedu machembere aipururudza mupururu*' (loosely translated: 'back home, this would be applauded by elderly women') is accompanied by video footage of young people rallying others to go to the fields and watch tractors tilling the soil. Ululation, especially in patriarchal societies (which is implied in the lyrics of the jingle) is/was traditionally the preserve of women, and is a way of applauding, celebrating and validating male exploits, such as successful hunting trips and the installation of chiefs. In this context, then, women in general – and elderly women in particular – are being called upon to assume a celebratory role; celebrating the masculine national project of 'restoring the land to its rightful owners' or 'taking the decolonisation struggle to the further level of economic liberation from the snares of neo-colonialism' (Ndlovu-Gatsheni 2009: 62). On this note, Ranjoo Seadou Herr (2003: 136) cautions 'Third World feminists [to beware] of the danger of nationalism and [to] try to avoid falling into the traps of patriarchal nationalists'. The choir women may not be feminists, but Herr's comments are pertinent to this context in which the women are engaging with the national project through their music. Since there is an intimate connection between gender and nationalism, the women's music cannot be blind to the underlying gender issues.

The jingles are obviously in the service of the national project, as conceived by ZANU-PF. Achille Mbembe (2006: n.p.), writing on nativism, asserts that this kind of national project pretends to redress the sad history of colonialism 'by creating a common language of grievance'. This pretence, according to Mbembe (ibid.), thrives on repetition and populist rhetoric – precisely what the jingles do. A characteristic feature of jingles in general is that they derive their effectiveness from repetition – in this context, from continuous airplay on radio and television stations in Zimbabwe, and in terms of lyrical content.

The objectification and metaphorisation of the female body

The choir's audiovisual political propaganda jingles, as represented by their debut album '*Nyatsoteerera*' (here cast as a form of advertising), illustrate the objectification of women and their bodies in political discourses and practices. Propagandists are psychological operators who manipulate the emotions aroused through music, and the choir's jingles, due to their repetitive nature, have effects that are not only provocative but also divisive, in certain ways, as the subsequent analysis will show.

The objectification of women in the context of audiovisual propaganda entails the use of female bodies and voices to make political statements. The female body has always been cast as nurturing, providing sexual pleasure, and, at a symbolic level, representing the land, which is at the core of rhetoric in Zimbabwean nationalist politics. These attributes are often exploited in art forms that are propagandist. The fecund female body is often exalted as a metaphor for the authoritarian creed. Here, a strong sense of maternity, which sacrifices both body and voice to perceived nationalistic ideals, is systematically propagated through the jingles under investigation. It is the materiality of the female body that is exploited. The outcomes have far-reaching implications for gender and nationalism.

Usually, for the propagandist, the best means of communication is through face- to-face interaction, for instance at rallies, but 'audio-visual media such as television, electronic tape recordings, and sound motion pictures are the second most effective means of communication available to the psychological operator' (The Army Institute of Professional Development 1983: n.p.). Effectiveness, as noted by The Army Institute of Professional Development (ibid.), 'is based on seeing and hearing the persuasive message', which is precisely what this choir's album attempts to do. Martina Pachmanová (2000) argues that the social terrain of Western civilisation is divided into the private sphere (traditionally belonging to women), on the one hand, and the public sphere (belonging to men), on the other. She argues further that this dichotomy has, for centuries, 'prohibited women from playing an active role in the public life of society' (ibid.). In a non-Western civilisation such as Zimbabwe, the division of the social terrain into private and public persists as a derivative of British colonialism, as well as of the patriarchal nature of local societies in general. Pachmanová engages with the implications of women's entry into public life and how women's roles are being re-cast in new spaces. Thus, by performing propagandistic musical jingles, these women are being re-cast in Zimbabwe's political space, albeit in an ambivalent manner. At one level their political party applauds their role as reproducers of the party's ideological standpoint, while at another level these women are viewed as pawns (and possibly with some irritation) by those who oppose ZANU-PF's version of Zimbabwe. The objectification of female bodies provokes varied reactions towards women's roles in public and political spaces.

One way of viewing women in the context of the presence of their bodies in visual propaganda material, is as metaphors for the mediation of men's political projects. The signification of women as metaphors derives largely from their position of otherness. N'Gone Fall (2007) submits that the mission of women in Africa was clearly codified as guardians and vehicles of African identity, who should have their feet anchored in tradition and their minds in modernity. She argues (Fall 2007: 72) that 'in Africa, everything is negotiable. Women know that their body [sic] is a perpetual object of desire, fantasy and submission – like a parcel of land that men feel free to own and explore, sometimes without permission.' Political elites in the Zimbabwean nationalist movement mine this female potential to further male nationalist projects. The argument made here is that this is the case with the performance of the choir, where African female bodies are shown as instruments of propaganda. As Fall further posits, 'female bodies and voices are used to articulate propaganda, conformity with and submission to, current power structures' (ibid.). The gyrating female bodies in propaganda videos, as is the case with this choir, make tangible both the objectification and metaphorisation of women.

Here, the authors posit that the gyrations of the female body are an invitation to mediate men's political projects and commune with the politics of power, as envisioned by men. Eva Feder Kittay (1988: 63) argues that women have relational and mediational importance in men's lives, therefore 'women's activities and relations to men are persistent metaphors for man's projects', and in provocative mode, she goes on to 'query the prominence of these and the lack of equivalent metaphors where men are the metaphoric vehicle for women and women's activities'. The authors of this article believe that the women's gyrations radically undermine the idea of an African feminine art/dance that is presumably beautiful and not challenging or disturbing in any way.

Seen at one level, the propaganda jingles locate the women in supportive roles, as their obscene dances translate into a metaphor for the 'political obscenity' that has characterised post-2000 politics in Zimbabwe. Female bodies are sacrificed on the altar of supposedly national/ist priorities at the expense of appropriating or extracting direct political benefits from the vocabulary of their music and the articulated projects in the political propaganda jingles. Having women derive benefits from the nationalist project is the domain of nationalist feminism. The mobilisation of women, that can be achieved through nationalist feminism, can foster grassroots power because the patriarchal form of nationalism, according to Shireen Hassim (2003: 53), '[lacks] serious attention to women's issues and to the potential for women to emerge as leader'. Women can thus '[step] beyond the ambitions of the national liberation movement (ZANU-PF is a former liberation movement) … [to develop their] agency and autonomy to effect changes in gender relations' (ibid.).

One example is the song 'Team', which articulates the power hierarchy in ZANU-PF, where President Mugabe, Vice-President Joice Mujuru and Vice-President John Nkomo are hailed in that order, yet the singers insist we should *'chimbomirai makadaro'* [maintain the status quo]. There is nothing that precludes these singers from asking for more powerful positions for women in the top hierarchy of the party, outside the women's league, where it appears male politicians are comfortable with women organising themselves politically, without encroaching into the male-dominated sphere. It is, however, possible that the choir women may have benefited from the land reform.

Women as symbolic reproducers of the nation

Nations consist of sexed and gendered beings, and so the trinity of nation, sexuality and gender cannot be separated when attempting to understand the objectification of women and the exploitation of the female body in the service of particular political creeds and national ends. The 'imagined community' of the nation 'has been constructed as a hetero-male project, and imagined as a brotherhood' (Anderson in Mayer 2000: 6). In the case of Zimbabwe, a popular war song, *'Zimbabwe ndeyeropa remadzibaba'* [Zimbabwe is born of the blood of the fathers] typically brings out the construction of the Zimbabwean nation as hetero-male. This discourse erases the contribution of women in constructing Zimbabwe, yet it is a historical fact that Zimbabwean women also shed their blood in the liberation war that birthed the country. As various scholars have noted (see, e.g., Mayer 2000; McClintock 1993) this 'masculine' notion consigns the role of protector and defender of the nation to men, and the role of reproducing the nation (biologically and culturally) to women. In this respect, therefore, women's bodies function as markers of the boundaries of the nation, and in national struggles such as those between rival political groups or parties, as is the case in Zimbabwe, they can be used to promote and privilege one particular version of the nation at the expense of others.

The contention here is that this is the case with the choir in Zimbabwe's polarized and contested political terrain, where different versions of the nation are vying for supremacy: a nativist-cum-Afro-radicalist strand represented by ZANU-PF and a neo-liberal-inclined strand represented by the MDC. The album title, 'Nyatsoteerera', is a clarion call and an invitation to all and sundry to register a particular reality which, in this case, is the privileged status of a particular view of the Zimbabwean nation, as represented by ZANU-PF, and of which the women are the ideological reproducers. In 'Nyatsoteerera' the women urge listeners to listen carefully or to take note of the reality that Mugabe holds the reins of power. In the visual accompaniment to the song, the lead vocalist addresses this call to a young man whom she exhorts to acknowledge Mugabe's incumbency.

An iconography of motherhood is depicted through the female singers' maturity and dress, most notably the long waist-cloth tied around the waist: in Zimbabwe, this is regarded as a symbol of motherhood and socially approved wifehood. In this way the women become 'privileged bearers of cultural authenticity' (Kandiyoti in Chitauro, Dube & Gunner 1994: 171), and therefore worthy ideological reproducers of the nation. Emblazoned portraits of the ZANU-PF leader and president, Robert Mugabe, as well as ZANU-PF party slogans such as '100% total empowerment' on their attire, cast the singers as embodiments of ZANU-PF's nationalist discourses which are centred on the indigenisation of national wealth.

The singers are also bearers of a personality and leadership cult, as the titular song shows. The song glorifies the incumbency of Mugabe as the one and only, against perceived and known but unnamed aspirants, and refers to him fondly by the name 'Bob'. In this way the song attempts to write out the other partners in the inclusive government, and symbolically from the national narrative. The principle of power-sharing which is implied by the current inclusive government, is erased.

At a higher level it (unwittingly) subverts the work of higher regional and continental institutions such as the Southern African Development Community (SADC) and the African Union (AU), who are the guarantors of the global political agreement (GPA) which gave birth to the inclusive government. In addition, the dances and lyrical content also subvert the dominant global neoliberal agenda whose leading exponents – the United States, Britain, Canada, Australia and the EU block – are abrasively critical of ZANU-PF and its land reform programme. The neoliberal agenda views the crisis of the Zimbabwean state as a result of ZANU-PF's populist rejection of capitalist market principles, as manifested through its re-appropriating of land from minority white farmers to address colonial imbalances in land tenure, along with 'indigenisation' policies targeted at transferring 51 per cent of shares in mining, industry and commerce to black Zimbabweans. The celebratory lyrics and visuals thus become a counter-narrative to those opposed to Zimbabwe's domestic policy. This multi-layered subversion is testimony to the semantic volatility of the messages contained in the jingles.

The same applies to the song 'Team', which singles out the aforementioned ZANU-PF leadership triumvirate as the team at the helm of Zimbabwe's leadership, and exhorts them: 'Chimbotongai makadaro' [Stay put for the time being]. The visuals accompanying the song exploit the iconography of the Zimbabwean national football team – an iconography which invests the three leaders referred to in the song with the vitality, energy and youthfulness associated with soccer players. The song title implies the existence of an opposing team that must be vanquished, while the iconography of the national football team subtly casts the opposing 'team' as foreign. This fits in well with ZANU-PF's casting of the political opposition, even in the context of the inclusive government, as a Trojan horse for foreign imperialist interests. In this way it attempts to foreclose other competing political discourses and achieve a monologic status for its cultural nationalist narrative.

The ZANU-PF nationalist discourse invoked by the choir is rooted in the war of liberation, as the song 'MuZimbabwe' clearly shows. The accompanying visuals link the present discourse with that of the war of liberation (the Second Chimurenga) through flashbacks of scenes from that war; and the toyi-toying of the dancers invokes the same spirit of the war, now in the form of the Third Chimurenga, which is about correcting colonial imbalances such as institutionalised land segregation in the former Rhodesia through the 'fast-track' land reform programme. The song's invocation of the ancestors and of land tropes in ZANU-PF's nationalist discourse resonates with its nativist strand. Although the song emphasises unity, it is referring to the unity between ZANU-PF and PF-ZAPU, the two former liberation war movements, which signed a unity accord in 1987, celebrated each year on 22 December as Unity Day. The current unity, represented by the Government of National Unity, is completely written out. This shows that the only unity ZANU-PF privileges, is one in which it subsumes the other party – which is not necessarily the case in the current inclusive government.

Propagandistic jingles and the carnivalesque

The propagandistic jingles exploit the notion of the carnivalesque through their highly sexualised, libidinous, excessive hip-gyrating dances. As far as Zimbabwe is concerned, one is immediately reminded of the *mbende/jerusarema* fertility dance which, under colonialism, was banned by the missionaries for its 'obscenity' and overtly sexualised choreography. Stuart Hall (1993: 108) submits that popular culture, as such, links with what Bakhtin terms 'the "vulgar" – the popular, the informal, the underside, the grotesque'. The choir's dancing exploits the notion of carnival to foreground the idea of subversion. In the current context, then, the dances could be seen as subverting/undermining the principle of inclusivity and power-sharing in the inclusive government. In the same sense, therefore, the dances in the propagandistic jingles exploit the negritudist representation of the black body – particularly that of the female – as being full of rhythm, and so, to an extent, are in service of the cultural-nationalist project of the post-2000 period. The term 'negritude' was coined by Aimé Césaire, Leon Damas and Leopold Sedar Senghor and others in the 1930s as a counter-discourse to Western negative stereotypes of Africans (Thompson 2002). These authors exploited the trope of the beautiful and rhythmic black body to celebrate blackness and counter white racist stereotypes about black people. In this sense, the carnivalesque jingles, besides their propagandist role, can also be seen to function not only as a kind of diversion, but also as an outlet, as a release and catharsis in the face of debilitating challenges. In this way the women can be said to be readily at the service of, and furthering the interests of, certain political agendas. According to Hall (1993: 108), carnival, which is part of popular culture, 'is rooted in popular experience and available for expropriation at one and the same time'. Yet, the carnivalesque is celebrated by Bakhtin as being subversive of authoritarian power, and liberatory in many respects. The carnival is also about laughter (often satirical and derisive), but in this case it is appropriated by an overarching regime of power. This contradiction is articulated by Stallybrass and White (1986), who point out that carnival is open to the play of power and can be exploited by the elite; making it a site of contestation. This is something which Bakhtin failed to appreciate in his theory of the carnivalesque, according to Stallybrass and White (ibid.). A certain ambivalence exists in figuring the choir women as reproducers of the ZANU-PF view of the nation. Ironically, the carnivalesque dances appear to cast the singers within the discourse of 'loose' women, and therefore unfit reproducers of the nation – or, at least, the version of the nation that they are supposed to represent. Therefore, their obscene gyrations altogether undermine/deflate their symbolic role as mothers and reproducers of the nation. Nevertheless, this can be counterbalanced by the iconography of motherhood and wifehood described earlier, and so in this way the dances are not necessarily divested of their political symbolism, and the carnival potentially fits into the traditional ceremonial, as described above.

Writing about the postcolony, Mbembe (2006) notes that 'power dons the face of virility', due to the sexualised and gendered nature of political power in which domination is masculinised and subordination is feminised. It provides another context for interpreting the political jingles. This seems to be reflected in those dances where hip-gyrations predominate, namely in songs dealing with power and domination ('*Nyatsoteerera*' and 'Team'), rather than those that focus on other themes. These dances project the sexualised body as spectacle, and are symbolic of the fecund female body. Sex is often an instrument of domination, and it is as such that it is inseparable from political discourses which are underpinned by power and domination. It is in this respect that Mbembe (ibid: 163) posits that 'rulers subject the ruled to various forms of copulation', and so the dances/jingles can also be located in the context of the power-play characterising the post-2000 Zimbabwean political landscape, and the current inclusive government.

The ambivalent iconography of motherhood in the jingles

The song '*MuZimbabwe*' talks of how '*vaMugabe vari kutonga*' [Mugabe is in power] and '*Tauya kuzosimudzira nyika yatakatora tose nehusiku*' [we have come/are here to develop the nation we fought for even in the darkness of night]. The implication is that no one can speak of empowerment or development outside the framework of Zimbabwe's nationalist struggles. The women are also articulating a conveniently abstracted collective will; they foreclose any other ideological paradigm in terms of development. They are, therefore, at a critical moment in Zimbabwe's historical and political trajectory, posing as mothers of this discourse. The discourse of motherhood potentially carries certain ambivalences: motherhood can refer to birthing, or, alternatively, to nurturing what has already been birthed. In this regard, it is problematic to place the choir 'mothers' in the discourse of motherhood in the context of the nation. The 'mothers' in this choir in effect consign their role to nurturing a male-generated version of Zimbabwe, while failing to exploit the mothering potential of birthing new or alternative narratives of Zimbabwe based on a fusion of male and female aspirations.

Considering the idea that nations are constructed as hetero-male projects, is it possible that nations can be reconstructed on the basis of a fusion of male and female aspirations? In most former colonial societies (as is the case with Zimbabwe), the role of women in national projects is rooted in the way the struggle for national liberation was organised.

Joyce Chadya (2003: 154), in discussing the role of women in Africa and in anti-colonial nationalism, submits that women 'internalised th[e] link between maternity and the struggle and thus appropriated the iconography of motherhood'. The choir women have continued to hold on to this iconography. Chadya (ibid.) highlights the fact that 'while during the struggle, "those" men, such as Nyerere of Tanzania, were sons who had to be taken care of; after independence, they became the fathers who had to be listened to'. The song 'Nyatsoteerera' resonates very well with this observation in that it denotes the largely marginal role of women in national projects. During the struggle, the men hailed women as mothers, but after the war they have continued to hail themselves as fathers in an ironic subversion of relations. In discussing the dangerous liaisons between women and nationalist movements, McClintock (1991: 109) posits that 'nationalisms are from the outset constituted in gender power, but, as the lessons of international history portend, women who are not empowered to organise during the struggle will not be empowered to organise after the struggle'. McClintock adds that 'if nationalism is not transformed by an analysis of gender power, the nation-state will remain a repository of male hopes, male aspirations, and male privilege', which women will continue to reproduce.

Conclusion

The women of the choir project a celebratory role in both their lyrics and dances. By continuing to applaud ZANU-PF leadership, they have infused the ideology of motherhood with the increasingly radical cast of the party's politicians. While it may be argued that recording their music is an insistence on their right to political agency and their right to access the technologies of political propaganda, they are still figured as the handmaidens of the male nationalist revolution. Their case illustrates the hidden power of discourse to hail subjects into particular subject-positions (Hall 2000). The women have remained entrapped in a nationalist discourse that is male generated and they have not transcended that paradigm. Judging by the lyrical content of their songs, the choir women seem to be suggesting that women cannot and should not conceive of their own and national emancipation outside the terms of the predominantly male-dominated national liberation movement. With their uncritical adoption of the patriarchalist iconography of motherhood, the women singers/dancers have failed to demand the right to refashion the terms of nationalist feminism to meet their own needs. Through nationalist feminism they could, as Herr (2003: 151) argues, '[take] an active part in the transformation of their own national culture, collaborating with [male nationalists] when national dignity is at stake, but at the same time resisting patriarchal constructions of nationalist discourses'. From a feminist perspective, the songs-turned-jingles show the need to strategically rethink how to transform levels of political visibility for women, in order to obtain measurable gains from the national project they are articulating.

References

Bakhtin, M. 1984. *Rabelais and his world*. New York: Indiana University Press.
Chadya, J. 2003. Mother politics: anti-colonial nationalism and the woman question in Africa. *Journal of Women's History* 15(3): 153–157.
Chitando, E. 2002. Music in Zimbabwe. *Zambezia* 29(1): 82–91.

Chitauro, M., C. Dube and L. Gunner. 1994. Song, story and nation: women as singers and actresses in Zimbabwe. In *Theatre and performance in Africa: intercultural perspective*, ed. E. Breitinger, 169–198. Bayreuth: Bayreuth University.

Fall, N. 2007. Providing a space of freedom: women artists from Africa. In *Global feminisms: new directions in contemporary art*, ed. M. Reilly and L. Nochlin, 71–77. London and New York: Merrell.

Hall, S. 1993. What is this 'black' in black popular culture? (Rethinking race). *Social Justice* 20(1/2): 104–114.

Hall, S. 2000. Who needs 'identity'? In *Identity: a reader*, ed. P. du Gay, J. Evans and P. Redman, 15–30. London: Sage.

Hassim, S. 2003. The limits of popular democracy: women's organisations, feminism and the UDF. *Transformation: Critical Perspectives on Southern Africa* 51(1): 48–73.

Herr, R.S. 2003. The possibility of nationalist feminism. *Hypatia* 18(3): 135–160.

Kittay, E.F. 1988. Woman as metaphor. *Hypatia* 3(2): 63–86.

Mayer, T. 2000. Introduction. In *Gender ironies of nationalism: sexing the nation*, ed. T. Mayer, 1–20. London and New York: Routledge.

Mbembe, A. 2006. On the postcolony: a brief response to critics. *African Identities* 4(2): 143–178.

McClintock, A. 1991. 'No longer in a future heaven': women and nationalism in South Africa. *Transition* 51: 104–123.

McClintock, A. 1993. Family feuds: gender, nationalism and the family. *Feminist Review* 44: 61–80.

Ndlovu-Gatsheni, S.J. 2009. *Do Zimbabweans exist? Trajectories of nationalism, national identity formation and crisis in a postcolonial state*. New York: Peter Lang.

Pachmanová, M. 2000. The politicization of the private, or the privatization of politics? A view of recent Czech art by women. *ARTmargins Online*. http://www.artmargins.com/index.php/8-archive/427-the-politicization-of-the-private-or-the-privatization-of-politics-a-view-of-recent-czech-art-by-women (accessed 15 February 2012).

Stallybrass, P. and A. White. 1986. *The politics and poetics of transgression*. New York: Cornell University Press.

The Army Institute of Professional Development. 1983. Propaganda media. www.psywarrior.com (accessed 22 January 2012),

Thompson, P. 2002. Negritude and new Africa: an update. *Research in African Literatures* 33(4): 143–153.

Discography

Mbare Chimurenga Choir. '*Nyatsoteerera*'. Grammar Records, 2010.

Stylin': The Great Masculine Enunciation and the (Re)Fashioning of African Diasporic Identities

Christine Checinska

ABSTRACT

In this article, Christine Checinska aims to: (i) outline the carnivalised theoretical approach that characterises her analysis of African diasporic cultural expressions, (ii) explore the creolised aesthetic that shapes the styling—or stylin', in colloquial terms—adopted by African diasporic men in the Caribbean, and (iii) to posit the notion of stylin' as a creolised non-verbal Nation Language (a term coined by Kamau Brathwaite; see *History of the Voice*. London: New Beacon, 1984). In this schema, the (re)fashioning of the body facilitates the reconfiguration of diasporic identities that are in constant flux as a result of geographical, psychological, and social border crossings. The Haitian Revolution (1791–1804) is central to the discussion, since it arguably galvanised what the author calls "the Great Masculine Enunciation", a form of democratisation of dress that marked the shift from the functional, anonymous (un)dress of enslaved Africans to the elegant, embellished, individualised swagger of African diasporic peacock males. This constituted the reverse of the Great Masculine Renunciation in the West, which saw the abandonment of adornment in favour of understatement in fashionable male dress after the French Revolution (1789–1799), as described by J. C. Flugel (*The Psychology of Clothes*. London: Hogarth, 1966).

In their text *Stylin': African American Expressive Culture from its Beginnings to the Zoot Suit* (1998), Shane White and Graham White examine the way in which African Americans have used their bodies to (re)fashion and express their identities from the period of enslavement in America to the 1940s. They trace African American style back to its origins in West Africa to suggest that there are certain cultural imperatives underpinning the modes of fashionable dress favoured by African diasporic peoples. The term "stylin'", used by White and White, and which I borrow for the title of this article, is African American urban slang for "showing off" or looking excessively fashionable. It has migrated into everyday Jamaican language, hence its use here to refer to men in the Caribbean. Stylin' describes both a transformative act and a form of countergaze at a personal and collective level. It encompasses dress, accessorising, grooming, and gestures. I argue that stylin' could be regarded as a creolised, non-verbal form of what Kamau Brathwaite (1984) calls "Nation Language", one which ultimately speaks of cultural and racial autonomy.

The Haitian Revolution (1791–1804) is key, since it arguably sparked what I call "the Great Masculine Enunciation": a democratisation of dress that marked the shift from the functional, anonymous (un)dress of enslaved West Africans in the Caribbean to the elegant, embellished, individualised swagger of African diasporic peacock males. Modern menswear in the West is said to have started with the Great Masculine Renunciation (Flugel 1966), which occurred during the period after the French Revolution (1789–1799). In fashionable male dress, adornment was abandoned in favour of understatement. This shift reflected the egalitarian ethos of the French Revolution. The Great Masculine Enunciation that I outline, whilst underpinned by a striving for equality, effectively constituted the reverse of this Western phenomenon; it is characterised by dressing up as opposed to dressing down.

Embracing White and White's use of the term "stylin'" and expanding on the idea of the Great Masculine Enunciation, I (i) outline the carnivalised theoretical approach that characterises my analysis of African diasporic cultural expressions, (ii) explore the creolised aesthetic that shapes the styling—or stylin', in colloquial terms—adopted by African diasporic men in the Caribbean, and (iii) posit the notion of stylin' as a creolised non-verbal Nation Language. In this schema, the (re)fashioning of the body facilitates the reconfiguration of diasporic identities that constantly shift as a result of geographical, psychological, and social border crossings.

Carnivalising Theory

The travelling, ever-evolving communities that constitute the global African diasporas could be viewed as synonymous with diversity and syncretism. Herein lies the problem: what investigative methods can be used to analyse the cultural expressions produced? Finding one theory or theorist on which to hang one's thesis is ill-advised. One has to engage in a search for models that encourage the use of multiple methods from a diverse range of sources; methodological and theoretical boundaries have to be negotiated. Writing as a black British writer/artist of African Caribbean descent, I do not dismiss Western theorists; instead, I go "a piece of the way with them", to cite Carol Boyce-Davies (1994), by taking up a carnivalised approach. Going "a piece of the way with them", as a model for negotiating relations with strangers, is founded on an African tradition whereby the host travels part of a journey alongside a stranger or friend before returning home, the distance travelled, or the "piece of the way", depends on the closeness of the relationship between the two or more parties. When used as a means of engaging with theory, it becomes a metaphor for a critical relationality, where a number of theoretical positions are examined for their efficacy in the analysis of diasporic cultural forms. Critical relationality has an inherent sense of fluidity, almost an inbuilt homelessness, that mirrors that of diasporic experiences. It suggests an integrated approach to theory, one that resists binary oppositions whilst challenging hierarchies of value and the privileging of Eurocentric viewpoints or "master" discourses, encouraging dialogue instead of separation or essentialism. It aims to be conscious of the plural self and diverse other(s).

The term "carnivalising theory" is proposed by Joan Anim-Addo (2006) as a means of reading the creolised literary text. I utilise it to create a methodology that is sympathetic to the syncretic cultural practices found in the Caribbean. There is a reflection of the schism of migration central to diasporic experiences, the notion of cultural exchange characteristic of creolised culture and the concept of the past, albeit a fragmented one, acting as an incubator for, and cutting into, the present.[1] It encourages theoretical complexity, relationality, and depth, whilst grounding the analysis in empirical investigation. Subsequently, the range of investigative methods that I apply to my research includes oral testimony and auto-ethnography. Although there is currently considerable interest in the efficacy of oral testimony in fashion studies,[2] my use of it allows for the rediscovery of forgotten voices from within the African diasporas whilst referencing oral (hi)storytelling traditions.

In working from a Western perspective, I draw on Roland Barthes's (1990; 2006) semiotic approach to the history and sociology of clothing, where fashion, dress, and— by extension—stylin' are languages and texts waiting to be "read". As a human being, one constantly "speaks". Language and dress, for example, are both systems that operate at the level of the individual and the collective. Structurally, systems of language and dress are shaped by particular cultural contexts. The displacement of just one element changes the whole, producing a new structure. Verbal language and stylin' cannot be separated from their cultural roots or, indeed, routes. Brathwaite (1984), in his analysis of Caribbean language structures, makes a distinction between the imposed imperial languages of Standard English and Creole English—the form of English that evolved in the new Caribbean environment—and Nation Language, the language of the enslaved. He notes that verbal Nation Language is strongly influenced by West African models. It consciously ignores the pentameter in order to express the everyday from African Caribbean, and by extension African diasporic, perspectives.

Whilst I do not advocate outmoded forms of essentialist thinking, in my view the African diasporic stylin' emerging from the Caribbean is also in some instances influenced by West African models. Referencing Brathwaite's (1984, 2) analysis of the lexical features of verbal Nation Language, "in its contours … it is not English", even though the garments being worn "might be English to a lesser or greater degree". Tracing the history of creolised African Caribbean self-fashioning back to plantation slavery, the attention paid to stylin' was instrumental in keeping alive fragments of shattered histories and traditions, mirroring the role played by verbal Nation Language. The sound explosions that punctuate the verbal are alive in the details of an outfit, for example the use of statement accessories such as a hat strategically placed at an angle, the glint of an earring worn with an otherwise sombre ensemble, a flash of colour, or a principled clash of pattern. The performativity of stylin' parallels the "total expression" or "orality" of verbal Nation Language (Brathwaite 1984, 18). The audience is key to the generation of meaning. Echoing the "call and response" of the spoken word, the styled body in movement demands a response (Checinska 2012).

A Creolised Aesthetic

The interrelated systems of colonisation and enslavement drove the seventeenth-century Caribbean plantation slave economy, providing a breeding ground for complex, layered cultural exchanges between Europe, the New World, and Africa. In their article *In Praise of Creoleness* (1990), the Guadeloupean linguist Jean Bernabé, the Martinican novelists Patrick Chamoiseau and Raphaël Confiant, together with Mohamed T. B. Khyar, discuss what it is to be creole, to be both French and Caribbean, yet not fully recognised as French. Twentieth-century overseas governance served to maintain the uneven power dynamic between metropole and colonies that had been established centuries before. Bernabé, et al. (1990) seek to reconcile the resulting tensions by reclaiming *creolité* and creolisation, and embrace the concept of "Caribbeanness" posited by the Martinican Édouard Glissant.

Glissant (1989) resists Western scholars' framing of the Caribbean solely against issues of dislocation and fragmentation. He notes that the tensions inherent within the processes of colonisation, enslavement, and displacement were necessary for the emergence of creolisation. However, by acknowledging plurality, diversity, exchange, and transformation as well, Glissant (1989) redefines Caribbean histories, languages, and identities. He emphasises the continual transformation and reinvention that distinguish creole societies and the cultural expressions that emerge. He also suggests that creolisation as a theory of creative disorder might be expanded to apply to histories, societies, and cultures beyond the Caribbean. Importantly, issues of power, domination, and subalternity are always present (Hall 2003).

Prior to Glissant's observations, Brathwaite (1971) asserted that the foundation of contemporary Caribbean societies is rooted in, and through, the creole societies created by the plantation slave system. He defines creolisation as a cultural process that emerged as people from mainly Britain and West Africa interacted with one another to create a distinctive culture that was neither British nor West African. However, creolisation was a process of contention rather than blending. Echoing Glissant's writings, the dynamics of domination and subordination characteristic of the plantation slavery system were central to it. A recurring theme in Brathwaite's work is the relationship between language, culture, and the structure of Caribbean society. He describes West Africa as the "submerged mother of the Creole system", since it was both the physical and psychological home of the majority of the enslaved (Brathwaite 1971, 6). Similarly, James Walvin (1971, 148), discussing the slave society on the eighteenth-century Jamaican estate Worthy Park, notes that traces of West Africa were apparent in social attitudes, culture, and identity. Even up to emancipation, one-third of the slaves at Worthy Park had been born in West Africa. The constant influx of the newly enslaved kept memories of home alive. Absenteeism on the part of the Jamaican planters enabled these traditions to be retained. The Haitian Revolution (1791–1804), together with the American Revolution (1775–1783), gave an increased impetus to the creolisation process.

There were physical, psychological, and spiritual aspects to the enslavement process instigated by the plantation slave owners. It began with "seasoning": a three-year procedure of naming, branding, and re-clothing. The enslaved would learn a new language and become acclimatised to his/her role. Then came "socialisation", involving integration into recreational activities such as drumming, dancing, and slave festivals. Thereafter followed "identification" with the group and authority figures such as the driver and the *obeah* man.[3] The collision of the enslaved and the plantation owners may have been violent, but it was also creative. The development of a creolised language structure amongst the enslaved was integral to the cultural exchanges that took place (Brathwaite 1971).

Brathwaite (1971) suggests that the fragmentation in history and culture that occurred in Jamaica when the indigenous Taino were wiped out by Europeans and replaced by enslaved West Africans gave rise to creolised cultural expressions. One aspect of this was verbal Nation Language (Brathwaite 1984). I suggest that non-verbal Nation Language developed simultaneously. The concept of a language of fashion and/or style is by no means a new one (see, in particular, Barthes 1990 and 2006). Indeed, Barthes's semiotic approach is fundamental to fashion theory.[4] However, where Barthes's approach has been applied to dress styles developed beyond the West, it has been done from an all-too-narrow, Eurocentric viewpoint that pays little attention to the cultural imperatives of the wearer. Such dress is read against the Western fashion system and is consequently seen as subversive, subcultural, exotic, something *other* than the norm. A binary system is established. Some examples that illustrate this include writings by Christopher Breward (1995), Stuart Cosgrove (1989), and Dick Hebdige (1979). By drawing on and developing Brathwaite's concept of Nation Language as a means of defining or reading African diasporic stylin', I trouble the narrow confines of Barthes's *The Fashion System* (1990). The fashion systems referenced by African diasporic peoples in the Caribbean were informed by a creolised aesthetic—the same aesthetic that spawned new language structures in spoken and written form. There is a symbiosis between vernacular linguistic and sartorial expression; both are underpinned by the negotiation of identities.

Brathwaite (1984, 5) begins his analysis of Caribbean language structure by defining the region's language as a "process of using English in a different way from the 'norm'. English in a new sense ... English in an ancient sense. English in a very traditional sense. And sometimes not English at all, but *language*". Since the enslaved were drawn from a number of different tribes, no single West African language existed. However, according to Brathwaite, there were common semantic and stylistic forms. He identifies the Ashanti, Congo, and Yoruba languages. These languages had to be submerged, since the language of public discourse was Standard English. Nevertheless, this submergence served an important "interculturative" purpose (Brathwaite 1984, 7), which allowed creolised languages to develop. The submerged language of the slaves constantly transformed itself, influencing and transforming the contemporary English of public discourse as it did so. Nation Language can be defined as the emergent language of an emergent people. Its primary purpose was to express the everyday from African Caribbean perspectives. It was English in some of its lexical features, but it was strongly influenced by West African models: "[I]n its contours, its rhythm and timbre, its sound explosions, it is not English, even though the words as you hear them, might be English to a lesser or greater degree" (Brathwaite 1984, 13).

As the language emerged from an oral (hi)storytelling tradition, performance is integral to Nation Language. It echoes the sounds of Caribbean carnival, *kaiso*,[5] and calypso. Brathwaite (1984, 18) describes the play of sound and performance as "total expression". The voice moves in an intervallic pattern rather than in a single forward plane, as it does with the iambic pentameter. There are intricate syncopated rhythmic variations that play sound off against silence. As with Barthes's language of fashion and the notion of stylin', the audience is key to the generation of meaning. In Brathwaite's words (1984, 19), "'[t]otal expression' grew from conditions of poverty, where people had to rely on their own resourcefulness in order to exist: they had to rely on their very *breath* rather than on paraphernalia like books and museums and machines ... they had to depend on *immanence*, the power within themselves, rather than the technology outside themselves". Nation Language became a strategy for survival and overcoming, and an act of free creative expression. The fragments of histories and traditions embedded within it carried with them bodies of knowledge with which the enslaved re-imagined or remembered themselves and, in so doing, resisted their allotted place in the plantation hierarchy.

Brathwaite (1984) contends that the roots of Nation Language can be traced back to *shango*, *anansesem*, the Spiritual Baptist movement or Africanised Church, yard theatres, ring games, and tea-meeting speeches. These were vernacular spaces, routed through West Africa and the Middle Passage, hidden from the planters' gaze. This brings me to the relationship between Brathwaite's Nation Language and the creolised aesthetic of African diasporic stylin' in the Caribbean.

26th December 1804:

> Nothing but bonjoes, drums, and tom-toms, going all night, and dancing and singing and madness, all the morning … Some of our blackies were most superbly drest, and so were several of their friends, who came to join in the masquerade; gold and silver fringe, spangles, beads, &c. &c. and really the most wonderful expense altogether. General N. gave the children money, and threw some himself among them from the gallery, and in the scramble all the finery was nearly torn to pieces, to my great vexation. However, they seemed not mind it, but began dancing with the same spirit as if nothing had happened, putting their smart clothes into the best order they could. We gave them a bullock, a sheep and a lamb, with a dollar to every person in the house, from the oldest individual to the youngest infant; besides a complete new dress, with two changes of linen. This is the case every Christmas, and at all the festivals they have a present of clothing. (Nugent 1839, 129–130)

The above is an extract from Lady Nugent's 1839[6] diary, *A Journal of a Voyage to, and Residence in, the Island of Jamaica, from 1801 to 1805, and the Subsequent Events in England from 1808 to 1811*. The diary entry cited above refers to the Jonkonnu Christmas masquerade.[7] The military costumes, European dress, West African-inspired masks, ox-horn headdresses, and animal skins of the Jonkonnu masqueraders are a microcosm of plantation slave dress. These masquerades performed an important interculturative function in terms of the development of non-verbal Nation Language (Brathwaite 1984, 7). Those who were not in masquerade costume were "most superbly drest", with "gold and silver fringe on their robes"; all were "dressed with a variety of trinkets and finery, and many not unbecomingly, though very fantastically" (Long 1970, 426).

Feast days and holidays, like Sundays and Christmas, allowed the enslaved to display their "better cloaths" (Long 1970, 426). These were of a "very superior description" and often exceeded in value "those possessed by the generality of European peasantry" (De la Beche 1825, 12). Lady Nugent's *Journal* is peppered with comments about the "odd appearance" of the "blackies". She notes their "finery" and the novelty of seeing them in European dress. For example, her diary entry of 13 September 1804 reads: "Lady M., her young people, and myself in the sociable, with our two black postillions, in *scarlet liveries*, but with black ankles peeping out of their particulars, and altogether a rather novel sort of appearance, to Europeans just arrived" (1839, 100–101, emphasis added). I use this image of the "two black postillions, in *scarlet liveries*", together with slavery apologist Edward Long's (1970, 500–504) observations that the "better cloaths" of the enslaved were chiefly made in the "finest and costliest fabrics", invariably dyed in the "gaudiest colours", to consider the traces of West African cultural expressions in the enslaveds' tastes in colour, pattern, and use of cloth.[8]

Traditional West African cloth was woven from a range of materials, including local silk and cotton, bark, bast, goat's wool, and raffia (Picton 2004). The use of draped, uncut cloth was a distinctive feature of indigenous dress. This stemmed from a concern with the elegance of the body in movement; draped cloth enhanced performance. Before the nineteenth century, male dress from Benin, Ghana, and the Ivory Coast, for example, was characterised by cloth draped over the left shoulder and under the right. Traditional dress to the east of Benin consisted of a wrap "skirt" worn with a long tunic over it (Picton 2004). As Olaudah Equiano (1998, 4) writes regarding the "manners and customs" of his country: "The dress of both sexes … generally consists of a long piece of calico or muslin, wrapped loosely around the body, somewhat in the form of a Highland plaid."

In order to wear these voluminous wrapped styles, one had to stand upright and be aware of one's posture in movement; if not, the garment would fall away. It had to be checked and adjusted accordingly if it was found to be lying or hanging incorrectly (Picton 2004). This awareness of the body in movement translates into the "total expression" of verbal Nation Language. Stylin' is as much about deportment, gesture, and stance as it is about individual items of clothing. As with spoken Nation Language, if the performance is ignored, meaning is lost.

Voluminous draping communicated the wearer's status. Expensive cloths, due to their finer weave, draped more readily. Furthermore, if, as J. C. Flugel (1966) suggests, dress is an extension of the bodily self, the increase in the perceived bulk of the wearer that results from draped and wrapped clothing, particularly when in movement, increases the wearer's perceived status in the eyes of the audience.[9] West African leadership dress was layered further still in a visual display of status, wealth, and power. As a result, an abundance of draped cloth became synonymous with prestige. The layers of cloth in leadership dress were combined with jewellery, headgear, and handheld regalia to reinforce the wearer's position at the pinnacle of the social hierarchy. Considering this use of draped cloth, could one say that there is a trace of West African tastes in the draping and wrapping of "coloured petticoats" about the waists of the newly arrived gang of "Eboe Negroes", whom Lady Nugent (1839, 136–137) met on her morning drive on 22 January 1805?

West African leaders appropriated European garments from the earliest contact. Items were traded on the basis of regional aesthetics and included such pieces as printed chintz, taffetas, damask silks, linen shirts, and "scarlet cloth" (Bradley-Foster 1997, 18–43). Particular colours, such as scarlet, had political and ritual meanings. In Benin, for example, scarlet in ceremonial leadership dress symbolised anger, blood, war, and fire. When worn, it communicated a threat to the viewer whilst simultaneously warding off evil. Other common colours in Beninean dress included white, yellow, scarlet, green, and the bright indigo blue that Equiano (1998, 5) recalls. For example, a trading ship left Benin in 1769 carrying a cargo of "360 slaves and … red, blue, violet and yellow dyewoods … and cloths"; similarly, a ship that left in 1789 carried "1,000 cloths … and red, yellow, blue and violet dyewoods" (Bradley-Foster 1997, 56). Although the draping and folding of fabric described above obscures colour and pattern, both were vital to creating the desired impression. Patterning was made complex by the construction of the cloth. European trade cloths were sometimes unravelled and rewoven to suit local West African tastes. Scarlet cloths were particularly hard to dye, so cochineal or kermes-dyed commercial cloths, such as those from Lyon and the Middle East, traded through the trans-Saharan caravans, were recycled (Schneider 1987, 428). Imported cloths were also used as bases onto which geometric patterns were printed using calabash shell stamps. Alternatively, tie-dye techniques were deployed to personalise the fabric (Bradley-Foster 1997, 56–58). Common cloths, such as West African *kente*, were woven in narrow ten-centimetre strips. These were then cut into sections and stitched together edge to edge, forming a patchwork length.

There is a correlation between the unravelled and reworked European cloths, the patched effect of *kente* cloth, the bricoleur's approach to dress displayed by the enslaved, and the percussive "sound explosions" of Brathwaite's Nation Language. In *kente* cloth, for example, multicoloured chequerboard patterns were stitched against simple two-colour stripes— pink against green, gold against scarlet. Additional layers of colour and pattern were introduced through the use of floating or non-structural weft threads. These floating threads generated a melange of effects. Three-dimensional weaves were simultaneously created (Perani and Wolff 1999, 26). Such complex patterning was punctuated by the simplicity of blocked colour, reminiscent of the interplay between speech and silence in Brathwaite's Nation Language. In this way, a polyrhythmic effect was created across each length of cloth. Harmony was achieved in spite of the juxtaposition of seemingly clashing colours. The play of light on these cloths created a luminosity that echoed the use of opalescent materials and mirrors in West African masquerade, where shininess was said to have magical properties, such as the ability to deflect evil by reflecting it back onto its source (Picton 2004, 32).[10] With this in mind, could the "gold and silver fringe, spangles, beads, &c. &c." that Lady Nugent (1839, 129–130) observed be related to this earlier use of opalescent materials?

Evidence of *riddimic* (rhythmic) patterns in slave dress has been difficult to find. Available visual imagery, for instance as found in the writings of Henry de la Beche (1825), show either the elaborately decorated Jonkonnu masquerade costumes or madras checks and ticking stripes like those found in Agostino Brunias's paintings. However, was Jemmy, who ran away from his master in 1793, carrying a blue coat with striped yellow buttons and a purple and white-bordered waistcoat, displaying a flair for syncopated colour co-ordination? Or was Billy, who escaped in 1790 wearing blue pantaloons and a sailor's jacket, showing a taste for striking colours that reveals an alternative fashion aesthetic to that of the Anglo-Saxon West (Brathwaite 1971, 203–204)? Do their sartorial preferences evidence the development of a distinctive, creolised, non-verbal language structure?

The propensity to drape and wrap cloth was exhibited in the attention that the enslaved paid to the dressing of their heads. Long (1970, 412) notes: "They are fond of covering this part of their bodies at all times, twisting one or two handkerchiefs around it, in the turban form, which, they say, keeps them cool, in the hottest sunshine". He adds that "they buy the finest cambric or muslin for the purpose, if their pockets can afford it". This preoccupation with dressing the head can be traced to the importance of the human head in certain West African ritual possession masquerade and figurative art. For example, if one acknowledges that in the Dahomean Yoruba religion, the head is regarded as the receptacle in which the spirit resides, paying attention to the dressing of the head is key to the (re)fashioning of identities in the midst of plantation slavery's "ungendering", feminisation and infantilisation (Checinska 2009). Majors and Mancini Billson (1992, 56–57) suggest that West African spirituality was an important survivor of the Middle Passage. Furthermore, they argue that the behavioural patterns of the African diasporas across the Black Atlantic today are informed by this trace. By the term "spirituality", Majors and Mancini Billson mean taking a vitalistic rather than a mechanistic approach to life, one that believes that supernatural forces impact daily events. In the Jamaican context, the West African possession rituals that took place during the initial stages of slave rebellions point to this spiritual aspect of dressing the head; it was believed that through these rituals, the enslaved would be able to expel "Massa's spirit from Quashies's head" (Burton 1997, 244–248).[11] Cuffee, the 1730s leader of the Maroons, wore a silver-laid hat. The 1750 rebel leader, Cudjoe, wore a feathered one (Burton 1997, 245). The re-enactment of possession rituals had the effect of empowering the enslaved to appropriate the power of their masters by drawing on spiritual powers. The physical and metaphorical masks in possession rituals enabled the (re)fashioning of identities in performance that contested those of the everyday (Picton 1990).

To summarise, enslaved West Africans emerged from the limbo of the Middle Passage carrying with them Old World knowledge, which provided models which then informed new creolised cultural expressions, including language structures. Certain interrelated dimensions of indigenous West African culture, such as spirituality, movement, and expressive individualism, rather than specific material artefacts, were retained. On the plantations, the Africanised Church and Caribbean carnival performed a pivotal interculturative function. Aspects of West African and European culture collided in these spaces. Both were re-inscribed and a bricoleur's approach was employed to create distinctive creolised forms. Without suggesting an essentialist West African culture, the detail of the outfits worn by the enslaved—such as the waistcoat with purple and white trimming, the colourful draped petticoats, the yellow-and-white-striped buttons placed on a bright blue background, and the turbaned heads—reveals traces of the wearers' pasts. Tastes in colour, pattern, and use of cloth, alongside exaggeration and abstraction in styling and the preoccupation with dressing the head, reference previous traditions. The clothing worn by the enslaved was given a creolised inflection. Like the relationship between standard and vernacular English in Brathwaite's verbal Nation Language, the garments may well have been European, but the manner in which they were worn was not. Stylin' became a strategic non-verbal Nation Language, in effect an act of transformation and freedom from the constraints of plantation life.

On Sundays, feast days and Saturday nights, the enslaved achieved a temporary freedom from the ungendering, infantilisation, and feminisation that characterised the Caribbean plantation system (Checinska 2009). The everyday dress of the enslaved reiterated the plantation's social hierarchy that fixed enslaved West Africans as social non-persons. The enslaved majority were clothed, fed, and housed by the European minority, whose hegemonic masculinity equated "being kept" with the feminine and therefore the inferior. (Infantilisation, for example as evidenced in fictitious characters from slave literature, such as Quashee, was an adjunct to this feminisation.) Restrictions in clothing were fundamental to the negotiation of gender roles. For example, until the age of 12–14 young boys wore just a simple coarse linen overshirt or smock, as did young girls. This denial of clothing that signified the transition into manhood, at a crucial point in male development, could be regarded as a disavowal of masculinity or a form of ungendering. Moreover, although slaves were issued with new clothes at Christmastime, in the early decades of plantation slavery, both male and female slaves in Jamaica were almost naked for much of the year once these clothes wore out (Sloane 1707). During carnival and feast days, as the boundaries between master and slave became blurred, dehumanisation was transformed into a "numinous experience", to reference Gloria Anzaldúa (1987, 73). New consciousnesses of self were created through the act of dressing and re-*presenting* the body—through stylin'. The enslaveds' state of emergence was made visible. However, freedom was ritualised and temporary; oppression was resisted and challenged but not permanently overcome. Poignantly, the masquerade ends, in the case of Lady Nugent's "superbly drest" "blackies" (1839, 129), when money is thrown from the gallery and all their finery is torn to pieces in the scramble to catch it. The plantation's social hierarchies come back into play. This brings me to the Haitian Revolution and the inspiration of the *ancien régime* elegance embraced by its leaders.

Haiti: The Great Masculine Enunciation

The Haitian Revolution (1791–1804) gave impetus to a process of creolisation already underway. Haiti, being the first independent black republic, represented cultural and racial autonomy. According to Western fashion history and theory, modern menswear began with the democratisation of dress galvanised by the French Revolution (1789–1799). This period is typically referred to as the Great Masculine Renunciation, for example in the writings of Barthes (2006), Breward (1999), Chenoune (1994), and Flugel (1966). Fashions in male dress shifted from an *ancien régime* emphasis on embellishment as a means of displaying social rank towards the foregrounding of function, discretion, and suitability. The French Revolution's ethos of equality and the resulting new social order demanded simplification, sobriety, and uniformity. In my view, from the perspective of African diasporic stylin', the Haitian Revolution sparked an alternative form of democratisation. Here, dress shifted from the functional and anonymous (un)dress of the enslaved to the elegant, embellished, and individualised, announcing the status of the wearer as free, equal, and part of humanity. This interpretation, driven by a striving for personhood, was characterised by dressing up rather than dressing down.

When the African diasporic male entered the global political stage, he was dressed. If one considers the issues of ungendering, of feminisation and infantalisation, of dominance and subalternity (Checinska 2009), and if one contemplates portraits of the Haitian revolutionary leaders Toussaint L'Ouverture, Jean-Jacques Dessalines, and Citizen Jean-Baptiste Belley against this, what is revealed is a visual representation of the African diasporic man's standing. These portraits represent the affirmation of masculinity and the articulation of personhood. Each symbolic male figure re-*presents* himself. The stylin' of each is underpinned by the dignity and self-respect of the sitter. These creolised sartorial compositions represent visual strategies where elaborate costume and an attention to detail come to signify the journey from powerlessness to power. They anticipate the "new shapes and consciousness" of African diasporic selves, to draw an analogy with Brathwaite's (1984, 49) verbal Nation Language. If being in diaspora means being situated between different cultures, holding the complex layered tensions between differing cultural imperatives, there is a further connection with Homi K. Bhabha's (1994, 177) assertion that the "in-between space" is the space of emergence. Thus stylin' becomes an enunciative practice.[12]

In the portrait shown on the next page, Dessalines stares directly at the viewer, his plumed bicorn hat set at an angle, the squareness of his jacket's shoulders accentuated by heavily tasselled epaulettes. His jacket facings are embellished with a laurel leaf design, resonating with the symbolic use of the laurel wreath in visual representations of imperial Rome. There is an echo of the *ancien régime* reliance on ornamentation to display wealth, status, and power in the use of extravagant surface decoration. These excessive trimmings legitimise Dessalines's authority; his appearance demands respect. However, this apparent embracing of the ostentation of the pre-revolution ruling classes is interrupted by the presence of a geometrically patterned skullcap, worn discreetly underneath his bicorn hat. Barthes (2006, 63–65) describes jewellery as the "soul" of an outfit, a "*next-to-nothing*" that is "the vital element in getting dressed, because it underlines the desire for order, for composition, for intelligence". Drawing on Barthes's assertion that "meaning" is revealed in the "detached detail", the depiction of Dessalines wearing a skullcap underneath a Napoleonic bicorn hat is significant. The addition of the skullcap moves Dessalines's dress beyond mimicry. Furthermore, the skullcap punctuates the outfit; it breaks the flow of the eye in a manner that parallels the syncopated sound explosions in verbal Nation Language.

Figure 1 Book illustration showing Jean-Jacques Dessalines (The Louverture Project 2005)

Dessalines had been enslaved and transported to San Domingo at the age of 16. His formative years were spent in West Africa. Could the skullcap reference his West African past?[13] When juxtaposed against Western dress, the skullcap is re-inscribed, becoming a potent cultural symbol. In one sense, the artist is conveying Dessalines's West African-ness and his metaphorical journey: from slave to soldier, to general, to emperor. However, by including the skullcap, the artist also shows the creolised nature of Haitian society and the creolised aesthetic of the formerly enslaved. By depicting Dessalines in this way at a time when blackness, with the advent of the Haitian Revolution, became a political force, the artist alerts the viewer to both the reversal of the plantation system's hierarchies of power and the contestation of the aesthetic values of the master classes. Worn with a French dress uniform, the skullcap becomes an ideological weapon. However, since meaning does not reside in the material object itself, both the skullcap and the dress uniform are re-inscribed when worn together in the moment of revolution and independence. Haitians at this historical juncture were a people in the process of becoming, of (re)fashioning identities by returning to their heritage and adapting key cultural symbols such as the skullcap to visually communicate that identity. The significance of this portrait lies in the sitter's use of dress to simultaneously signify the removal of Western domination and the entry of men of West African descent into the international political arena on an equal footing with Europeans.[14]

Dessalines succeeded L'Ouverture after his capture, having been the latter's lieutenant in the fight against the British and Spanish attempts to seize San Domingo from the French (James 1980, 250). Their leadership styles differed greatly. Whereas L'Ouverture was reserved, seeking advice from no one and neglecting to inform the masses of the rationale behind his strategies, Dessalines was decisive, did not pander to the colonists, and communicated directly with the people during the fight for independence. At Crête-à-Pierrot, for example, whilst awaiting the approach of the French, Dessalines patrolled the fort, naked to the waist, wearing dirty boots and a hat through which a bullet had passed (James 1980, 315).

Once the French were driven out in 1803, Dessalines became governor general of San Domingo. In January of the following year, he renamed the island "Haiti". By October he was declared Emperor Jacques I:

> Private merchants of Philadelphia presented him with the crown, brought on the American boat the Connecticut, his coronation robes reached Haiti from Jamaica on an English frigate from London. He made his solemn entry into Le Cap in a six-horse carriage brought for him by the English agent, Ogden, on board the Samson. Thus the Negro monarch entered into his inheritance, tailored and valeted by English and American capitalists, supported on the one side by the King of England and on the other by the President of the United States. (James 1980, 370)

In this carefully stage-managed entry into Le Cap, Dessalines's naked torso, dirty boots, and bullet-holed hat are replaced by a coronation robe and crown. He marks the legitimacy of his imperial leadership by being "valeted by English and American capitalists" (James 1980, 370). By surrounding himself with symbols of luxury from a Western perspective, Dessalines's visibility on the international political stage is amplified.

Conclusion

The leaders of the Haitian Revolution appropriated the elegance of the *ancien régime*, re-inscribing it with a West African inflection, thereby creating a creolised effect. On the ground, the military attire adopted by the Haitian army was seen as an act of defiance. Napoleon, for example, vowed not to leave one gold epaulette on the shoulders of those "gilded Africans" (James 1980, 271). The image of these revolutionaries is as important to the history of African diasporic male stylin' as the French Revolution is to the history of European male dress. However, unlike its French counterpart, the Haitian Revolution sparked the Great Masculine *Enunciation*—the reverse of the Great Masculine *Renunciation*. On a collective level, it represented cultural and racial autonomy. Moreover, it marked psychological freedom. The sight of the Haitian revolutionary leaders sporting personalised military uniforms awakened the Caribbean region to a new level of consciousness, founded on dignity and pride in being black-skinned. The reversal of the everyday ungendering, infantilisation, and invisibility of the enslaved was given impetus. Stylin' was an embodied non-verbal articulation of this reversal.

The portraits of Dessalines, first patrolling the fort naked to the waist wearing a hat through which a bullet had passed, then seated with a geometrically patterned skullcap clearly visible underneath a French bicorn hat, represent a strategically (re)fashioned identity. Read against the tensions noted by Brathwaite (1971; 1984), Glissant (1989), and Bernabé et al. (1990), stylin' allows the border between the interior self and the outside, or between the private and the public, to be temporarily ruptured. This mirrors Brathwaite's (1984, 49) assertion regarding verbal Nation Language: "The detonations within Caribbean sound-poetry have imploded us into new shapes and consciousness of ourselves". The articulation of a transformed, (re)fashioned identity through the process of stylin' momentarily fuses the sense of inner conflict, allowing for "new shapes and consciousnesses" of the self to be seen. This amplification or presencing of the inner self simultaneously acts as a countergaze.

Setting the findings discussed here into a broader context, stylin' is a vital visual marker of the continual process of fashioning and refashioning identities. What is being articulated is a particular state of emergence that is integral to the negotiation and contestation of geographical, psychological, and social borders. By definition, this is an ongoing feature of African diasporic experiences. Dessalines's self-fashioning and the appearance of Lady Nugent's (1839, 129) "superbly drest" "blackies" reveal a creolised aesthetic shaped by a language structure routed through particular cultural experiences and environments. In this schema, stylin' as Nation Language acts both as a facilitator and a symbol of transformation and emergence, and as a mediator of the process of (re)fashioning identities, a process that never reaches completion.

Notes

1 Mark McWatt (1982), writing on the pre-occupation with the past in West Indian novels, highlights the irony of this concern with history, since, regarding the formerly colonised Caribbean region, the past is "buried" or "absent". For this reason, the object of the writers' focus is, in fact, the "historyless-ness" or the invisibility of Caribbean history. I would go beyond that to suggest that this condition of perceived "historyless-ness" is inextricably linked to a perceived culturelessness, which feeds the absence of the African Caribbean within the fashion theory canon, hence the concern with speaking into certain absences in this article.
2 Examples of this trend include the exhibition *Fashion Lives* (November 11, 2005 to February 7, 2006, The British Library, London), the lecture series *Talking Design: Fashion Fiction* in which presenters discussed the links between autobiographical storytelling and fashion (2006, V&A, London), the *Nova* magazine exhibition (March 27 to August 26, 2006, The Women's Library, London), and the *Fashion Lives* study day (2006, The London College of Fashion, London).
3 The *obeah* man is a spiritual leader in the Jamaican Spiritual Baptist Church.
4 Barthes (1990) demonstrates the way in which high fashion functions as a process of signification. In doing so, he also exposes the social constructedness of language. He applies the theory of semiotics to examine the way in which fashion communicates varied meanings shaped by the context in which garments are worn and/or read. Through semiology (Saussurean analysis), Barthes translates fashion into a non-verbal language, governed by specific structures and systems. Through close readings of fashion magazine editorials, he identifies the signifiers, signifieds, signs, and sign systems that generate meaning.

The signifier is the concept that one applies to an individual garment or accessory, which is the signified. The signifier and the signified combine to produce the sign. The sign system is the cultural and/or historical context that frames meaning. The sign system can be subdivided into particular norms and forms. For Barthes, the detached detail of an outfit ultimately fine-tunes meaning; changing just one detail of an outfit changes the meaning just as the context changes one's perception of that outfit. All objects have multiple potential meanings. Hierarchies of value are reproduced, communicated, and maintained through fashion systems (see also Barthes's collection of essays in *Language of Fashion*, 2006).

5. *Kaiso* is a genre of Trinidadian vernacular music that originated in West Africa and later evolved into calypso. It has a narrative form usually containing a satirical or political subtext. In Barbados the term is used to refer to the staged performances of calypso that coincide with public festivals.
6. Lady Nugent was the wife of the governor of Jamaica during the time of the Napoleonic War.
7. Also known as John or Johnny Canoe. The Jonkonnu festival is a creolised art form that grew out of the collision and exchanges between West African masquerade and English folk festivals.
8. Mirroring the relationship between power and dress, cloth visually consolidates social relations based on hierarchies of power, as well as communicating individual and cultural identities. Cloth production, trade, and consumption are woven into the history of the slave trade. For example, slaves were purchased by British merchants in Africa "with a variety of woollen goods" (Long 1970, 491), cotton produced in the Americas supplied the raw materials for the textile industry in France, and Haiti produced quantities of indigo needed for dyestuffs. Meanwhile, Jamaica imported "mill-work of all sorts" from London, cottons, and ready-made clothing from Liverpool, and cottons from Lancaster to clothe the enslaved (Long 1970, 500–504).
9. Clothing—or, in my interpretation, cloth—by adding to the perceived mass of the body, allows the wearer to fill more physical space, promoting an increased sense of power and authority: "a sense of extension to our bodily self" (Flugel 1966, 34).
10. Contemporary *kente* cloth also incorporates lurex yarns to achieve a heightened level of shininess.
11. Here the word "Quashie" refers to the enslaved (Burton 1997, 244–248). The spiritual aspect of the *presentation* of self is a recurring issue in the interviews and reminiscence workshops with African Caribbean elders that were conducted as part of my doctoral research (Checinska 2009). There is, for example, an equation between spirituality, "coolness", and "fine dressing". In particular, the "coolness" of Jamaicans is regarded as a spiritual gift; at an individual level, style is regarded as a reflection of one's soul. This is not the forum in which to go deeply into the relationship between spirituality and "coolness". I raise it because this connection, which is highlighted by African Caribbean elders themselves, is worthy of further research.
12. Bhabha (1994, 177) writes that if culture as epistemology prioritises function and intention, reflecting its empirical referent, then culture as enunciation prioritises signification, troubling, and re-inscribing social hierarchies such as notions of ours/theirs or high/low. The possibilities of *other* narrative spaces are opened up.
13. In the 1810s, Osifekunde, an Ijebu (between Oyo and Benin), wrote: "[T]he common people … contend [sic] themselves with the *botiboti*, a simple cap made in the country. The more well-to-do prefer the *akode* or brimless hat" (as quoted in Bradley-Foster 1997, 268).
14. A parallel can be drawn between the wearing of West African dress in the moment of political strength in Haiti and the wearing of indigenous dress in newly independent Nigeria during the 1960s. As Jennifer Craik (1993, 27) points out, in the early days of colonialism, the educated classes adopted Western dress. However, with Nigerian independence, as nationalisation became a strong political movement, indigenous clothing re-emerged; meaning had shifted.

References

Anim-Addo, J. 2006. *Touching the Body: Dynamics of Language, History and Publication*. London: Mango.
Anzaldúa, G. 1987. *Borderlands/La Frontera: The New Mestiza*. San Francisco: Aunt Lute Books.
Barthes, R. 1990. *The Fashion System*. Los Angeles: University of California Press.
Barthes, R. 2006. *The Language of Fashion*. Oxford: Berg.
Bernabé, J., P. Chamoiseau, R. Confiant, and M. B. T. Khyar. 1990. "In Praise of Creoleness." *Callaloo* 13 (4): 886–909. https://doi.org/10.2307/2931390
Bhabha, H. K. 1994. *The Location of Culture*. London: Routledge.
Boyce-Davies, C. 1994. "Negotiating Theories or Going a Piece of the Way with Them." In *Black Women, Writing and Identity*, edited by C. Boyce-Davies, 38–58. London: Routledge.
Bradley-Foster, H. 1997. *New Raiments of Self: African American Clothing in the Antebellum South*. Oxford: Berg.
Brathwaite, E. K. 1971. *The Development of Creole Society in Jamaica 1770–1820*. Oxford: Clarendon.
Brathwaite, E. K. 1984. *History of the Voice*. London: New Beacon Books.

Breward, C. 1995. *The Culture of Fashion*. Manchester: Manchester University Press.
Breward, C. 1999. *The Hidden Consumer: Masculinities, Fashion and City Life 1860–1914*. Manchester: Manchester University Press.
Burton, R. D. E. 1997. *Afro-Creole: Power, Opposition and Play in the Caribbean*. Ithaca: Cornell University Press.
Checinska, C. 2009. "Colonizin' in Reverse: The Creolised Aesthetic of the Empire Windrush Generation." PhD thesis, Goldsmiths, University of London.
Checinska, C. 2012. "Every Mickle Mek a Mockle: Reconfiguring Diasporic Identities." In *Beyond Borders*, edited by J. Hutnyk, 135–152. London: Pavement Books.
Chenoune, F. 1994. *A History of Men's Fashion*. Paris: Flammarion.
Cosgrove, S. 1989. "The Zoot Suit and Style Warfare." In *Zoot Suits and Second-Hand Dresses: An Anthology of Fashion and Music*, edited by A. McRobbie, 3–22. London: Macmillan.
Craik, J. 1993. *The Face of Fashion*. Oxford: Routledge.
De la Beche, H. T. 1825. *Notes on the Present Conditions of the Negroes in Jamaica*. London: Harvey, Darton & Co.
Equiano, O. 1998. *The Interesting Narrative of the Life of Olaudah Equiano, the African*. London: X Press.
Flugel, J. C. 1966. *The Psychology of Clothes*. London: Hogarth Press.
Glissant, E. 1989. *Caribbean Discourse*. Charlottesville: University Press of Virginia.
Hall, S. 2003. "Creolité and the Process of Creolization." In *Creolité and Creolization: Documenta 11 Platform 3*, edited by O. Enwezor, 27–41. Michigan: Distributed Art.
Hebdige, D. 1979. *Subculture: The Meaning of Style*. London: Routledge.
James, C. L. R. 1980. *The Black Jacobins*. London: Allison & Busby.
Long, E. 1970. *History of Jamaica or a General Survey of the Ancient and Modern State of that Island: With Reflections on its Situations, Inhabitants, Climate, Products, Commerce, Laws and Government*. London: Frank Cass.
Louverture Project. 2005. [Image]. Accessed April 24, 2017. https://thelouvertureproject.org/index.php?title=File:Jj_dessalines.jpg
Majors, R., and J. Mancini Billson. 1992. *Cool Pose: The Dilemmas of Black Manhood in America*. New York: Lexington.
McWatt, M. 1982. "The Preoccupation with the Past in West Indian Literature." *Caribbean Quarterly* 28 (1 & 2) March–June: 12–19. https://doi.org/10.1080/00086495.1982.11671999
Nugent, M. 1839. *A Journal of a Voyage to, and Residence in, the Island of Jamaica, from 1801 to 1805, and the Subsequent Events in England from 1808 to 1811*. London: n.p.
Perani, J., and N. H. Wolff. 1999. *Cloth, Dress and Art Patronage in Africa*. Oxford: Berg.
Picton, J. 1990. "What's in a Mask?" *African Languages and Cultures* 3 (2): 181–202. https://doi.org/10.1080/09544169008717719
Picton, J. 2004. "What to Wear in West Africa: Textile Design, Dress and Self-Representation." In *Black Style*, edited by C. Tulloch, 22–45. London: V & A.
Schneider, J. 1987. "The Anthropology of Cloth." *Annual Review of Anthropology* 16: 409–448. https://doi.org/10.1146/annurev.an.16.100187.002205
Sloane, H. 1707. *A Voyage to the Island Madera, Barbados, Nieves, S. Christophers and Jamaica, with the Natural History of Herbs and Trees, Four-Footed Beasts, Fishes, Birds, Insects, Reptiles, &c, of the Last of Those Islands*. London: B. M.
Walvin, J. 1971. *The Black Presence*. London: Orbach and Chambers.
White, S., and G. White. 1998. *Stylin': African American Expressive Culture from Its Beginnings to the Zoot Suit*. London: Cornell University Press.

Part III
Afropessimism/Afrofuturism

Afropessimism: A Genealogy of Discourse

Boulou Ebanda de B'béri and P. Eric Louw

Afropessimism is an important issue for all Africans as well as for anyone interested in African development and socio-cultural analysis. Although there are bits and pieces and research works on Afropessimism, none has as yet brought it all together in a coherent way. When we decided to undertake this examination of Afropessimism, however, we discovered that it is more complex than first meets the eye, because there is more than one perspective on this phenomenon. In fact, there seem to be at least five different views on Afropessimism, which can be represented as in Table 1. Views 1 and 2 reject the very existence of Afropessimism, seeing it as an unjustified 'Western construct'. In contradistinction to this, Views 3, 4 and 5 see Afropessimism as justified. However, Views 3, 4 and 5 do not see Africa or Afropessimism in the same way; nor do they conceptualise the 'solution' to Afropessimism in the same way.

For all of these reasons, it becomes important that the phenomenon of Afropessimism be examined. This *Critical Arts* issue on Afropessimism should be seen as a small step on the road to an intellectual conversation around this phenomenon. Undeniably, Africans have inherited socio-political institutions from other cultures, mostly unrelated to the African past and framework of knowledge production; as have African intellectuals eager to articulate alternative, contextual insider knowledge about the continent. Now, more than ever, Africa is in need of a new contextual development for the days ahead. This is so important today, because the African nations as we now know them have inherited patterns of thought and models of knowledge production that are not only foreign to the continent's historical experience, but that have also shown their limitations in their own milieu of emergence. Because it is at these crossroads of socio-political, economic and theological ideologies that both the discourses and practices of representation of Afropessimism have emerged, we are certain that it is also on that same field that potential optimism about Africa will surface. Though we have no consensus today about Afropessimism, this volume of *Critical Arts* raises many key questions which, for Africa's sake, demand answers. Generally, we admit that the naturalised low ranking of the continent or the validity of the measurement criteria by which it is judged should be re-evaluated in taking into account some of the values specific to Africa. Therefore, the articles of this special issue of *Critical Arts* can be seen as a small intervention in trying to denaturalise the measurement-standards used, and to begin unpacking the genealogy of a discourse that is so undermining of Africa's future in a world where image and impression management means so much.

Table 1 Perspectives on Afropessimism

	(1) Africa is misrepresented by racists	(2) Africa is misrepresented by Western media	(3) Africa is in trouble but it can be fixed Version 1	(4) Africa is in trouble but it can be fixed Version 2	(5) Africa is hopeless and cannot be fixed
What is the problem?	Africans are portrayed negatively by Western racists	Africa is portrayed negatively by Western media	African client states are run by poor leaders	Africa is badly run and Africans are incapable of governing themselves	Africans are incapable of running things
Who is to blame?	Racists negatively stereotype Africans (Western racism is the problem, not Africa)	Journalists construct negative representations (Western media are the problem, not Africa)	Bad African governments and neo-colonialism (The West is complicit in the problem)	Africans are to blame (The West is not the problem, it is the solution)	Africans are to blame (The West is not the problem or the solution)
What is the solution?	Attack racist portrayals	Rebrand Africa to create good representations	New African leaders are needed to create better governance	Recolonisation (by the West, the UN or China)	Give up on Africa, excise it from the world community

All of the contributions in this volume address the rise of Afropessimism discourses and the implications some of these discourses have for Africa and Africans, with a particular focus on the southern African cultural and political context. Many of these contributions focus on 1) defining Afropessimism; 2) analysing the role Afropessimism plays in driving donor fatigue and in promoting a kind of anti-development dis'course; 3) determining what role the media play in producing and circulating an Afropessimism discourse; 4) investigating the response from development agencies (e.g. Have they modified their messages/PR?) to Afropessimism; and 5) interrogating to what extent some African political figures have helped to produce, elude or silence multiple practices of Afropessimism.

This phenomenon of Afropessimism nonetheless seems much more complex and its impact much deeper, not only in terms of how Africa is imagined and perceived, but also as regards the ways in which Africans view themselves. This later aspect of pessimism about themselves has been deeply engrained in Africans' minds, and has helped to produce negative impacts, as is evident from the following discussion with a colleague and friend – an African Professor of Mechanical Engineering at the University of Ottawa – who once asked if I do not think that Africans (read 'black people') are naturally doomed (read 'naturally unintelligent').

So, Afropessimism is more than a discourse, it is also a state of mind: a naturalised world view of African countries, African peoples, and the inner and outside knowledge of both the continent and its people. For example, in the 13–19 May 2000 issue of *The economist*, Africa was characterised as the hopeless continent. Such damning indictments generate enormous penalties for Africans, because they both aggravate donor fatigue and keep foreign investors out of the continent. The negativity encoded in the notion of the 'hopeless continent' forms part of the phenomenon of Afropessimism, which has been growing over the past two-and-a-half decades, but the discursive origins of which can be traced back at least to the 15th-century Western consciousness.

As a discourse, Afropessimism produces the meaning that something is wrong with Africans. The heart of this discourse derives from the fact that Africans are failing to live up to a set of criteria generated by Westerners who want to develop Africa. Specifically, Westerners want Africa to function socially and economically in such a way that the continent would mesh neatly into the globalised economy built by Europeans and Americans over the past two centuries.

Reading the justifications provided by the British as they built their African empire provides some wonderful insights into the roots of the Afropessimism discourse. In a nutshell, British justifications for their empire (i.e. Globalisation I) run as follows: 1) the British said they wanted to trade with Africa; 2) the problem they encountered was that Africans apparently did not have either the requisite entrepreneurship to make use of Africa's resources or the skills to build a viable economy; 3) Africans were seen as unable to establish the good governance needed to run a viable economy or a trading network; 4) consequently, British imperial discourse argued that if Africans could not do it themselves, then Britain would annex these territories and develop Africa themselves. Once developed by the British, these territories were integrated into Britain's global trading network.

This British imperial discourse was naturalised throughout Europe and came to underpin the governance of Africa for half a century. But then, during the 1950s and 1960s, a shift took place, and this imperial discourse was demonised and attacked as racist. In its place arose a wave of Afro-optimism, which swept the globe as independence was granted to African countries.

With the death of Europe's formal empires came a new phenomenon, however – that of an informal empire run by the Americans (Louw 2010). The Pax Americana (i.e. Globalisation II) is also a trading empire. Not surprisingly, the Pax Americana has sought to 'develop' Africans so that Africans could be taught to run viable economies and establish the 'good governance' required for trade to flourish. In the 1960s it was assumed that this 'development' would result in a well-governed and economically flourishing continent – a continent plugged into global networks as a viable partner in global trade.

Inside Africa itself, however, this Pax Americana vision resulted in two divergent responses: some Africans decided to accept the logic of this informal empire and to become willing (comprador) partners of the West, while other Africans rejected what they called neo-colonialism and set about developing strategies of resistance. This pattern was also found amongst Asians, Latin Americans and people in the Middle East.

However, it turned out that those Africans who had opted to become partners of the West were poor compradors. And so, ultimately, only one group of Africans came to be seen as viable trading partners – the South Africans, who were descendants of white settlers, rather than indigenous Africans. Outside of South Africa, the West's comprador partners were seen, by the 1980s, to have failed to build successful economies or to instil what the West would regard as 'good governance'. And so the optimism of the 1960s melted away and in its place emerged a new discourse – Afropessimism.

Significantly, this Afropessimism discourse sounded a great deal like the language used by the early builders of the British Empire, because it concluded that Africans were incapable of running viable states and economies. Effectively, Afropessimists have concluded that

'Africa is doomed' because it is either run by corrupt and incompetent (failed) compradors, or by those who resist working within neo-colonial frameworks. For Westerners, both of these groups are a disaster, because neither is able to serve as worthwhile partners of Globalisation II.

The resultant Afropessimism as we know it today has gained widespread currency in the global mass media. Worse, for Africans, is the fact that 'Afropessimism' has acquired a taken-for-grantedness, so that journalists now regularly use it as a shorthand commonsensical expression which means that there is no hope for sub-Saharan Africa, because the continent is poorly run and unable to govern itself. This pessimistic discourse has seemingly even become deeply seeded in the minds of African youths, as reflected by their non-stop migration toward Western countries – an embarrassing situation that led Nicolas Sarkozy, the president of France, to argue that *France cannot welcome all of the misery of the world*, an idea many other European politicians in Germany, Italy and the United Kingdom seem to carry on effectively. Not surprisingly, African politicians do nothing but constantly complain about Afropessimism and the damage it inflicts (Angula 2007; Jordan 2004; Mogae 2007).

The current discourse of Afropessimism has now been active for at least 30 years. In some ways, the deeply negative portrayals of Africa encoded in these pessimistic discourses are entangled in, and a reaction to, an earlier wave of 1960s euphoria generated by African decolonisation. Particularly, many African countries were decolonised over a span of 12 years (between 1957 and 1968, and the 1970s and 80s in some rare cases like that of Zimbabwe), during which there was a flood of optimism about African independence, not only in the countries concerned but also across Europe and North America. Indeed, prolific intellectuals like Basil Davidson and Thomas Hodgkin did much to popularise a sense of goodwill and high expectations about Africa's future, with Davidson's writings serving to make the nationalist leaders of these new states fashionable in the West (Howe 1993). Western journalists continued to popularise the idea that Africa had a bright and prosperous future ahead of it, now that the continent had been freed from the rapacious and greedy colonial powers. These expressions of optimism did not, however, count on several well-oiled political factors and their consequences in the African political and economic systems, such as the East/West division of the world, which legitimated Western support for dictatorships, and the apartheid and tribalism which became constitutive of the political systems in all African countries. As Kofi Buenor Hadjor argues:

> Africa has been ill-served by its leaders. […] Africa's independence has been mortgaged and the attempt to assert control over the continent's destiny has been abandoned. Africa is less free and more divided than it was in the sixties. At least, then Africans shared a common dream and a common purpose. The first generation of leaders [has] succeeded in destroying that dream as Africa becomes engulfed by their nightmare. (1993: 120)

The 1960s seemed to bear out this optimism as the new African states made good progress. However, by the late 1970s political and economic difficulties began to manifest themselves. Initially this was blamed on the legacies of colonialism and imperialism. As Ngũgĩ wa Thiong'o would argue, imperialism is not just a slogan: 'It is real, it is palpable in content and form and in its methods and effects. […] Imperialism is total: it has economic, political, military, cultural and psychological consequences for the people of the world. It could even lead to holocaust'(2005/1986: 2). Indeed, the manifested economic difficulties of the 1970s created a political environment in which all of these young African countries would emerge as the pantry of Western imperial powers. They had to execute the orders coming from the West, period. The few ideologues who tried to take different directions (Lumumba, Sankara, Mandela, to name but a few) were either assassinated, jailed or forced into exile. Exile, a later solution which formed part of the West's hegemonic political world view, was applied to another black country of the Western hemisphere, namely Haiti. Indeed, multiple dictators succeeded in ruining Haiti for centuries, without consequences. Some of them even found safe refuge with their former Western supporters, for instance Jean-Claude (Baby Doc) Duvalier in France. However, the first democratically elected president since the independence of Haiti (twice democratically elected) was forced into exile by the United Nations, a.k.a. the United States (US) government. Here, Aristide was accused of being a dangerous socialist. Some respected American media even labeled him a 'crazy', corrupt populist who had endangered the political stability of the region (the southern part of the United States, i.e. the State of Florida, which overlooks the infidel Castro's Cuba). Aristide's presidency became linked to the increase of drug imports to Florida, the leitmotiv of the Reagan/Bush presidency, thus legitimating Uncle Sam's intervention in Haiti. In his articles, *Who removed Aristide?*, Paul Farmer (2004) reported that both the French and US governments had vested interests in having a dictator (*not* Aristide) in power.

> Aristide was a proponent of liberation theology, with its injunction that the Church proclaim 'a preferential option for the poor', but liberation theology had its adversaries: members of Reagan's brains trust, meeting in 1980, declared it less Christian than Communist. 'US policy,' they said, 'must begin to counter (not react against) . . . the "liberation theology" clergy.'[1]

As Palmer adds: 'The Haitian President, Jean-Bertrand Aristide, was forced from power. He claimed he'd been kidnapped and didn't know where he was being taken until, at the end of a 20-hour flight, he was told that he and his wife would be landing "in a French military base in the middle of Africa". He found himself in the Central African Republic.' (ibid.). This location is important, because why would both the US and France decide to exile Aristide in the Central African Republic, instead of in France, as was the case with Baby Doc Duvalier? Some of the answers are that this sub-Saharan location is of particular importance: it is a clear referent of the Western possession of Africa, recalling the saga of the 'Diamond of Bokassa', which involved the former presidents of both France (Giscard d'Estaing) and the self-proclaimed dictator of this country, the Emperor Bokassa. Indeed, like Aristide, Bokassa was removed from power in the middle of the night, after meeting with another Western-declared infidel, Muammar Gaddafi. Unlike Bokassa, however, Aristide was not removed from power because he was 'playing with an infidel', but because he was promoting the 'liberation theology' which seemed to be the only sure route that would help Africans get rid of the poverty of the mind in which they had imprisoned themselves, and which had legitimated African pessimism discourses. Indeed, as Palmer (ibid.) argues:

> The United States might not have been able to prevent Aristide's landslide victory [67% with no necessary run-off according to the Haitian Constitution], but there was plenty they could do to undermine him. The most effective method, adopted by the first Bush administration, was to fund both the opposition – their poor showing at the polls was no reason, it appears, to cut off aid to them – and the military. Declassified records now make it clear that the CIA and other US groups helped to create and fund a paramilitary group called FRAPH, which rose to prominence after a military coup that ousted Aristide in September 1991.

The Haitian experience is similar to what has been happening in Africa. African leaders must follow a certain set of rules if they would like to stay in power; thus Africa became divided into two clear ideologies that prevail to this day: pro-humanist (i.e. traditionalist) and pro-imperialist. The humanist is a kind of traditional resistant class, comprising students, intellectuals and other progressive minds – they are mostly voiceless, politically speaking. Imperialism is viewed as transnational monopolies which are *othering* everything as different, and for which every other world view becomes zeroed. The current political division in the Ivory Coast could actually be reflective of this traditionalist/imperialist trend. On the one side, we have a candidate supported by a transnational and international community, on the grounds that he is the winner of an 'open and democratic election' – as if such a thing could exist in Africa. On the other hand, a traditionalist candidate (who paradoxically spent many years in prison for fighting against corruption and for democracy) refutes the choice of the majority of Ivorians on the grounds that his country's wealth would continue to be sold out to (and thus controlled by) Western powers. The pessimism, in the contest of Africa, grew from similar situations of bi-polarity, forged with two different, mainly unconcealable states of mind: imperialism and traditionalism.

The shifts to democracy which emerged in the late 1980s and early 1990s, in shedding new light on attitudes towards Africa, failed to take into account this African bi-polar reality. Indeed, in the wake of the second round of globalisation, when Washington and Paris began pressuring African states to democratise their political systems and liberalise their economies, many in the World Bank, the International Monetary Fund and the overall international development community came to reinforce the idea that Africa's state-centric development approach was at the heart of Africa's problem. Democracy, according to Western standards, was necessary. Nevertheless, this Western definition of democracy quickly became obsolete and impossible to implement in the African context of tribal and racial divisions, as well as in view of the bi-polar ideologies outlined above. In Africa, people do not seem to express their democracy or cast their vote for a particular political programme or political party, but rather for the closest ethnic, tribal or racial candidate – especially if this candidate represents the current power-holder. Nowadays, this is the naturalised tradition of demo/autocracy, which manifests throughout Africa. In addition, the idea that a liberal economy would cure this problem also became obsolete, because as we moved into the new millennium, the expected improvements in African conditions were nowhere to be seen. As a result, Afropessimism actually deepened during the first decade of the 21st century, and Western portrayals became harsher. This growing harshness was derived from a number of different sources, namely:

- The World Bank, aid donors and the development industry which have all grown increasingly critical of Africans. This has generated a constant flow of aid fatigue stories;
- The African Studies network (which used to serve as a cheerleader for Africa) became pessimistic and then 'died'. This sent a very negative message into the world about Africa;
- The ever-growing African diaspora has fed the idea that something has gone terribly wrong on the continent. The growth of a South African diaspora since 1990 has, in particular, served to spread 'bad news stories' about Africa into the West;

- The 'Bono phenomenon' has generated a great deal of bad publicity for Africa;
- The behaviour of African politicians and bureaucrats has kept Western media supplied with an endless flow of bad news stories.

Nowadays, despite the 'democratisation' of many African countries in the late 1980/90s, pessimism amongst Western governments and donors about Africa's political instability has continued to grow. Indeed, economic decline, social decay across the continent, Africa's deteriorating health services and organised corruption count among many other palpable elements that have fuelled this pessimism. Further, there is concern that development projects in Africa are not delivering the expected results, while a number of Eastern and south-east Asian countries have made enormous economic progress. Comparing the differences between Africa and Asia has led to a growing portrayal of Africa as being to blame for its own ills and its lack of agency. In particular, the media have focused the blame on Africa's poor governance as the source of the continent's economic decline.

Current forms of Afropessimistic discourses – especially those related to an incapacity when it comes to self-governance – emerged in the 1980s. As we would suspect, the notion of self-governance is closely tied to that of emancipation, autonomy, qualification and certainly agency. Any lack of self-governing abilities would legitimate neo-colonial interventions in the form of 'aid' for example – which in the best-case scenarios could only generate between 28 and 32 cents for every dollar spent by Western donors. As we know today, only a few 'beneficiaries' would end up benefiting in reality. Perhaps, as Dambisa Moyo (2009) would argue, African countries should turn down all foreign aid, and start making an inventory of their own wealth, because aid has never solved any of the challenges faced by the continent, but has rather widened the gap between the haves and the have-nots.

The articles presented in this special issue of *Critical Arts* raise interesting questions that will help us continue this conversation on the Afropessimism phenomenon, and perhaps track down and reflect on the complex production of a certain kind of discourse in Africa today. For example, Noah Bassil's article, 'The roots of Afropessimism: the British invention of the "dark continent"' deals with the early formation of pessimistic discourses in relation to the continent. Historically, the qualification of Africa as the 'dark continent' is not a recent production. Indeed, we would argue that with the legitimation of 'Africa's darkness' comes the Western imperial extension of power over the entire continent, from north to south; east to west. One could trace back the production of paternalistic discourses vis-à-vis Africa to the *Code noir* of Louis XIV and Louis XV. In the *Code noir*, for example, both French kings articulated the rights of imperial extension of power over Africans, arguing that advanced people have the 'highest rights' to exert control over lower peoples and nations; not necessarily to elevate them to become French subjects, but rather to control their lives. As Bassil's text rightly puts it, 'this system of knowledge production about Empire and the subjects of Empire remained institutionalised' in 'British colonies' as well. Nowadays these discourses of lack of agency, that have come to define the continent and its people, have also sealed off Africa from anything positive, allowing in pessimistic ideologies.

As Osée Kamga's article, 'The weakness of "social capital" as a key infringement to African development' suggests, linkages between models of administration of traditional society and modern states, where individuals matter more than social structures and where power remains concentrated in the hands of a strongman who has pre-eminence over institutions, have generated a lack of confidence in social institutions and have undermined the trust needed for social cohesion. However, in many African countries, alternative associative formations are working to empower everyday people, despite the fact that the human benefits derived from these forms of social capital have been overlooked by many Afropessimistic discourses.

It is precisely the condition of possibility of counter-hegemonic practices that Daniel McNeil attempts to analyse in his article, 'Black devils, white saints and mixed-race *femme fatales*: Philippa Schuyler and the winds of change'. Inspired by Fanon's intellectual activism, McNeil opposes this to Schuyler's figure of whiteness – an African-American child prodigy who grew up to be a peripatetic concert pianist and who represented anti-black caricatures in order to promote white male heroes as the only possible way out for Africans' intellectual emancipation. In this comparison, McNeil notes that a colonised mind, such as that of Schuyler who craved whiteness, also helps to produce counter-discourses, legitimated by intellectual activists searching for new forms of humanism. This is the case with Fanon, who rejected the premise that a Western takeover of Africa and Africans was a prerequisite for Afro-optimism.

In search of a different kind of alternative discourse, H. James Garrett and Sandra J. Schmidt's 'Reconstituting pessimistic discourses' identifies three forms of discourse narrative: 1) of progress; 2) of memorialisation; and 3) of hope. Their fieldwork in South Africa shows that although these forms of pessimistic discourse dominate Western knowledge about the everyday life experiences of people in Africa, they might also fit into a broader narrative, not of Afropessimism itself, but of global pessimism. In mobilising the work of several postcolonial theorists, they conclude their analysis by suggesting that the effective production of an Afropessimism counter-discourse must emerge from within Africa, and must be contextual. For example, African leaders must work to shape different economic and social images of their country, because the pessimism expressed in relation to Africa is about global political and economic systems of privileges, designed to reproduce particular centers and margins across the globe, thus maintaining the global system of power (defined above as the bi-polar system of domination).

Afropessimism is, however, more than just a discourse that has become popular with journalists and which is now widely circulated by the global media. It is a vision of Africa and Africans that has real political and economic consequences, because this discourse impacts on contemporary policymakers. It is the link between this discourse and everyday politics that Martha Evans analyses in her article. Specifically, she focuses on the Internet commentaries of post-apartheid white South African expatriates. Evans found that this racialised group of expats produces negative predictions about their country's future in fuelling negative portrayals of political conditions in South Africa, and in predicting that this country will fail just like other black African countries have. Some of these post-apartheid South African whites are openly racist and link the future failure of the South African economy to the devastating effects of HIV/AIDS on the country's black population. Evans concludes that although such negative and pessimistic discourses circulate on the Internet, their impact is wide and it leads to the internalisation of writing off Africa – in particular, producing difficult conditions to fight against them or to set up counter-discourses.

Afropessimism is certainly a practice of representation, perhaps more so than anything else. This is clear in Susan Falls' article 'Picturing blood diamonds'. In the case of the film *Blood Diamonds*, the Western NGOs and retailer discourses would appeal to Western ethical consumerism, helping people to feel good about 'clean' stones but, ironically, as Falls concludes, also feeding the black markets by reproducing exclusionary 'licit' channels.

These practices of representation that have produced Africa as a naturalised pessimistic object of knowledge also formed the cornerstone of liberal discourses, which have a profound effect on some Western policies toward Africa and on the development of other genres of African self-representation. This triple articulation is interesting, as it effectively forges links between policies, ideologies and the representation of the continent. In their article, 'HIV/AIDS and discourses of denial in sub-Saharan Africa: an Afro-optimist response?', forthcoming in the *International Journal of Cultural Studies*, Abraham Mulwo, Keyan Tomaselli and Michael Francis examine the discourses surrounding the HIV/AIDS pandemic within the broader context of the global representation of Africa. As with HIV/AIDS, Africa is represented with images of sorrow that help reinforce the stereotypical 'dying African' who is in need of an 'external gaze' to become an acceptable human, as with Edward Said's articulation of *Orientalism*. The theoretical *coup-de-force* this article produces is a practical demonstration of links between ideological formations and discursive productions, which naturalise the images of and ideas about Africa in becoming commonsense interpretations of the continent and its people. So, Africa has been fixed in an external gaze that ranks Africans badly. This is a ranking system that has been around for so long that the basis of the original ranking has been all but forgotten. Therefore, so naturalised has the ranking become that few now pause to ask about the origins or the validity of the measurement criteria by which the continent is still judged. This special issue signifies a small intervention, because the individual articles try to denaturalise the measurement standards used, and begin the task of unpacking the pessimistic genealogy of discourse that has been so undermining of the continent's future.

Note

1 Also available online at http://www.lrb.co.uk/v26/n08/paul-farmer/who-removed-aristide (accessed 19 March 2011).

References

Angula, N. 2007. Afro-pessimism: can Africa rebrand its image? Opening address by the Prime Minister of the Republic of Namibia to 19th All Africa Students Conference, Windhoek, 2 July.
Farmer, P. 2004. Who removed Aristide? *London Review of Books* 26(8), 15 April: 28–31.
Hadjor, K.B. 1993. *On transforming Africa: discourse with Africa's leaders*. New Jersey/ London: Africa World Press/Third World Communication.
Howe, S. 1993. *Anticolonialism in British politics*. Oxford: Clarendon Press.
Jordan, Z.P. 2004. Address by Minister Pallo Jordan at the launch of the Centre for African Literary Studies. University of KwaZulu-Natal, Pietermaritzburg, 7 September.
Louw, P.E. 2010. *Roots of the Pax Americana: decolonization, development, democratization and trade*. Manchester: Manchester University Press.
Mogae, F.G. 2007. A crisis of image. *Harvard Review* 29(2). http://hir.harvard.edu/courting-africa/a-crisis-of-image
Moyo, D. 2009. *Dead aid: why aid is not working and how there is another way for Africa*. New York: Farrar, Straus and Giroux.
Wa Thiong'o, N. 2005/1986. *Decolonizing the mind: the politics of language in African literature*. Suffolk (UK)/Portsmouth (NH): James Currey/Heinemann.

The Roots of Afropessimism: The British Invention of the 'Dark Continent'

Noah R. Bassil

ABSTRACT

This article aims to interrogate the history of British perceptions of black Africa, to come to an understanding of the notions that set black Africans apart from Europeans at the time of the conquest and colonisation in the late-19th century. It is asserted that it is only during the time of the expansion into black Africa in the late-19th century that British perceptions of the barbarity, backwardness, idleness and inferiority of black Africans congealed into a discourse that largely subverted positive and ambivalent perceptions that Europeans had long held, dating as far back as the era of the Ancient Greeks. In exhuming the history of Greek and Roman knowledge of black Africa, as well as those of medieval times, it becomes possible to draw a picture of black Africa as the 'other' through an analysis of the way that black Africa's place in the modern world system was shaped by slavery, colonialism and notions of race, and how this has contributed to contemporary views of black Africa as the 'dark continent'.

Introduction

Common perceptions of European–African relations have been framed by false impressions that Europeans from the earliest times have found people of black complexion savage and inferior. The idea that a common thread of racism towards Africans can be discerned from the Hellenic age to the modern is a misconception that this article challenges. If racism is institutional, discursive and legal discrimination to ensure the domination of a specific group(s) of individuals against others (Miles 1989: 41–66), then racism against black Africans is an entirely modern phenomenon. Attempts by some scholars, most notably Bernard Lewis (1990), to contend that Muslim cultures had an equal, if not greater, antipathy to black Africans as a way of diminishing Euro-American responsibility for the African slave trade can be dismissed as polemical (Aidi 2005). The trans-Atlantic slave trade played a large part in shaping modern perceptions of Africans, but as this article sets out, such perceptions remained contradictory, fluid and contested right through the 18th and into the 19th centuries.

Colonialism, it should go without saying, was not specifically a British practice. Neither were European ideas of Africa entirely British. Nonetheless, privileging the history of the formation of the British ideas of Africa, as this discussion does, can be viewed as fundamental for an understanding of modern discourses pertaining to black Africa. Britain's considerable colonial system (both in Britain and in Africa) operated in a way that led to the formation of intricate patterns of knowledge production about Africa, which were designed to serve imperial interests. This system of knowledge production about Empire and the subjects of Empire remained institutionalised even as British colonies gained independence. The power of the English language to shape discourses beyond Anglophone countries was a direct result of the international dominance enjoyed by Britain during the age of Empire. While Britain's formal dominance over the world may have been greatly diminished in the second half of the 20th century, British ideologies of Empire remain an important component of modern conceptualisations of the world (Said 1993; Young 2001).

The practice of colonialism had a profound impact on Africa and what was 'known' about Africa. Yet, there was a rich and varied history of ideas about Africa in the European imaginary prior to the colonial project in Africa taking shape at the turn of the 20th century. Certain precolonial ideas of Africa were appropriated by the imperial project and provided the foundations for justifying colonialism in Africa. Ronald Robinson and colleagues argue that the British colonial project in Africa was pursued by Victorian politicians who had never visited Africa, but relied on an idea of what they believed Africa to be (1978: 21). For Victorian politicians and the wider public, as Robinson and colleagues remark, '[a]ll that was generally known about Africans consisted of horrible tales of the "Middle Passage", fables about noble savages degraded by muskets and gin, and infant races awaiting the Gospel's dawn' (1961: 27).

By the 1880s, this version of Africa had become widely accepted as an accurate depiction of the continent and its people. However, there is much more to the narrative of British perceptions of Africa.

Rather than take the view that black Africa was perpetually seen in the way that Robinson et al. describe, this article will demonstrate that it was not until the late-19th century that black Africa came to be perceived in these resolute terms, and it was only in the 19th century that the British came to perceive that black Africans were significantly different from themselves. Nancy Stepan notes that there was a

> 'change from an emphasis on the fundamental physical and moral homogeneity of man, despite superficial differences, to an emphasis on the essential heterogeneity of mankind, despite superficial similarities ...' so that, 'By the middle of the nineteenth century, everyone [in Britain] was agreed, it seemed, that in essential ways the white race was superior to non-white races.' (Stepan, in Wheeler 2001: 33, this author's addition in parenthesis)

Explaining the shift in the second half of the 19th century away from the earlier fluid and contradictory ideas and practices towards Africans, is one aim of this article.

The idea of Africa as the 'dark continent' was only possible by neglecting a whole history of interaction with, and knowledge of, Africa. When the term finally came into regular use, popularised by Livingstone's *Expeditions into the dark continent* (1876), the British had been in close contact with black Africa for centuries. The first black Africans to arrive in England did so in 1554, and by the 1800s the black population of England numbered over 15 000 people. England established its first trading post on the West-African coast in 1631.

This article argues that it was not that Africa was discovered by Europeans in the 19th century, but rather that it was rediscovered. By word of further introduction, this study focuses on black Africa and not on the geographic Africa. Africa north of the Sahara occupies a different place in the European consciousness than the lands inhabited by the 'black races' south of the Sahara. North Africans were portrayed as Moors, Orientals, Muslims and Arabs – another discourse on which much has been written (Lockman 2004; Said 1978). When speaking of Africa, most Europeans were referring to the people who inhabited the lands of the 'blacks' south of the Sahara. To ensure that this distinction is clear, I will refer in this article only to black Africa; which in the European imaginary is distinct from North Africa's Arab and Berber populations.

Ancient attitudes towards Africa

In the 18th and 19th centuries, the poetry, prose and visual arts of antiquity were reanimated by European nation-builders anxious to erect historical foundations for the newly emerging nation-states (Turner 1981; Vance 1997). While in earlier times Europeans were conscious of Plato, Aristotle and numerous other cultural legacies of the ancient world, a new-found glorification of Hellenic and Roman achievements, as a part of the construction of a distinctly European heritage is noticeable from the 18th century onwards. In the process, Greco-Roman attitudes towards black Africa were interpreted through the prism of 19th-century prejudices, as evidence that black Africa had been considered inferior by earlier European civilisations. More recent scholarship has challenged the idea that the ancient Greeks and Romans perceived black Africa exclusively as savage and backward.

Frank Snowden, in *Blacks in antiquity* (1970), contends that the ancient Greeks and Romans were very aware of the physical differences that existed between black Africans and themselves. Snowden's principal point is that despite this awareness the Greco-Roman perception of black Africa was not determined by the existence of what were apparent physical differences. He also suggests that there was an absence of racism in Greco-Roman culture. The most convincing element of Snowden's argument is that he shows that the Greeks and Romans engaged with black Africans without specifically formed racial prejudices. As Snowden remarks: 'Racial diversity, then, was explained in a uniform manner that applied to the Ethiopian as to any other people, and any special racial theory about darker peoples was completely absent' (ibid: 176).

In no way is it suggested that skin colour can be altogether discounted by analysts of the ancient Greek and Roman perception of Africa. While, as Snowden makes clear, there was not a specifically strong negative stereotype attached to black Africans, there was also certainly no doubt that colour and other physical differences were evident in the depictions in Greek and Roman art and literature. The important feature for the Greeks and Romans, Snowden argues, was not colour, but rather a perception of the cultural achievements of a particular society.

Evidence of this attitude can be found in the numerous references to Ethiopians, by the Greeks and Romans as people honoured by the Gods, as Homer remarked in *The Iliad*. Herodotus (211) stated: 'The Ethiopians ... are said to be the tallest and best-looking people in the world.' The praise afforded the Ethiopians and the Nubians, two nations clearly a part of black Africa, is illustrative of the racially undetermined attitude towards black Africa, even by the Greeks whose tendency towards ethnocentric chauvinism has been well recorded. Snowden comes to the conclusion that in regard to black Africa, 'there was a remarkable lack of bias in the classical commentaries' (1970: 120).

Christopher Miller, for one, finds Snowden's perspective problematic. In particular, Miller has difficulty with the ease with which Snowden comes to the conclusion that racial prejudice was absent in the Greco-Roman era (1986: 25). While Miller shares Snowden's position regarding the way that skin colour and physical differences were noted by Greek and Roman societies, he differs as regards the conclusions he draws from literary and other depictions of black Africans in ancient sculpture and painting.

Miller insists Snowden has misread the trope that existed in ancient times. That trope, Miller contends, attached inferiority to people with black skin. Miller accepts that a positive image of black Africa existed and that 'there is clearly a whole tradition of literature that runs counter to the more familiar-negative-representations of Africa' (ibid.). However, Miller suggests that the negative images of black Africa have been underplayed by Snowden and argues that the familiar belief in Greco-Roman literature and mythology of monstrosity and savagery residing in black Africa is too common and consistent to be ignored (ibid: 22–28). Cornel West's analysis also differs from Snowden's, in that he argues that 'the minority status of black people in Greece and Rome still rendered black statues, proportions and measurements marginal to cultural life. Hence, the black presence, while tolerated and at times venerated, was never an integral part of the classical ideals of beauty' (2002: 108–109). Here, West raises a high standard for Greco-Roman culture to attain in terms of its relationship with the black image. Conversely, one could ask what level of veneration of the Greco-Roman form was evident in the art, literature and culture of the Ethiopians or Nubians, and whether the neglect of the 'white' form is evidence of an equal condescending attitude by blacks towards whites. Snowden's point, which is a very important one, is that in the ancient world the black race was not conceived of as inferior, nor was blackness constructed as a binary opposite of 'whiteness' in the way that it would become a feature of the relationship between Europeans and black Africans in the late 18th and 19th centuries.

Miller argues that the Greco-Romans represented black Africa as a savage place of danger – an unknown place on the edge of the world. While Miller interprets this to be specifically about black Africa, Snowden comes to a different conclusion. Snowden is alert to such less-flattering representations of Africa in both the Greek and Roman literature, but prefers to see this as part of their predilection for sensationalising the unknown. For Snowden, such representations are not racial and were certainly not representations which the Greeks and Romans restricted to black Africa. Greek and Roman ignorance of the very north of Europe produced equally fantastical tales of monstrosity and savagery, such that it would be possible to surmise that it was not racial difference, nor black Africa *per se*, that led Greek and Roman societies to produce a view of Africans as savage and semi-human. Black Africa was not *sui generis* savage and backward in the ancient imaginary, and by no means was all of black Africa considered in such a way. The second issue of importance to be drawn from Miller's work, and for that matter also from the work of Snowden, is that Greco-Roman societies were not unfamiliar with black Africa and its people. Whether positive or negative, the ancients had knowledge of, and interacted with, the people and cultural practices of black Africa.

Even though Miller's interpretation fails to place the negative commentaries of black Africa within the general prejudices the Greco-Roman world held towards 'barbarians', there is still merit in his work. The major importance of Miller's work is his examination of the negative discourse of black Africa that existed in the Greco-Roman tradition – a negative discourse that would be reinterpreted by 19th-century British commentaries of black Africa. But to view the perception of black Africa in the ancient world from the vantage point of more recent discourses is to read history back to front. The Greco-Roman civilisation was not entirely ambivalent to colour, but neither were there the same embedded notions of backwardness and savagery that have become a feature of modern European perceptions of Africa. To read the representations of black Africa, as evident in Greco-Roman texts, without attempting a historical contextualisation may draw readers to interpret that black Africa was something for the ancients that it was not. In Greco-Roman perceptions of black Africa there is evidence of negative perceptions towards black Africans, just as there is evidence of positive attitudes. The difference between then and more recent times is that in the ancient world black skin was not a marker of inferiority. An illustration of this difference can be ascertained by partly redirecting Ali Mazrui in this context: Mazrui makes the point that 'Arabs alerted the people of sub-Saharan Africa that they were *black*. Europe tried to convince Black people they were inferior' (2005: 70, emphasis in the original).

The attitude of Arabs towards the black Africans they encountered as the Islamic Empire spread across North Africa into West Africa and down the East-African coastline, exemplified a non-racial pattern similar to that which existed in the ancient world. Despite the long history of Arab conquest, proselytising, colonisation and enslavement, in black Africa 'there is a lack of consistent literature that theorises the inferiority of black people. Islam did not have its Gobineau' (Hunwick & Powell 2002: xx). Arabs denigrated and enslaved any black Africans who had not been Islamised, but for those who were Islamised there is a long history of Arab–African intermarriage and assimilation. It may be overstating things to argue that the Islamic world was unified, but where disunity existed it was not due to racial differences marked by skin colour. The Islamic Empire became as much African as it was Arabian, and without a level of ambivalence towards skin colour the Arab–African character of Islam could not have come into existence. The expansion of Islam and the retreat of Christianity from the southern Mediterranean largely created a barrier between Europe and black Africa, that would restrict contact between the 'white' world and the 'black' one for almost a thousand years.

Black Africa in the European imagination in the age of European exploration

Medieval Christian European attitudes to black Africa were ambiguous, and at certain times contradictory, to say the least. The age of European exploration increased knowledge of the non-European world and laid the foundations for centuries of expansion. Yet, black Africans had a presence in England and across Europe during the Middle Ages that has often been overlooked by perspectives that privilege notions of Europe discovering a largely unknown world. The idea that black Africa discovered Europe has been suppressed by a Eurocentric historiography founded on the discoveries of Western explorers.

Paul Edwards (1992), however, explains that during the late-Middle Ages and Renaissance, black Africans were regularly employed by Europe's most prestigious royal courts. Edwards adds: 'Furthermore, far from being slaves or even servants, many of the Africans at these courts were free men, sometimes of high status' (ibid: 23). One literary example of the phenomenon Edwards describes is found in Shakespeare's *Othello*. Shakespeare's choice of Othello as hero of Venice could easily have drawn on commonly understood conventions of the time, including the widely read 14th-century work *Mandeville's travels* (written around 1371), which Eldred Jones states was the most important pre-Shakespearean publication to deal with Africa. Jones adds that '[m]any of the commonest notions which were held about the continent (Africa) by Elizabethans can be traced back to this book' (1965: 5, this author's addition in brackets). Jones' analysis suggests that Mandeville's representation of Africa was similar to that put forward by ancient writers. The continent was a place of wonder, mystery and monstrosity, but some of the black inhabitants (notably the Christian Ethiopians) were depicted as possessing great beauty and power. The ambivalence towards skin colour and race can be seen to have held in Mandeville's work, and Othello's status and achievements, regardless of his skin colour, were a feasible proposition for Shakespeare's English audience. There is little doubt about Othello's skin colour. Numerous instances in the play refer to Othello as black, including Othello's own famous enunciation: 'I am black' (III. iii, 263). Philip Butcher is one scholar of Shakespearean literature who argues that Othello was both Moor and 'black', which was not uncommon for the time (1952: 246). Othello is the hero of tragic events that are not entirely of his own making, and in a similar way to Shakespeare's other tragic heroes, he is undone by a fatal character flaw that had little to do with his skin colour. It is not Othello's identity as a black African that leads to his demise, but a universal human weakness that leads to his downfall.

Othello's virtues resonate throughout the play, more so than his vices – this, despite Iago's efforts to denigrate the Moor. In fact, Bartels argues that it is the crude depictions of Othello made by Iago, Roderigo and Brabantio that place them 'outside polite society' – it is not Othello who is the outcast (1997: 45). Othello is but one of a range of black characters who appeared in Elizabethan and Jacobin literature. In fact, Shakespeare made use of black characters at other times in *Titus Andronicus*, *The tempest* and *The merchant of Venice*. There is, however, something particularly important in the way Othello was cast as the black hero, which for Martin Orkin (1987) and Phyllis Branxton (1990) make the play about the injustice inherent in racism. Apart from all the ambiguity around race and skin colour in Shakespeare's other plays, *Othello* is a play where the black character suffers from the pernicious injustice committed by a white villain. Whether Shakespeare intended to confer the play upon his English audience as a didactic message about the evils of racial prejudice (as Orkin argues) is uncertain, but the centrality of the black character and the cause of his fate may lend themselves to questions about English attitudes to black Africans at that time. It is likely that modern scholars read too much 'race' into Shakespeare, as Othello's racial identity, rather than his religious and political affiliations, only became principal issues of concern in the 19th century, overturning the tendency to view religion and rank as more important indicators of merit than skin colour. Shakespeare's character provides one example of the medieval propensity to diminish the importance of skin colour and race by concentrating on individual character, rank and religion in designating human achievement.

The pre-Victorian England that Shakespeare and his later compatriots inhabited viewed the world through a different optic than that which would emerge in the 19th century. For Shakespeare, and those from his age, skin colour was not considered a determinant of human character and ability. Even the case of Queen Elizabeth's exhortations in 1599 and 1601 against the growing number of 'Neggars and Blackamoors' residing in England was formulated in religious terms, not necessarily on the basis that blacks were inferior or savage. The origin of Elizabeth's assault on these particular undesirables who were increasingly migrating to her realm was that they were 'infidels, having no understanding of Christ or Gospel' (in Jones 1965: 4). Religion and not race lay at the centre of English perceptions of the world during this period.

The world of the 17th and 18th centuries was framed within the classical episteme of divine order and of the universality of mankind. Social status and religion, which were inseparable and co-dependent, 'were *more explicitly* important to Britons' assessment of themselves and other people than physical attributes such as skin colour, shape of the nose, or texture of the hair' (Wheeler 2001: 7, emphasis in the original). This perception would change in the late-19th century, as the English increasingly constructed an imperial cosmology whereby skin colour came to distinguish ruler from ruled, and British from non-British (Said 1993). Even so, as Lorimer points out: 'When a black visitor entered mid-nineteenth century England, his social position, not his colour, determined the quality of his reception' (1978: 56). The shift from prejudices encrypted by status and education to those of race was a gradual one, and would only take full shape at the apogee of British imperialism in the high-Victorian era.

Richard Hakluyt's *The principall navigations voiages and discoveries of the English nation* (1589) was written at a time when the New World promised greater riches than Africa. Hakluyt's intention in this work was to drive English expansion at a time when Spain and Portugal had created huge overseas empires in the Americas, where it was believed an immense unsettled continent was awaiting European colonisation (Bartels 1997). Africa also played a part in Hakluyt's narrative as a source of gold, spices and slaves. In particular, North Africa loomed large as the location in which Hakluyt could place the struggle between Christianity and Islam, which was becoming a motif of the age. For Eldred Jones, sub-Saharan Africa served merely as a backdrop in Hakluyt's chronicles for the clashes between Europe and the Moors along the North-African coast (1965: 15).

In this religious *mis-en-scène*, the appeal of the legend of the Ethiopian kingdom of Prester John is unsurprising. Mandeville had earlier written of the extensive power and reach of black Ethiopia, which Hakluyt repeated for his Elizabethan audience:

> In the East side of Afrike beneath the red sea, dwelleth the great and mighty Emperour and Christian king Prester Iohn, well knowen to the Portugales in their voyages to Calicut. His dominions reach very farre on euery side: and hath under him many other Kings both christian and heathen that pay him tribute. This mightie prince is called Dauid the Emperour of Aethiopia.

The earlier depictions of the Ethiopians by the ancients, as already noted, along with the widely held belief during the early-Middle Ages that the Ethiopians had a common Christian identity, and uncertainty regarding the vast majority of the continent combined to ensure that Africa remained an ambiguous idea in the English imaginary in the 16th through 18th centuries. While increasingly accurate accounts of the coastal kingdoms along West Africa were being reported in 16th and 17th- century England, the African interior remained a great mystery. Stories of the African interior as a place of danger and monstrosity are common in the literature of this period, and over time a distinction formed between a coastal Africa which Europeans were engaged with, and reliant upon, for access to trade goods, and the unknown interior, where many of those goods (especially slaves) originated. In England and across Western Europe, in the 16th and 17th centuries ideas of Africa were still being formulated. Amongst the multiple discourses that existed, black Africans could be Christianised Ethiopians, Moors or Muslim enemies of Christian Europeans, or beasts from the interior. There is a clear indication of the awareness of difference, and questions of skin colour were central to this difference, but inherent inferiority or a sense of racial difference cannot be deduced as part of the English attitude to black Africans.

Black Africa and Britain in the age of European expansion

The relationship between Europe and Africa in the age of European expansion was shaped by the requirements of the Atlantic slave trade. Initially, the trans-Atlantic slave trade and the ideas of the enslaved were dominated by the Portuguese, Spanish and Dutch. In particular, Anthony Barker argues that the early notions which the British held of black African slaves were influenced by the Portuguese (Barker 1978: 4). While the Atlantic slave trade was a cruel and brutal affair, even for that age, it was legitimated by established notions of religious duty to convert non-Christians. Britain's involvement in the trans-Atlantic slave trade and ideas about enslaved Africans came later, when English slave traders supplanted their European rivals with the signing of the Treaty of Utrecht in 1733. The British dominance of the slave trade was short-lived, as slavery came under intense pressure from religious and economic reformers in England before the end of the 1700s. Before tracing the impact of contestations over African slavery, a brief depiction of the perceptions of black Africans – as held by Europeans in the New World and in the Old, and actions towards them in the 16th and 17th centuries – will help to contextualise the changes that would come to redefine Africa in the later period.

In the earliest period of the colonisation of the Americas there is strong evidence that the racialism and prejudice which permeated the relationship between blacks and whites in the late-18th and 19th centuries was far less prominent in some areas. Slavery and the treatment of slaves was a brutal affair, premised on the power differentials between slave-owner and enslaved, but slaves were treated that way because they were slaves, not because they were black Africans (Banton 1999: 36; Frederickson 1999: 74). Eric Williams, in his immensely influential study of slavery in the Caribbean, argues: 'Slavery was not born of racism; racism was the consequence of slavery' (1994: 7). The debates that Williams inspired in regard to the relationship between economics, slavery and racism, continue over a half century after the first publication of *Capitalism and slavery* in 1944. Numerous studies now reiterate Williams' key point regarding the relationship between slavery and the development of racism, and extol his assertion that 'subhuman characteristics so widely pleaded, were the later rationalisations to justify a simple economic fact: that the colonies needed labour and resorted to Negro labour because it was the cheapest and the best' (ibid: 20). Williams contends that slavery became a solution to the problem of a shortage of labour, and states that before the expansion of the plantation economies in North America and the Caribbean, slavery coexisted with indentured servitude and neither form of labour was predicated by a colour bar. This is a point affirmed by Wheeler, who argues that in the 16th and even into the 17th century, slavery could have happened to almost anyone regardless of 'religion, national origin, or skin colour' (2001: 58).

Indentured labour and fixed-term servitude were common after the establishment of the first English colonies in North America and the Caribbean in the early 17th century. Barbados was settled in the 1620s primarily to produce tobacco for an increasing, if illicit, European demand. The tobacco grown in Barbados proved to be of poor quality and less profitable than tobacco grown in Virginia. However, within a half century, Barbados would be a flourishing English colony with a burgeoning economy and a growing interest in acquiring black African slaves. The reason for this transformation, historians have largely agreed, was due to the introduction of sugar to the island (Blackburn 1997; Williams 1994). Robin Blackburn calculates that in 1938, Barbados had a population of 6 000 people, with

2 000 of these indentured servants and only 200 African slaves (1997: 230). African slaves were more expensive than European indentured servants, and until the 1650s blacks and whites worked side by side in the cane fields. In the 1640s, however, the higher cost of European labour and a drop in the price of black African labour (as English merchants established slave-trading enterprises), as well as a hike in the price of sugar prepared the ground for a transformation of the Barbadian economy. By 1653 there were 20 000 black African slaves in Barbados and only 8 000 European indentured labourers, and by the turn of the 18th century, English colonies in the Caribbean would be almost exclusively dependent on black African slave labour. This was the beginning of a long period of English exploitation of black labour in the Caribbean, where conditions for slaves were far more onerous than in the British colonies in North America. The reason for this, Blackburn suggests, was that in England's North-American colonies the larger free population operated to restrain the practices of land-owners, whereas a Caribbean plantation owner had immense power and was 'subject only to the opinion of his fellows' (1997: 240). In time, Caribbean slave-owners would become a source of some of the most noxious ideas, including claims of black African sub-humanity and savagery.

While the slave economies of the English Caribbean quickly developed into segregated societies and sugar plantations were dependent on black African labour further north, in the colonies of Virginia, Massachusetts and Maryland there was a different attitude towards black Africans. The colour-bar in North America developed more gradually than in the English colonies in the Caribbean. In some of England's North-American colonies in the 17th and early 18th centuries, black Africans were considered by law, at least, to be equal members of society and they

> had little difficulty in acquiring property or exercising an equal right to vote; some even took legal action against whites or held minor public offices. (Frederickson 1999: 76–77).

In addition, George Frederickson explains that marriages between white women and black men occurred in the colonies of Virginia and Maryland, and only came to an end in the 18th century when laws were passed prohibiting interracial marriages (1999: 75–76). The era of ambivalence towards race in England's American colonies has become obscured by, as William A. Green argues, '[t]wentieth century historians, obsessed by contemporary race problems, (who) have attributed race prejudice to seventeenth-century settlers for whom discrimination was unimportant and essentially benign' (1987: 34).

The rights and freedoms permitted former slaves and freed black Africans in the Americas, as Williams and others since have argued, were subsequently lost with the transformation of race relations resulting from the expansion of the slave trade and the increasing dependence of New World production on unfree black African labour. Unfree labour in the colonies increasingly came to mean black African labour, but much evidence points to the development of racism in the Americas to justify a mature form of institutionalised slavery, rather than racism preceding slavery. In England, attitudes towards black Africans were shaped by a different history than that experienced in the North-American and Caribbean colonies.

The first black Africans to arrive in England came with John Lok in 1554. Peter D. Fraser makes the very important point that many black Africans were 'interpreters for the traders rather than commodities of the trade' (2001: 257) and that the status of black Africans in England in the period from the 16th to the 19th century was more complicated than just that of servitude. By the end of the 18th century, black Africans had become an established element of English society, with as many as 15 000 residing in England. In addition, countless black Africans had travelled to England to be 'educated' before they returned to Africa as missionaries or doctors, and to act as officials in expanding Afro-European settlements along the West-African coastline (Winthrop 1999: 68–69).

The elements that sustained a somewhat benign relationship between Britain and black Africa were a mixture of Christianity as a world view and the inability of the British to project military power into black Africa. Christianity, in particular, was a powerful force for maintaining a positive belief in black Africa amongst the British. Christianity provided a coherent lens for people throughout the 16th through early 19th centuries, producing a view of black Africans as potential converts and brothers (and sisters) in a shared faith. Since in Christian philosophy all humans were made by God and descended from common origins, those 'fallen' peoples could be brought back into the fold (Loomba 1998: 105). Just as the Christian kingdoms of Europe viewed the mythological Prester John and his Ethiopians through a religious lens that transcended skin colour and physical features, the British of the early-modern era believed very strongly in the power of Christianity to cleanse the soul, if not the colour of a person's skin.

Increasing reports and narratives of black African customs and rituals led to a stronger belief within British society in the urgency for a Christianising mission in Africa. The cultural practices and beliefs of black Africans relayed back home to Britain were increasingly viewed as inimical to the code of conduct expected of Christian societies. The measure of black Africa in the age of exploration was based on the extent that Africans could become good Christians and good Britons. What this reveals is, without doubt, a deep sense of cultural superiority and prejudice towards black African culture and black Africans. What is less obvious is the extent to which skin colour was considered a more important measure of a person's value than his or her Christian behaviour. While in the colonies, regardless of achievement, black skin came to represent a mark of perpetual inferiority, in Britain the association was not as obvious and ingrained as it would later become.

In the 17th and 18th centuries, ideas about black Africa were often fragmentary, contradictory and ambiguous. This is reflected in the behaviour towards black Africans in England and towards the black Africans who controlled the slave trade along the West-African coast. A coherent discourse of black Africa had yet to be embraced by British society, and the construction of a savage and backward black Africa was only partially completed. It was in the 19th century that this altered, as debates about the most effective means to end slavery and save black Africa led to the consolidation of the belief that Africa was a continent in need not only of British generosity, but of direct British intervention.

Slavery and abolitionism: black Africa reinvented

In the 1780s, 75 000 slaves a year were 'exported' from West Africa, with British merchants responsible for over half the trade. The segments of British society that benefited from the slave trade included the traders and British owners of Caribbean sugar plantations. Both these influential groups were represented at the highest levels of British politics and society, including the considerable number of aristocrats who, as absentee landlords, happened to 'own' many black African slaves. In any case, the British who profited in one way or another from black African slavery had much to lose if abolition won government sanction. As the slave trade increasingly came into conflict with British humanitarian and economic ideals in the late-18th century, the prospect of an end to slavery in the British dominions became possible. With the danger that slavery would be outlawed, this wealthy and powerful group within British society instigated a whole programme of justifying slavery and the slave trade. For almost a century, beginning in earnest in the 1770s, arguments for slavery were mounted by pro-slavery elements of the British intelligentsia who utilised ethical, economic, nationalistic and scientific reasons for maintaining a practice many in Britain were rejecting due to their increasing awareness of the horrific nature of the slave trade, and emerging doctrines of the economic benefits associated with wage-labour.

The pro-slavery lobby advanced numerous arguments pertaining to the benefits of the slave trade for British national interests. The potential economic cost and instability that might eventuate if slavery were outlawed served to inhibit parliamentary support for abolitionism in the closing years of the 18th century. Even that vocal opponent of colonialism, Edmund Burke (1729–1797), was unable to support the immediate abolition of slavery, arguing instead for the gradual eradication of that 'incurable evil'. In 1792, Burke would argue that 'the cause of humanity would be far more benefited by the trade and servitude, regulated and reformed, than the total destruction of both or either' (in Davis 1966: 398). Burke and his contemporaries would rely on arguments put forward by Caribbean plantation owners and slave traders that economic imperatives demanded the continuation of slavery and the slave trade, and as a consequence the pro-slavery position remained in the ascendancy until the end of the 18th century, despite the zeal of the growing abolitionist movement.

Advocates for slavery in the Caribbean and for the continuation of the slave trade, unconvinced that economic arguments would prevent the surge of abolitionist opinion in Britain, worked another angle that relied on depicting slavery as a necessary stage in the development of black Africans. In essence, the pro-slavery argument was based on the belief that 'African life was so "degraded" that even slavery in the West Indies was preferable' (Curtin 1964: 53). The pro-slavery lobby profited little from this argument, as the abolitionists seized on the same basic premise that black African 'degradation' required addressing. Abolitionists, though, placed the blame for the denigration of black Africa on the violence perpetrated by the slave trade. Abolitionists argued that Africa experienced insufficient legitimate labour (the natives were indolent) or legitimate commerce to enhance African life. The resolution, therefore (as far as the abolitionists were concerned), was to be found through intensified Christian teaching and via the introduction of private property rights which, in time, they believed would inspire Africans towards legitimate labour and commerce. Naturally, abolitionists argued that there could be no progress in Africa unless the slave trade was abolished. In 1807, the House of Lords accepted the Abolition of Slavery Act by a vote of 41 to 20, thus bringing into law a bill that had first been passed by the House of Representatives in 1805.

For over a century the British government's abolition of slavery and opposition to the slave trade was represented as among the 'three of four perfectly virtuous pages comprised in the history of nations' (Lecky 1869: 153). This view, that the abolition of slavery was a victory of moral progress by a society led by virtuous men and women inspired by Christian ethics, remained unchallenged in the British psyche until Eric Williams' *Capitalism and slavery* argued that the end of slavery could be attributed to a change in the political economy of the British Empire and a decline in the economic importance of the Caribbean colonies. For Williams, British opposition to slavery and the slave trade had little to do with moral progress, religion or humanitarian considerations (Drescher 1987a: 180–196; Turley 1991: 1–2). In the 65 years since the publication of *Capitalism and slavery*, scholars have subjected Williams' thesis to scrutiny, often disputing the economic determinism on which his conclusions are based, but without completely discrediting the challenge he poses to the dominant historical motif that the British abolition of slavery was an exclusively philanthropic achievement. Williams' legacy has been to inspire successive generations of scholars to revisit important questions regarding the history of racism, slavery and anti-slavery.

There is evidence that as the economic argument waned, pro-slavery advocates turned to an increasingly virulent racially based campaign during the first decades of the 19th century, calling for increased intervention in black African affairs on the basis that slavery was beneficial to the 'savages' and 'sub-humans' who inhabited the continent (Curtin 1964: 159–165). More recent scholarship by David Brion Davis (1984), Seymour Drescher (1987b) and David Turley (1991), for example, has favoured a reinterpretation of the history of British abolitionism as a convergence of moral and economic imperatives, where class and culture were not mutually inclusive, but were mutually reinforcing. A similar if distinctive history of the development of a more systematic form of racism in the United States (US) also emerged in this period. The appearance in the US of racist doctrines based on a belief in the natural inferiority of negroes slowly filtered through to Britain, with little overall impact, at that very time when pro-slavery advocates continued to make arguments that black Africans were incapable of progress unless coerced to change their natural inclinations.

What emerged during the period of slavery and abolition was a recurring motif from pro-slavery advocates and abolitionists alike, that black Africans lived in a state of degradation which was antithetical to the British sense of appropriate morality. The clear differences between advocates of slavery and abolitionists on the issue of slavery obscured a commonly held view that black Africa was largely inhabited by a population that was savage, backward and indolent, and in need of redemption through British intervention. This view of black Africa would resonate beyond the debates surrounding slavery and abolition, and would shape the idea of Africa in the Victorian Age.

Racism and imperialism: British paternalism and ideas of black Africa

The life of Samuel Crowther, according to Douglas A. Lorimer (1978: 60–62), provides a very useful illustration of the change in attitude of the British towards black Africans in the 19th century. Crowther was rescued from slavery and sent to England in 1826 to receive an education. He climbed the ranks of the Anglican Church, becoming Bishop of Niger in 1864 at which time he also received an honorary doctorate from Oxford University, in recognition of his translation of the scriptures into African languages. On returning to his diocese, Bishop Crowther faced considerable opposition from 'white' missionaries and clergy, but he reasserted his authority which remained largely unchallenged until the 1880s. Crowther resigned his post in 1892, since his authority as bishop was impugned by 'a new younger breed of white missionary', '[i]nspired by a more rigid evangelical paternalism, and by new anthropological notions of the master race and the childlike attributes of the Negro' (ibid: 62).

What this brief example demonstrates, is that in the 19th century, British attitudes towards Africans, and hence Africa, transformed from strong governmental and societal opposition to slavery, accompanied by British generosity towards assimilated black

Africans like Crowther, into a position that assumed that physical attributes – especially black skin – determined people's character and that those racial characteristics could be quantified. This change can be attributed to a number of inter-related factors, such as the transformation of Britain in the 19th century into the pre-eminent global imperial power, the role of Empire in reshaping British nationalism (Said 1993), the reconfiguration of class relations within Britain as an industrially advanced imperial power (Lorimer 1978) and the consolidation of British scientism and technological advances (Adas 1989).

Racist doctrines emerged in the late 1700s without having had much affect on the way in which the majority of people in Britain viewed black Africa. Edward Long's *History of Jamaica* (1774) claimed black Africans were 'brutish, ignorant, idle, crafty, treacherous, bloody, thievish, mistrustful, and superstitious people' not due to culture and environment, as commonly believed in the 18th and early 19th centuries, but inherently so, with only the power of 'white' authority able to curb these 'savage' tendencies. The belief in the inherently inferior black African was evident in the propaganda of numerous advocates of slavery, but the views of Long and others like him existed on the margins of knowledge about black Africa. Even in the Victorian Age, racist views by James Hunt, which were similar to those expounded by Long, proved unpopular with English society (Lorimer 1978: 138–140).

More common was the view put forward by churches and various missionary organisations across Britain. Prior to the advent of mass literacy and the popular press, church groups and congregations performed an important function in circulating information and ideas throughout society. Missionaries, in particular, played a large part in the invention of a black Africa. Churches had significant interest in encouraging missionary activity by promoting the idea of black Africa as a *tabula rasa* where increased British involvement would lead to the conversion of the 'natives' and ultimately to the congregation's moral and spiritual fulfilment. Curtin (1964) makes the argument that self-interested depictions of black Africans as requiring the urgent salvation of Christian moral values, the introduction of a work ethic and legitimate trade, led to a widespread belief in the degeneration of the entire continent. His conclusion on the role of the church in constructing a wild and wicked black Africa, is that

> [i]t is hard to escape the conclusion that the systematic representation of African culture in the missionary press contributed unintentionally to the rise of racial and cultural arrogance. (Curtin 1964: 328)

Despite the increasing racialism apparent in the middle decades of the 19th century, the conventional wisdom in Britain remained that much could be achieved by continuing to support missionary activity and the introduction of legitimate commerce into black Africa. While various forms of racism, including the more racially virulent forms of social Darwinism, led to some change in the way black Africans were viewed by British society, such ideas remained on the fringes of polite society. David Livingstone, at Cambridge in 1857, directed his attention to uplifting black Africans when he implored his audience,

> to direct your attention to Africa. I know that in a few years I shall be … in that country, which is now open; do not let it be shut again! I go back to Africa to make an open path for commerce and Christianity; do you carry out the work which I have begun. (in Nkomazana 1998)

Two decades after Livingstone argued for continued British involvement in black Africa for the benefit of the 'natives', the Belgian king would argue that European paternalism was urgently needed to save black Africa. This appeal on humanitarian grounds was warmly received by the British public. The reason for this, as Thomas Pakenham (1991) describes so effectively, was due to King Leopold's familiarity with the British image of Africa. Leopold unfailingly read British newspaper reports and gauged that the dominant view of Africa in the British imagination was that of a continent requiring the disciplined and tough guiding hand of a father towards his children. The British accepted Leopold's civilising mission with very little resistance and there should be no astonishment that they did, as Leopold offered the British a mirror image of their own perceptions of Africa. Leopold successfully disguised his lust for wealth and power as well as his imperial appetite in the clothes provided by British paternalism and cultural arrogance towards Africa.

The relationship between Europe and Africa had evolved by the late-19th century to a point where European domination of the continent was established by consent (where possible) and by coercion and conquest (where necessary). Colonialism altered the relationship between 'black Africa' and 'white Europe', with the emerging racialism sometimes providing justification for the policies of exploitation and oppression that followed. We should not underestimate the burden of racialism on the colonial experience of black Africa and the oppression it caused. However, Britain's 'civilising mission', which professed an inherent belief in universalism, was a far more dominant and insidious paradigm for legitimating control of black Africa. The construction of a savage, primitive, indolent and historically isolated black Africa was a more powerful and sustaining invention than the scientific racism that emerged in the late-19th century, as Lorimer (1978) concludes. In black Africa, missionary zeal and a belief in uplifting the 'natives' from the so-called state of nature that was so abhorrent to British sensibilities, were the premises on which the modern perception of black Africa became institutionalised.

Conclusion

The reinvented black Africa of the 19th century is most vividly expressed in the depiction of the Tarzan novels which appeared first in 1912, authored by American writer Edgar Rice Burroughs. Burroughs himself never ventured to Africa and his knowledge of Africa was wrought from British representations of the 'dark continent' in the late-19th century. The black Africa which had interacted with Britain and other European societies for centuries was lost to the world, as an image of savage, primitive and isolated continent came to the fore, transferred from the British to the American imaginary. Immediately upon the release of Rice's *Tarzan of the apes* the reproduction of this savage and wild black Africa was appropriated by the film industry, radio, and then later by television. In the 1930s, Tarzan's exploits occurred in a *mis-en-scène* of a black Africa populated by savage, cruel and very primitive tribes. Kevin Dunn suggests that the Tarzan movies of the 1930s were 'arguably the largest shaper of the West's perception of Africa' (1996: 155).

The reinvention of the image of black Africa occurred in an age of British ethnocentrism and national pomposity. Prior to the second half of the 19th century, British images of Africa were fluid, ambiguous and contested. In Britain in the second half of the 19th century it hardly mattered whether a person supported or opposed slavery, or was inclined to racialist theories or found them unethical and unscientific – a belief in British superiority was an unquestioned norm, as was an acceptance of the cultural inferiority of all those with black skin. Social Darwinism and explicit racism were hardly necessary in determining the place of Africa in the British global hierarchy. There was nothing deterministic about the development of the British discourse that black Africa required European tutelage to overcome historically embedded savagery, backwardness and isolation. Nonetheless, such a view proved to be a very convenient discourse for empire builders to exploit to legitimate conquest and colonisation. A century on from the height of European conquest and control of Africa, similar views of black Africa continue to underwrite 'Western' intervention in a continent which remains in the 'Western imaginary' as a place that is savage and backward.

References

Adas, M. 1989. *Machines as the measure of men: science, technology and ideologies of Western dominance*. Ithaca, New York: Cornell University Press.

Aidi, H.D. 2005. Slavery, genocide and the politics of outrage: understanding the new racial Olympics. *The Middle East Research and Information Project* 234(Spring).

Banton, M. 1999. The racialising of the world. In *Racism*, ed. M. Bulmer and J. Solomos, 36–40. Oxford: Oxford University Press.

Barker, A.J. 1978. *The African link: British attitudes to the negro in the era of the Atlantic slave trade, 1550–1807*. London: Frank Cass and Company Limited.

Bartels, E.C. 1997. Othello and Africa: postcolonialism reconsidered. *The William and Mary Quarterly* (Third Series) 54(1): 45–64.

Blackburn, R. 1997. *The making of new world slavery: from the Baroque to the Modern, 1492–1800*. London: Verso.

Braxton, P.N. 1990. Othello: the Moor and the metaphor. *South Atlantic Review* 55(4): 1–17.

Butcher, P. 1952. Othello's racial identity. *Shakespeare Quarterly* 3(3): 243–247.

Curtin, P.D. 1964. *The image of Africa: British ideas and actions 1780–1850*, Volumes 1 and 2. Wisconsin: The University of Wisconsin Press.

Davis, D.B. 1966. *The problem of slavery in Western culture*. Oxford: Oxford University Press.

Davis, D.B. 1984. *Slavery and human progress*. Oxford: Oxford University Press.

Drescher, S. 1987a. Eric Williams: British capitalism and British slavery. *History and Theory* 26(2): 180–196.

Drescher, S. 1987b. *Capitalism and antislavery: British mobilization in comparative perspective*. Oxford: Oxford University Press.

Dunn, K. 1996. Lights …camera … Africa: images of Africa and Africans in Western popular films of the 1930s. *African Studies Review* 39(1): 149–175.

Edwards, P. 1992. The early African presence in the British Isles. In *Essays on the history of blacks in Britain: From Roman times to the mid-twentieth century*, ed. J.S Gundara and I. Duffield, 9–29. Aldershot: Ashgate Publishing Limited.

Fraser, P.D. 2001. Slaves or free people? The status of Africans in England, 1550–1750. In *From strangers to citizens: the integration of immigrant communities in Britain, Ireland and Colonial America, 1550–1750*, ed. R. Vigne and C. Littleton, 254–260. London: The Huguenot Society of Great Britain and Ireland and the Sussex Associated Press.

Frederickson, G. 1999. Social origins of American racism. In *Racism*, ed. M. Bulmer and J. Solomos, 70–81. Oxford: Oxford University Press.

Green, W.A. 1987. Race and slavery: considerations on the Williams Thesis. In *British capitalism and Caribbean slavery: the legacy of Eric Williams*, ed. B. Solow and S.L. Engerman, 25–50. Cambridge: Cambridge University Press.

Hakluyt, R. 1589. Principall navigations, voiages, traffiques and discoveries of the English nation, ed. E. Goldsmid. http://ebooks.adelaide.edu.au/h/hakluyt/voyages/ (accessed 27 March 2008).

Hunwick, J.O. and E.T. Powell. 2002. *The African Diaspora in the Mediterranean lands of Islam*. Princeton: Markus Wiener Publishers.

Jones, E. 1965. *Othello's countrymen: the Africans in English Renaissance drama*. London: Oxford University Press.

Lecky, W.E.H. 1869. *A history of European morals*, 6th edition, 1884, vol. 1. London.

Lewis, B. 1990. *Race and slavery in the Middle East: an historical enquiry*. Oxford: Oxford University Press.
Lockman, Z. 2004. *Contending visions of the Middle East: the history and politics of Orientalism*. Cambridge: Cambridge University Press.
Loomba, A. 1998. *Colonialism/postcolonialism*. Routledge: London.
Lorimer, D.A. 1978. *Colour, class and the Victorians*. Leicester: Leicester University Press.
Mazrui, A.A. 2005. The re-invention of Africa: Edward Said, V.Y. Mudimbe and beyond.*Research in African Literatures* 36(3): 68–82.
Miles, R. 1989. *Racism*. London: Routledge.
Miller, C. 1986. *Blank darkness: Africanist discourse in French*. Chicago: The University of Chicago Press.
Nkomazana, F. 1998. Livingstone's ideas of Christianity, commerce and civilization. *PULA: Botswana Journal of African Studies* 12(1 & 2). http://archive.lib.msu.edu/DMC/African%20Journals/pdfs/PULA/pula012001/pula012001004.pdf (accessed 28 February 2008).
Orkin, M. 1987. Othello and the 'plain face' of racism. *Shakespeare Quarterly* 38(2): 166–188.
Pakenham, T. 1991. *The scramble for Africa: white man's conquest of the dark continent from 1876–1912*. New York: Avon Books.
Robinson, R., J. Gallagher and A. Denny. 1978. *Africa and the Victorians: the official mind of imperialism*. London: Palgrave Macmillan.
Said, E.W. 1978. *Orientalism*. New York: Pantheon Books.
Said, E.W. 1993. *Culture and imperialism*. London: Chatto & Windus.
Snowden, F.M. 1970. *Blacks in antiquity: Ethiopians in the Greco-Roman experience*. Cambridge, Mass: Belknap Press of Harvard University Press.
Turley, D. 1991. *The culture of English anti-slavery: 1780–1860*. London: Routledge.
Turner, F.M. 1981. *The Greek heritage in Victorian Britain*. New Haven: Yale University Press.
Vance, N. 1997. *The Victorians and Ancient Rome*. London: Wiley-Blackwell.
West, C. 2002. A genealogy of modern racism. In *Race: critical theories*, ed. P. Essed and D.T. Goldberg, 90–112. Malden, MA: Blackwell Publishing.
Wheeler, R. 2001. *The complexion of race: categories of difference in eighteenth century British culture*. Pennsylvania: University of Pennsylvania Press.
Williams, E. 1994. *Capitalism and slavery*. Chapel Hill, NC: The University of North Carolina Press.
Winthrop, J.D. 1999. First impressions: initial English confrontations with Africans. In *Racism*, ed. M. Bulmer and J. Solomos, 66–70. Oxford: Oxford University Press.
Young, R.C. 2001. *Postcolonialism: an historical introduction*. Oxford: Blackwell Publishers.

Rainbow Worriers: South African Afropessimism Online

Martha Evans

ABSTRACT

The relationship between the rise of Afropessimism and the growth of global communication networks is more or less proportionate with the deepening of the digital divide. With fewer internal sources of information, news networks are portraying events in Africa as more tragic, more mysterious and more distant than ever before. This, in turn, has an off-putting effect on foreign investors and donors, who are becoming increasingly impatient with mounting reports of African corruption, misrule and political unrest. While South Africa's relatively advanced media infrastructure should exempt it from this trend, the discourse of Afropessimism is highly visible, both in news about the country and in posted responses to headlines. This article is concerned with the reception of reports on South Africa by one of the most vocal online groups commenting on events in the country: white expatriates. Focusing on the web presence of a number of popular sites, ranging from the Afro-dystopic to the Afro-optimistic, the article analyses the ways in which some South Africans living abroad are active in spreading pessimistic views about their homeland – a trend that is important because these views are beginning to dominate online responses. The article concludes that the high visibility of Afropessimism on blogs and on platforms such as YouTube is cause for concern, firstly because it indicates that events in South Africa are rapidly distancing it from world opinion, and secondly, because the country's future failure is increasingly being represented as a *fait accompli*.

Introduction

The relationship between the rise of Afropessimism – the view that Africa is incapable of progressing (Olukoshi 1999: 451) – and the growth of global communication networks is more or less proportionate with the deepening of the digital divide. With African Studies in a state of decay (Hydén 1996; Olukoshi 1999) and fewer internal sources of information, news networks are portraying events in Africa as more tragic, more mysterious and more distant than ever before. In turn, the spread of Afropessimism has an off-putting effect on potential foreign investors and donors (Onwudiwe 1995), who are becoming increasingly impatient with mounting reports of African corruption, misrule and political unrest.

While South Africa's relatively advanced media infrastructure should exempt it from this trend, the discourse of Afropessimism is highly visible, both in news about this country and in posted responses to headlines. Because it is perceived as the gateway to Africa's future development (Guest 2005), reactions to events in South Africa are crucial, and the Internet provides a useful means of examining what the global community is thinking about current affairs. Forums provide open access to users, and the increasing number of self-published blogs offers unedited predictions about the country's future. Because the Internet can mask participants, allowing them to 'hide' behind anonymous user names, pseudonyms and personae, it offers a fairly transparent forum, as commentators are not hampered by audience expectations and speak without presupposing a critical audience. The Internet thus offers new ways of intersecting the communication loop, collapsing boundaries between sites of creation and consumption.

This article is concerned with the reception of reports on South Africa by white expatriate Internet users – one of the most vocal groups commenting on events in the country. Many South Africans' decision to emigrate, particularly in the post-apartheid period, is predicated on nervous predictions about the country's future, especially in the context of other African countries. The expectation that South Africa will follow their trajectory of economic and political decline (Davidson 1992; Guest 2005) is summed up in the popular defence, 'but look at the rest of Africa,' described on one blog as the 'Sierra Leone syndrome moving south' (*Die nuwe Suid-Afrika*).

In particular, the article analyses the ways in which, and the reasons why, some South Africans living abroad are active in spreading pessimistic views about their homeland – a fact that is important because these views are beginning to dominate online responses. The article focuses on the web presence of a number of popular sites, ranging from the Afro-dystopic to the Afro-optimistic.

Afropessimism or Afrorealism? The difficulty in talking about Africa

On the surface, questioning the reasons for the spread of Afropessimism may seem anomalous; the 1994 Rwandan genocide, the protracted violence in the Congo and events in the Sudan and Zimbabwe suggest that the continent will be afflicted with continued strife during this century, and make it near impossible to view Africa in a positive light. In South Africa, social crises such as crime and the HIV pandemic, the government's perceived shortfall in dealing with these issues, infrastructural challenges as well as conjecture about corruption among leading politicians[1] (including South Africa's president) suggest that the country's challenges have as much to do with state weakness and social decay as they do with negative stereotyping. Africa's difficulties, in short, 'are not imagined' (Martin 2008: 340) and there appear to be solid reasons for worrying about South Africa's future. The news out of Africa is bad, these events declare, because bad things are happening there.

An increasing impatience with the continent is also reflected in the number of books on what Adebayo Olukoshi refers to as the 'basket-case' (1999: 452) thesis on Africa – many of which move away from the postcolonial tendency to link the continent's problems with imperial representation. New analyses acknowledge that the continent's woes began in the colonial era, but go on to explore the effects of the complex combination of technological underdevelopment, corruption and dictatorship (Museveni 2000), dwindling resources and disease (Kaplan 1994), as well as the unproductive focus on the 'old refrain about imperialism, colonialism, apartheid, dependency, and globalisation' (Mbembe 1999, in Robins 2004: 18) – all of which have less to do with the West than was previously argued. Exploring Afropessimist discourse in such a climate rapidly lands one in an impasse; what Achille Mbembe calls the 'dead end' of reflection on the African experience (2002: 242).

Another difficulty facing an analysis of expatriate responses is that South Africans living abroad do not present a homogenous group and their online activity is not representative. According to the South African Institute for Race Relations, an estimated 800 000 white South Africans emigrated between 1995 and 2005 (in Jooste 2008), their stated reasons for leaving are diverse and they have moved to various parts of the globe.[2] Also, although the largest migratory wave started in 1992 (Louw & Mersham 2002: 313),[3] they left at different stages of the country's metamorphosis and have vastly differing experiences of its transformation.

In spite of the diversity of the group, expatriate responses to the post-rainbow period have not only been consistently negative but are also increasingly racialised, as numerous articles on expatriate activity suggest (see Cinman 2008; Eaton 2005; Jordan 2008; Richman 2007; Roper 2008; Moerdyk 2008). At a glance it would appear that they no longer reflect the findings of a 2004 Research International survey which concluded that only 22 per cent of expatriates were negative about the country's future (*Homecoming revolution* e-newsletter, 13 December 2005).

Although an imbalanced focus on the continent's failures is undoubtedly a key feature of the discourse, in its purest form Afropessimism is more than the continual depiction of negative events. As the term implies, Afropessimists believe that news coming out of Africa will *always* be bad, unless (as extreme versions propose) recolonisation is allowed. John Lonsdale defines the core premise of Afropessimism as 'the assumption that African citizenries cannot exist' (2004: 75). Such predictions rapidly regress into essentialist and racist positionings.

Online expatriate responses to events in South Africa perpetuate this thinking to varying degrees, with openly racist declarations and fantasies of recolonisation sitting at the extreme end of the continuum, and predictions about the country's decline and apologetic speculations about the benefits of apartheid situated further along the scale. Though triggered by political and social events, what some of these comments imply is that white South Africans' despair about their homeland (particularly as it is expressed online) has as much to do with perceived political disempowerment, the effects of geographical displacement and the preservation of racial and cultural identity (Steyn 2004) as it does with the situation described.

The analysis by Alexander, Eyerman, Giesen, Smelser and Sztompka of the 'trauma process' in *Cultural trauma and collective identity* (2004) provides a useful schema for assessing the link between Afropessimism and group identity revision. The theory posits that trauma as a cultural process is mediated through varied forms of representation and linked to the overhaul of collective memory and identity.

The horror, the horror: fantasies of persecution and power

The number of websites serving South Africans living abroad is mushrooming and the advent of social networking sites such as Facebook and MySpace has resulted in the creation of several expatriate groups (e.g. 'Homesick South Africans' and 'South Africans Abroad'). These sites and groups all purport to harness the 'scatterlings' of what is increasingly being termed the South African 'Diaspora'. Ironically, the Internet, often imagined as a kind of borderless space, is sought by clusters of (mainly white) expatriates wishing to express a sense of themselves that is inextricably tied to a geographical place. New media technologies bring a fresh dimension to understanding diasporic communication, providing much stronger links to home than was possible in earlier decades and operating as a crucial factor in the development of diasporic identity (see Moyo 2007; Tsagarousianou 2004).

Most expatriate sites offer information on host countries and details on where to buy South African products. They also operate as social and business networks and set up forums where participants can share their experiences. Many post news about South African events, so that expatriates can keep abreast of affairs in their homeland, and the number of responses to these links indicates that South Africans are eager to stay informed.

In addition to these networking sites, the rise of web logs has led to the creation of a number of vitriolic blog spots with titles such as *Die nuwe Suid-Afrika* [The new South Africa][4], *I luv South Africa, but I hate my government*[5] and the elusive *South Africa sucks* (which at last count had been through eight manifestations, was last located at www.zasucks.com and, at the time of writing appears to have been removed by Wordpress). These all proclaim to be dedicated to exposing the 'real' situation in South Africa and are typically makeshift collages of writing on the shortcomings of ANC rule (with links to negative news reports on crime, corruption, mismanagement and the failings of affirmative action), images of deteriorating infrastructure and gruesome photographs of victims of crime.

The creators and supporters of these sites conform to one of Martin Hall's predicted prototypes of South African Internet users: 'subject to mood swings, racially insensitive, and a client of hate sites such as those of the AWB and the Boerestaat Party' (2000: 476). Hall points to Orania's quick trek into cyberspace[6] and the use of new media technologies as a 'psychological centre for Afrikaner education' (ibid; see also Stephney 2000). Adopted user names include Kaffir Hater, Laager, Koos de la Rey, Turd World and Refugee, and, for the most part, discussion is reduced to racist, self-congratulatory banter and radical conspiracy theories about 'Boer' genocide and 'communistic' plots.

Two of the sites with a more sophisticated appearance are *African crisis* – 'Africa's premier hard news website'[7] and *Stop Boer genocide*: 'South Africa in crisis: what people don't want to talk about'.[8] The creator of the *African crisis* site, ex-Zimbabwean Jan Lamprecht, operates out of South Africa, but has appeared in conservative American media channels. The *Stop Boer genocide* site is run, somewhat surprisingly, by an English-speaking South African couple now residing in England. Both websites have a special focus on farm attacks and situate them within the context of racially motivated violence and genocide.

Although *Stop Boer genocide* deplores the fact that 'no one batted an eyelid' in response to a 'farm attack' awareness-raising event held in 2004, the British media has started to take notice of the phenomenon. Both the *Telegraph* (2005) and *The Sunday Times* (2006) have reported on the violence, while Sky News included an insert, 'Farmers killed in South Africa' (2006), and the BBC produced an hour-long documentary, *Blood and Land* (2007). Yet, although sympathetic to the dangers of farming in Africa, official reports are not inclined to entertain the idea of a genocide campaign against 'Boers'. The Sky News insert, for instance, includes an official government comment from the then Minister of Safety and Security, Charles Nqakula, which contradicts the suggestion that the attacks are part of a racially motivated government campaign.

Similarly, while one might have expected the April 2010 murder of farmer and white supremacist Eugene Terre'Blanche to draw global attention to the 'farm murder' phenomenon in South Africa – the killing made headlines on CNN, the BBC and Reuters – most of the reporting focused on his politically divergent viewpoints[9] rather than his identity as a farmer.

The statistics on farm murders are hotly debated – a situation that is not helped by the fact that the South African Police Service (SAPS) stopped releasing figures in 2007. One report estimated that between 1991 and 2001 there were 6 122 farm attacks in farming communities, and 1 254 people were murdered (Committee of Inquiry into Farm Attacks, *Final report* 2003: 417). The Transvaal Agricultural Union (TAU) recorded 1 266 murders and 2 070 attacks in the period 1991–2009 – an average of 0.2 murders a day (in Vena 2010). The seriousness of the problem, as well as the activism of agricultural unions, compelled the SAPS first to implement a 'rural protection plan' in October 1997, followed by a 'rural safety summit' a year later. Later investigations[10] into the phenomenon illustrate some of the difficulties in covering farm attacks in South Africa; because of their remoteness and because socio-economic divides still run along racial lines in commercial farming areas, white farm owners feature more frequently (but certainly not solely) as victims, which gives the crimes the appearance of racism. But the suggestion that the attacks form part of an orchestrated government plan to exterminate the 'Boer' people seems unlikely.

In addition to reporting on farm attacks, *Stop Boer genocide* and *African crisis* host forums and hold petitions against violence, crime and affirmative action in South Africa. There are links to pages that publish views on events, including reports such as 'Are you being watched?' (which speculates that the motivation behind the Regulation of Foreign Military Assistance Act was to 'persecute' Afrikaners who had been 'forced abroad as security guards'), 'Mandela beneath the halo' (from *Stop Boer genocide*), which sports an iconic image of Madiba with devil's horns, and 'How Nelson Mandela brought crime and murder to South Africa' (from *African crisis*), which illustrates crime increases since 1994 via graphs.

Some of the writing appears to have been generated by the creators of the site, while other articles have been submitted by supportive users. One example from *African crisis*, titled 'South Africa: what whites can do practically' (26 August 2006) encourages white South Africans living in the country to engage in a 'covert race war' by withholding tax where possible, refusing to 'prop up' BEE enterprises and teaching black South Africans incorrect job skills. Other articles hypothesise about the plight of the Afrikaans language and the future of the Boer.

The reclamation of the term 'Boer', because of its link with suffering endured during the Anglo-Boer War, can be seen as an attempt to emphasise a culture and way of life that are under attack (Stephney 2000: 1–2) as well as an ability to retaliate and endure. Similarly, the link with Diaspora and the refugee status that users bestow upon themselves can also be seen as a means of claiming a marginalised identity. As Melissa Steyn points out, we associate Diaspora with 'those displaced through slavery, through forced, involuntary, limited choice migration' (2001: 11). Yet, since white power in South Africa still retains much of its economic and social muscle (Steyn 2001; Van der Westhuizen 2007) this self-perception is arguably skewed.

The association with genocide[11] takes the sense of discrimination one step further, linking it with seriously persecuted groups. Ironically, the sites also demonstrate the racist converse of this in their celebrations at the devastating effects of HIV/AIDS on the country's black population. Inflammatory titles such as 'AIDS, a curse or a blessing?' (from *Stop Boer genocide*) are frequent, and the effects of the virus are interpreted as the manifestation of God's will – as 'God's Grim Reaper going about his business among the black population' (from *African crisis*). As Michel Wieviorka points out in *The arena of racism*, racist thinking can be seen to operate along a continuum that begins with difference (or racialisation), moving on to discrimination and concluding with extermination (or purification) (in Berger 2001: 81). Celebrating the effects of HIV/AIDS can be seen as an implicit example of this (ibid.).

For the most part, the explicit nature of these opinion pieces makes them less interesting than the straight news reports taken from other online sources. Topics that find their way into the archive include articles about increasingly racialised issues such as crime and corruption, Minister of Safety and Security, Charles Nqakula's 2006 comment on crime and white flight,[12] the 2008 debate about the ANC's plan to disband the Scorpions,[13] and the 2008 electricity crisis.[14] Alongside the other material on the sites the reports make for worrying reading, and generally sketch a picture of South Africa (and Africa) as a hellish place that is swiftly sliding into anarchy under black rule.

The mission of the websites – to expose the hidden 'truth' about South Africa – is ironic in light of these reports. In spite of the fact that sites appear to have been set up to counter what is perceived as the conventional media's inadequate reporting, much of their content is taken from mainstream media sources, which refutes their argument that coverage of events is conspiratorially 'liberal' and pro-ANC.

Some of the material is, however, doctored in order to safeguard preferred readings. These fabricated and altered news reports take on the appearance of official journalism. Some pages use South African Press Agency (SAPA) reports and insert interpretative phrases to ensure that the information is understood 'correctly'. (See, for instance, 'Are you being watched?' on *Stop Boer genocide*.) To untrained readers the merger of straight journalism and commentary, together with the SAPA accreditation, gives the report an authentic and seemingly objective appearance. Similarly, headlines are rewritten to reframe articles. (On *African crisis*, 'Question mark over farmer's killing' becomes "Farm murder: a white farmer shot dead by blacks wanting to claim his land?' and 'Another racist attack?' is rewritten as 'Another racist attack? Its [sic] only RACIST, if Whites are the attackers ...')

The visual features of *Stop Boer genocide* and *African crisis* also break the boundaries of conventional journalism and are perhaps the most shocking. Whereas YouTube polices the publication of graphic photographs, the websites feature disturbing images of corpses, badly beaten survivors of violence, and grieving widows and widowers. Short, factually questionable captions accompany some of the photographs on *Stop Boer genocide* (e.g., 'Alwyn Labuschagne grieving for his loss' and 'Necklacing happen [sic] all the time in SA'), and the following opener precedes a gory display on *African crisis*:

> All the photos you see on this page are white people who were murdered or attacked by blacks. Kindly note, our government falls over itself to spread news across the world when a Police dog attacks a black man. They then shout RACIST! RACIST! At the top of their voices. The trained Police dog does not even draw blood. They find this, and parade it as a white hate crime against a black. Now come and take a look at a very small sampling of black hate crimes on whites and compare them. (Lamprecht n.d.)

Instead of contextualising the images the commentary has the opposite effect, and the photo 'albums' are experienced as a gratuitous series of random images of African horror. While *Stop Boer genocide*'s mission is to expose racially motivated violence in the post-apartheid era, oddly, it features photographs of black victims of lynchings and necklacings[15] – which appear to have been taken in townships during periods of political unrest under apartheid – images from campaigns against Afrikaner instruction (labelled 'anti-Afrikaner campaign') as well as images from Zimbabwe. In this case, the lack of political context serves as prime example of one of the defining features of Afropessimist discourse, which tends to paint all African countries with the same brush.

According to commentators discussing the journalistic ethics of the sites on other forums (see http://www.africans.com), some of the photographs on *African crisis*[16] were recognised by site visitors as originating from the website http://www.rotten.com, which bills itself as 'an archive of disturbing illustration'. Research into other photographs on *Stop Boer genocide* shows that they derive from subversive sites such as http://littlemidgets.com, which features pornographic material alongside images of excessive bodily deformity and injury, as well as the now-dismantled http://www.ogrish.com, which displayed uncensored news material from wars, accidents and executions.

The actual sources of the majority of the photographs remain unknown, although site administrators claim they come from members of the TAU (pers. comm., 14 February 2008).[17]

Recognising the subversive power of the Internet, the TAU, representing over 6 000 farmers, has frequently tried to galvanise government into action by threatening to publish images of farm murders in order to 'show the world' what 'really is going on in South Africa' (Niemann cited in Sara 2001: 1). As Inez Stephney points out, the Internet allows authors 'to hide and resurface at will' and they are 'not obliged to make a full disclosure of their identity or even a truthful one' (2001: 2). Similarly, the lack of journalistic codes governing the revelation of sources allows users to publish material without fear of censure, although website hosts are growing increasingly reluctant to publish offensive material.

In the first half of 2006, another controversial site (*Crime expo South Africa* – now defunct) also published extensive photographs of alleged crime victims in an effort to discourage tourism and investment in South Africa (Swart & Kirk 2006: 1). As is evident from discussions on other forums (see, for instance, the Wikipedia discussion page for the 'crime in South Africa' entry), violent crime is one of the most emotive and challenging issues in the country. A United Nations (UN) survey involving 60 (mainly developed) countries for the period 1998–2000 ranked South Africa first for rape per capita and second for assault and murder (UN Office on Drugs and Crime 2002). The effects of violent crime are purportedly racialised in the media, which has long been criticised for its skewed focus on white victims (Balseiro 1997: 6; Shaw 2002: 50). Experience and fear of crime are also the most oft-cited reasons for emigrating (Louw & Mersham 2002: 315). The release of statistics, the large number of individuals directly affected by crime in some way, and the perception that the security and safety service are unable to control the problem have contributed hugely to post-apartheid emigration figures, as South Africans seek out countries seen as 'safe'. As Richard Ballard argues, 'crime, both real and imagined, provides the justification to avoid areas where one lacks direct control' (2004: 50). *Crime expo*'s focus on the issue, coupled with its explicit nature, attracted numerous visitors (both from within South Africa and abroad) as well as the attention of the mainstream South African media. Once news of the site entered the official public sphere, however, investigative journalists uncovered irregularities and dubious ethical activity. Derrick Spies (2006) of the *Herald* discovered that some photographs purportedly submitted by the South African public were in fact taken from other websites (including *African crisis*), while others were taken at accident rather than crime scenes, and Werner Swart and Paul Kirk from the *Citizen* revealed links between the website creator and a bogus organisation.[18] Three days after the *Citizen* report was published, the *Crime expo* website was taken down and there have since been calls for a criminal investigation on account of the website's abuse of public funds – donations channelled via direct deposit and SMS (Williams 2006).

Other extremist sites, however, pass under the radar and their anti-crime façade and emotive appeals attract foreign readers who are sometimes taken in by their ideology. Responses along the following lines (both taken from *Stop Boer genocide*'s guestbook archives) abound:

> Dear Sir, I have read your website with shock, anger and sadness. This is a side to South Africa we definitely DO NOT see in the UK, what a surprise. Words fail me, what can I say that in any way will help you? (Anonymous)
>
> I have recently become aware of the plight of white South Africans and I didn't realize that it was this dire. I am an African American and I am totally ashamed and heartbroken of what the people of South Africa are doing. (Anonymous)

Conservative (and Christian) America's fear of communism has arguably been replaced by anti-terrorism, as proponents of Herman and Chomsky's propaganda model argue (see Klaehn 2005: 88); because of this perhaps, and because the continent is seen as ripe for terrorist activity (see Davis 2007; Mentan 2004), America has a particularly sympathetic ear for former residents who warn of the continent's dangers. In some cases, denouncers slip out of cyberspace and into other forms of American media. The controversial former talk-show host Jani Allan has, for instance, featured on the Republican Broadcasting Network, speaking, among other things, against 'Boer' genocide, calling for aid for Afrikaner 'refugees' (*Sunday Independent*, 20 June 2004: 3) and linking events in Africa to a 'new world order'.

Even in the United States, though, there are few public platforms willing to entertain the extremist viewpoints of these expatriates, whose arguments are too openly skewed by their sense of marginalisation and political disempowerment. Their attempts to dramatise a collective cultural trauma (in Alexander's [2004] terms) out of white South African experience is thus relegated to cyberspace. As Alexander points out:

> Mediated mass communication allows traumas to be expressively dramatized and permits some of the competing interpretations to gain enormous persuasive power over others. At the same time, however, these representational processes become subject to the restrictions of news reporting, with their demands for concision, ethical neutrality and perspectival balance. (2004: 18)

The Internet not only provides a permissive forum for seditious viewpoints restricted by conventional media, but its 'inherent malleability of content' also offers a platform for the 'acting out of mythic realities' (Novak 1993: 6). This description of the virtual environment reads like Jacqueline Rose's definition of fantasy itself: 'Fantasy is supremely asocial. Doubly licentious, it creates a world of pleasure without obligation to what it is either permissible or possible, outside the realm of fantasy, to do' (1996: 2).

In this respect, the doctoring of news articles and videos can be seen as a kind of fantasy of news production.[19] The Internet generally offers the 'promise of control over the world by the power of will' (Novak 1993: 228), a world in which a 'combination of computer and verbal skills equals high status and prestige' (Bromberg 1996: 149). The formal title of 'editor', the cult-like fan mail from appreciative users, even the attention from less complimentary visitors to the site, can be seen as strategies of imagined re-empowerment.

The acute sense of marginalisation is nowhere more evident than in the plethora of letters addressed to prominent political figures, such as former South African president Thabo Mbeki, in which expatriate writers take on an imagined advisory capacity:

> Dear Mr Mbeki
>
> We are two of the tens of thousands of expatriate South Africans who are frequently bombarded with requests to return to help build the 'rainbow nation'.
>
> Unlike many we did not leave because of crime, instability or because of racial issues. Instead we were working in Mozambique and after receiving a job offer in Australia we decided to try it out.
>
> When we look at news from 'home' it is not the horror stories that prevent us from considering a return. Instead, Mr President, it is the way that you and your government are systematically reducing the Afrikaner's existence, language and legacy to a small pathetic resemblance of what it once had been. (Van Rensburgs 2007: 1)

Letters such as these provide writers with some sort of relief from their perceived political emasculation, as there is a good chance that they will be read by *somebody* in cyberspace at some point. The informal and direct address ('Mr Mbeki', 'you') implicitly plays with power reversal. Jani Allan's 'Letter in response to President Mbeki' also employs overly familiar terms:

> I have no personal vendetta against South African President Thabo Mbeki. Admittedly, when I had a radio show in Cape Town, I used to good-naturedly refer to him as M-Bek-One, since his name resembles the license plate of a car. But M-Bek-One evidently has a vendetta against me. (2004: 1)

The casual tone of the letter belies the inflated sense of self-importance at ever having received a response from Mbeki.

On another website frequented by expatriates (*Homecoming revolution*, discussed later in the article), forum users engaged in other forms of power-play, holding a mock election at one point, in which participants voted themselves and peers into political positions of power. Similarly, on the *I luv South Africa but I hate my government* blog, viewers are invited to participate in a poll: 'What do you think will be the end game for whites in South Africa?'

Alexander et al.'s (2004) exploration of cultural trauma and collective identity also explains some of the actions, specifically with regard to the very public nature of the memorialising some expatriates engage in. In a chapter on psychological and cultural trauma, Niel Smelser points out that in order for psychological trauma to transcend its individual boundaries, those interested in establishing the event as historically traumatic 'must speak in a language that will reach individuals as peoples' (2004: 41). For this reason, symbolic language, the language of 'negative affect' plays an important part. Entrance to the *Stop Boer genocide* website is preceded by visuals of moving cogs in a machine and a 12-day 'soul walk' across England to raise awareness of the farm attacks, which involved tying yellow memorial ribbons on lampposts and other public structures. This links to actions taken by farmers within South Africa; in Limpopo province, farmers erected a memorial to victims of farm attacks on a green hillside. A large white cross made up of scores of small white crosses sits below the word '*plaasmoorde*' [farm murders].

Such activities, together with the production of Afropessimist discourse, the adoption of the persecuted 'Boer' identity and the attempted portrayal of violence in South Africa as racially motivated genocide, speak not only of a profound sense of marginalisation which skews much of the commentary on events in the country, but also of attempts to redefine white South African identity in the global sphere.

'This used to be my playground': remedies for homesick South Africans

White expatriates' involvement in the spread of Afropessimism is also evident on sites that are less explicitly engaged in identity revision. The trauma of geographical dislocation transpires in what might be seen as an 'appetite' for Afropessimism in the flood of responses to a blog called *Death of Johannesburg*.[20]

Seemingly less a-social, *Death of Johannesburg* bills itself as a 'blog illustrating the collapse and urban decay of inner-city Johannesburg in the "new" South Africa … the things that tourists are not told about'. Run by a one-time resident of the city, who refers to himself as 'Real Realist' and whose current location is not disclosed, the blog is featured on *African crisis*, *South Africa sucks* and is discussed in a host of other blog forums on the web. Its graphic nature has attracted the collective gaze of the online expatriate community, and the majority of commentators appear to be living outside of South Africa. Though it shares a similar aim with previously discussed sites – i.e. to unveil issues not covered in mainstream media – the blog's content and methods differ markedly. Apparently simple, it features photographs of landmark buildings, parks, monuments and streets (such as the Carlton Hotel and Jeppe Street), which have, for various reasons, fallen to wrack and ruin. Sometimes the photographs are featured alongside earlier images of the areas. Where there are no earlier images to give a sense of narrative, stirring captions accompany the photographs:

> Once the Carlton Hotel was a rich status symbol for Johannesburg; an internationally renowned establishment where the moneyed and the famous wined, dined and slept in style … The 600-room hotel, which took seven years to build, opened in 1972 – and closed in 1997 – because it became too dangerous for people to stay there, attacked as they were if they dared venture out into the surrounding streets. Today it stands empty, a slowly crumbling and deserted ruin, stripped of its finishings, symbolic of the New South Africa, just waiting to die …[21]

One obviously intended interpretation of the blog's formula is that the current government's mismanagement is slowly eroding South African infrastructure. The underlying interpretation is more insulting, exposing the flimsy line between Afropessimist and racist thinking. As one anonymous visitor put it: 'THEY build nothing; THEY only destroy.' And another: 'This is typical of what Africans do to there [sic] countries they have no real concept of how to run any enterprise or venture they are very often too tribal and parochial.'

In general, there is a direct proportion between the severity of the Afropessimist discourse expressed on sites and the anonymity provided by the web interface, with groups on seemingly transparent social networking groups (such as MySpace and Facebook) attracting fewer members and little conversation, whereas blogs that permit anonymous postings frequently regress into overtly prejudiced discussion. Since most of the postings on blogs such as *Death of Johannesburg* and *South Africa sucks* are anonymous, alarmingly racist sentiments, fuelling pessimistic content, proliferate. In addition, the nameless nature of the comments makes it virtually impossible for visitors to engage in discussion with one another, so that viewpoints remain unchallenged.

Once again, as with the more extremist sites, the *Death of Johannesburg* blog is occasionally visited by foreigners who are quick to express their dismay and sympathy (e.g. 'What a terrible loss for everyone who worked so hard to build your beautiful country' and 'God help you'). But most of the comments come from nostalgic South Africans living abroad, many of whom have not returned to the country for some time. The photographs appear to have a profound effect on these expatriates, whose most common refrain is brokenheartedness. Tearful comments pour forth in response to the photographs:

> We lived in Swaziland in the 70s and used to travel to Joburg and stay at the Carlton often … what a shame to see these pics.! I can't believe this can happen in S.A. in the middle of Joburg. What is going to happen to the centre? Just crumble and decay! (Anonymous)

> Looking at these pictures have sent a chill down my spine and the realisation how bad Jo'burg has deteriorated. (Jim)

> These pictures shocked me to the core. (Anonymous)

> How sad to see the Carlton Hotel like this. It used to be just awesome to go to The Top of The Carlton for drinks and snacks after work on a Friday … What on earth is happening there? (Rene Halstead, Perth, Western Australia – ex Jhb)

> I cry as I see these pictures. I lived there once. It was my home. (Anonymous)

> Man i am saddened by these pictures. Hillbrow used to be my playground in the early 80s as well as Rockey Street with the speak easy etc ... (Anonymous)

> Oh my God how can this be … I will cry tonight. (Jasmine Ogden Richards)

In spite or perhaps because of the heartbreaking effect of viewing the photographs, the site has found its way into most expatriate forums, and the stark graphics appear to be trusted more than conventional news media. Site visitors frequently praise the blogger for his 'honesty' and thank him for establishing the site. In addition, requests for further images of once-familiar areas and old haunts flood in.

The Johannesburg narrative is a powerful one, reflected on other Internet platforms like YouTube (see Evans 2009) where expatriate users have posted emotionally charged videos documenting the city's decline. The link between landscape, space and identity provides a useful means of examining expatriate responses to these images. Richard Ballard points out that 'our sense of space and self are mutually constitutive' (2004: 50) and that emigration can be seen as an extreme response to a sense of dislocation (ibid: 52), with gated communities, for instance, representing a less radical reaction. Indeed, on many of the sites, emigration is referred to as 'voting with the feet'. The majority of respondents to the site resist what others term South Africa's 'Africanisation', which is equated on the site with decline and eventual death. The 2010 Soccer World Cup loomed large in these predictions. Photographs of the Johannesburg Municipal Bus Depot elicited the following responses:

> Maybe I can catch a nice bus there, after leaving my pleasant safe hotel, to go to a World Cup game? Well, maybe not. (Anonymous)

> So what's the problem … looks ready for the world cup soccer ahead of schedule!!!!! ha ha ha. (Anonymous)

Responses such as these indicate a reaction other than heartbreak, and the enjoyment of the city's supposed demise is difficult to understand. A certain predictable glee often attends expatriate responses to news of national crises or failures. Elsewhere, discussants claim to participate in debate about the country's future for 'pure amusement' (UKandLovingIt on *Homecoming revolution*), widening the chasm between them and white South Africans still living in the country.[22] Events such as the 2008 electricity crisis (which numerous expatriates and much mainstream media attributed to the failings of affirmative action) and reports on corruption and incompetence quickly find their way into expatriate channels, and continued negativity and pessimism seem to operate as a panacea for any form of residual doubt and/or guilt about having left.

Thus, just as photographs of South African landscapes pull at the heartstrings of homesick expatriates, so images of urban decay have the effect of alleviating this sentiment and confirming the rightness of their decision to emigrate. Scores of respondents express their relief at having fled. User 'Happy to be here' succinctly sums up the effect:

> Someone sent me a link to this site, and I have to say that it's both the most depressing and most gratifying thing I have seen in a long time.
>
> Most depressing because I can remember the way the place used to be back in the late 80s and early 90s even. I can remember walking home from Bella's at 3am on New Year's day, unmolested. Look at the place now. No way could I do that safely.
>
> It's also the most gratifying thing I have seen, because it makes me really appreciate what I have now, having made the decision back in '98 to pack up and get out of there.

The satisfaction of being 'proved right' frequently comes up in discussion, with one expatriate describing the feeling of hearing bad news about South Africa thus: 'Basically it's affirmation of what is probably the biggest decision in your life' (SuperJohn, 28 July 2008, *Homecoming revolution*). For some, the perceived chaos projected by the images also soothes homesickness or nostalgia:

> I have lost hope for South Africa yes, but I still miss it, when I see documentaries I miss the nature, and everything. Then I hope again, I hope that someday my children will be able to live where I grew up. But that doesn't last long, I will get a txt from a friend telling me that you now pay R11 for a bread! what?! Then I loose it all again. each time I'm dissapointed in myself for believing that it can work out. Maybe I'm naive… I don't know, but no, we don't find glee in things that goes wrong, it saddens me deeply and then like Daxk said, it is a feeling of: 'I knew it was going to happen.' (Cecile, 31 July 2008, *Homecoming revolution*)
>
> *sigh* … those were the days.
>
> Now its all just f%$*!d … so so sad. Where's the nostalgia for us now?!?!
>
> FYI - nostalgia [nos·tal·gi·a} n. feeling of longing for the past or bygone things, sentimentality.
>
> None of that here my friend. 'Proudly se moer!!' (Anonymous, n.d. *Death of Johannesburg*)

As with many Afropessimist texts, the overriding feature of the *Death of Johannesburg* blog is imbalance, which some visitors point out, citing instances of urban development elsewhere in Johannesburg to counter the negative portrayal of the city's reality. Once again, the site appears to constitute a kind of fantasy of news production, as mainstream media coverage tends to focus on urban renewal and development.[23] In some cases, the blogger appears to have fabricated, or at least oversimplified, the reasons for the city's transformation. One commentator pointed out that the once-famous Three Castles Building, featured now as 'just another ruin', was in actual fact burnt down as part of an insurance scam, and the photographs cannot be viewed as factual evidence of the blogger's central thesis. Others argue that the decay featured on the site has more to do with integration after apartheid and that it is narrow-minded ever to have viewed South Africa as First World. Elsewhere on the blog, South African locals point out that some of the photographs are out of date, sometimes even emailing updated versions of the area, and that the featured areas (such as Wits Drill Hall) have been or are being upgraded. Others list the various agents and sites of urban renewal.

Although these oppositional voices usually come from informed locals still living in the country, whereas the blogger's location is undisclosed, the tenor of the blog remains cynical, at times sliding into dubious speculation about the benefits of apartheid and interpreting the images as a justification for recolonisation:

> This may sound very strange, but maybe south africa was better off with the apartheid system. yes, it was true that the former nationalist gov't was very harsh, but at least JoBurg was a so called 'showcase city'. (Anonymous)

> I am somewhat of a liberal, but I have to say, I am not pleased with the New South Africa. I really think moderate white governing was the answer. I honestly think all African countries were better off as British Colonies. (Anonymous)

> We should take back the country, it belongs to the Whites, we built it up, in which other African country have Black people made a success of what they do? (Anonymous)

The disclaimers that precede so many of the user comments – 'this may sound very strange, but …' and 'I am somewhat of a liberal, but …' – like the 'I am not a racist, but …' rider are frequently followed by commentary rooted in racist thinking, which often forms the backbone of expatriate attempts to explain their decision to leave.

Confirming the accuracy of predicted reasons for emigrating appears to be one of the central factors behind much of the Afropessimist discourse expressed by expatriates (Moerdyk 2008: 2). Nowhere is this more evident than in the discussions that take place on the *Homecoming revolution* website, which aims to reverse the so-called 'brain drain'.

The Homecoming revolution: *emigration, disempowerment and revenge*

Launched in 2003 by Angel Jones of MorrisJones&Costet, the *Homecoming revolution* was initially an independent non-profit project. Its success in making contact with potential homecomers[24] attracted the sponsorship of First National Bank in 2004 and a series of adverts was launched at the beginning of 2005, sporting slogans such as: 'Don't wait until it gets better, come home and make it even better.'

In addition to high-profile conferences, e-newsletters and corporate advertising, the initiative, run by a small group with PR and advertising expertise, involves the website, which, like other sites such as *South Africa: the good news*[25] publishes optimistic news about the country to counter what they see as the negative publicity it receives overseas. Patriotic optimism sums up the tone of the site, which tries to portray South Africa if not as a country of promise, then at least as 'just another country', with problems like any other. 'There are always going to be government policies you aren't going to agree with or social issues that require some work' (e-newsletter, 25 November 2005), their newsletter tells its readers.

As with the *Death of Johannesburg* blog, many of the responses on the site can be seen as ordinary reactions to geographical displacement. Finding oneself in the milieu of an alien culture has been identified as a major source of cultural trauma in the 20th century (Sztompka 2004: 162–163), and the feverish online activity in which expatriates increasingly engage suggests that the Internet is sought as a means of alleviating the trauma of large-scale geographical shifts. The rush of requests for more photographs from the *Death of Johannesburg* blogger attests to this, as do other expatriate websites such as http://www.zimdays.com, which features photographs of Zimbabwean landscapes and suburbs. *Homecoming revolution* users have created long threads listing aspects of South African life that they miss (many of them from childhood), and one commentator openly states:

> Why do I feel homesick so often? Does Africa run so strong in one's veins! Not a day passes where I am not thinking about SA and reading the online newspapers, it's almost like I wish myself to be there. The stories in the newspaper are enough to scare the hell out of any God fearing man but still there's something that I cannot get out of my system. Some say 'that's because your heart is in SA' and 'home is where the heart is'. (Silverfox 5 May 2008)[26]

Because of its mission, however, over the years, the site has attracted a number of vehemently pessimistic commentators who, because of their lack of faith in the country's economic and political future, see the initiative as irresponsible. Many are highly suspicious of the site's motives, seeing the postings as 'propaganda' and ANC funded. The forum has undergone numerous transformations in an attempt to keep forum postings in line with its aim. First, proper login procedures were imposed in the belief that getting participants to identify themselves would curb the invective. When this did not work, the forum was dissolved because, as Megan Woods explained, it 'started attracting the worst kind of racists and pessimists who were just looking for a place to whinge' (pers. comm., 25 February 2005).

The forum was resurrected as a blog, administered by an embattled moderator. While this resulted in the elimination of overtly racist sentiments, Afropessimism still pervaded discussions. According to MD Martine Schaffer, the same core group of people commented on the blog for over four years (pers. comm., 33 July 2008), and the site administrators considered 'banning' these users from commenting on the blog (see Jordan 2008). In April 2009 the team dissolved the blog, stating that 'within the context of current strategy and operations, there is no alignment'. It was re-launched in August 2009, with stricter measures put in place and the declaration that 'The Homecoming Revolution has taken ownership of the space in which we operate'. There are now only a select number of comments that filter through the gatekeepers.

Understandably, the organisation is eager to distance itself from expatriate projections, but in all kinds of ways, and largely because of its white expatriate target market, the initiative finds itself trapped by Afropessimist discourse, and at times displays discomfort with its own identity and purpose. In the former blogs, posts from users describing their 'reasons to return' were, for instance, increasingly replaced with posts citing 'reasons to stay', and users commonly asked why the website needed to advertise South Africa, arguing that if the country were a land of real opportunity, then expatriates would soon return.

In an attempt to steer conversations towards optimistic conversation, typical threads opened with a posted article reporting on a positive event in South Africa (e.g. 'Living standards have improved: Stats SA'), a stirring photograph of a landscape (e.g. of a lion kill in the Kruger Park) or simply an analysis of a political or social trend. These were then refuted by many of the site visitors, either through discussion or through pasted links to articles that paint a different picture – frequently reports on crime. In most cases the postings attempted to sabotage the mission of the initiative. When queried about their presence on the site, many defended their actions by adopting an activist stance, claiming that it is their patriotic duty to raise awareness of the implications of events in their country: 'We roundly criticise, not to justify our decision (in fact that argument applies far more readily to those who stayed or returned which is why they get so irrationally defensive), but to shout the warning and show possible paths to redemption' (god, 12 February 2008). A similar point is made on another forum elsewhere on the site: ' … my little voice is out there pointing out their [the ANC's] little tricks and attempts to hide things. and it's just as effective as the little shopgirls in Dunnes, Dublin, refusing to sell Outspan oranges because of apartheid' (Daxk, 23 April 2008).[27]

The reference to apartheid sanctions is interesting, since other users openly confess to adversely influencing foreign investment, wherever possible, in order to cripple the country:

> And I save them [investors] money. loads of it. By doing projects all over the world (except South Africa, of course). And they are listening. Because of the input I give into decision making processes regarding expansions and developments in South Africa.
>
> So yes, they are listening. As you will soon find out in the news – specifically regarding investment in South Africa. Unfortunately, for South Africa, it wont be good news. but then, they brought it upon themselves, didn't they? (Born2Run, 1 February 2008)[28]

The vengeful tone of this and other statements implies that some expatriates utilise their economic clout as well as the prevailing nervousness around Africa in the West not only to restore a sense of control over the country, but also as a means of exacting some form of revenge.

Linked to this is the complaint about the global community's role in the fall of apartheid. On various online platforms, expatriates claim that the parties that put pressure on the government to end apartheid will now see the results of their actions. 'Where is the rest of the world now? They were the ones who pushed for this,' user butchkatravis (now living in Australia) asks in response to a dystopic portrayal of the 'new' South Africa on YouTube. Similarly, HansieSlim (an active YouTube user now residing in the UK) claims to create a distorted picture of South Africa because it is the 'same technique that the mass media used for decades to create the false impression that apartheid SA was an evil place'. Many expatriates now live in the very countries which put pressure on the government to end apartheid. A frustration with host countries' 'complicity' in their disempowerment is evident in numerous comments: 'I am in complete agreement with the points you make about the hippocritical Australians, who killed their indigenous peoples and maintained a whites only policy at the same time as they were condemning Apartheid South Africa internationally and with sanctions' (Rensburg, 19 February 2008, *Homecoming revolution*).

The video postings and user comments, which in many cases utilise existing media portrayals, can be seen as an attempt to draw the attention of the global sphere to their mistake in meddling in South African affairs under apartheid. In most cases, the error that they wish to highlight links back to one of the core premises of Afropessimism: the belief that Africa is incapable of self-rule.

Conclusion

Edward Said points out in *Reàections on exile* that 'exile is a jealous state … Exiles look at non-exiles with resentment … an exile is always out of place' (2002: 208). While a distinction needs to be made between the expatriate and the exile, this goes some way to explaining the heated debates that occur between those who decided to leave and those who chose to stay. Frequently, responses from white South African expatriate Internet users appear to be informed by more than the events themselves, and perceived marginalisation, a skewed sense of political disempowerment, the urge to justify the decision to emigrate and the traumatic effects of geographical displacement colour their responses to the country.

Although Internet forums do not necessarily provide a survey of trends in expatriate thinking, the high visibility of Afropessimism on blogs and on platforms such as YouTube is cause for concern. Firstly, because it indicates that events in South Africa are rapidly distancing it from world opinion, and secondly, because the country's future failure is increasingly being represented as a *fait accompli*. The profusion of blogs and the cut-and-paste way in which links are created hastens the effect.

In addition, the Internet is just one medium in which the future of South Africa is discussed by white expatriates. The vehemence of the discussion suggests that their involvement in the scattering of Afropessimism extends to other spheres as well, particularly since they are able to feed into 'an existing strand of international sympathy which writes off Africa' (Steyn 2001: 21). Their discourse, persistently negative and implicitly racist, is increasingly dominating online reactions to events in the country, making it more and more difficult to set up counter-discourses at a time when astute analysis is needed.

Notes

1. See, for instance, Andrew Feinstein's *After the party* (2007) and Terry Crawford-Browne's *Eye on the money* (2007), which allege that there was widespread government corruption in connection with the arms deal of the late 1990s. Other widely reported scandals include the 2004–2006 travel 'scam' (also referred to as 'Travelgate'), in which 14 members of parliament pleaded guilty to abusing parliamentary travel vouchers, as well as the 2006 ruling on Schabir Shaik (in which Shaik was found guilty of soliciting a bribe for then Deputy President Jacob Zuma from arms dealer Thomson-CSF).
2. According to the South African Network of Skills Abroad, the most popular destinations for South Africans are the United Kingdom (UK), Australia, New Zealand, the United States and Canada (Louw & Mersham 2001: 304).
3. An estimated 70 000 *South Africans* are thought to have left the country between 1989 and 1992 (*Economist* 2005). Because of the anonymous nature of Internet postings, however, it is sometimes difficult to determine exactly when participants emigrated. Where possible, the details of commentators have been included.
4. http://dienuwesuidafrika.blogspot.com
5. http://iluvsa.blogspot.com/2011/02/south-africa-sucks-v8.html
6. Orania refers to an all-Afrikaner enclave in the Northern Cape province of South Africa. Forty Afrikaner families bought the town in December 1990, the year the ANC was unbanned. See http://www.orania.co.za/ for the official website.
7. http://africancrisis.co.za
8. http://stopboergenocide.com
9. Terre'Blanche was the leader of the white right-wing *Afrikaner Weerstandsbeweging* [Afrikaner Resistance Movement].

10 There have been two inquiries into the attacks in farming communities. Pressure from unions led to the 2001 Inquiry into Farm Attacks. In the same year, Human Rights Watch produced a report. The SAPS report concluded that the attacks are particularly violent in nature (ibid: 420) and that the elderly are common targets (ibid: 419) – both issues raised by the agricultural unions and featured frequently on the *Stop Boer genocide* and *African crisis* sites, which appear to have strong links with the unions. But one of the major suspicions of the unions – i.e. that the attacks are racially motivated – was dispelled by the report findings, which concluded that in 89.3 per cent of cases the motive was robbery, while in only 2 per cent of the attacks could a political or racial motive be discerned (Committee of Inquiry into Farm Attacks, *Final report* 2003: 419).

While the independence of the SAPS investigation may be questioned (and was heavily criticised by agricultural unions), the findings of Human Rights Watch would suggest that the SAPS investigation is fairly sympathetic to unions and (mainly white) farm owners. Titled 'Unequal protection', the 2001 report concludes that the rural protection plan has led to the 'increased insecurity' of black farm residents, who have become the targets of 'sometimes indiscriminate "anti-crime" initiatives', and that the plan has 'failed to respond to crime committed against black farm residents, particularly crime committed by white farm owners' (Human Rights Watch 2001). Contrary to the portrayal of the SAPS as 'doing nothing' and as 'openly hostile towards the Boer nation' (*Stop Boer genocide*), the Human Rights Watch report concludes that 'the police in commercial farming areas have been mobilised to treat crime against farm owners as a particular priority' (2001), and are 'frequently unresponsive, even hostile', to farm workers and residents wishing to report assaults by farm owners or managers (ibid.).

11 See also the website titled 'Stop white genocide' (http://stopwhitegenocide.praag.org).

12 In 2006, Charles Nqakula famously made the following comment, directed at negative opposition members of parliament:

They can continue to whinge until they're blue in the face, they can continue to be as negative as they want to or they can simply leave this country so that all of the peace-loving South Africans, good South African people who want to make this a successful country, can continue with their work. (cited in Da Costa 2006: 1)

The comment was much criticised in the South African media and was quoted extensively in South African expatriate forums.

13 In 2007, after Zuma was elected as president of the ANC, the new NEC suggested that a high-profile crime-fighting group, affectionately referred to as 'The Scorpions', be disbanded because of its potential to abuse its power. The suggestion met with much criticism in the media, which widely interpreted the move as an attempt to protect potentially corrupt political elite targeted by the Scorpions. The Scorpions have since been disbanded.

14 An electricity supply 'crisis' in early 2008 saw numerous blackouts and widespread 'load-shedding' throughout South Africa. Various explanations were offered in the media, ranging from theft of cables and skills shortages, to demand outstripping supply.

15 Necklacing refers to a method of lynching that became common during South Africa's struggle against apartheid in the 1980s and 90s. Necklacing sentences were frequently used to punish black community members who had been exposed as apartheid spies or collaborators.

16 Now located at http://www.africancrisis.co.za/Article.php?ID=47276. Many of the photos originally viewed were not available when last viewed in April 2011, due (according to Lamprecht) to indiscriminate hacking as well as the Internet host's refusal to continue hosting the website: 'So the real reason the Farm Murders and many other photos disappeared was because of Readyhosting shutting my site down despite me discussing the matter with them several times.'

17 Queries to members of the Transvaal Agricultural Union about the origins of the photographs remain unanswered.

18 The *Citizen* uncovered links with an organisation calling itself the Gay and Lesbian Alliance, which had previously provoked public outcry by threatening to have its members donate blood without disclosing their sexual status as a protest against a ban on gay blood donors. The Alliance was largely dismissed as bogus by other gay and lesbian organisations, which were unable to establish any proof of membership (Evans 2006).

19 I am indebted to André Wiesner for this observation.

20 http://deathofjohannesburg.blogspot.com/
21 See URL above.
22 This is evidenced by denigrating titles such as 'ostrich', 'chicken runner' and 'nimby'. The term 'ostrich' is frequently used to describe whites who chose to stay in post-apartheid South Africa because of expatriate perceptions of their sticking their head in the sand and remaining in a blinkered state to the realities of transformation. 'Chicken runners' is used to describe expatriates who are seen as cowardly. Nimby stands for 'not in my back yard' and refers to middle-class individuals not wishing to tolerate integration.
23 A *Sunday Independent* article, for instance, featured the city's 'regeneration' (see Corrigall 2008: 2).
24 In 2007, the average number of monthly visitors was 12 391 (pers. comm. 14 February 2008).
25 http://www.sagoodnews.co.za/
26 Silverfox left South Africa in 2001, citing 'crime, BEE and AA' as his reasons for emigrating.
27 Daxk left South Africa for Ireland in 2005, describing himself as a 'refugee from crime' after experiencing an armed hijacking only to be confronted by his attackers one month later.
28 Born2run left South Africa 'a few years ago', claiming he has 'little hope for South Africa's future'.

References

African crisis. 2006. South Africa: what whites can do practically, 26 August. http://www.africancrisis.co.za/Article.php?ID=8599& (accessed 14 March 2008).

Alexander, A. 2004. Toward a theory of cultural trauma. In *Cultural trauma and collective identity*, ed. A. Alexander et al., 1–30. Berkeley: University of California Press.

Alexander, J.C., R. Eyerman, B. Giesen, N.J. Smelser and P. Sztompka. 2004. *Cultural trauma and collective identity*. Berkeley: University of California Press.

Allan, J. 2004. Letter in response to President Mbeki, *JRNY Quist*, 6 October: 1. http://www.jrnyquist.com/jani_allan_letter_on_mbeki.htm (accessed 5 May 2008.)

Ballard, R. 2004. Assimilation, emigration, semigration and integration: 'white' peoples' strategies for finding a comfort zone in post-apartheid South Africa. In *Under construction: 'race' and identity in South Africa today*, ed. N. Distiller and M. Steyn, 51–66. Sandton: Heinemann.

Balseiro, I. 1997. *Simunye*? Searching for nationhood in post-apartheid South Africa. *Communicare* 16(1): 1–18.

Berger, G. 2001. Problematising race for journalists: critical reflections on the South African Human Rights Commission Inquiry into Media Racism. *Critical Arts* 15(1 & 2): 69–96.

Bromberg, H. 1996. Are MUDs communities? Identity, belonging and consciousness in virtual worlds. In *Cultures of Internet: virtual spaces, real histories, living bodies*, ed. R.R. Shields, 143–152. London and New Delhi: Thousand Oaks and Sage Publications.

Cinman, J. 2008. The pitter patter of expats. *Mail & Guardian* Thoughtleader blog, 21 July. http://www.thoughtleader.co.za/burningpaper/2008/07/21/the-pitter-patter-of-the-ex-pats/ (accessed 29 July 2008).

Committee of Inquiry into Farm Attacks. 2003. *Final report*, 31 July. http://www.saps.gov.za/statistics/reports/farmattacks/farmattacks_2003.htm (accessed 1 July 2008).

Corrigall, M. 2008. Recycling a city: exploring Jo'burg's regeneration. *Sunday Independent*, Sunday Life Section, 10 February: 2.

Crawford-Browne, T. 2007. *Eye on the money: one man's crusade against corruption*. Cape Town: Umuzi.

Da Costa, W.J. 2006. Crime whingers can leave, says Nqakula. *CapeArgus*, 2 June: 1. http://www.iol.co.za/index.php?set_id=1&click_id=13&art_id=vn20060602104812572C523307 (accessed 2 February 2008.)

Davidson, B. 1992. *The black man's burden: Africa and the curse of the nation state*. London: James Curry.

Davis, J., ed. 2007. *Africa and the war on terrorism*. Hampshire and Burlington: Ashgate Publishing.

Eaton, T. 2005. Homecoming devolution. *Mail & Guardian*, 14–20 January.

Economist, The. 2005. Home sweet home – for some. Issue 376 (8439), 13 August.

Evans, J. 2006. Gay blood protest: did it really happen? *Mail & Guardian online*, January 16. http://ww2.mg.co.za/article/2006-01-16-gay-blood-protest-did-it-really- happen (accessed 9 July 2008).

Evans, M. 2009. *Uit die blou*: nostalgia for the 'old' South Africa on YouTube. *Journal of Global Mass Communication* 2 (1&2): 47–65.

Feinstein A. 2007. *After the party: a personal and political journey inside the ANC*. Cape Town: Jonathan Ball.

Guest, R. 2005. *The shackled continent: Africa's past, present and future*. London: Macmillan.

Hall, M. 2000. Digital SA. In *Senses of culture: South African culture studies*, ed. S. Nuttall and C.A. Michaels, 460–478. Cape Town: Oxford University Press Southern Africa.

Homecoming revolution. 2005. *Homecoming revolution* e-newsletter, 13 December.

Human Rights Watch. 2001. *Unequal protection: the state response to violent crime on South Africa's farms*. USA: Human Rights Watch. http://www.hrw.org/reports/2001/safrica2/(accessed 9 July 2008).

Hydén, G. 1996. African studies in the mid-1990s: between Afropessimism and Amero-skepticism. *African Studies Review* 39(2): 1–17.

Jooste, B. 2008. Packing for Perth and Piccadilly. *Cape Times*, 30 March: 8.

Jordan, E. 2008. Citizen ex. *Sandton online magazine*. http://www.sandtonmag.co.za/pages/421483389/Articles/2008/August/citizen-ex.asp (accessed 30 July 2008).

Kaplan, R.D. 1994. The coming anarchy: how scarcity, crime, overpopulation, tribalism, and disease are rapidly destroying the social fabric of our planet. *The Atlantic Monthly* (February).

Klaehn, J. 2005. *Filtering the news: essays on Chomsky's propaganda model*. Montreal: Black Rose Books.

Lamprecht, J. n.d. Farm murders in South Africa (1994–present). http://www.africancrisis.org/photos45.asp (accessed 4 May 2008).

Lonsdale, J. 2004. Moral and political argument in Kenya. In *Ethnicity and democracy in Africa*, ed. B. Berman, D. Eyoh and W. Kymlicka, 73–95. Oxford and Athens: James Currey and Ohio University Press.

Louw, E. and G. Mersham. 2001. Packing for Perth: the growth of a southern African Diaspora. *Asian and Pacific Migration Journal* 10(2): 303–333.

Martin, W.G. 2008. Africa's futures: from north-south to east-south? *Third World Quarterly* 29(2): 339–356.

Mbembe, A. 2002. African modes of self-writing. *Public Culture* 14(1): 239–273.

Mentan, T. 2004. *Dilemmas of weak states: Africa and transnational terrorism in the twenty-first century*. Aldershot and Burlington: Ashgate Publishing.

Moerdyk, C. 2008. Expats are trashing SA. *News24*, 12 February: 1–2. http://www.news24.com/News24/Columnists/Chris_Moerdyk/0,,2-1630-2224_2269003,00.html (accessed 6 May 2008).

Moyo, D. 2007. Alternative media, diasporas and the mediation of the Zimbabwe crisis. *Ecquid Novi: African Journalism Studies* 28(1 & 2): 81–105.

Museveni, Y.K. 2000. *What is Africa's problem?* Minneapolis: University of Minnesota Press.

Novak, M. 1993. Liquid architectures in cyberspace. In *Cyberspace: first steps*, ed. M. Benedikt, 225–254. Cambridge (MA): MIT Press.

Olukoshi, A. 1999. State, conflict, and democracy in Africa: the complex process of renewal. In *State, conflict, and democracy in Africa*, ed. R. Joseph, 451–466. Boulder Colorado and London: Lynne Rienner Publishers.

Onwudiwe, E. 1995. Image and development: an exploratory discussion. *Journal of African Policy Studies* 1(3): 85–97.

Richman, T. 2007. Bitter expats. In *Is it just me or is everything kak? The whinger's guide to South Africa, from AA to JZ*, ed. T. Richman and G. Schreiber, 20. Cape Town: Two Dogs.

Robins, S. 2004. 'The (third) world is a ghetto'?: looking for a third space between 'postmodern' cosmopolitanism and cultural nationalism. *CODESRIA Bulletin* (1 & 2): 18–26.

Roper, C. 2008. A hypothetical apocalypse. *News24*, 9 July. http://www.news24.com/News24/Columnists/Chris_Roper/0,,2-1630-1649_2354327,00.html (accessed 12 July 2008).

Rose, J. 1996. *States of fantasy*. Oxford: Clarendon Press.

Said, E.W. 2002. *Reflections on exile and other essays*. Cambridge (MA): Harvard University Press.

Sara, S. 2001. White farmers threaten to publish farm murder photos on net. *AM*, 24 March, ABC radio transcripts. http://www.abc.net.au/am/stories/s265479.htm (accessed 3 March 2008).

Schaffer, M. 2008. Personal communication (via e-mail), 23 July.

Shaw, M. 2002. *Crime and policing in South Africa: transforming under fire*. Bloomington and Indianapolis: Indiana University Press.

Sky News. 2006. Farmers killed in South Africa, 23 May. http://news. sky.com/skynews/Home/video/Farmers-Killed-In-South-Africa/Video/200605414158849?lid=VIDEO_14158849_Farmers%20Killed%20In%20 South%20Africa&lpos=searchresults (accessed 21 July 2008).

Smelser, N. J. 2004. Psychological trauma and cultural trauma. In *Cultural trauma and collective identity*, ed. A. Alexander et al., 31–59. Berkeley: University of California Press.

Spies, D. 2006. 'Sabotage' claim by SA crime website's creator. *Herald*, n.d. http://www.epherald.co.za/herald/2006/07/14/news/n08_14072006.htm (accessed 10 July 2008).

Stephney, I. 2000. Technology beyond the frontiers of history: the role of the Internet in reshaping peoples' place in time. *International Conference on Memory and Forgiving in the Life of the Nation and the Community*, 9–11 August 2000, Cape Town: 1–9.

Steyn, M. 2001. 'White talk': white South Africans and the management of diasporic whiteness. *The burden of race?: Conference on Whiteness and Blackness in Modern South Africa*, 5–9 July 2001, History Workshop and Wits Institute for Social and Economic Research, University of the Witwatersrand, Johannesburg: 1–30.

Steyn, M. 2004. Rehybridizing the creole: new South African Afrikaners. In *Under construction: 'race' and identity in South Africa today*, ed. N. Distiller and M. Steyn, 70–85. Sandton: Heinemann.

Sunday Independent. 2004. Whites are facing genocide, says Jani Allan. 20 June: 3.

Swart, W. and P. Kirk. 2006. Crime website linked to shady gay 'activist'. *Citizen*, 13 November. http://www.citizen.co.za/index/article.aspx?pDesc=27414,1,22 (accessed 9 January 2008).

Sztompka, P. 2004. The trauma of social change. In *Cultural trauma and collective identity*, ed. J.C. Alexander, 155–195. Berkeley, Los Angeles, London: University of California Press.

Transvaal Agricultural Union. 2008. Personal communication (via e-mail), 14 February.

Tsagarousianou, R. 2004. Rethinking the concept of Diaspora: mobility, connectivity and communication in a globalised world. *Westminster Papers in Communication and Culture* 1(1): 52–65.

United Nations Office on Drugs and Crime. 2002. *The eighth United Nations survey on crime trends and the operations of the criminal justice system*. Austria: Centre for International Crime Prevention.

Van der Westhuizen, C. 2007. *White power: the rise and fall of the National Party*. Cape Town: Zebra Press.

Van Rensburg, T. and R. van Rensburg. 2007. Open letter to Mr Mbeki. *Die Burger* blogspot, 3 May: 1. http://dieburgerblogs.mweb.co.za/ViewBlog.aspx?blogid=43&pageno=8 (accessed 6 May 2008).

Vena, V. 2010. Anatomy of a farm murder. *Mail & Guardian online*, 8 April. http://mg.co.za/article/2010-04-08-anatomy-of-a-farm-murder (accessed 18 April 2011).

Wieviorka, M. 1995. *The arena of racism*. London: Sage.

Williams, J. 2006. Crime expo website disappears from the net. *Independent online*, 22 November. http://www.iol.co.za/index.php?set_id=1&click_id=13&artid=iol1164192268745C651 (accessed 9 July 2008).

Woods, M. 2005. Personal communication (via e-mail), 25 February.

'Did He Freeze?': Afrofuturism, Africana Womanism, and Black Panther's Portrayal of the Women of Wakanda

Tiffany Thames Copeland

ABSTRACT

Some have viewed the internationally acclaimed blockbuster hit, the Black Panther film, as feminist; meanwhile, others have highlighted its aspects of African culture focusing on its traditional elements and Afrofuturistic aspects. One of the main characters, Actress Lupita Nyong'o, who played Nakia said that *Black Panther* signifies a balanced representation of women and men, and she later alluded to feminism as she explained the balanced idyllic gender representation between the sexes. This study found that the roles of the leading women characters in this Afrofuturistic film—the top characters were derived from the IMDB's list—represented Africana womanism. The women at the heart of this study are warriors including Nakia, a War Dog of Wakanda; Okoye, the first lieutenant of the *Dora Milaje* and Ayo, a member; Princess Shuri, the head of Wakanda's technological division; the Queen Mother of Wakanda, Ramonda, who was King T'Challa and Princess Shuri's mother; and the *Merchant Tribe Elder* and the *Mining Tribe Elder of the Wakandan Tribal Council*. The egalitarian relationship between the women and the men in the film, and the representation of the women, showed a revisioning of African history in the recreation of an Afrofuturistic present. Thereby, the women's portrayal emerged from the wider egalitarian Wakandan society, which depicted a mythological African utopian nation, and yet, simultaneoulsy reignited an African historical reality.

The superhero science fiction film, *Black Panther*, which was directed by Ryan Coogler, grossed over a billion dollars globally and has been described by some as feminist (Harris, 2018; Spencer, 2018), while others focus on its Afrofuturistic components, considering it to include a hodgepodge of traditional African cultural elements (Sere et al., 2020). A New York Times article suggested that the film portrayed 'a futuristic African alternate reality – made up of diverse tribes and untouched by colonizers' (Ryzik, 2018) – ultimately showing an African utopia, also known by its racially-specific reference, a Blacktopia. Sere et al. (2020) described the African imagery in the film including a 'representation of African civilization through a symbol of vibranium, cultural ritual, [and] traditional costume.' Meanwhile, others concentrated on the representation of women. Harris (2018) said, '[T]his comic book movie might dare to become arguably the most feminist example of its kind to date.' *Black Panther* Actress Lupita Nyong'o said that *Black Panther* signifies a balanced representation of women and men, and she later alluded to feminism as she explained the balanced idyllic gender representation between the sexes:

> [Women are] allowed to realize their full potential alongside the men; and the men are not threatened by the power of the women, that the powers are complementary... So it's a real lesson for the real world. The feminist struggle is not to strip men of their power, it's a struggle for equality. (ABC News, 2018)

Spencer (2018) said in her popular *Medium* article called, *Black Feminist Meditations on the Women of Wakanda*, 'I asked myself how could a Black feminist lens enrich the vibrant conversations about the political meaning and historical resonance of this film?'

Black Panther has had such a wide-spreading reach – earning almost one and a half billion dollars internationally (The Walt Disney Company, 2018) – that it has become crucial to understand its ideology. Furthermore, Black Panther has been described as a celebration of Black culture (Johnson, 2018), making it highly important to assess the various aspects of this film.

Africana womanism and the women of Wakanda

This analysis incorporated Africana womanism as a framework for understanding the film's portrayal of women. Womanism was first used by Alice Walker (Glass, 2017), and it was theorized by Clenora Hudson-Weems. It was utilized as the ideal gendered approach to studying the representation of African women in Wakanda, rather than Intersectionality. Intersectionality stresses the importance of recognizing the interplay of race, class, and gender on women's lives, yet Africana womanism does not center in on socioeconomic class and instead considers the predominating influence of traditional African culture on Black women's behavior, making it ideally suitable for this study. The women under investigation comprise of the top characters in the film, and since they are the leaders of Wakanda and are either royalty themselves or are dealing directly with royalty, socioeconomic class is not a distinguishing factor in determining the differences or similarities in their portrayal – in fact, all these women are the elite of Wakanda. Further, Africana womanism was utilized because of its grounding in Africana culture, and because of its delineation of an egalitarian relationship between African women and men, making it well suited for this Afrofuturistic film. Further, this film's incorporation of black actresses and actors from all throughout Africa and the African diaspora, exposes its Pan-African orientation, or its centeredness in Africa along with its imbedded message for African unity.

Africana womanism is an Afrocentric theory that enables the researcher to investigate women of African descent from an African cultural standpoint instead of a European one. According to Sofola (2020), 'As a race, the most painful part of our experience with the Western world is the "dewomanization" of women of African descent.' She continues, 'Africana Womanism strongly makes the point that the Eurocentric definition of woman is alien and destructive to the woman of African heritage' (p. xii). Although, in an Afrofuturistic nation, the women adhere to positive traditional African values. Hudson-Weems described how Africana womanism is different from all the other attempts at theorizing women's experiences:

> *Africana Womanism* is an ideology created and designed for all women of African descent. It is grounded in African culture, and therefore, it necessarily focuses on the unique experiences,

struggles, needs, and desires of Africana women ... The conclusion is that *Africana Womanism* and its agenda are unique and separate from both White feminism and Black feminism, and moreover, to the extent of naming in particular, *Africana Womanism* differs from African feminism. (Hudson-Weems, 2020, p. 15)

Africana womanism's descriptors were used as a guide in critiquing *Black Panther*'s portrayal of the African women of Wakanda. Hudson-Weems described an Africana womanist as having eighteen positive descriptors based on African culture: she is a self-namer, a self-definer, family-centered, genuine in sisterhood, strong, in concert with men in the struggle, whole, authentic, a flexible role player, respected, recognized, spiritual, male compatible, respectful of elders, adaptable, ambitious, mothering, and nurturing (Hudson-Weems, 2020) – all of which are positive aspects, easily ideologized in an Afrofuturistic society. Therefore, this research conducted on the *Black Panther* film was completed with these outlining principles used as a guideline.

The women's roles in Black Panther were not in competition with men's roles. Even though the top two leading roles were played by men: the late American Actor Chadwick Boseman starred as King T'Challa and the Black Panther, and the American Actor Michael B. Jordan starred as his cousin and antagonist, Eric Killmonger – the women were all represented as the trusted leaders of Wakanda; they were the king's confidants and his wise and savvy advisors. These women – who lived in a patrilineal society – had strong and noble roles that were centered around T'Challa, who inherited the throne, becoming the *Black Panther* after his father, King T'Chaka (played by the South African Actor Bonisile John Kani) passed away after a detonated bomb attack at the Vienna International Centre. The Kenyan-Mexican Actress Nyong'o, who portrayed Nakia, a *War Dog* for Wakanda (a member of Wakanda's central intelligence), had a passion for community service. Nakia was King T'Challa's ex-girlfriend, and she helped him to realize the importance of engaging in community service and using their strong international position in the world to provide aid to the more vulnerable countries. Danai Gurira, the Zimbabwean-American actress who calls herself a "Zimerican," played the role of a *Dora Milaje* general in King T'Challa's all-women security unit. Florence Kasumba, a German actress born in Kampala, Uganda, played Ayo, who was also a member of the *Dora Milaje*. They helped him to win the battle for the throne as the head of the armed forces of Wakanda. The Guyanese-born British Actress Letitia Wright portrayed Princess Shuri, King T'Challa's junior sister, who was the head of Wakanda's innovative technical program. The American Actress Angela Bassett portrayed the Queen Mother of Wakanda role; she was King T'Challa's mother, constantly supporting him as he transitioned from being the prince to the king of Wakanda. The late American Actress Dorothy Steel, at 92 years old, played the role of the *Merchant Tribe Elder* and the South African Actress Connie Chiume played the *Mining Tribe Elder*, they both were advisors to King T'Challa. Most of these main characters aided T'Challa in regaining the throne from his cousin, Killmonger. Killmonger began using Wakanda's vibranium to create weapons and wage war on the world's oppressors, in order to liberate Africans around the world, but T'Challa was against using Wakanda's natural minerals for violent purposes. Not only were the aforementioned women in a close relationship with the main male character, King T'Challa, who would oftentimes transform into the Blank Panther, but they significantly aided in advancing the film's storyline.

This analysis sought answers for the following research questions:

RQ1: What is the portrayal of the top women characters in the film?

RQ2: How does the top women characters' representation relate to traditional African cultural and historical realities?

RQ3: How does the African representation of the top women characters relate to Afrofuturism?

Black women have been traditionally misrepresented in Western media. They have been stereotypically portrayed as a mammy, jezebel, welfare queen, and sapphire or the angry black woman archetype (Gilman, 2014; Brown Givens & Monahan, 2005; West, 1995). Further, Givens and Monahan (2005) found that these mediated portrayals negatively impact people's real-life perceptions of African American women.

Black Panther not only portrayed Black women differently through the showcase of traditional African customs, but it has refashioned African traditions, creating a utopian world where an African country is successfully managed independently, and has neither been influenced by the West nor colonized by a Western nation. Although, by the movie's end, King T'Challa would learn through Nakia's persuasion, that it was not sufficient to be independently successful, but that Wakanda must use its resources to provide support to other countries in need.

Literature review

Afrofuturism strategically places people of African descent in a post-human world, becoming reimagined as 'trans-human anamorphosis, cyberspace, and digital souls' – essentially renegotiating and reconfiguring racial power (Kim, 2017). Mark Dery (1994), creator of the term Afrofuturism said, 'Can a community whose past has been deliberately rubbed out, and whose energies have subsequently been consumed by the search for legible traces of its history, imagine possible futures?' Derrick Bell expounded on Dery's concept by connecting science fiction to critical theory, essentially using science fiction while searching for social justice; Afrofuturism is also incorporated into film, art, music, literature, and scholarship.

Afrofuturism includes the merging of the past, present, and future. According to Yaszek (2013, p. 2), Afrofuturism is 'not just to remember the bad past, but to use stories about the past and the present to reclaim the history of the future.' Eshun (2003, p. 290) said that these histories of the future are being taken over globally by a new space that he refers to as 'the future industries.' Afrofuturism becomes an empowering epistemology because the world then transforms into a raceless society, thereby eradicating the deterministic outcomes of race, as opposed to the incorporation of an overarching allegiance to a Eurocentric worldview through assimilation.

The European dominance on the construction of knowledge has led to many misconceptions and misunderstandings about African people's lifestyle, since Africa is traditionally shown in American films with contempt. So whoever controls the means of communication can construct a reality that others adhere to. Yaszek said that the main-stream media treats Afrodiasporic people as though they are either the unlucky offspring of slaves or Africans who have been the victims of colonization:

> What you tend to see in the mainstream media, again and again and again, is the sense that blackness is a catastrophe. Black spaces are zones of absolute dystopias where either capitalism

hasn't had a chance to intervene yet or where capitalism has failed. We see this again and again in the news: black cities are always depicted in dystopic ways. Africa is a gigantic continent, with lots of different ecosystems and cultures and nations and people and events and histories, and yet it's always treated somehow as the place of dystopia, plagued by drought, AIDS, and famine, and we rarely hear positive things about progress in Africa unless it is in terms of capitalist intervention. (Yaszek, 2013, p. 3)

In fact, African people in general along with African women's presence in the film industry are lacking. The USC Annenberg's Institute for Diversity and Empowerment at Annenberg released a report called, 'Media, Diversity, and Social Change Initiative,' which showed their findings for research conducted on media stories, including 109 motion pictures and 305 series productions for cable, broadcast, and a digital series (Smith et al., 2016). These stories were released by major media conglomerates, including NBC Universal-Comcast Corporation, 21st Century Fox, The Walt Disney Company, CBS, Sony, Viacom, Time Warner, Netflix, Hulu, and Amazon. The researchers found that a gender-balanced representation was only shown in 8% of all the films investigated; and further, women only had 29% of the speaking roles in films and were just 26.5% likely to be a lead character. They also found that women were more likely to wear sexy or revealing clothing, shown in nudity, or referenced as being physically attractive in films. Behind the scenes, women only represented 3% of film directors and 29% of writers across media. The findings are even more bleak when one factors in race; 87% of film directors are white (and mostly men) and people of African descent are not represented:

> No platform presents a profile of race/ethnicity that matches proportional representation in the U.S. Over 50% of stories featured no Asian speaking characters, and 22% featured no Black or African American characters. The complete absence of individuals from these backgrounds is a symptom of a diversity strategy that relies on tokenistic inclusion rather than integration. (Smith et al., 2016, p. 16)

Methodology

This qualitative research study includes the Africana womanism methodology. Since this movie had such a profound impact on popular culture, this research was conducted in order to understand its true representation of African women.

The sample size for this research was drawn from the IMDB online database (IMDB (Internet Movie Database), 2018). Their 'top cast' listing for the Black Panther included seven women and census sampling was applied; although, one actress was excluded from this analysis and another was added. The Brazilian and Jamaican Actress Nabiyah Be (the daughter of Jimmy Cliff, the legendary Jamaican recording artist), who starred as Linda, was eliminated from this assessment because she was not a woman from Wakanda, and instead portrayed an American. Her role centered around aiding Killmonger in stealing a vibranium artifact from the Museum of Great Britain. In addition, since the *Merchant Tribe Elder* was a part of the top cast list, her counterpart, the *Mining Tribe Elder was added to the list*. This resulted in a sample size of seven women, including the following: 1) Nakia, a War Dog of Wakanda; 2) Okoye, the first lieutenant of the *Dora Milaje*; 3) Ayo, a member of the *Dora Milaje*; 4) Princess Shuri, the head of Wakanda's technological division; 5) the Queen Mother of Wakanda, Ramonda, as well as King T'Challa and Princess Shuri's mother;

6) the woman known as the *Merchant Tribe Elder* of the *Wakandan Tribal Council; and 7)* the woman known as the *Mining Tribe Elder* of the council.

The researcher independently decoded the information. The coder watched this film six additional times from the original screening, in order to conduct this research study. The first two times she jotted down notes. She then listed all of the eighteen categories of Africana womanism on the second row of a spreadsheet. After the researchers third and fourth time watching the film, she placed key portrayals onto the spreadsheet. The relevant scenarios were displayed as codes, and assessed on the characteristics outlined in Africana womanism, which is reflective of eighteen positive qualities of African women. Then she watched the movie two more times to ensure that all relevant scenarios were included.

Results

The women of Wakanda showed Africana womanism by consistently displaying most of its key descriptors. These women were wholeheartedly self-namers, self-definers, family-centered, in concert with men in struggle, strong, whole, ambitious, flexible role players, authentic, respected, recognized, spiritual, nurturing, ambitious, and adaptable. These well-rounded women were confident and passionate about the work they performed. They projected a communal orientation, while simultaneously showing their independence. They also showed additional qualities of being witty, savvy, loyal, and brave. These qualities, including the Africana womanism descriptors, will be elaborated on as each of the top women characters in the movie are discussed.

These women did not show any of the stereotypical portrayals of Black women in Western media, including the mammy, jezebel, welfare queen, and sapphire archetype. Although, these roles are attributed to African American characters, and yet the women of Wakanda were represented as African women.

The Wakandan Tribal Council *members*

The *Wakandan Tribal Council* positions consisted of elders whose main duty was to advise the king, so these elders had leadership roles and were always in consultation with King T'Challa. The *Wakandan Tribal Council* comprised of four members, two men and two women, and included the following people: Dorothy May Steel from Flint, Michigan, USA, who represented the *Merchant Tribe Elder*; Connie Chiume from Benoni, South Africa, starred as the *Mining Tribe Elder*; Issaach De Bankolė, born in Abidjan, Côte d'Ivoire, portrayed the leader of the *River Tribe*; and Danny Sapani, of Ghanaian descent and born in Hackney, London, played the role of the *Border Tribe Elder*. All of the elder tribal leaders had to give their permission in a formal public coronation ceremony at Warrior Falls before T'Challa could be granted the kingship. Showing a comradery among the ethnic groups, in this Afrofuturistic film where tribalism in its derogatory sense does not prevail, each one uniformly stated that T'Challa's anticipated role as Wakanda's new king 'will go unchallenged' (Coogler, 2018). Afterwards, the *Jabari Tribe,* consisting of those who removed themselves from the mainstream Wakandan society, challenged T'Challa's ascent to the throne, but later in the film they would aid him in regaining it.

All members of the tribal council were at liberty to have their own unique style that was representative of their specific ethnic group – this showed an acceptance of other people's cultural traditions. The *Merchant Tribe Elder* stemmed from the Sahara's Tuareg people, and this group was responsible for Wakanda's trade in crafts, including art, clothing, and artifacts (Chutel & Kazeem, 2018). The women of the *Tribal Council* were dressed in oversized Fulani gold hoop earrings, and had traditional African hairstyles, including the loc style of the OvaHimba ethnic group in Namibia. The *Mining Tribe Elder's* red-ochred locs, with puffs at the ends, complemented her colorful red and orange clothing patterns and her adornment of matching jewelry—the bright red color was inspired by the Maasai ethnic group of Kenya and Tanzania. The *River Tribe Elder* wore a lip plate, which is an item embraced by the Mursi, Chai, and Tirma women of Ethiopia (Chutel & Kazeem, 2018).

The *Merchant Tribe Elder* showed courage in speaking truth to power when she said to King T'Challa at a *Tribal Council* meeting in the Citadel, the palace that the royalty who are members of the *Golden Tribe*, inhabit, 'Wakanda doesn't need another warrior right now, we need a king' (Coogler, 2018). She made this assertive statement after listening to King T'Challa's plan to visit South Korea in pursuit of the arms dealer Ulysses Klaue, who had stolen some of Wakanda's vibranium. The *Mining Tribe Elder* also showed bravery when she was the first of the elders to laugh at Killmonger, after he initially announced his intention to challenge King T'Challa for the throne.

The existence of the *Wakandan Tribal Council reflects* African societies historically while addressing the deference that Africans have for elders. Africans traditionally live in communal societies; the elders from those communities are seen as the ones who have wisdom, which can only be gained from the aging process (Khapoya, 1998). Councils of elders have been widely used thoughout Africa as a source for conflict resolution; these councils have existed in countries like Botswana, South Africa, Uganda, Ethiopia, and Kenya (Kariuki, 2015). The elders are viewed as the transmitters of African cultural practices, and they are also seen as the ones who can preserve the peace in a society (Michel et al., 2019). When the elders die, Africans traditionally believe that the spirits of these deceased become actively engaged in their communities (Khapoya, 1998) – so in the African worldview one never loses power, instead one gains power through the aging process, and this deference follows the person into death. Death is simply just another stage of life (Ekore & Lanre-Abass, 2016). So the *Wakandan Tribal Council* has its basis in African historical traditions.

Overall, the Africana womanism themes are apparent from the portrayal of the elder women of the Wakanda Tribal Council. The *Merchant Tribe Elder* and the *Mining Tribe Elder* showed the following qualities: 1) self-namer and self-definer, including their willingness to embrace their own ethnic group's traditional culture; 2) 'in concert with the male in struggle,' as they worked in alliance with the elder men from different ethnic groups as well as King T'Challa; 3) strength and authenticity, in their willingness to challenge the two main characters, King T'Challa and Killmonger; and 4) they were recognized and respected for their role in the community. The gender-balanced Tribal Council's involvement in such important matters showed an equality between the sexes in Wakanda, a respect for elders, and a comradery among the ethnic groups.

The *Dora Milaje*, Wakanda's woman warriors

King T'Challa had an all-women guard of fierce warriors protecting him on a daily basis called the *Dora Milaje*, some of which included his first lieutenant, Okoye, and a general member, Ayo. Christopher Priest introduced this group into the Black Panther comic strip after becoming the head writer in 1998. These women were an 'amazon-type' who displayed excellent abilities in using swords to fight, and their tall spears and red armor were based on the Maasai ethnic group (Chutel & Kazeem, 2018, February 19). These women wore rings around their neck and arms, like the married Ndebele women of South Africa who are known for their copper or brass rings. The Ndebele wear rings to show their faithfulness to their husband, after the building of their home. The *Dora Milaje* were not only portrayed as being physically strong but also mentally strong, since they were independent thinkers.

One scene showed modern items associated with women's oppression, as empowering. While King T'Challa, Nakia, and Okoye went to a club together in North Korea to investigate a security issue, Okoye was repulsed by a wig she was wearing. Although, in order to overpower their opposition, Ulysses Klaue and his entourage, she used her wig and her high heel as a weapon in a club fight. Therefore, this showed that Okoye is a self-definer and would not become a victim of the objects used for the so-called beautification of women.

Okoye and Ayo showed strength and bravery when they went against the orders of Killmonger after he was declared the king of Wakanda. Killmonger decided to attack T'Challa again, when the true king of Wakanda, T'Challa, reappeared after Killmonger threw him over a mountain cliff. Okoye said to Killmonger, 'You, your heart is so full of hatred, you are not fit to be a king' (Coogler, 2018). When she drew her weapon on him, every member of the *Dora Milaje*, including Ayo, went against Killmonger, and as the *Black Panther* he fought the four of them. This scene exemplified this all-women military unit's sisterhood, flexibility, and adaptableness, because when Okoye went against Killmonger, the other members immediately followed. The *Dora Milaje* was always in concert with the Africana man in his struggle, specifically King T'Challa, since they continued operating as his security, even after his throne was taken from him.

Another scene also signified the independent thinking of Okoye. She confronted her husband W'Kabi, portrayed by the British actor Daniel Kaluuya, who was head of security for Wakanda's *Border Tribe* and also was T'Challa's best friend. W'Kabi betrayed T'Challa by fighting on behalf of King Killmonger after T'Challa seemingly reappeared from the dead. In Wakanda's *Battle of Mount Bashenga*, Okoye confronted W'Kabi with her weapon, since he was fighting against the former king, T'Challa. W'Kabi pierced into her eyes and said, 'Would you kill me my love?' Okoye responded by aiming her spear at him and said, 'For Wakanda, without question' (Coogler, 2018). This scene signified her loyalty to Wakanda, which is a highly respectable quality to project.

One of the latter scenes showed the power of the *Dora Milaje*, especially Okoye, when she placed herself in between a fast-charging rhinoceros that was racing towards Winston Duke. Duke is an actor born in Trinidad and Tobago, who played M'Baku, the head of the *Jabari Tribe, which was based on the Dogon ethnic group of Mali and the Karo ethnic group of Ethiopia*. M'Baku once challenged T'Challa's rule, but now he was fighting on his behalf. As the rhinoceros charged towards Okoye, it suddenly stopped right in front of her; instead of trampling over her, it licked her cheek. This scene indicated the high level of respect shown to this military unit, even by the animals of Wakanda, adhering to Africana womanism's respected and recognized characteristic. The *Dora Milaje* is not just a fictitious group in the Afrofuturistic Wakanda, but they are also part of a historical African reality.

During the eighteenth and nineteenth century, there existed an elite group of women soldiers in West Africa, which other Africans called 'Ahosi,' meaning 'king's wives' or 'Mino,' meaning 'our mothers'; Europeans referred to this group as the 'Dahomey Amazons,' who were members of the Fon ethnic group (Coleman, 2018; UNESCO, 2014). Although, women from conquered group would also become soldiers of this unit to evade becoming a prisoner of war. These women in the Kingdom of Dahomey, located in what is now the Republic of Benin, protected the king and devoted their life to weapons training and fighting wars. They were fierce women soldiers committed to a life of celibacy. These soldiers were comprised in different units, at one time consisting of 4,000 people, and each group had their own dances, battle songs, flag and uniforms (UNESCO, 2014). According to UNESCO, these solders fought many important battles:

> Women soldiers distinguished themselves on many occasions in the history of the Kingdom of Dahomey, particularly in the battles of Savi (1727), Abeokouta (1851 and 1864) and Ketu (1886), as well as during the two wars against the French, until the fall of Abomey in 1892. This final battle resulted in the dissolution of their army. (UNESCO, 2014, p. 7)

An unfortunate aspect lead to the rise and eventual decline of the Kingdom of Dahomey: its involvement in the slave trade. It was an elaborate system of trading African prisoners gained through wars or raids, in exchange for European goods, like firearms, knives, bayonets, spirits, and fabrics; due to their involvement in slavery, the Kingdom reached considerable levels of wealth (UNESCO, 2014). Although, there was no connection between the women warriors in Black Panther and slavery, in this Afrofuturistic society. In fact, slavery was never directly mentioned, and was alluded to just once when T'Challa asked Killmonger if he would like them to save his life. Killmonger said right before dying, 'Bury me in the ocean, with my ancestors that jumped from the ships, because they knew death was better than bondage' (Coogler, 2018).

The Black Panther used the Afrofuturistic concept of an African king with an all-women security team of warriors, to highlight a real aspect of African history. These women warriors exemplified Africana womanism's descriptors and were self-definers, genuine in sisterhood, strong, in concert with men in the struggle, authentic, flexible role players, respected, recognized, adaptable, and ambitious.

Princess Shuri, head of Wakanda's technological division

Princess Shuri, T'Challa's junior sister, was not only the princess of Wakanda but was the head of the Wakandan Design Group, and was a technological genius of an Afrofuturistic society. Princess Shuri oversaw Wakanda's defenses, weaponry, transportation and communications systems. In Wakanda, a place that had never been colonialized, women were shown to have as much knowledge and confidence as men. Princess Shuri designed an artificial intelligence system called the *Griot*, sound absorbent sneakers made with nanotechnology, remote access *Kimoyo Beads* that controlled her lab console, *Vibranium Gauntlets* that fired shots that could knock people into the air, and she upgraded the *Panther Habits* which redistributes energy, like bullets. As Princess Shuri told T'Challa, 'How many times do I have to teach you, just because something works does not mean that it can't be improved' (Coogler, 2018). She showed that she was just as smart as her brother, and they had a mutually respectful relationship.

Princess Shuri had a personality with grit, which is unlike the traditional Western portrayal of women. Traditionally, American films show women as patriarchal society victims (Cadilhe, 2020, p. 146; Maity, 2014, p. 28); however, Princess Shuri excelled in Wakandan society, she rehabilitated people and could even resuscitate them from an unresponsive state. When her expertise was sought after in helping the American CIA operative Everett Ross, played by Martin Freeman, after he became injured while trying to save Nakia from getting shot, Princess Shuri casually said, 'another broken white boy to fix' (Coogler, 2018). She alluded of the Africana womanism descriptors of being strong, a self-definer, flexible, adaptable, ambitious, respected, and recognized.

Princess Shuri also showed her willingness to defend herself as a combatant who is proficient with spears, while showing support to the lead male character, King T'Challa. In the beginning of the movie after he arrived from a mission, she was shown giving her brother an obscene gesture as he joked about her clothes. Although, when T'Challa asked for help on a mission, she used her innovative technological systems and assisted him with enthusiasm and bravery. Shuri told T'Challa, 'The Black Panther lives. And when he fights for the fate of Wakanda, I will be right there beside him' (Coogler, 2018). After Killmonger became the King of Wakanda, she told him very boldly while they were fighting, 'You'll never be a true king' (Coogler, 2018). T'Challa rescued her from Killmonger's wrath. This showed the Africana womanism traits of being family centered, since Princess Shuri showed that she was still loyal to her brother even after he was defeated in the fight for the throne.

Ultimately, Princess Shuri's role provided a connection between being a smart young woman and being cool, because she frequently made jokes and had a good time, while working as a master scientist and engineer on groundbreaking new technology. During the coronation ceremony she made a public announcement after Zuri, played by the American Actor Forest Whitaker, who was her father's trusted advisor, asked if anyone of royal blood would contest T'Challa's reign as the next King of Wakanda. As Princess Shuri raised her hand, the cermony attendees gasped. She then said in amusement, 'This corset is really uncomfortable, so could we all just wrap it up and go home' (Coogler, 2018). Another scene showed King T'Challa in Princess Shuri's lab. When he tested her Panther Habits—a fully protective body suit that incorporated innovative technology like kinetic energy—for the second time by kicking it, she recorded him and laughed as he was thrust onto the floor. King T'Challa abruptly said, 'Delete that footage' (Coogler, 2018). She made an outspoken comment, after it was announced to M'Baku that T'Challa was 'murdered,' M'Baku said that he was defeated more-so than murdered. Princess Shuri responded, 'do not rub our noses in it' (Coogler, 2018). These scenes showed that Princess Shuri was not only a technological genius, but she had a playful and humorous side, which made her portrayal reflective of the Africana womanism descriptors of being whole, ambitious, authentic, a nurturer, and a self-defining figure.

The Queen Mother of Wakanda

The Queen Mother of Wakanda respected the traditions of Wakanda and was the bedrock of her family after the death of her husband, King T'Chaka.

Queen Mother Ramonda was immersed in the African traditions of Wakanda. She wore a Zulu-style hat or headdress that was inspired by Winnie Mandela, a South African activist of Xhosa descent (Allure, 2018). All of the women of Wakanda had natural hairstyles, including the queen, whose hair was in the form of downy white natural 'locs' (the colonized term for dreadlocks; Thames Copeland, 2021).

Queen Mother Ramonda's esteemed position was apparent, and she was respected by others. She was protected by the *Dora Milaje*. Nakia did a slight curtsey to her as a show of respect for her and the royal family. Without even glancing in her direction, when Princess Shuri made an obscene gesture directed towards T'Challa, the queen mother sternly called her name and she responded with, 'Sorry mother.'

Queen Mother Ramonda was savvy and she supported her children throughout the film. After T'Chaka was killed, she caressed her son, T'Challa, and asked him how he was doing. Next, when M'Baku challenged T'Challa for the throne with a physical fight to the death, his mother screamed out to him, 'show him who you are!' when it appeared he was losing (Coogler, 2018). He instantly gained momentum and defeated the Great Gorilla M'Baku. Towards the film's end she spearheaded a spiritual ritual involving the heartshaped herb, and helped in saving her son's life. She called upon the ancestors for healing. Eventually, T'Challa arose; he gasped for air as he came out of his coma and asked for a blanket. The queen adhered to the Africana womanism descriptors: she was family centered, spiritual, strong, respected, and recognized.

The queen mother is a recognized traditional role in parts of Africa, and the position is still prevalent today. The queen mother holds a leadership role in a community and operates in duality with the chiefs (Stoeltje, 2021). The queen mother role in Ghana is traditionally based on matrilineal descent of royal lineage. For instance, queen mothers and chiefs exist among the Akan ethnic group; they reside over the towns and villages. Further, the Asantehene, the Asante king, and the Asantehemaa, the Asante queen, rule over the entire Asante ethnic group.

Queen Ramonda was a representation of Africana womanism. She showed the Africana womanism traits of being in concert with men in the struggle, authentic, flexible, spiritual, adaptable, mothering, and nurturing.

Nakia, a War Dog of Wakanda

The Wakandan women had dominant roles in their society, while simultaneously supporting their male counterparts. Nakia was a Wakandan War Dog and T'Challa's ex-girlfriend. Even though they were no longer together, they were still friends and played supportive and nurturing roles in one another's life.

The movie opened showing a woman, Nakia's prowess and power over a man, T'Challa. As she was secretly transported in the back of a truck in Nigeria, in an effort of preventing the trafficking of women and girls. Okoye had previously warned T'Challa about his apt towards freezing upon encountering Nakia, so before they left to locate her, she told him, 'Just don't freeze when you see her' (Coogler, 2018). As the Black Panther, his response was, 'I never freeze,' but he later stood frozen and mesmerized when he saw her in Nigeria – although he was saved by Okoye who threw a spear into a person who was trying to kill him, while he stood frozen (Coogler, 2018). Nakia was also physically powerful and helped T'Challa fight the human traffickers. She showed her bravery while in the midst of a dangerous situation when she said to T'Challa, 'Why are you here? You ruined my mission' (Coogler, 2018).

Nakia exhibited a pinnacle example of Africana womanism's woman in concert with men in the struggle descriptor, after initiating a plan to save Wakanda from Killmonger's rule, which ultimately lead to saving T'Challa's life. The Wakandans believed that T'Challa was dead after Killmonger won the fight for the throne and threw him over the Warrior Falls cliff. Although, Nakia had devised a plan to visit M'Baku, to ask for his assistance in regaining control of Wakanda. She brought Queen Ramonda; Princess Shuri; and Ross, the American CIA agent into the mountains with her. When they arrived, they learned that a fisherman had found T'Challa, who was in a coma. They gave T'Challa a heart-shaped herb, from which the Black Panther's strength derives, and eventually he came out of his coma. Before leaving, T'Challa asked M'Baku to help him in his fight for the throne of Wakanda; he refused, but eventually changed his mind.

Nakia was a warrior who also participated in African cultural traditions. During the coronation ceremony dance scene, drums were heard in the distance. A session of wooden rafts were moving down a river, with a black panther sculpture on top of each one, representing the *Panther Goddess Bast*. T'Challa spoke of this Goddess (which was derived from Bastet, an Egyptian Goddess shown as a cat and a lioness) and another one in Captain America: Civil War when he said, '"In my culture, death is not the end. It's more of a stepping off point. You reach out with both hands and Bast and Sekhmet, they lead you into a green veld where, you can run forever" (Russo & Russo, 2016). These rafts held people from each group. The *Dora Milaje* was collectively dancing with their spears, Princess Shuri and her mother lead in the traditional dances of the *Golden Tribe* on another raft, and Nakia took the lead in the dances among the *River Tribe,* and its people were adorned in green African patterned clothing. The *River Tribe* was based on the Suri and Mursi ethnic groups of Ethiopia. Nakia was dancing with a circular weapon in each hand. Her face was painted to represent her ethnic group and cowrie shells were a part of her ethnic attire.

Nakia constantly showed care and concern for T'Challa. Nakia showed family centeredness as she brought T'Challa's family together, playing a seminal role in saving his life. She eased T'Challa's pain by giving him advice after he had difficulties accepting that his father, T'Chaka, killed his uncle, N'Jobu, played by the American Actor Sterling K. Brown. Nakia said, 'You can't let your father's mistakes define who you are, you get to decide what kind of king you are going to be' (Coogler, 2018). This comment showed that Nakia represented Africana womanism's traits of being a self-definer, a flexible role player, and a nurturer, while also honoring her cultural traditions.

In a later scene, as King T'Challa and Nakia were talking in an urban center, she spoke about how she wanted to live her life dream of helping others. King T'Challa asked her to stay and Nakia said, 'I came to support you and to honor your father, but I can't stay. I just have my calling out there. I've seen too many in need just to turn a blind eye. I can't be happy here knowing there are people out there who have nothing' (Coogler, 2018). She urged him that Wakanda could assist other countries by providing technology, aid, and refuge. He responded jokingly, 'If you weren't so stubborn, you would make a great queen,' and Nakia said, 'I would make a great queen because I am so stubborn – if that is what I wanted' (Coogler, 2018). In this scene, when Nakia rejected the traditional Western notions of what a woman should be and indicated that she could not sacrifice her dream (of helping others) to be with T'Challa, she displayed Africana womanism's qualities of being a self-namer, self-definer, strong, whole, authentic, and ambitious.

Nakia told T'Challa, 'Wakanda is strong enough to help others and protect ourselves at the same time' (Coogler, 2018). Nakia said that if other countries could do it then they could do it, but he was reluctant and wanted to maintain a form of isolationism, believing that exposing Wakanda to the world would recede their way of life. At the end of the movie,

King T'Challa was positively influenced by Nakia, as she spearheaded the successful effort to place him back on the throne, and as he started to participate in community service overseas.

Nakia had a warrior spirit, unlike the traditional western depiction of women, including the stereotypical portrayal of Black women, but like the *Dora Milaje*, and in the tradition of other notable African women. She resembled those African warrior queens of an African past, like Queen Nzinga from Ndongo (Angola); Queen Ndete Yalla from Senegal; Sarraounia Mangou from Niger; Queen Mother Yaa Asantewa from Ghana; as well as Kimpa Vita a prophet from Kongo (the former Kingdom of Kongo's present location is the Democratic Republic of Congo and Angola); and anti-apartheid activists, like Charlotte Maxeke and Winnie Mandela from South Africa, along with other women who fought on behalf of African people from their own respective African country (UNESCO (United Nations Educational, Scientific and Cultural Organization), 2015).

Nakia was a representation of Africana womanism. The womanism themes included the following: 1) self-namer and self-definer, due to her self-definition and encouraging T'Challa to define himself too; 2) in concert with men in the struggle, a nurturer, and being family oriented, as she continued to build her alliance with King T'Challa, his mother Romana, and his sister Princess Zuri; and 3) her aptitude for being strong, authentic, flexible, and adaptable, by leading the effort in saving Wakanda.

Discussion

Wakanda is a patrilineal society that showed an egalitarian relationship between the sexes. The top women characters greatly contributed to T'Challa's outcomes, or to the future of Wakanda, including his mother, the Queen Mother Ramonda, whose encouragement fueled him in winning his original fight for the throne; his younger sister, Princess Shuri, whose technological inventions helped him to defeat his enemies; his first lieutenant, Okoye and security member, Ayo, who guarded his life; the members of the *Wakandan Tribal Council*, the *Merchant Tribe Elder* and the *Mining Tribe Elder* who advised him; and his ex girlfriend, Nakia, the former War Dog who initiated the rescue effort that lead to the Black Panther's resurgence in the film. 'And as you can see, I am not dead,' shouted T'Challa (Coogler, 2018). He said this phrase after appearing for the first time from a presumed death, as he fought to regain the throne from Killmonger.

The questions guiding this research were ascertained to gain an understanding of the portrayal of the women in the film, and their relationship to traditional African cultural values and Afrofuturism. Connections were made between Africana womanism's descriptors and the qualities of the top women characters in the film. The results found that this film portrayed an egalitarian and non-competitive relationship between the sexes, which is a display of traditional African culture.

In the *Invention of Women: Making an African Sense of Western Gender Discourses* text, Oyewumi (1997) mentioned that the term 'woman' was a term imposed onto African societies. He suggested that African societies, unlike the European ones, have never based one's position in life on body anatomy. Historical assessments of the sexes determined that gender roles in Africa were more flexible, egalitarian, and complementary (Anyidoho, 2020). Even when investigating a traditional African language, such as Yoruba, there is an absence of gendered languages as well as any form of sex autonomy related information (Oyewumi,

1997). In fact, as it relates to African languages, the *Jabari Tribe* spoke Yoruba, while all the other ethnic groups spoke Xhosa. Although, European men, based on their historical situation and into modernity, have consistently subjugated white women. Further, during the colonization of Africa, Europeans invented the term 'women' in Africa, for the subjugation of African women (Oyewumi, 1997; Steady, 2005).

Agbaje (2020) mentioned how gender roles, identification, and stratification were imports of colonialism. European anthropological scholarship promoted acculturation theories, Social Darwinism, and structural/functionalism, which were used as proof that African culture was so-called inferior. Meanwhile, as Oyewumi (1997) said, '[Women] were dominated, exploited, and inferiorized as Africans together with African men and then separately inferiorized and marginalized as African women' (p. 122). For instance, women were excluded from the 'colonial public sphere'; they did not receive as much education as boys; the women chiefs were not recognized, unlike the men chiefs who were recognized and given more power; citizenry was only recognized for women through their husbands (Oyewumi, 1997, p. 123). More specifically, among the Yoruba, 'females became subordinated as soon as they were made up into women – an embodied and homogenized category – by definition they became invisible' (Steady, 2005, p. 153). It is only until this European effort in separating the private and public spheres into 'gendered spheres' that men have had the advantage in the public sphere; before colonization, African societies were not stratified according to body type (Steady, 2005; Sudarkasa, 1987; Nzegwu, 2001). Finally, European missionaries with school systems in Africa began to impose this worldview onto Africans (Steady, 2005).

The Black Panther's portrayal of African women involved in various aspects of life, did not only depict a mythological African utopia, but it reignited an African historical reality. Women were involved in politics, the military, the spiritual realm, and science and technology. This film also showed the importance that African women placed on their family and wider community. So prior to the colonialization of Africa, women assumed political roles and served as advisors and elders of equal standing to men, and even the African spirits, whether they were male or female, were of a similar status (Steady, 2005). Therefore, it is not unusual that the Wakandas believed in Goddesses.

European evolutionists of the nineteenth century created theories concerning family kinship patterns that placed communal African egalitarian gender patterns at the bottom of the social ladder and individualistic Eurocentric patriarchal gender patterns at its top. According to Amadiume (2005, p. 84), 'they postulated a progression from barbarism and savagery in primitive sexual promiscuity, to matrilineal descent, to matriarchy . . . and, finally, to masculine imperialism and patriarchy, monogamy and the nuclear family.' Further, Diop mentioned in, 'Pre-colonial Black Africa,' that Africa was the matriarchal and agricultural South, Europe was the patriarchal North, the Mediterranean basis was where matriarchy came before patriarchy, and Western Asia was classified as the 'zone of confluence' (Diop, 1989). Further, some societies were simultaneously male and female oriented or had a female line of descent and focus. For instance, the Ashanti's of Ghana have a matrilineal and a matriarchal system, the Uduk of Sudan and Ethiopia have a matrifocal and patrilineal organization (Amadiume, 2005); and the Nigerian Igbo of Nnobi and the Igbos in general, have a matriarchal system; and Amadiume (1987) argued that mostly all African groups have a basis in a matriarchal system – making women rights not a foreign concept in Africa, since African kinship patterns were historically egalitarian.

Consequently, the Black Panther used an African historical reality in the creation of an Afrofuturistic utopia; although, a casual observer might assume that the film is simply a feminist portrayal of the top women characters. In actuality, the Black Panther is more accurately described as a showcase of traditional African gender relations, which is represented in Africana womanism.The portrayal of the top women characters in the Black Panther represented women from an Africanhistorical reality, including, as mentioned earlier: the portrayal of the *Dora Milaje* which reflected the women warriors of the Kingdom of Dahomey; the portrayal of the elder women in *Wakandan Tribal Council* that represented African's traditional council of elders system; the representation of a queen mother which suited a historical reality of African queen mothers; the representation of Nakia, a War Dog of Wakanda, who had an African warrior spirit like many other women in African history who succured leadership roles in their country; and the representation of Princess Shuri who showed bravery, quick wit, and an outspoken nature at a young age, like many other African woman of our past.

Conclusion

'Did he freeze?' Princess Shuri eagerly asked Okoye. She was referring to T'Challa's initial reaction when he saw Nakia. 'Like an antelope in headlights,' Okoye said with a grin and blinked her eye. Princess Shuri laughed. T'Challa, who was standing beside them with his mouth open wide during their conversation, said to Okoye in an tone that spoke to his embarrassment, 'Are you finished?' This lighthearted scene is a vivid representation of the films non-conformity to stereotypical gender roles, and in this instance the gender roles were reversed. Nakia was not looking for a prince charming to 'sweep her off her feet' (Maity, 2014, p. 30), but instead a man was now the one who was standing in awe of a woman. This scene showed the capacity of a woman – who was not dressed scantily clad but was wearing modest clothing – to overpower a man by her presence alone.

Africana womanism accurately describes the qualities of the women in Wakanda, which were realistic portrayals of the traditional African relations between the sexes. The leading women characters complemented their male counterparts and consistently showed that it was appropriate and even celebrated for them to have the following characteristics: to be self-namers, self-definers, family-centered, in concert with the men in the struggle, strong, whole, a flexible role player, authentic, respected, recognized, spiritual, ambitious, nurturing, and adaptable. The women of Wakanda had a communal orientation while simultaneously showing their independence. They also displayed traits outside the scope of Africana womanism, including bravery, loyalty, wittiness, savvyness, an adherence to African cultural and historical traditions and a non-adherence to traditional Western female stereotypes, including those strictly imposed on Black women.

This film's equitable relationship between the sexes did not exist in isolation, but emerged from an isolationist egalitarian African nation, which was able to maintain its traditional African values in a modern and technologically advanced society (emerging from the mining of their rare vibranium metal, to which they had full control). Therefore, in the Black Panther, egalitarian relationships existed between the sexes in Wakanda, among the different ethnic groups, between the young and the elderly, and there was no sign of racism or the inferior thinking that stems from it – so equality was a societal norm in

Wakanda. Moreover, any situations that could likely lead to discrimination, were mended or resolved.

T'Challa told his deceased father about his decision to allow Killmonger to be raised in America after killing his father, that he was 'a monster of our own making' and he continued by saying, 'I must right these wrongs' (Coogler, 2018). Thus, friction existed between the African character, T'Challa, and the African American character who was his cousin, Killmonger – representative of the real and lingering conflict between the two groups. Thus, this antagonism spanned back at least one generation in the film, and began with the rift between his father and uncle. Although, by the movie's end, T'Challa invested in three buildings in an African American community in Oakland, California. This was his effort in opening a community center, called the *Wakandan International Outreach Centre*, at the site where his father killed his uncle and where Killmonger was raised. He announced that two women (Princess Shuri and Nakia) would be in charge of this new initiative. This move reflected a new way of life for the Wakandans, and further, it represented a mending of the relationship between Africans and African Americans, showing movement towards African unity. This initiative adhered to the desires of Killmonger and his father, N'Jobu, for Africans to work together on behalf of their own liberation, and it showed that ultimately their efforts would not be in vain.

'We must find a way to look after one another as if we were one single tribe,' King T'Challa (Coogler, 2018) said earlier, during his speech at the United Nations. King T'Challa made a personal declaration to use Wakanda's resources to aid countries in need. On a micro level, this comment spoke to the Black Panther's inclusion of actresses and actors from all throughout Africa and its diaspora, stressing a Pan-African vision in its production and ideology. Ultimately, on a macro level, this movie allowed its viewers to visualize a utopian society where female oppression does not exist, equality is the norm, and efforts are in effect to help others in need.

This Afrofuturistic, *Black Panther* film not only showed what African countries can become, but it also showed what Africa was already in the recreation of its history on behalf of its own future. It showed the possibilities for revisioning traditional African cultural systems in an Afrofuturistic reality, one that merges the past, present, and the future, in the creation of an ideal and truly democratic present.

In conclusion, the most popularized phrase from the film is 'Wakanda forever,' (and it is the namesake of its sequel). It operates in conjunction with the crossing of one's arms in front of the chest, and it seeps of meaning. This greeting becomes more than just a sign of Wakandan patriotism dating back to the ancient Egyptian tombs that showed the deceased pharaohs' arms crossed. It becomes more than a catchy phrase that moviegoers delightfully repeat. The "Wakanda forever" greeting has become symbolic of human beings' desire to live in a society where every person matters, where gender and racial oppression and stereotypes are nonexistent, and where differences among others are welcomed, recognized, and celebrated– if all of this is possible in an Afrofuturistic society, then perhaps one day it can actualize in the real world too.

Disclosure statement

No potential conflict of interest was reported by the author(s).

References

ABC News. (2018, February 16). *Black Panther' star Lupita Nyong'o on the powerful role of women in the film*. [Video]. Available from: http://abcnews.go.com/Nightline/video/black-panther-star-lupita-nyongo-powerful-role-women-53144641

Agbaje, F. I. (2020). Colonialism and gender in Africa, A critical history. In O. Yacob-Haliso, & T. Falola (Eds.), *The Palgrave handbook of African women's studies* (pp. 1275–1294). Palgrave Macmillan.

Allure. (2018, October 9). *Angela Bassett breaks down her most iconic movie looks | Pretty detailed*. [Video]. YouTube. https://www.youtube.com/watch?v=Cvz_KDmjmqY

Amadiume, I. (1987). *Afrikan matriarchal foundations: The Igbo case*. Karnak House.

Amadiume, I. (2005). Theorizing matriarchy in Africa: Kinship ideologies and systems in Africa and Europe. In O. Oyewumi (Ed.), *African gender studies: A reader* (pp. 83–98). Palgrave Macmillan.

Anyidoho, N. A. (2020). Women, gender, and development in Africa 2019. In O. Yacob-Haliso, & T. Falola (Eds.), *The Palgrave handbook of African women's studies* (pp. 155–169). Palgrave Macmillan.

Brown Givens, S. M., & Monahan, J. L. (2005). Priming mammies, jezebels, and other controlling images: An examination of the influence of mediated stereotypes on perceptions of an African American woman. *Media Psychology*, 7(1), 87–106.

Cadilhe, O. (2020). Feminism and dissident femininity in popular culture. Cher's role and the role of religion in *Moonstruck*. *Pontos de Interrogação*, 10(2), 145–164. https://doi.org/10.30620/p.i..v10i2.10843

Chutel, L., & Kazeem, Y. (2018, February 19). *Marvel's 'Black Panther' is a broad mix of African cultures—here are some of them*. Quartz. https://qz.com/africa/1210704/black-panthers-african-cultures-and-influences/

Coleman, A. L. (2018). There's a true story behind Black Panther's strong women. Here's why that matters. *Time*. http://time.com/5171219/black-panther-women-true-history/

Coogler, R. (Director). (2018). *Black Panther* [Motion Picture]. Marvel Studios.

Dery, M. (1994). *Flame Wars. The Discourse of Cyberculture. Black to the Future: Interviews with Samuel R. Delany, Greg Tate, and Tricia Rose*. Durnham, North Carolina.

Diop, C. A. (1989). *The cultural unity of Black Africa: A comparative study of the political and social systems of Europe and Black Africa, from antiquity to the formation of modern states*. Lawrence Hill & Company.

Ekore, R. I., & Lanre-Abass, B. (2016). African cultural concept of death and the idea of advance care directives. *Indian Journal of Palliative Care*, 22(4), 369–372. https://doi.org/10.4103/0973-1075.191741

Eshun, K. (2003). Further Considerations on Afrofuturism. *CR: The New Centennial Review*, 3(2), 287–302. https://doi.org/10.1353/ncr.2003.0021

Gilman, M.E. (2014). The Return of the Welfare Queen. *American University Journal of Gender, Social Policy & the Law*, 22(2), 247–279.

Glass, Q. (2017, April 13). Womanist is to feminist as purple is to lavender? *Huffington Post*. https://www.huffingtonpost.com/entry/womanist-is-to-feminist-as-purple-is-to-lavender_us_57eed0c0e4b0972364deb308

Harris, A. (2018, February 23). Black Panther is the most feminist superhero movie yet. Yes, including Wonder Woman. *Slate*. https://slate.com/culture/2018/02/black-panthers-feminism-is-more-progressive-than-wonder-womans.html

Hudson-Weems, C. (2020). *Africana Womanism Reclaiming Ourselves* (5th ed.). Routledge.

IMDB (Internet Movie Database). (2018). *Black Panther*. https://www.imdb.com/title/tt1825683/

Johnson, T. (2018, February 23). Black Panther is a gorgeous, groundbreaking celebration of black culture. *Vox*. https://www.vox.com/culture/2018/2/23/17028826/black-panther-wakanda-culture-marvel

Kariuki, F. (2015). Conflict resolution by elders in Africa: Successes, challenges and opportunities *Challenges and Opportunities*. http://kmco.co.ke/wp-content/uploads/2018/08/Conflict-Resolution-by-Elders-successes-challenges-and-opportunities-1.pdf

Khapoya, V. (1998). *The African experience, an introduction* (2nd ed.). Prentice Hall.

Kim, M. (2017). Afrofuturism, science fiction, and the reinvention of African American culture. [Doctoral Dissertation, Arizona State University]. ASU Library. https//hdl.handle.net/2286/R.I.45002.

Maity, N. (2014, October). Damsels in distress: A textual analysis of gender roles in disney princess films. *IOSR Journal Of Humanities And Social Science*, 19(10), 10. https://doi.org/10.9790/0837-191032831

Michel, J., Stuckelberger, A., Tediosi, F., Evans, D., & van Eeuwijk, P. (2019). The roles of a grand-mother in African societies - please do not send them to old people's homes. *Journal of Global Health*, *9*(1), 1–7. https://doi.org/10.7189/jogh.09.010306

Nzegwu, N. (2001). Gender equality in the dual-sex system: The case of Onitsha. *Jenda A Journal of Culture and African Women Studies*, *1*(1), 1530–5686. https://www.africaknowledgeproject.org/index.php/jenda/article/view/30

Oyewumi, O. (1997). *The invention of women*. University of Minnesota Press. http://www.jstor.org/stable/10.5749/j.ctttt0vh.9

Russo, A., & Russo, J. (Directors). (2016). *Captain America: Civil War* [Motion Picture]. Marvel Studios.

Ryzik, M. (2018). The Afrofuturistic Designs of 'Black Panther'. *The New York Times*. https://www.nytimes.com/2018/02/23/movies/black-panther-afrofuturism-costumes-ruth-carter.html

Sere, S., Muarifuddin, M., & Masri, F. A. (2020). The Representation of African Cultural Identity in Black Panther Film by Ryan Coogler, the Application of Stuart Hall's Theory. *The Journal of English Language and Literature*, *3*(1) . http://journal.fib.uho.ac.id/index.php/elite/article/view/876

Smith, S., Choueiti, M., & Pieper, K., (2016). *Inclusion or Invisibility? Comprehensive Annenberg report on diversity in entertainment* (report). Retrieved from Institute for Diversity and Empowerment at (USC) Annenberg. https://annenberg.usc.edu/sites/default/files/2017/04/07/MDSCI_CARD_Report_FINAL_Exec_Summary.pdf

Sofola, Z. (2020). *Africana Womanism: Reclaiming Ourselves* (5th ed.). Forward.

Spencer, R. C. (2018, February 21). Black feminist meditations on the women of Wakanda. *Medium*. https://medium.com/@robyncspencer/black-feminist-meditations-on-the-women-of-wakanda-5cc79751d9cd

Steady, F. C. (2005). An investigative framework for gender research in Africa in the new millennium. In O. Oyewumi (Ed.), *African gender studies: A reader* (pp. 313–340). Palgrave Macmillan.

Stoeltje, B. J. (2021). Asante Queen Mothers in Ghana. *Oxford Research Encyclopedia*. https://doi.org/10.1093/acrefore/9780190277734.013.796

Sudarkasa, N. (1987). The status of women in indigenous African societies. In R. Terborg-Penn, S. Harley, & A. Benton Rushing (Eds.), *Women in Africa and the African Diaspora* (pp. 25–41). Howard University Press.

Thames Copeland, T. (2021). *"We Are Not Scared to Die": Julius Malema and the New Movement for African Liberation*. Peter Lang Publishing.

The Walt Disney Company. (2018, August 16). *'Black Panther' becomes third film ever to reach $700 million domestic milestone*. https://thewaltdisneycompany.com/black-panther-becomes-third-film-ever-to-reach-700-million-domestic-milestone/

UNESCO (United Nations Educational, Scientific and Cultural Organization). (2015). *African women, Pan-Africanism, and African resistance*.

UNESCO. (2014). *The women soldiers of Dahomey*. The United Nations Educational, Scientific and Cultural Organization. http://unesdoc.unesco.org/images/0023/002309/230934E.pdf

West, C. M. (1995). Mammy, Sapphire, and Jezebel: Historical Images of Black Women and Their Implications for Psychotherapy. *Psychotherapy*, *32*(3), 458–466.

Yaszek, L. (2013). Race in science fiction: The case of Afrofuturism and new Hollywood. In L. Schmeink (Ed.), *A virtual introduction to science fiction* (pp. 1–11). Web 13. http://virtual-sf.com/?page_id=372

Fashioning Africanfuturism: African Comics, Afrofuturism, and Nnedi Okorafor's *Shuri*

James Hodapp

ABSTRACT

Internationally renowned Nigerian-American sci-fi writer Nnedi Okorafor recently wrote that she no longer wants her work to be considered Afrofuturism, preferring her own term Africanfuturism. Okorafor argues that despite the potential for Afrofuturism to underscore global Blackness, in practice it has privileged African American concerns while marginalising those of Africa. Okorafor, whose work includes several comics including Black Panther, Shuri, and LaGuardia, argues that her work should be understood as explicitly African rather than part of the Black diaspora. She puts this notion into practice by writing novels and comics set in Africa with African characters 'sometimes with aliens, sometimes with witches, often set in a recognizable, future Africa, with African lineages – that are not cultural hybrids but rooted in the history and traditions of the continent, without a desire to look toward Western culture.'

Okorafor's need to assert the notion of Africa as an important site of Blackness in comics highlights the marginal standing of representations of Africa in discourses of global Blackness in comics, even in the contemporary era of diversity, inclusion, and equity. This article examines Okorafor's Marvel comic Shuri to further elucidate Africanfuturism and consider the concept as a paradigm for approaching African comic content.

In a blog post from October of 2019, Nnedi Okorafor – arguably the most prominent contemporary Black science fiction and fantasy writer – makes a case against the use of the term 'Afrofuturism' to describe her novels, short stories, and comics. Okorafor's definition of Afrofuturism, which aligns with conventional usage, focuses on the Black diasporic nature of the term and how it has become a catch-all for Black science fiction in general, when in practice many categories of Black science fiction that are not diasporic, but explicitly African, also exist. Okorafor, who is Nigerian-American, expresses frustration at her work being considered Afrofuturist, and thus diasporic, when she has explicitly created characters and plots that are African, rather than diasporic. Okorafor does not disparage Afrofuturism for its ability to name and harness the zeitgeist of African American sci-fi and fantasy literature and comics, but is adamant that her writing does not fit the category. She contends that despite the potential for Afrofuturism to underscore global Blackness, in practice it has privileged African American concerns while marginalising those of Africa itself. To wit, she argues for a schism via a new term that captures Africa-centric writing that she and others from Africa produce.

Her suggestion is 'Africanfuturism' (Okorafor 2019a, 'Africanfuturism Defined'). For Okorafor, Africanfuturism asserts the explicitly African, rather than Black diasporic, nature of her work, which includes ten novels and many comics, including issues of *Black Panther*, *LaGuardia, Wakanda Forever, Venomverse, Antar, Mystery in Space*, and *Shuri*.

[1] According to Okorafor, Africanfuturist literature and comics are set in Africa with African characters 'sometimes with aliens, sometimes with witches, often set in a recognisable, future Africa, with African lineages – that are not cultural hybrids [diasporic] but rooted in the history and traditions of the continent, without a desire to look towards Western culture' (Okorafor 2019a, 'Africanfuturism Defined'). In contrast to Afrofuturism's concern with recovering lost African sensibilities for African Americans, Africanfuturism is self-referential, having access to African culture and traditions that continue to inform the way Africans live in and see the world.

To demonstrate how African diasporic literature is conflated with African literature, Okorafor highlights comics that could potentially be Africanfuturist or Afrofuturist, depending on authorial decisions. She gives the following example from *Black Panther*, a series that she has helped reshape in the wake of its popular film adaptation:

"**Afrofuturism**: Wakanda builds its first outpost in Oakland, CA, USA.

Africanfuturism: Wakanda builds its first outpost in a neighboring African country" (Okorafor 2019a, 'Africanfuturism Defined').

In this example, *Black Panther*'s fictional African country of Wakanda can be Afrofuturist if the authors chose to imbue it with diasporic stories set in places like Oakland (where the first Wakandan outpost is located) or Africanfuturist if they chose African stories set in Africa. In several *Black Panther* narratives, the technologically advanced and powerful nation of Wakanda desires to stop pretending to be an impoverished nation in order to aid outsiders. For Okorafor, the decision in those narratives to make the United States, rather than any number of closer, more relevant, and more necessitous African countries the beneficiaries of Wakanda's largess is problematic for preferring a distant western Black diaspora over local Africans. She argues that Wakanda as an African nation should be more attuned to the acute needs of its neighbours in Africa, as well as more respectful of their cultures. Okorafor finds the dislocation of an African country to the United States via an outpost a strange act of marginalisation that takes the futuristic African creation of Wakanda and turns it diasporic as part of a larger project to centre the American experience of Blackness over the African one. Okorafor's coining of Africanfuturism, then, both describes her work to date more accurately than Afrofuturism, and aspires to centre Africa in discourses of Blackness in Black literature and comics.

Many futuristic African comics could serve as useful case studies for considering the Africa-centred ideology of Africanfuturism in comics. African comics such as *Malika, Kwenzi, Karmzah, Blackmoon, Captain South Africa, Danfo, Jember, Hawi*, and *Eru*, among many others, use African settings and characters with little reference to the diaspora. However, Okorafor's own work is well suited because she has a significant body of comic work featuring Black African characters on the cusp of Africa and the diaspora. By analysing her work, we can flesh out Africanfuturism as an ideology as well as understand how it works in practice on the comic page. In particular, the Marvel comic *Shuri* is well suited for this analysis because it exists in the *Black Panther* universe, therefore retaining the latent qualities of *Black Panther* regarding the dislocated position of Africa within the series, but is largely Okorafor's creation as the character was marginal and underdeveloped until Okorafor's *Shuri* series.[2] In the *Shuri* comics, we see a fully realised version of Africanfuturism as Okorafor was given licence to (re)create the character and its publication coincides with Okorafor's development of Africanfuturism. Ultimately, this article scrutinises the ideology of Africanfuturism while using *Shuri* as a case study to understand how it manifests in practice in comics.

Afrofuturism and Africanfuturism

At the heart of considering the new term Africanfuturism is the definition of the extant term Afrofuturism, and specifically whether it adequately represents Black African science fiction and comics. Like many literary movements, Afrofuturism is a sensibility more than a strict ideology with rigid criteria. Just as 'postcolonial' and 'world' in literary studies have asserted the value of non-western literary cultures traditionally maligned and/or ignored by the Euro-American literary world, Afrofuturism asserts Black elements of science fiction that have been suppressed, misunderstood, and generally eschewed by traditional literary powerbrokers. Afrofuturism pushes back against the absence of Black people in much mainstream science fiction, arguing that science fiction can at times appear to be a white fantasy in which Blackness has been erased from the future. Octavia Butler, often cited as a literary proto-Afrofuturist, opined in 1980 that 'I don't think anyone seriously believes the world of the future will be all white any more than anyone believes the present world is all white. But custom can be strong enough to prevent people from seeing the need for science fiction to reflect a more realistic view' (Butler 2018). Afrofuturism shares Butler's observation that representations of the future in popular western media have been mostly white and, like Butler, (re) imagines Blackness as central to the future.

Although a comprehensive genealogy of Afrofuturism is not necessary here, briefly tracking its development provides insight into its ambitions, purview, and fidelity to African experiences. The seminal text of Afrofuturism is Mark Dery's 1994 article and interviews 'Black to the Future' (1994). In it, Dery defines Afrofuturism explicitly as an African American ideology, arguing that African Americans 'are the descendants of alien abductees' made to inhabit a 'sci-fi nightmare' in which 'impassable force fields of intolerance frustrate their movements; official histories undo what has been done; and technology is too often brought to bear on Black bodies' (180). In this context of prolonged and continuing historical trauma, a Black future offers liberation for African Americans. By turning to the future, African Americans can imagine a new relationship with Africa to potentially suture their disconnect from it. Dery also reads the marginalised and denigrated history of African Americans as a corollary to the history of science fiction as a dismissed genre, concluding with the provocative rhetorical question: 'Can a community whose past has been deliberately rubbed out, and whose energies have subsequently been consumed by the search for legible traces of history, imagine possible futures?' (210). In short, Afrofuturism seeks to build imaginary Black futures from fragmented African and African American displaced pasts.

Dery's original usage explicitly constructs Afrofuturism as an ideology to mobilise the African American literary imaginary in the context of not being fully at home in the United States, and yet not African either. The loss of an African homeland via transatlantic slavery weighs heavily on Afrofuturism as African American identity is disconnected from Africa, even as the continent constitutes it. The African past in which one could identify with specific ethnicities, languages, and cultures is largely irretrievable. However, the future represents a creative discursive space where a rejoining of African American identity with Africanness is possible, even if only in the imagination.

However focused on African American identity this initial foundation was, Afrofuturism has come to be defined subsequently via Blackness. Some of the most salient texts after Dery are *Afrofuturism: The World of Black Sci-Fi and Culture* (2013) by Ytasha L. Womack and *Afrofuturism 2.0: The Rise of Astro-Blackness* (2017), a collection edited by Reynaldo Anderson and Charles E. Jones in which Blackness is serially conflated with being African American. Their very titles gesture towards a shift to equating Afrofuturism, not only with African Americans, but with Blackness – an idea furthered in their pages. *Afrofuturism 2.0* in particular argues that Africa is clearly included in Afrofuturism's claims to Pan-Africanism, yet demonstrates a familiarity with no particular African cultures. For example, *Afrofuturism 2.0* devotes an entire chapter to the Kenyan artist Wangechi Mutu, yet only mentions her Kenyan birthplace once with no attention to linguistic or ethnic group, attributes no Kenyan influences to her work, and relies almost exclusively on theory from Americans Donna Haraway and Octavia Butler with no reference to African theoretical constructs of art (of which there are many).[3] The other works of Afrofuturism mentioned here similarly displace Africa in their Pan-Africanism. In other words, proponents of Afrofuturism often proclaim Blackness as inclusive of Africans and African Americans, but in practice the term has come to signify the Black diaspora. Other important texts in establishing Afrofuturism (and its western bent) are a 2002 special issue of *Social Text* edited by Alondra Nelson, *The Black Imagination: Science Fiction, Futurism and The Speculative* (2011) edited by Sandra Jackson and Julie E. Moody-Freeman, and Rasheedah Phillip's *Black Quantum Futurism: Theory and Practice Vol. 1* (2015). Many iterations of Afrofuturism have been articulated by scholars, mostly American, that gesture to international liberation movements. I do not have space to address all of those here, but these are largely aspirational – rarely addressing, and never centring, Africa or any specific African cultures or traditions. This article seeks to move beyond these ambiguous admissions that Black liberation looks different for Africans and centre discussion of a Black future in Africa via specific African cultural references.

Okorafor herself is often mentioned in most of these works as a paragon of Afrofuturism. A recent example represents this phenomenon well. Bennett Capers' 2019 'Afrofuturism, Critical Race Theory, and Policing in the Year 2044' offers a comprehensive 30,000 plus word overview of Afrofuturism, that deploys Dery's definition as 'speculative fiction that treats African American themes and addresses African American concerns . . . ' (Dery in Capers). The article calls Okorafor an Afrofuturist and labels her novel *Who Fears Death* as Afrofuturism despite the novel being set in Sudan with an African woman as its main character. We can see from these examples that Afrofuturism conveniently claims self-referential African science fiction as its own while espousing an ideology that is almost exclusively diasporic, even when ensconced in discourses of Blackness.

In short, there are two problems with Afrofuturism's ability to incorporate African sci-fi fiction and comics. First, it was not initially meant to include Africa, but rather to give voice to the anxieties of African American conceptions of futurity. Secondly, its move to Blackness as a primary intersecting discourse reflects the way Blackness has been conflated with Africa-Americanness in other ideologies, perhaps most notably Black Internationalism which signals primarily how African Americans have called for solidarity beyond the United States.[4] These manoeuvres use Black and African American interchangeably so that Black signals African American without closing off the horizon to Africa itself, yet routinely failing to address the perspective of the majority of Black people in the world who overwhelmingly live in Africa. It is understandable, then, why African science fiction and comic producers would feel that their work is being incorrectly identified via a western-orientated understanding of their writing, however sympathetic they are to Black diasporic discourses. Tegan Bristow bluntly argues the lack of Africa in Afrofuturism in 'We want the funk: What is Afrofuturism to the situation of digital arts in Africa?' when she argues 'Unlike what it suggests, Afrofuturism has nothing to do with Africa, and everything to do with cyberculture in the West' (Bristow 25). For Bristow and subsequently Okorafor, Afrofuturism represents an important critique of Blackness in western culture, but does not adequately account for African experiences or their projections into the future.[5] To wit, Okorafor articulates her alienation by citing the inadequacies and misuses of Afrofuturism, but also by asserting the importance of an Africa-specific sense of futurity in literature and comics. For Okorafor, Africanfuturism both describes her work and that of other writers on the continent more accurately and serves as aspirational to encourage African content to be normalised in comics.

Shuri

The above articulates the theoretical context within which Okorafor makes her assertion for an Africa-specific term for African speculative fiction and comics, but what makes a comic Africanfuturist in practice? The following sections outline how in *Shuri* Okorafor asserts a strong African, rather than diasporic, sensibility in her work while ensuring it remains accessible to global readers.[6]

Although the character of Shuri plays a significant role in the *Black Panther* film (2018) which reinvigorated interest in the franchise, Shuri is a fairly new addition to the *Black Panther* universe. The character Black Panther was created by Stan Lee and Jack Kirby, premiering in *Marvel*'s *Fantastic Four* #52–53 in 1966 and subsequently appearing in *The Avengers, Captain America*, and *Daredevil* before featuring in his own stories entitled *Jungle Action featuring The Black Panther* starting in 1973.[7] In 1977, he became the titular character of his own comic and *Black Panther* comics have appeared in various forms since.[8] By contrast, Shuri first appears in 2005, temporarily becoming the Black Panther in a series of 2009 issues.[9] She features prominently in 2018's *Wakanda Forever*, written by Okorafor, before appearing as the titular character of her own comic in 2019. To date, *Shuri* has run for ten issues, two of which were written by Vita Ayala and eight of which were authored by Okorafor.

Shuri's history within the *Black Panther* comics and Marvel universes is significant because while she is a known figure, her relatively recent appearance gives new writers significant creative licence to shape her character. Okorafor has built a rounded backstory. Shuri is affable to the insights of the hitherto underrepresented female elders of Wakanda and her stories rely less on non-African elements than those of *Black Panther* (which have been detailed at length elsewhere). For our purposes, Shuri's trajectory as a late arriving minor character who Okorafor develops into an Afro-centric titular hero, allows us to gauge the development of the comic and the character's Africanfuturism.

The primary indicator that I will use to gauge the Africanfuturism of *Shuri* is the degree to which the comic develops as an African comic as opposed to an African diasporic one. In her short treatise on Africanfuturism, Okorafor points out that *Black Panther* has been constructed as African yet is concerned almost exclusively with affairs within the fictional Wakanda and the west, but rarely with other parts of Africa (Okorafor 2019a, 'Africanfuturism Defined'). In contrast, in *Shuri* Okorafor locates all of the action in Africa (with a brief detour through space and an alien planet) with almost exclusively African characters. The story shifts between Wakanda, Timbuktu, an alien planet, and the *Djalia* (the plane of Wakandan ancestral memory), foregoing western locales all altogether. The only white character is Iron Man, though he must travel to Mali, while the main villain (outside of alien insects) is Ethiopian.[10] These broad overarching gestures that explicitly place the comic in Africa with African characters significantly positions *Shuri* as squarely Africanfuturist. Moreover, by analysing the granular level of this Afro-centrism we can see how the comic mobilises its ideology to code Shuri as Africanfuturist via the mixing of particular African cultures.

African languages and metonymic gap

Although *Shuri* is an English language comic, Okorafor uses African languages within it to develop an African world. The comic includes words or phrases from Amharic, Swahili, and Yoruba mingled with English, sometimes explaining the insertion of the foreign language and other times not. A brief example from the fourth issue is indicative of Okorafor's African linguistic strategy. A girl named Mansa who has the unique ability to communicate with an invading insect is whisked away by chief Ikoko to the Wakandan palace. Ikoko tells her that tea is waiting for them and asks 'Would you like a cookie, muffin, or *maandazi*?' She replies 'Ooh, *maandazi*!' (Okorafor 2019a, *Shuri*). The Swahili word is inserted in a context alongside sweets such as muffins and cookies but is never explained or translated. The insertion of foreign words from formerly colonised peoples in the literature of colonial languages has been termed 'metonymic gap' by prominent postcolonial theorist Bill Ashcroft (Ashcroft et al. 2000). For Ashcroft, these non-European linguistic intrusions into European linguist texts 'constructs a "gap" between the writer's culture and colonial culture' through the use of 'unglossed words, phrases or passages from a first language, or concepts, allusion, or references that may be unknown to the reader' (Ashcroft et al. 2000). These gaps created by the insertion of African languages purposefully alienate readers in colonial languages metonymically to represent the gap between the reader's culture and the one in the text. These insertions jolt readers out of a text that has largely smoothed over cultural and linguistic difference by coming to them in their familiar and culturally dominant language. These jolts both remind readers that the speech of the story they are reading almost certainly would not take place in English, and that despite the work the text has done to welcome the reader into a foreign culture they do not know, there remain many elements of that culture that are inaccessible to them. Their knowledge is partial, not totalising.

These gaps are a form of resistance to the totality of interpretation by readers in dominant colonial languages in stories about and by those who have been the linguistic victims of that language. A Marvel comic written in Swahili or Igbo is unlikely today, but a Marvel comic with scattered references and gaps that refuses the total erasure of African languages as an important marker of culture in a comic centred on Africa is possible. This minor gap signals an important moment of Africanfuturism as Okorafor disrupts her own narrative, however briefly.

In the case of the *maandazi*, the cultural gap created is fairly small as a reader can glean from the context of muffin and cookie that accompanies tea that *maandazi* is a kind of sweet bread. However, the decontextualised reader would still not know what exactly it is, in this case popular and cheap fried dough balls (akin to a donut) that are popular street food in East Africa. The gap consists of not knowing the denotation of the word as fried dough, though perhaps being able to glean it from context, but also not knowing the larger cultural connotation. The connotation for *maandazi* is that it is primarily a street food yet on offer at the Wakandan palace. The gap here for non-East African English readers with no knowledge of *maandazi* and East Africa is minor so the alienation of missing out on the contents of a comic written in one's own language is also minor. However, Okorafor signals in this minor moment, articulated in a single word via common street food, that Wakandan royals imagine a connection to common Africans, though the connection may be lost to most western readers.

Numerous metonymic gaps appear in the eight issues of *Shuri* penned by Okorafor. We see another example when the villain Moses Magnum says 'Yah-min-deh-no?' just before being sucked into a Black hole near Timbuktu. A footnote tells us that the phrase is 'Amharic for what is that?' The alienation is less here because the phrase is translated, but its presence is a gesture to a depth inaccessible to some readers and the footnote does not mention that Amharic is the language of Ethiopia, a few thousand miles from where the events are taking place. In this example, the meaning of the African text is translated, but a layer of linguistic specificity remains, like a barely visible underlayer of a palimpsest or as Ashcroft argues 'the writers is saying 'I am using your language so that you will understand my world, but you will also know by the difference in the way I use it that you cannot share my experience' (Ashcroft et al. 2000). Why does Magnum in this moment revert to his native Amharic? What does it mean to him to do so? Okorafor does not make her text illegible to the Anglophone reader, but stresses that despite its legibility, important differences in the non-Anglophone culture cannot be glossed over via English.

Things fall apart and intertextuality

Beyond employing linguistic resistance to the totalising systems of colonialism, Okorafor expresses an Africanfuturist ethic in *Shuri* when she embeds references to African arts and culture. Her references are not simply quick allusion for the sake of African reader fan service (if such a thing exists) or a way to confirm her African *bona fides*, but work as pivotal moments in the narrative. These moments move the plot along and create a complex intertextuality with African art. Okorafor references music and other African cultural products in *Shuri* but the most illustrative example in the series comes in the climax in issue 10. Shuri's mysterious mutant hacker friend, Muti, has joined her in the supernatural *Djalia* (Plane of Wakandan Memory) where he meets thousands of years of Wakandan legends (ghosts essentially) who are assisting Shuri to defeat an invasion of powerful alien insects. Muti taps into the fabric of the *Djalia*, allowing him to understand how the insects work. When a group of soldier insects attack he realises 'I can see how they work! They're just like weak programs!' As he taps into his mutant hacking ability via the power of the *Djalia* he meditatively closes his eyes, conjuring up a series of ones and zeros. He finally destroys the soldiers with the incarnation 'Things fall apart. The center cannot hold,' a reference to the most important literary work of the print era in Africa, Chinua Achebe's 1958 novel *Things Fall Apart*, which itself borrows its title and epigraph, from the poem 'Second Coming' by Y.B. Yeats.

As a Nigerian Igbo writing in English, Okorafor's decision to allude to the most well-known Igbo to ever write in English is a fitting homage. It is certainly true that Okorafor's allusion here to Achebe is low hanging, or highly accessible, Africanfuturism in that it is a reference to the most well-known book to come out of Africa, regularly included in lists of the 100 most important books of the 20th century. Hence, it is a reference to a book that is at once African and yet accessible to non-Africans – a feat difficult to achieve. However, the moment represents more than a quick reference to African or Igbo culture, in itself a rarity in global popular culture, but embodies an intertextual moment deepened by understanding the text being deployed. In the plot of *Shuri*, the moment *Things Fall Apart* is mentioned is crucial as Shuri, who has become the Black Panther again, knows how to defeat the main enemy but cannot get past the soldiers. Moreover, the reference is uttered at the moment in the comic when the tide finally turns in favour of the Wakandans who had been unable to slow the progress of the alien invasion for nine issues. Muti reaches his hands into the material of the ancestral plane of memory, exclaiming 'I can literally read the stories of the Djalia through my hands,' inferring that a knowledge of African stories can be mobilised for contemporary problems.

Set during the early years of British colonialism in Nigeria in the 1890's, *Things Fall Apart* begins: 'Okonkwo was well known throughout the nine villages and even beyond' (1). The opening and much of the book celebrates the prowess, intelligence, and moral fortitude of Okonkwo while expositing the traditional values of Igbo society. Slowly though British colonists arrive and disrupt Igbo society. The book ends with the British profanely disrupting a sacred Igbo ritual and the disgrace of Okonkwo when he kills a British messenger. In the ultimate act of humiliation, Okonkwo commits suicide and a colonial officer overseeing the area decides that Okonkwo's life deserves 'Perhaps not a whole chapter but a reasonable paragraph (299).' The next line is the last of the novel and informs the reader as to the title of the officer's memoir: '*The Pacification of the Primitive Tribes of the Lower Niger* (299).'

The thing that is falling apart in Achebe's novel is traditional African culture. It 'cannot hold' itself together against the onslaught of European colonialism. In *Shuri*, the phrase 'things fall apart' is upended and repurposed to strengthen an African culture against a foreign invader. The trauma of colonialism is transformed into power against foreign incursion when Muti utters these words. African cultural is harnessed through an Igbo novel in English to save Wakanda, Africa, and the world. Rather than Africa being the centre that 'cannot hold,' it is the foreign oppressors of Africa who cannot withstand the power of ancestors, such as Achebe. Where Okonkwo failed, Shuri and Muti succeed.

Clearly, Okorafor could have found a way for Shuri and Muti to beat the aliens without invoking the most iconic piece of African literature, but by doing so she both stakes a claim for the African qualities of *Shuri* and Wakanda (even to western readers) and creates narrative depth for the comic via a complex intertextual relationship that further unlocks and illuminates the moment for those with the requisite understanding. In doing so, Okorafor demonstrates an African intertextual literary model for Africanfuturist comics.

The Egungun

As an epilogue to issue ten of Shuri, Okorafor pens a short page-long letter in which she expresses her excitement at being asked to develop Shuri and explains the various difficulties she encountered in writing it, such as how to combine the movie and comic book versions. She also details 'some things I set out to do.' In keeping with her statements aimed at making *Black Panther* more African, she admits that she 'wanted to reintroduce Wakanda to Africa and plant some seeds for that budding relationship with Shuri at the helm.' We have seen above a few shrewd strategies that Okorafor employs to link the world of *Black Panther* to the African world, but in her last word on *Shuri* she explicitly points to where her Africanfuturist agenda for the comic is embodied most: 'This came in the shape of the Egungun.'

In issue four, Shuri's mother calls her to a mysterious meeting. When she enters a community centre, her mother begins immediately 'This is the Egungun, a secret Pan-African alliance.' Three women and two men sit at a table. All wear a shirt that is divided vertically with Black on one side and a national flag on the other, including Nigeria, Senegal, South Africa, and Kenya. Over three panels the members of the Egungun explain that Egungun refers originally to 'the Yoruba collective ancestral spirits' and a member of the Egungun explains that the reasoning behind the name: 'We used the naming of our alliance as an exercise in being able to honor *one* of our nations without everyone else feelings slighted. It's better than making up a new name that doesn't have any weight.' This brief exposition of the alliance's name represents a challenge to the modus operandi of *Black Panther* comics to date.

As in other uses of words from African languages, the borrowing of a Yoruba word and the connotations it carries imbues *Shuri* with specific African cultures. As in the other instances of metonymic gap in which a word and its connotation creates a gap that the western reader must bridge, this reference operates on multiple registers. The simplest version of this reference allows readers to understand that this group confers with and advises the Black Panther and Wakandan royalty on their relations with and responsibilities to Africa. Beyond that lies centuries of the tradition of Egungun in Yoruba culture that inform the *raison d'etre* and the ethics of the group.

Egungun in Yoruba religious ceremonies are masked figures. In *Shuri*, this allusion to masked figures indicates the clandestine nature of the council and the significance of them revealing themselves to Shuri. In traditional Yoruba culture, Egungun serve as a type of medium to the ancestors who have power in the real world, usually interested in compelling the living to meet the ethical standards set by previous generations. The role of those who dress as Egungun is at once to communicate with the ancestors and to represent the traditional values of the community, whether that be for a family, town, or larger entity. Tunde Yusuf and Kayode Olusegun aptly articulate the Egungun sensibility in their article on the philosophy of indigenous knowledge:

> An individual does not own indigenous knowledge because it is a product of the culture, tradition and way of life of a community. It is thus community owned. It is usually passed orally from generation to generation; it is not codified or documented anywhere except in the minds of the community and the community's knowledge custodians, such as chiefs, traditional doctors, etc. (1).

In keeping with the Yoruba foundations of the Egungun, the pan-African alliance in *Shuri* is a site of cultural knowledge intent on compelling Wakanda to meet its commitments to the rest of Africa. The Egungun are a repository of the wisdom of different cultures in Africa passed down over centuries from others who were also told it orally first hand. Wakanda and others cannot know these cultures and their wisdom as outsiders as each is not only communally owned, making it exclusive in nature, but also collective in that no single person within each culture can fully represent the culture. Instead, one must consult with a variety of insider cultural experts who have been the recipients of cultural knowledge to gain the wisdom of a culture. The Egungun in *Shuri*, like Egungun in Yoruba culture, mediates their cultures and ancestral wisdom which Wakanda, under Okorafor's guidance, is coming to see as essential for its future. While this level of nuance may be lost on the average Anglophone reader, it represents an unapologetic assertion of non-diasporic African culture that helps unlock key moments in the comic.

Adding to the above depth available to the reader via the group, is a not so subtle critique of *Black Panther* comics as lacking an African ideological bent, despite purporting to be about an African. The comment by the Egungun member that 'It's better than making up a new name that doesn't have any weight' is a critique of Wakanda as a fictional African country whose name has no meaning connected to African culture. The Egungun is grounded in centuries of African traditions and mobilises African culture to help Africa while the name Wakanda is an ungrounded fiction referencing no African traditions, unfortunately mirroring its evasion of connections with Africa.[11] Clearly, African locales abound in which *Black Panther* could be grounded. One cannot help but notice that Black Panther's Marvel colleagues, most notably Captain America, are allowed real homelands to represent and defend. The origins of nearly every other human Avenger is an actual place, and one cannot ignore the Marvel Universe's obsession with New York City which is also home to many of its characters such as Spider-Man and Iron Man, as well as the headquarters of the Avengers.

For Okorafor, fictionalising an African country as Black Panther's home represents a missed opportunity to depict African life and cultures as equal to those in places like New York City. Marvel characters regularly find themselves fighting and travelling around the iconic sights of New York, such as the Statue of Liberty and the Empire State Building, pausing at times to nosh at a Jewish deli or save passengers in an MTA subway car. *Black Panther* could also introduce quotidian African contexts to represent an equally substantive and viable African way of life to Marvel readers. Wakanda could have been headquartered inside the iconic African Renaissance Monument in Senegal. Black Panther could be depicted fighting villains outside The Agostinho Neto Mausoleum in Angola, a structure taller than the statue of liberty. These real-world African locales and the Africans that inhabit them could bring Africa into focus for readers who are often unaware of the richness of specific African cultures, or even more damagingly, accept derogatory notions of Africa as poor, diseased, backwards, uncivilised, and war-torn. Via the words of the Egungun, Okorafor openly critiques the implication that an African country that is technologically advanced and powerful must be fictionalised, even in a fantastic comic world where boys are bitten by radioactive spiders to gain spider-like qualities and a glove with a gemstone can be snapped to extinguish half the life in the universe. Okorafor's intervention is minor in the grand scheme of the Marvel universe, but it demonstrates that comic writers can put real Africans and African cultures on the page alongside the spectacular as equals to their western counterparts.

Although Okorafor criticises the western orientated representation of Africa in comics, she also brings to the foreground critiques of Africa. Rather than simply reversing critical notions of Africa into positive ones, Okorafor's corrective gesture highlights problems facing Africa, refusing a naïve and idyllic view. Embedded in that short quip about how to 'honor one of our nations without everyone else feeling slighted' is a critique levelled at Africans themselves, specifically at the petty squabbles that have emerged from real-life attempts at Pan-Africanism. This critique adds yet another layer to the already significant depth given to the African world in *Shuri* and introduces African self-critique as an important element of Africanfuturism. Here Africanfuturism does not ignore the past in its creation of an African future but admits how politically fraught African unity has been historically. While not eliding a past fundamentally upended by trans-Atlantic slavery, colonialism, vulture capitalism, neo-colonialism, and other forms of Euro-American domination, Okorafor's Africanfuturism admits that Africa has also failed itself at times. This quick critique of the shortcomings of Pan- Africanism is perhaps the most self-referential African moment in *Shuri*, thus cementing it as Africa-specific and Africanfuturism rather than Afrofuturism. In short, this is insider African self-critique that like much of *Shuri* brackets the diaspora.

After Shuri's initial meeting with the Egungun she meets them again in Timbuktu after defeating the Ethiopian villain Magnum. They meet inside one of the legendary Timbuktu libraries. Both Shuri and the Egungun mention the destruction of many ancient manuscripts by Ansar Dine, an extreme Islamist group, in 2013. One member says they are at 'the scene of one of the worst crimes against Africa' and other members chime in with reference to similar attacks by Boko Haram and Fulani Herdsmen in Nigeria and Al-Shabaab in Kenya. The attacks by Islamist extremist groups Boko Haram and Al-Shabaab are widely reported the world over, but the Fulani herdsmen attacks are a string of violent assaults deadlier than Boko Haram's in Nigeria that have received significantly less worldwide attention (CNN). These groups and the infamous crimes they have committed are yet another reference to purely African acts – ones perpetrated by Africans on Africans. The Fulani herdsman allusion is also a call for recognition of an overlooked crisis. As above, Africa is the subject of criticism but in the wake of Shuri's defeat of Magnum, which prevented many causalities, the comic and real worlds are blurred by insinuating that Wakanda could have mitigated these other crises in Africa if it had been more engaged with the continent. As Shuri leaves, the hijabi Senegalese member of the Egungun urges Shuri to 'bring Wakanda back to us [Africa]' so that as a whole continent Africa can protect itself. Another member chimes in that 'Africa is a false creation that over time grew a soul. It still needs a unifying symbol' in imploring Shuri to lead the unification of Africa, a colonial invention that is constituted by the greatest variety of languages, religions, and ethnicities of any continent. Okorafor pushes back against the pervasive notion that Africa has become a singularity (i.e. Africa is a country) in the world's imagination despite its broad and disparate societies. The Egungun are asking Shuri to join them in harnessing this problematic inheritance to do justice to Africa. Just as Africans must decide how to mobilise the problematic colonial inheritance of Africa as a singular unit, Shuri must decide what to do with her own problematic inheritance of the Black Panther mantel and Wakanda's historical inaction on the continent.

Conclusion

There can little doubt that Okorafor is putting into practice her own notion of Africanfuturism. Her *Shuri* comics deploy multiple techniques to bring African issues to the forefront of the narrative, while bracketing those of the Black diaspora. The comic does this in large part via a series of allusions to African languages, foods, and cultures in general. The slippages, or gaps, created by asserting Africanness that is likely unfamiliar to readers are intentionally minor as to only mildly alienate the non-African reader, but they gesture to an available depth of field regarding topics as complex as the subject formation of Africa, Pan-Africanism's potential and shortcomings, and the ancient rituals of the Yoruba Egungun. These narrow but deep gaps are bridgeable in the sense that the narrative maintains legibility for non-African readers while offering historical, cultural, ideological, and political depth for readers with the requisite understanding, or those willing to seek out new knowledge about Africa.

In many comic theories, the unseen is highly significant in analysis. Whether the generally acknowledged referencing to blank space in the gutters between panels to give the illusion of movement, the process Scott McCloud terms 'closure,' to explain the way readers fill out comic worlds with what is inferred but not explicitly shown, or Maaheen Ahmed's argument about the importance of 'gaps' in meaning creation in her *Openness of Comics*, comics are often understood as oscillating between the seen and unseen to create meaning (Ahmed 1). Similarly, Okorafor represents a visible, manageable Africa while gesturing to a larger, more robust, unwieldy, and largely underrepresented and immense Africa. Readers may skim over the presence of a few unfamiliar allusions to *maandazi*, Fulani herdsmen, *Things Fall Apart*, and the nature of Yoruba Egungun, but nonetheless *Shuri* asserts an ethics of representation that refuses to elide Africa, and Okorafor imagines that such representational ethics should inform how writers craft *Black Panther* and other comics about Africans.

Disclosure statement

No potential conflict of interest was reported by the author(s).

Notes

1. Okorafor's short story 'On the Road' has also been adapted by other writers into a graphic novel called *After the Rain*.
2. For a discussion of Black Panther and Africa from a Euro-American perspective through the lens of the Cold War, see Martin Lund's '"Introducing the Sensational Black Panther!" Fantastic Four #52–53, the Cold War, and Marvel's Imagined Africa.' Lund, like many others such as William Schulte and Nathaniel Frederick, has much to say of import about situating *Black Panther* in comic studies, but like other commentators very little to say about Africa for its own sake, instead commenting on what Euro-America's views on Africa, race, etc. have to say about Euro-America. One can also turn to larger studies such as Bradford Wright's *Comic Book Nation* for a Euro-American perspective on race in comics which also lacks perspective on race from an African perspective. While these texts provide notable insight into comics, race, and Black Panther, they entirely lack careful analysis of Africa. At best, they acknowledge outmoded and often racist images of Africa portrayed in many American comics but do not take up alternative and substantive narratives about the continent.

3 One also finds this book's claim to encompass Africa difficult to reconcile with fact that Swahili is mentioned once in its 242 pages, Igbo twice, Yoruba three times, Arabic once, and Zulu not at all. One American city, New York, on the other hand, is mentioned by far more than all of these combined.
4 The Black Atlantic also falls into this category in that it primarily considers how to position Africa within the African American imaginary rather than visa-versa or how Africa positions itself in the world.
5 The authors of Afrofuturism are highly critical of Bristow, accusing her of articulating 'the Post-Cold War/Post-Apartheid existential crisis of some White South Africans' rather than the tangible lack of Africa-centric content in their notion of Afrofuturism. One wonders what they would make of Okorafor's nearly identical rejection of the term, especially given the fact that she is mentioned as an Afrofuturist in their book over twenty times.
6 The question of the audience of Marvel comics as a white American corporation is too large to address here, but my later discussion of metonymic gap, addresses how Okorafor subtly crafts her language as Africa-specific.
7 Ironically, *Jungle Action* before Black Panther was set entirely in Africa but featured white heroes, such as 'Jann of the Jungle,' 'Tharn the Magnificent,' and 'Lorna the Jungle Girl' while Black Africans were hapless bystanders often depicted as degrading stereotypes. With the addition of Black Panther, the comic shifted significantly to attempt, however imperfectly, to centre Black Africans rather than white Tarzan types.
8 The history of *Black Panther*'s publication is complex, featuring some publication gaps, but in general the character has appeared regularly in one form or another in Marvel comics since getting his own comic. A more detailed account of this history is available in Todd Burrough's *Marvel's Black Panther: A Comic Book Biography, From Stan Lee to Ta-Nehisi Coates*.
9 Noted Africa-American comic creator and director Reginald Hudlin created the Shuri character as a female addendum to Black Panther, stating in an interview that he created Shuri because 'I wanted girls to be as empowered as boys.' Given the trajectory of Black Panther and Shuri and statements such as 'Basically, I wanted a Halloween costume for my son and daughter' before Okorafor Shuri, we can see that initially Shuri was largely an extension of the world of Black Panther as an Africa-American fantasy (Johnson 2018).
10 Also noteworthy is that when Ayala takes over authorship of issues six and seven the setting shifts immediately to New York, and then back to Africa when Okorafor takes up authorship again in issue eight.
11 Again, the work of Lund et al. covers the non-African focus of *Black Panther* for a longer explanation.

References

Achebe, C. 1958. *Things Fall Apart*. London: Heinemann.
Adebayo, B. 2018. "Nigeria's Pastoral Conflict 'Six Times Deadlier' than Boko Haram in 2018, ICG Says." *CNN*, Cable News Network, 27 July 2018, edition.cnn.com/2018/07/27/africa/nigeria-herdsmen-boko-haram-report/index.html .
Ahmed, M. 2016. *Openness of Comics: Generating Meaning within Flexible Structures*. Jackson: University Press of Mississippi.
Anderson, R., and C. Jones, Eds. 2017. *Afrofuturism 2.0: The Rise of Astro-Blackness*. Lanham: Lexington Books.
Ashcroft, B., et al. 2000. *Post-Colonial Studies: The Key Concepts*. New York: Routledge.
Bristow, T. 2012. "We Want the Funk: What Is Afrofuturism to the Situation of Digital Arts in Africa?" *Technoetic Arts: A Journal of Speculative Research* 10 (1): pp. 25–32. doi:10.1386/tear.10.1.25_1.
Burroughs, T. 2018. *Marvels Black Panther: A Comic Book Biography, from Stan Lee to Ta-Nehisi Coates*. New York: Diasporic Africa Press.
Butler, O. 2018. "In 1980: Octavia Butler Asked, Why Is Science Fiction So White?" *Garage*, 4 Sept 2018, garage.vice.com/en_us/article/d3ekbm/octavia-butler.
Capers, I. 2019. ""Afrofuturism, Critical Race Theory, and Policing in the Year 2044" (February 8, 2019)." *New York University Law Review* 94: 101–157.

Dery, M. 1994. "Black to the Future: Interviews with Samuel R. Delany, Greg Tate, and Tricia Rose." In *Flame Wars: The Discourse of Cyberculture*, edited by M. Dery. Durham: Duke University Press. pp. 179–22.

Jackson, S., and J. Moody-Freeman, Eds. 2011. *Black Imagination: Science Fiction, Futurism and the Speculative*. Bern: Peter Lang Publishing.

Johnson, V. 2018. "*Black Panther* Writer Reginald Hudlin on T'Challa and the Future of Black Superheroes." *Vulture*. //www.vulture.com/2018/02/black-panther-reginald-hudlin-interview.html.

Martin, L. 2016. "'Introducing the Sensational Black Panther!' Fantastic Four #52–53, the Cold War, and Marvel's Imagined Africa." *The Comics Grid: Journal of Comics Scholarship* 6 (1): 7.

McCloud, S. 1994. *Understanding Comics: Writing and Art*. New York: Harper Perennial.

Nelson, A.Ed. 2002. *Social Text*. 71. (Summer)

Okorafor, N. 2019a. "Africanfuturism Defined." In *Nnedi's Wahala Zone Blog*. nnedi.blogspot.com/2019/10/africanfuturism-defined.html.

Okorafor, N. 2019b. *Shuri: The Search for Black Panther*. New York: Marvel Worldwide.

Okorafor, N. 2019c. *Shuri: 24/7 Vibranium*. New York: Marvel Worldwide.

Phillips, R. 2015. *Black Quantum Futurism: Theory and Practice*. Afrofuturist Affair/House of Future Sciences Books. New York.

Womack, Y. 2013. *Afrofuturism the World of Black Sci-Fi and Fantasy Culture*. Chicago: Lawrence Hill Books.

Wright, B. 2003. *Comic Book Nation: The Transformation of Youth Culture in American*. Baltimore: Johns Hopkins University Press.

Yusuf, T., and K. Olusegun. 2020. "Management of Indigenous Knowledge (Ifa and Egungun) in Osun State, Nigeria." *Library Philosophy and Practice*. 2015

Part IV
Troubling the African Diaspora

Random Thoughts Provoked by the Conference "Identities, Democracy, Culture and Communication in Southern Africa"

Stuart Hall

In February 1997. a workshop/conference was convened between four academic institutions: The Sage journal Culture, Media and Society, the Department of Media and Communication at the University of Oslo, Norway, the Department of English at the University of Zimbabwe and the Centre for Cultural and Media Studies at the University of Natal. Durban.

The workshop, which took place at the University of Natal. Durban, was designed to give international and South African delegates an opportunity to present papers on various topics relating to identities, as well as to explore ways of developing co-operation and exchange of staff, research interests, work in progress and information.

At the end of the conference, Stuart Hall summed up some of the main themes. Hall went on to expand on some of the issues touched on in the deliberations. Ruth Teer-Tomaselli transcribed and edited his remarks. (Ed.)

Stuart Hall

As far as I can, I've tried to group what I have been listening to into what seems to be some main themes. The first thing I'm going to do is just to indicate what those are. Most papers overlap the four basic themes that I have identified.

Then I want to say just a word about what the status of my own remarks are on these themes.

Four themes

A number of papers have been preoccupied with the very serious and important issue surrounding the question of *democratisation and the media* in the context of nation-building.

Circumscribing many of our deliberations, with people taking very different views of it, but nevertheless as a central theme and topic which couldn't be avoided, is the question of globalisation as a general context in which our debates have taken place and its potential dangers and problems. There is a major thread around the question of identity. This has proliferated in all sorts of ways, but I think one could go through the various sessions and try to gather together how we have been talking about the questions of identity. What its constituent elements are? How to think about it politically? How to think about it ideologically in a post-colonial setting specifically? I don't want to get hung up on terms, but I will come back to the question of 'post-colonial'. Then the question of identity I want to identify in a slightly different way in a moment; why we are talking about identity at all? So I'll give you *identity* as the second thing.

Thirdly, and I separate this from the substantive conceptual questions of how we think about identity, the problem of *negotiating cultural identities in Southern Africa* at this particular conjuncture. As it were though, the way I would shape the formal political problem and the substantive political issue which has circumscribed our deliberations.

Fourthly, in so far as we touch ground consistently around the political problem which is ours, and which we want to take ownership of, and in rather different ways from perhaps another conference, is the question of how central issues around cultural identity are to the development of a democratic society in Southern Africa.

Thoughtlines

Well, those are my four themes. None of them are terribly surprising. I want to warn you that I am going to express my own opinions. Inevitably, I am going to inflect them with what my own take is on those questions.

In addition to my formal agenda of four themes, I think there have been what I would call some underlying tensions, or what I would call *thoughtlines*. Now, this is the collective unconscious of conferences. The themes that really agitate, that create, constitute the flashpoints where you can see people suddenly spring out of a deep and profound sleep, and their eyes begin to flash and they grip the edge of the table. You know something has happened to them. It's not what the subject is *about*, quite, it's a kind of *underground current* which really makes conferences come alive. There are a lot of positions around the following issues. In so far as those issues create a kind of emotional and conceptual freezone in the room, we ought to know what they are because it's obvious there are some things at stake for us in them. There are tensions around what *models of analysis* underpin our discussion.

When people say

What about gender?

I see twenty people turn off and five people come alive — and I wonder whether they are talking about it in the same way. We've got to a common point, everybody knows what the *word* means, but some people, the five people who have been waiting to hear it for a day and a half, respond positively, and the other twenty people who knew it was going to come, just switched off. That's what I mean by 'thoughtlines'. Everybody knows it's there, but when it surfaces you can feel the waters part. As if you were in the Red Sea and the walls went up. You just know something awkward is passing through. What is the tension around that?

There is a tension around identity talk as such. Some people think we are talking too much about it and wonder where the hell it comes from. What happened to those old things we used to talk about? The really serious and important things. So we can't just swim into this with *'identities'* as our banner as if everybody is perfectly agreed, as a kind of settled conceptual universe as to where this word comes. It isn't at all. There are certainly tensions around *globalisation*. This is one of the points where the collective unconscious kind of became suddenly conscious. One of those moments in analysis when you look at your analyst and say,

I think we are talking about the same thing.

Well those are some moments when clearly globalisation is a tremendously important question. I am coming back to that.

The tensions around the notions of the struggle for *cultural identity* and cultural *diversity* are always there. I want to dwell on this particular aspect because I think it is so deep, and I think we are all uncertain where we line up about it. Let me describe it as tension which is within each of us. In so far as we think about cultural identity, we think about it and feel it and experience it as somewhere we would be placed, settled, at home, recognised. Where things would be *where they always have been*. Where we would be familiar with the codes being used. Where we wouldn't be looked at as if we were strangers. Where we would come home to after a long exile. For many of us, 'culture' means that. 1 suspect this is so partly because we are modem, and largely because we are urban intellectuals. That's a kind of fate and a destiny that we carry, rather than a privilege. But because of that, we are all so uneasy about that closed and settled notion of 'culture'.

We've all made our escape attempts at different times — although we don't talk about them very much. We've all waited for the moment when the culture did not close around us, did not claim us. We've always known that moment when we wanted to look over the horizon at something other than where we've been settled. We've experienced the tension between what we mean by culture between these two pulls — between *being at home* and *being in a world* which is no longer possible, because of the rapidity of social and human achievement. It's not possible to be at rest permanently until you are dead. You can be permanently at rest when you are dead, but otherwise culture continues to be something which is partly about *where you are going to,* what you *might become,* as well as *what you were* and *what your ancestors were.*

I want to describe this as a tension between *roots* and *routes.* Between thinking of culture, on the one hand, as what has rooted us in the ground — what *embeds us* in a place or in a context of recognition — and, on the other hand, thinking of culture as the *different staging posts* that we have been through in our lives, collectively and individually. The tension between these two ways of talking about culture are crucially at issue when we talk about securing the culture in nation-building. Securing the culture against external threats. This is what we have fought for. This is what is at stake.

There are important tensions around these two conceptions. Tensions around what I'd call the question of 'posts'. *Post-colonial* and *post-national* and *post-modern* and *post-enlightenment* and all of those things quite clearly are there, are serious issues of theory, theoretical development and conceptual development which we have not really talked about seriously and consistently. We've kind of stumbled across them. We've kind of taken aim and fired at one another occasionally about them. But we haven't really gone through the debate or the argument around them. And finally, there are tensions around *absences.*

That's a kind of map. Not a very good map — you can't map the unconscious because you don't know it. But you sort of know it when it erupts on you, when it sneaks up from behind you and hits you over the head. That's when you know that something has been repressed. Something which keeps on coming back, disturbing your discourse from underneath.

I have a feeling that what I have just said is shadowed by a lot of baggage. I don't want to make too many comments about South Africa, because I don't know anything about it. Nothing about it at all. I have been here for four days. South Africa is a mystical land for me. It's the one place in the world to which I couldn't go. None of us could come here for twenty — thirty years — though we know every name on the map as if we lived here. It's a curious experience of being here, of both being intensely familiar and completely at sea in relation to it. So, I don't want to make any prescriptions about South Africa at all. I do want to say that the questions that we've been debating are at a peculiar point of intensity in their coming together in their historical conjuncture.

It is interesting to me to have met so many people from Zimbabwe, who, it seems to me, have had a dubious benefit of settling in to their crisis. They are beginning to live with it like an old friend. They have heard some of those things before. But with South Africans, I get the feeling that each new statement is an annunciation of a crisis they haven't quite reached yet. Another crisis' And that's coming up the road and so is that and that! Heady excitement of an historical moment of profound transition. I am one of those unfortunate people who have only seen at first hand two historical transitions in my life. I was fortunate enough to set foot in Havana very early in 1960 before the Soviets moved in and before the Americans could quite make up their minds. That heady moment of freedom between one system and another, gives you an enormous historical opening up of the pores — which you never forget. In that moment, things become clear just as they become complicated. But they also become clear in ways which are enormously beneficial to others of us who have been thinking about them in very worn-out, well-occupied, well-grouped ways.

Democratisation and the media

About the deep question around the democratisation of the media, there are so many particular issues, but I don't have a great deal to say that will be helpful at this point. I acknowledge the point which was made sometime yesterday, about the way in which these two things are constantly involved together and the way in which they have actually failed to be profoundly theorised and analysed. It's a shocking thing that is so perfectly correct. I am sure that after the discussion we've had, we understand how important the media are, although they are by no means the only institutional force which is involved in the démocratisation of society. We know that no easy assumptions can be made about existing models of the press, and this is perhaps as apposite a point as any for me to say that the question of state and other forms or *modes of regulation* are going to be as difficult and as complicated in the areas of culture, information and communication as in any other.

Culture is one of the most unpredictable areas that we have, because of its intricacy and delicacy. It doesn't mean that we don't have to think what the modes of regulation are there, but nevertheless it seems to me that we do have to recognise the *complexity* of those modes. The only thing that we can say without fear of contradiction, is that we are in the middle of a global, *neo-liberal moment*. Whether it's generated from inside, or imposed from the outside, this is the moment when forms of global neo-liberalism are represented to us in the *language of deregulation* — but — they constitute a mode of regulation of their own. Just as free markets are not free, *deregulation is a form of regulation itself*. When we think of the conditions which even forms of liberal ownership require, when we think about the forms of regulation which might attempt to graft a social interest, or a public interest, or a national interest, or a community interest onto a prevailing market system. It's not as if we don't know what riding the tiger with two heads is like. That's what you are proposing to do.

This takes place in the middle of the decline of another kind of model which previously has had its impact on Africa. A kind of command economy model, a dissolution of the separation between state and economy, which is another way we thought opened a pathway for alternative development in Africa. You are in very much the same position as everyone else who has an emancipation project in the world: with the alternative having gone, much more intricate questions are open on how to *combine elements of regulation* with *elements of freedom*. Elements of *diversity* combine with elements of *control* to secure something like a social interest which is larger than the sum of the individual egoistic interests which are at play. Nevertheless, these elements do not do so in a form that reproduces the authoritarianism of the single, dominant political force in the form of the state.

This may feel to you like loading on to you the problems that the rest of the world hasn't solved. Yes, the rest of us are facing exactly the same problems in relation to all our social institutions. We are facing the barrage of a neo-liberated alternative and we are facing the question of how to devise new modes of social regulation which recognise institutionally the fact that we are interdependent, one on the other. We ask

What is the cost of that?

*What are the **forms** of that?*

*How do **people participate** in that?*

*How can we **extend the democratic reach** of that?*

These are the *political questions* with which we are struggling. There are no other political questions.

The one thing that I wanted to say about that to you — and not to give you hope — it's just to remind you — of course — that the alternative to a command economy comes from certain sources. Some people believe in it. Some people are paid to propagate it. But it would be an extremely simple world if it were simply being thought up in some conspiratorial committee just on the outskirts of Washington and projected by fast jet plane on to us. I have to tell you the reason why I attach some weight to the question of the post-colonial. It is not that those pressures externally don't exist, but what is *new* about the present conjuncture is that it is *deeply implicated with the internal crisis* of the post-colonial state. It is implicated in the very form of the national liberation moment and the aftermath.

It's not simply what *they* are doing to *us*. There is an old answer to that: Get rid of them if you can! But when *they* are doing that to *us,* and some of *us* are doing that to *us* as well, the question of who is *there,* and who is *here-,* where is *inside* and where is *outside,* becomes much more complicated.

When we say it's a complicated question, what we are talking about is *politics*. Politics, however complicated at a certain point, divides into *those* over there and *us* over here. In reality, some of *them* are over here, and some of *us* are over there. That is really what it is like. The colour of who is doing what to whom cannot be predicted from outside. It is necessary to know something about the local situation.

I need some term. *Post-colonialism* happens to be the one I like. If you don't like it, throw it away but don't lose sight of what is specific about that conjuncture. When the crisis has been internalised in so-called 'developing countries', they themselves are *internally* living the crisis of their relations with the rest of the world, with the rest of the globe.

Globalisation

Now let me turn to the question of globalisation.

I don't want to have a theological argument about globalisation. Whether we like it or not, we have to acknowledge that globalisation provides one of the historical domains in which the new nation-building is going on. I don't know whether it strikes you how extraordinarily paradoxical it is. The nation state, the national economy, the national cultures and globalised world market have always co-existed. The nation states, the big European nation states, were the engines of a system which lived, in part, by the globalisation of the economy. Now what is happening in the new forms of globalisation is that many societies, including of course post-colonial but not only those, many societies in eastern Europe for example, having seen the lessons of history, reach for the nation state at the moment it begins to weaken on a global level. To play the big game, everybody has got to become a nation. I can't be persuaded that there is any other reason for people in former Yugoslavia to tell themselves these fantastical stories, the former history of the Serbs, etc., plucking out this bizarre identity of the Soviet nation at this point in time, 1996/1997, unless they thought there was really some purchase in becoming a nation just now.

It is not my view that globalisation renders the nation-building useless. But it is my view that *globalisation reconfigures* the relationship between the *global,* the *local,* the *national* and the *regional.* They *don't disappear,* but the relations and the *balance between them shifts* in the context of globalisation. It's exactly as in the media context. When television was introduced, people said television will obliterate all the other media. That hasn't happened. What television has done, is to reconstitute all the other uses of the other media.

Radio for instance, in Britain, has disappeared as the voice of the *national community,* but has popped back up in a much reconstituted form, proliferating everywhere as a voice of *local communities.* It's still in the game, but the balance between the elements changed — that is what is happening to the nation. It's no longer that engine of modernity which it was in the nineteenth and early twentieth century, nor is it going to cease to exist. Therefore, it is a player, but is not a player in the same way as it has been before.

The question is:

> What does that **do** to a society **like** the society of Southern Africa, for which nation-building is the summation of the enormous struggle they have been through?
>
> What will be produced out of the ferocious, horrendous divisions and inequalities of the past?

Something like a *national culture,* something like a *national identity* which would transcend the internal divisions?

At that very moment, it is as if the big game shifts upwards a bit. It says,

> That's important, but look at what is happening in the global environment. Look at how what is happening there is contained, redefined. It is important, it is **repositioned in relation to the global.**

That is the reason why I think the question of globalisation is important. Whatever theoretical models we want to bring to bear on it, we've got to think about this question:

> What is the nature of the national culture and the national identities we are now struggling to build in an era of intensified global relationship?

Not to think about that, is not to be serious about our own project.

The notion of globalisation is *structured by power*. The suggestion that societies are entering this competition on a level playing field is just nonsense. They are *riven by power*. But whether that means that there is nothing to it but the incoming prize of power, I am not convinced.

If we think about globalisation in terms of migration of peoples forced and free, for example, the movement of cultures around the world; if we think about it in terms of the number of images of *the other* that is available to larger numbers of people, not necessarily the few rich people of the world; if we think about it as just the very proliferation of a sense of lives and cultures and worlds and forms of behaviour and ways of carrying on that are not like ours; then we must think of it as being able to *produce power,* and not simply to be produced *by* power.

The knowledge of *difference* which widens and spreads throughout our societies today, quite far down the social register, makes it impossible for us to imagine a form of national identity or national culture which could effect some form of workable cultural closure against globalisation. I mean *entire* cultural closure. But, let me warn you, that is not to say that people aren't going to try. The attempt to close cultures, to set up *defensive cultural barriers* against globalisation, usually against the failure of modernisation in societies, is a form which is widespread, not only in the Third World. *Fundamentalism* is alive and well in the United States and in Western Europe and in Britain. This is not a code word for Islam or something rubbishy like that. Again and again, cultures that feel under threat, live the fantasy that they could just lock the doors to go back at being British in the old way; or French in the old way. They try to protect their way of life in that sense.

Now if we can't do that — and I don't have the time to argue why I think we can't — If we can't do that, and we are not prepared to open the skies, to lie down and think of Manhattan — you know, to say,

Come in please. I'm yours.

If we are not prepared to do that, then we have to work out the most complicated and ingenious, imaginative compromises which allow our citizens to have a strong enough sense of themselves that they are not obliterated by what is coming in. But not so closed against the experience of others as to write themselves out of modernity.

The elite of the emerging nation state — out of the best will in the world, the best enlightenment will in the world — that says to its own people,

The best thing for you is not to have a stake in modernity

will go down. Deserves to go down. It's standing in the way of one of the deepest aspirations of human beings to experience life at its most advanced. People want that, and people will come towards that. They will create both new historic needs and desires and it's not our duty guarding their culture, guarding their old way of life, guarding their families and guarding our fantasies about the past. Guarding our investment in tradition which we have long since passed. But we like to go back to the village and find it just as it was before, in exactly the same way as the people in the Caribbean would love to go back to Africa to discover their roots, imagining that it still looks like it did when the slave ships left three hundred years ago. They are disappointed to find things have happened to Africa in the last three hundred years. It hasn't been waiting for them to go back to their roots to find it exactly as it was, frozen in time.

What is the balance between simply saying to the global culture,

> Come in and destroy ns. take us.

which is to cede the very things that we've been struggling for, or on the other hand to say,

> The only way we can survive is to tell our people that they must forget to be modern folks, they must go on being tribal, traditional, primitive folks that people take the plane to come and look at and photograph and go back home and say 'I saw some of them, I looked at the childhood of mankind in Africa'?

You will go down! And rightly so! Because they believe there are dominant modernities. But they don't believe they have no capacity to make a modem form of life of their own.

Identities

This takes me to the final point which is about the question of identities. If we conceive of *identity* as something which is given to us at birth, a little seed which is the *real* us, has grown into an acorn, and which hasn't been changed by time, by history by anything, then we *can* think of culture and identity as something that stands still. We can think of identity as something that is always unified and homogenous. But actually, none of us think identity is like that.

We keep talking about how history has changed. We keep talking about how people who *used to be like* that, are *now like* this. We keep talking about the birth of a new subject. We keep talking about the different histories that have made us what we are; what is specific to our identity. In the post-modem notion of identity we are nothing. We are just a sort of wandering star. We can choose to be this today, on the Internet, and be that tomorrow, etc. It's just crap. The one thing we are *not* is one, only one thing. What we are, are those different histories. Those different ways in which at different historical moments people have addressed us, have called us and the recognitions this implies.

> Yes, that is me.

That is a moment of identity, of identification. And thank God many of us are called in all sorts of ways, all day.
   Advertising is nothing but an attempt to call us.

> Hello, over here, this is what you look like, this is what you should wear.

Fortunately, not everybody answers all the time or we would have gone around the bend. Fortunately, every now and again we say,

> Yes, that's me.

That is the point where we take up an identity position. If we think we are going to take it up forever, forget it, because history is going to change on us. Someone is going to say,

> I know.

I can tell you this in terms of my own experience. I was born in the Caribbean. In my childhood, nobody in the Caribbean ever addressed me as *black*. The word was not used.

They used forty other synonyms for it, but nobody ever called me *black*. When I came to Britain, my mother said to me,

I hope they don't make you into one of those blacks over there.

I can tell you when I became a black intellectual. In the 1960s, after *black* was made to mean something different by a whole social movement, then it became a mirror into which I looked and said,

That's what I am. I am black, of course.

It's something I've always known. Identity is a kind of 'after the *event recognition*". This is what I've always been. I've never called myself *black* until now. What else could I be? It is that moment when identity surfaces and identification is made.

Identification is much more important than *identity*. Identification, the moment when we invest in how we are hailed from the outside. Or when we say,

No, I'm not one of those! I don't belong to that classification. 1 won't see myself in that mirror.

Those are the moments over which politics struggle. Political struggles can make us make those identifications. Although the question of identity and how we think about it is not unified, it is not just nothing. We all come out of very specific histories. We all come out of very specific languages. When I say that, what I mean is that we all have access to ways in which we express ourselves. Both at the high level and at the simple level. That is who we are. We are the sum of the positions that we've assented to. We are the sum of the ways in which we've been willing to be recognised. We are the sum of the claims we've been willing to make. We are the sum of where we hope we are going. What we are hoping to become. We are the sum of the subjects that we dream ourselves into.

The idea that identity might be some vaporous thing that happens in our heads, that it doesn't have anything to do with how we imagine ourselves, is just nonsense. The *nation* itself, and most collectivities of that kind, depend on material conditions, personal and social relationships. But they also depend on how we *imagine ourselves*. We don't actually know, we never actually know all the other people in communities. If we feel bound to a community, it is because we have taken an *imaginative identification* with other people like us. With people who have been oppressed or excluded because of their skins, or because of their gender, or because of their sexualities. *That is what identification means*. It has much to do with what is in your imagination.

That is why the question of the *media* is so crucial. It's not just crucial depending on the literal documentary information it gives us. It's crucial because it *trades in images* of us. It trades in possible identification. It says,

Invest in me. Give the feeling of emotion, assent to me and I will **recognise** *you.*

The idea that we could constitute a culture in which people would be perfectly happy, whatever the messages, whatever the stories that people told or recited one to another, whatever the songs they sang, is fictitious. It's not the case.

It isn't that we overvalue language in some crude way. It is that what we think of, what sets a lot of the processes into being that are certainly material conditions which limit what *is possible to be* and what is *not possible to be*. Unless that moment of identification is, or is not made, the body does not come into the place. We have an empty screen where the people or the party or the proletariat even should be, but nobody chose to go there.

We know a lot of historical circumstances in which we could say why everybody should be in the picture, in the frame, and yet they aren't. They just didn't identify. They didn't come in. There is still a notion that we could make a new society, a democratised society, make a society beyond the reach of the rigid classifications of ethnicity and race. Without the *moment of identification,* it just seems to me to be impossible to conceive. Exactly how the negotiations around that are happening in the new South Africa, is a question which I don't have the competence to answer.

I want to say two things in closing.

Every identity is an exclusion. Unless we are going to identify ourselves as nothing but members of the human race, every other identification leaves something out. To leave something out is an act of power. It's an act of symbolic power, which is to say:

> I am what I am because I'm not the other.

Difference of that kind isn't always invested with power. People have brown eyes and blue eyes. You don't create eye colour, except in science fiction. You don't have a ruling race because they have blue eyes. *Difference is an open invitation to power.* As soon as power sees differences, it knows it can begin to classify *them* and *us,* into the brown eyes and the blue eyes, the black eyes and the white, the sort-of-brown and the not-so-brown, the kinky-hair and the straight-hair and on and on it goes. Difference invites the play of power.

The question about those exclusions is that sometimes they are imposed with utmost violence including physical violence and the violence of the state. That is precisely what apartheid is. Many of the societies don't try to impose their classification in that way. But of course they discipline and normalise the institutionalisation of differences of class, of gender, of sexuality, of race and ethnicity all the time. Apartheid was a particularly extreme form of institutionalising difference with violence of the law.

When we constitute an identity which leaves some voices more marginal and leaves some voices out; that which is excluded almost always picks itself off the floor, gets itself together, walks around to the back door, breaks a window and comes back in. It comes back in to trouble the fixed, settled, well-ordered structure of who-is-in and who-is-out. Be careful that in that moment of constituting the *us* we don't forget to hear the *them.* Who is the *them* being left out? Who is in the margin? Who is excluded? The excluded aren't going to be excluded all the time! They are going to come back and trouble the way in which we are trying to organise and classify the world. That's the first thing.

The second thing about how those identities are being negotiated goes back to the point I made about *tradition and roots.* I come from the Carib-Ararach Indians and they were practically wiped out within a hundred years of the arrival of the Spanish. Everybody else who is in the Caribbean comes from somewhere else. We find it very difficult to be at home because we are exiles. The French are exiles, the British are exiles. Portuguese are exiles, the Indians came with indentured labour, the Blacks came as slaves. Everybody is from somewhere.

Out of that has come a very rich musical tradition of which I cite a figure like Bob Marley. I think the rest of the world imagines that Marley is somebody who heard a traditional

African music played in his home village, remembered it all the while. Somehow, when the circumstances were right, was able to breathe out exactly as he'd heard, exactly as it was brought from Senegal or where it came from. When at last the Jamaican people were independent, he presented it to them as a kind of monument:

> This was always our music and here it is. I've been keeping it in a bag for you.

Of course it is not true that Marley could have produced a single note — or especially a single rhythm — without the underground tradition of African rhythm. Of course memory plays an absolutely crucial part. But there has never been a traditional music in the Caribbean called reggae. There never was. It is the effect of what we call the *invention of tradition*. It was created as an old music the day before yesterday. It speaks to people because it combines enormous elements from the past and an address to today, to what is happening in downtown Kingston. It is made in downtown Kingston, which is one of the most unmemorable parts of the earth, familiar in every street and siding throughout the entire world. Everybody knows Trenchtown as if they were there. If I could describe it, Trenchtown could fit in this room. It's about forty houses, yet it is known throughout the world.

> *Is it known because it was always there?*
> *No!*
> *Is it known because it was created the day before yesterday?*
> *No!*
> *Is it the same music as was created with the music of the African slaves?*
> *No!*
> *Did they forget entirely their music?*
> *No!*
> *Is there an influence of western music on it?*
> *Yes!*
> *Is there an influence of religious music on it?*
> *Yes, of course!*

Jamaica is a more deeply religious society than any in the world. Any in the world. The only question is not whether you belong to church, but which *sect* you belong to. Nobody would dream of asking you whether you belong to church. It is only a question of which church, combining which bit of African and Christian and Calvinist religion. Deeply and profoundly religious.

Where does this music come from?

It comes out of the *transformation of culture*. The production of new culture out of what is already there. It is not the act of complete creativity from nothing, but of the specificity of the experiences made into something new. The end result has never existed before. It honours the past without being bound to it. It is about the present without being celebratory about it. It looks towards the future in a language which it borrows from Christian conversion although it's founded in a non-Christian philosophy. It's out of these *syncretic* things, borrowed here and there, that a music has been produced with which is practically the only thing Jamaicans fully identify. *That* they know is their music.

We need to begin to think about cultural identity with that notion of the fact of the *relationship*, the *forging of the relationship between past, present and future*. Not in an imitative or monumentalist way but in the way which enables *new subjects to be introduced*. We talk about there being rainbow subjects, we just have to spend a lot of time thinking about what it is. But it is a new subject. We are talking about the production of a *new subjectivity.* Something which has never yet been seen on earth in this part of the world, which will not forget the terrors out of which it has been constructed and the violence and the horror but which will also make something creative out of it. Which won't be afraid, as Bob Marley was not afraid, to use twenty-first century technology to spread his message across the world.

Marcus Garvey: The Remapping of Africa and Its Diaspora

Rupert Lewis

ABSTRACT

This article takes up the challenge of the United Nations (UN) Resolution which designated 2011 the Year of African Descendents by remembering Marcus Garvey's impact on anti-colonial and nationalist movements in Africa, which led to political freedom and the remapping of Africa and its diaspora. This solidarity was forged through the dissemination of Garvey's writings, as well as the establishment of branches of the Universal Negro Improvement Association and African Communities League (UNIA) in West and southern Africa, especially South Africa. This solidarity between Africans on the continent and African descendants in the diaspora laid the foundation for modern Pan-Africanism and African Nationalism. Focus is given to Garvey's thought and his solidarity with Sol Plaatje, an early leader of the African National Congress.

Introduction

The imperial remapping of the world over the past half a millennium was structured on very profitable economic systems undergirded by political, cultural and racial systems that shored up hegemonic power and gave legitimacy to the 20th-century global order of empire and racial oppression. Racial oppression created apartheid in South Africa, Rhodesia, Namibia, and many countries in Africa, while segregation was the name given to the racially discriminatory system in the United States (US). In all these conditions racial solidarity arose among the oppressed (Magubane 1987).

Solidarity may transcend ethnic boundaries and involve whites and non-African persons, but it implies a common bond of interests and empathy, an understanding of the circumstances of power and working through the strategies, tactics and organisational forms necessary to change power relations. Solidarity is premised on strategies of communication, and these take many forms: face-to-face, door-to-door campaigns; church meetings; legal, illegal and clandestine work; organising mass protests against a powerful state apparatus; joining the armed struggle against overwhelming military odds – as was the case in South Africa, so well documented for the period 1960–1994, in the six volumes of the *Truth and Reconciliation Commission of South Africa report*. It is this history of the 20th-century anti-colonial, civil rights and liberation struggles that lie behind the United Nations (UN) resolution which has designated 2011 the Year of African Descendents. The resolution starts out by reaffirming the Universal Declaration of Human Rights, which proclaims 'that all human beings are born free and equal in dignity and rights and that everyone is entitled to all the rights and freedoms set forth therein, without distinction of any kind'.[1]

The UN resolution governing the activities for 2011 calls for the strengthening of 'national actions, regional and international cooperation for the benefit of people of African descent in relation to their full enjoyment of economic, cultural, social, civil and political rights, their participation and integration in all political, economic, social and cultural aspects of society, and the promotion of a greater knowledge of and respect for their diverse heritage and culture'. Such a resolution requires struggles on many levels, among them, national and global. This was the case with the anti-colonial struggles and this has to be the case with the current struggles against national and global economic and political systems which impede the realisation of the goals outlined in the resolution. The resolution also requires paying tribute to the movements that struggled for a world where the rights of the subjects of European and American empires would include taking their place as human beings and so redraw the maps of colonial geographies. One such 20th-century movement was the Garvey movement.

Catalysts for the Garvey movement

Marcus Garvey was born in St. Ann's Bay, a northern seaport town of Jamaica, on 17 August 1887. From his early years in St. Ann's Bay until his death in London on 10 June 1940, just two months short of his 53rd birthday, Garvey used his knowledge of the world, the experience of extensive travels through Central America, Europe, the West Indies and the US, to develop a global perspective on the future of Africa and people of African descent, and to build an organisation that embodied the aspirations of millions of Africans for self-determination, justice and freedom.

The Universal Negro Improvement Association and African Communities League (UNIA) was launched in Kingston, Jamaica, in 1914. Prior to the launch Garvey said, in a pamphlet entitled *A talk with Afro-West Indians*: 'For the last ten years I have given my time to the study of the condition of the Negro, here, there, and everywhere, and I have come to realise that he is still the object of degradation and pity the world over, in the sense that he has no status socially, nationally, or commercially' (Hill 1983a: 55).

This degradation was due to the transatlantic slave trade, plantation slavery and colonialism – systems that had been organised by Portugal, Spain, Britain, France, Holland, the US, Belgium, Germany and Denmark. The scramble for Africa followed on the end of the transatlantic slave trade, and Africa thereby continued to be central to European economics and politics. In 1876 only 10.8 per cent of Africa had been colonised, but by 1900, 90 per cent of the continent had been carved up. These systems laid the basis for modern racism throughout the world, and Africans and their descendants bore the brunt of its impact for centuries.

In the US, the bloody Civil War of 1861–1865 claimed more than 600 000 lives, but brought freedom to four million African-American slaves. After a decade this freedom was aborted and racial segregation was legally justified to ensure economic exploitation under white supremacy. It took 100 years before civil rights were achieved in the US in the 1960s.

In many Latin-American countries which had gained independence in the 19th century, African descendants who had fought in these wars of liberation from European rule became second-class citizens. They did not have the right to vote, to access education, or to hold certain jobs, as there was public discrimination. In addition there was personal discrimination which restricted social relations between people of different races and shades of skin colour.

In general, the colonial world was one of limited opportunities where, for the majority of the population, employment on an estate and cultivating a small plot of land were the main options. Higher education was the privilege of whites, brown people and some blacks, and on graduation the racial ceiling in employment in the civil service, the police force, and in the educational system was rigorously reinforced by the preferential promotion and recruitment of young British white males and some females. It is not surprising, therefore, that there was considerable migration from the Caribbean islands to Panama, Cuba, Costa Rica and the US of people in search of a better life. Garvey was himself a migrant to Panama and Costa Rica. Between 1882 and 1915, when the Jamaican population was around 500 000, 168 888 Jamaicans left the island to work on the construction of the Panama Canal (Lewis 2006: 84). The West Indian migrant communities in these overseas territories were key areas in the growth of the Garvey movement.

Another factor which spurred interest in Garvey's message was World War I (1914–1918), in which, for the first time, colonial Caribbean soldiers saw class divisions among Europeans and recognised that there were also European workers and peasants, not only European plantation owners and bosses. They came into contact with radical ideologies, political parties and trade unions that were based on class principles. More importantly, the promises made to West Indian soldiers that they would be given the right to vote and receive grants of land were not fulfilled. As a result, many of the veterans of World War I adhered to radical Garveyism, both in the US and in the Caribbean.

Yet many colonial subjects in the British Caribbean were pro-monarchical in their sentiments. They believed that the evils of colonialism were perpetrated by local whites, and that the British king was the caring, albeit somewhat neutral, head of the Empire. Some of these ideas were fostered by the rituals of religion and school, and portraits of British sovereigns were hung on the walls of many black peasants' homes. Encounters with racism in Europe in its many and varied forms helped to explode the myth that the Empire was for all – black and white alike. Many black soldiers had inadequate clothing for the European winter and succumbed to frostbite, losing fingers, hands and toes in the process. Many were killed by the winter, not while in combat.

Garvey's Pan-Africanism

After taking part in activities around trade unionism, journalism and politics in Jamaica, and travelling to Central America and Europe, Garvey concluded that the problems facing Africa and African descendents were international.[2] In 1914, on his return from England to Jamaica, he formed the Universal Negro Improvement Association and African Communities League (the UNIA). He then left Jamaica in 1916 with the intention of meeting with Booker T. Washington, to try to raise money to develop a Tuskegee Institute for education in Jamaica. But he got caught up in the growth of a new consciousness and activism among African Americans, and the UNIA took off and grew in the US beyond his wildest expectations. This growth enabled the organisation to emerge as an international force of black resistance and affirmation. Yet Garvey did not build this movement by himself: there were many women and men who laboured in different parts of the world, helping to shape a new consciousness of our possibilities in the struggle for freedom.

Garvey continued the tradition of Caribbean contributions to the African liberation that was already evident in the work of the Trinidadian barrister, H. Sylvester Williams, who organised the 1900 Pan-African Conference from 23–25 July 1900, in London (Hooker 1975: 31), and who went to Cape Town from 1903–1905 to establish a legal practice and continue his activism (Mathurin 1976: 113–127).[3] Another Pan-Africanist from Trinidad was Malcolm Nurse, better known by his revolutionary *nom de guerre*, George Padmore (Baptiste & Lewis 2009). Padmore played a critical organisational and ideological role in the Pan-African movement from the 1920s until his death in 1959. He represented the trend in Pan-Africanism that was influenced by Leninist thinking about anti-imperialism and self-determination. Padmore was a mentor to Dr. Kwame Nkrumah and became his advisor when Nkrumah became the first Prime Minister of Ghana in 1957.

The distinctive feature of the Garvey movement in the 1920s and 1930s was its mass popular base and the successful communication strategies deployed in newspapers, public meetings and face-to-face communication, to influence the growth of a new consciousness of self-confidence and purposeful activities by Africans and African descendents. This was mass-based Pan-Africanism which had organisational roots in East, West and southern Africa. Divisions of the UNIA existed in Lesotho, Liberia (Monrovia and Brewerville), Nigeria (Kano and Lagos),[4] South Africa (Cape Town, Johannesburg and Pretoria) and Namibia (Lüderitz and Windhoek). Yet this organisational presence does not reflect the influence of the Garvey movement in Kenya, Senegal, Rhodesia, the Congo and other parts of the continent, where the *Negro World* newspaper was circulated clandestinely or where sailors, students and other travellers to the US, France or England were exposed to Pan-African ideas. Volume IX of *The Marcus Garvey and Universal Negro Improvement Association papers – Africa for the Africans (June 1921–December 1922)*, edited by Robert Hill, traces in detail the UNIA in Liberia, in Accra, Gold Coast, and in Freetown, Sierra Leone. Hill points out that

> [c]olonial police surveillance of Garveyism was a constant component of the movement's history. The *Negro World* was banned in French West Africa in January, in Nyasaland in March, in Nigeria in June, in The Gambia in September, and in the Gold Coast in December 1922. In the Belgian Congo, an official ordinance gave the colonial government the power to refuse entry to foreigners. South Africa and South West African police conducted extensive surveillance of Garveyite activities. In Kenya, colonial officials and police investigators sought to establish the existence of a connection between the UNIA and Joswa Kamulegeya of the Young Baganda Association. Police in Freetown interrogated a UNIA deportee from Senegal to ascertain the nature of the material confiscated in Dakar. (Hill 1995: xlviii)

Sol Plaatje, the first secretary of the ANC and certainly one of its co-founders, shared platforms with Garvey in New York in the 1920s (Meli 1988: 37). Moreover, Plaatje's writings, including his classic sociological work *Native life in South Africa*, were known to readers of the *Negro World*. During Plaatje's 1921–1922 visit to the US he published in the *Negro World* and was hosted by the UNIA (Willan 1984: 265). Brian Willan, Plaatje's biographer, wrote that in February and March 1921

> the *Negro World* carried reports of the many meetings Plaatje addressed in the city, most of them in churches (usually belonging to the African Methodist Episcopal Church) and private residences …. By far the largest audiences Plaatje attracted, in New York or elsewhere, were the packed meetings (six altogether) he addressed at Liberty Hall, which seated over 6,000

people; many thousands more were able to read the verbatim reports of his speeches in the columns of the *Negro World*. On the first occasion, the day after he arrived in New York, Plaatje and Garvey spoke together on the same platform. (Willan 1984: 266)

Plaatje also had ties with Dr. W.E.B. Du Bois and Du Bois' journal *The Crisis* published the American edition of *Native life in South Africa*. A correspondent from Cape Town, writing under the name of Peter Daniels, wrote the *Negro World* newspaper a letter in 1921 which enables us to understand how he perceived the ideas of Garveyism. Daniels wrote:

> Garveyism is a new doctrine, a doctrine with such far-reaching effects that it has revealed to the black race that there are good hopes for them as a race, and that there is a life for them that is really worth living. It has stirred up consciousness within the race, and it has demonstrated the value of organisation. Garveyism has taught the Negro that God Almighty created him a free Man, and that it wasn't God's intention that he should be a serf and slave all his life. It has taught the Negro to begin carving out his own destiny in the quarry of this great world. Garveyism has indeed caused a revolution within every right-thinking Negro and has unveiled to them those sterling qualities with which men are endowed. (in Hill 1995: 242)

This impact on consciousness, accompanied by a parallel organisational initiative, represented the platforms by which Garveyism became the ideology of a global movement.

In 1920, Clements Kadalie, pioneer of black trade unionism in South Africa and leader of the Industrial and Commercial Workers Union, in a letter to a colleague wrote: '[M]y essential object is to be the great African Marcus Garvey and I don't mind of (sic) how much I shall pay for that education' (Hill & Pirio 1987: 215). Garvey also had a major influence on James Thaele, a leader of the ANC in the Cape, described as the driving force of Cape Town Garveyism, and under whose leadership the 'Western Cape Congress, UNIA, ICU were virtually synonymous' (ibid: 232).

A final example of solidarity is the letter sent from Frank Mothiba – an ANC activist – to the *Negro World* in 1924, which concluded: 'May God bless our true leader, Marcus Garvey, and the UNIA till Africa, the land of our fathers, is redeemed, so that the red, the black and the green may fly on the hilltops of Africa. Nkosi, sikelela Africa (God bless Africa)' (Hill 2006: 277).

Given his ideological trajectory and widening influence, Garvey's resistance to white supremacy was met with repressive legislation, propaganda and force. As the movement gained in strength, the US and European governments took action against Garvey to restrict his travel and ban the *Negro World* newspaper. There was even an attempt to assassinate him in 1919. J. Edgar Hoover, later head of the Federal Bureau of Investigation (FBI), infiltrated the movement with special agents who made several attempts to build a case to imprison and deport Garvey from the US because he was regarded as a trouble-maker. Theodore Kornweibel Jnr. points out that 'no black militant drew more investigation and surveillance by the Military Intelligence Division, State Department, and Bureau of Investigation ... than Marcus Garvey ...' (1998: 100). Among the black agents who were placed in the UNIA headquarters and Black Star Line was a Jamaican in whom Garvey confided. In 1923, Garvey was charged and convicted of mail fraud as a result of the intended sale of Black Star Line stock. The charge arose from the fact that monies had been solicited by offers of the Black Star Line stock at a time when the business had not yet completed its purchase of a new boat. The officers directly involved in sending out the mail to potential purchasers were charged along with Garvey, but he alone was punished while the others went free. The case continues to be analysed by students of law, and most scholars point to the fact that the judge was a supporter of an organisation – the National Association for the Advancement of Colored People (NAACP) – hostile to Garvey; that the jury was all-white; and that Garvey was not directly involved in sending out the mail. In 1927, after spending nearly three years in prison, Garvey was deported to Jamaica. He remained there until 1935 when he relocated to Britain.

Aspects of Garvey's philosophy and praxis

Garvey had a profound understanding of the role of religion, as his sermons and the theological discussions in the UNIA showed. His theological writings form the base for the development of Black Liberation theology, which emerged in the US in the 1960s. But, more importantly, Garvey's location of the Bible in time and geographical place enabled the development of catechisms for teaching the young about the place of Africa and Africans in the Old and New Testaments. Hence, for example, the importance attached to Ethiopia and its role in the spread of early Christianity. At the same time the movement also recognised the importance of Islam in Africa. The UNIA took the position that it was a secular organisation open to a diversity of theological views, and what brought its members together was the struggle for freedom against colonialism and racism. Garvey's slogan, 'Africa for the Africans, those at home and those abroad' paralleled the cry at the time of 'India for the Indians' and of demands for Egyptian and Irish sovereignty. So Garveyite nationalism was part of a sentiment emerging in the colonial world which sought to develop sovereignty among colonial peoples.

Garvey placed great emphasis on organisation. In *Philosophy and opinions* he wrote:

> Organization is a great power in directing the affairs of a race or nation toward a given goal. To properly develop the desires that are uppermost, we must first concentrate through some system or method, and there is none better than organization. Hence, the Universal Negro Improvement Association appeals to each and every Negro to throw in his lot with those of us who, through organization, are working for the universal emancipation of our race and the redemption of our common country, Africa. (Jacques-Garvey 1992: 24)

The UNIA was organised in over 40 countries in nearly 1 200 divisions in Africa, the Caribbean, Latin America, Australia, and especially in the US, where it was strongest, with some 936 divisions – more than half of these were located in the apartheid southern states. Eight conventions of the UNIA were held in New York, Kingston and Toronto in the 1920s and 1930s, during August (the month which is associated with the emancipation from slavery in the West Indies). The first historic convention, held at Madison Square Gardens in August 1920, brought together representatives from many parts of the world and produced the historic 'Declaration of rights of the negro peoples of the world'. This declaration affirmed that 'Negroes, wheresoever they form a community among themselves should be given the right to elect their own representatives to represent them in Legislatures, courts of law, or such institutions as may exercise control over that particular community'(quoted in Hill 1983b: 573). It affirmed not only the right to representation, but the right to common human respect, religious worship, freedom of movement, freedom of the press and free speech. It protested the illegal seizures of land, lynching, flogging and segregation, and affirmed the freedom of Africa. This collective document represents the core philosophy of the Garvey movement.

Another quotation provides the three cornerstones of Garvey's philosophy:

> No Negro, let him be American, European, West Indian or African, shall be truly respected until the race as a whole has emancipated itself, through self-achievement and progress, from universal prejudice. The Negro will have to build his own government, industry, art, science, literature and culture, before the world will stop to consider him. Until then, we are but wards of a superior race and civilization, and the outcasts of a standard social system. (Jacques-Garvey 1992: 24)

The first pillar is that regardless of nationality, prejudice against Africans and their descendents is universal. Second, he affirmed the principle of self-reliance. Third was the centrality of Africa to his political thought. Yet Garvey did not advocate a mass repatriation to Africa. In a speech published in *The Negro World* on 13 November 1920, he stated:

> Understand this African program well. I am not saying that all the Negroes of the United States should go to Africa; I am not saying that all the Negroes of the West Indies should go back to Africa, But I say this: That some serious attempt must be made to build up a government and nation sufficiently strong to protect the Negro or your future in the United States will not be worth a snap of the finger ... Without an independent Africa – without a powerful Africa you are lost.

In clarifying this position Garvey argued in *Philosophy and opinions* that 'to fight for African redemption does not mean that we must give up our domestic fights for political justice and industrial rights' (quoted in Jacques-Garvey 1992: 35). There was, therefore, a relationship between the idea of the liberation of Africa and the efforts by blacks, wherever they were, to advance their positions. So, in keeping with the centrality of Africa, Garvey tried to set up an African headquarters of the UNIA in Liberia, and the organisation even acquired land there. However, by the mid-1920s, under pressure from France, Britain, the US and Firestone Rubber Co., the UNIA plan was frustrated.

Another important area of Garvey's thought was his insistence on practical economic programmes. The Black Star Line was the single-most important economic venture that gained Garvey mass support. The Garvey boats which plied the Atlantic Ocean and the Caribbean Sea were the expression of what blacks could achieve at a time when naval and commercial sea-power still symbolised Western economic and military strength. Garvey's supporters saw a bigger meaning in the small boats he put out to sea. Blacks at that time had difficulty travelling and getting their produce shipped; the UNIA's venture into shipping had a solid economic basis, particularly in the growth of trade between West Africa and the US after the 1914–1918 war. Part of the failure of Garvey's shipping venture had to do with poor management and too great an emphasis on the ideological and political dimension of blacks running a shipping line. Economic considerations gave way to political ones and this, together with the enormous obstacles put in the way of the UNIA by the American government and the sabotage of opponents, helped to wreck the venture.

There was also the Negro Factories Corporation which had investments in restaurants, laundries and a range of service enterprises. In the area of health, the development of the Black Cross Nurses was an important institution, providing health services to black communities. On the Atlantic coast of Nicaragua, Costa Rica and Panama, the UNIA developed a range of educational, burial and insurance schemes and other institutions geared to the needs of migrant West Indian labour. Moreover, Garvey published newspapers wherever he went. The best known was *The Negro World*, published in New York from 1918–1933.

Garvey's impact

Garvey had a huge impact on leaders of African independence such as Kwame Nkrumah of Ghana, Nnamdi Azikiwe of Nigeria and Jomo Kenyatta of Kenya, among others. At the All-African Peoples' Conference in Accra in 1958, Nkrumah stated: 'Long before many of us were even conscious of our own degradation, Marcus Garvey fought for African national and racial equality' (quoted in Jacques-Garvey 1970: 319).

For a younger generation in the US, the children of Garveyites became activists in the 1950s and 1960s Civil Rights and Black Power movements. An example of this is that Malcolm X's parents were themselves active in the Garvey movement, and this was also the case with hundreds of activists in the era of Martin Luther King.

Garvey was able to think through the problems and programmes to end universal racism and oppression and argued that, in the final analysis, African descendents would be their own problem-solvers. He created an organisational framework within which this process could take place. He identified the liberation and unity of the African continent as the central objective to which African aspirations in other places of the African Diaspora ought to be tied. The Garvey legacy is an indispensable reference point. Failure to consult this intellectual tradition is to perpetuate mental slavery.

It was Garvey who, in 1937, talked about blacks freeing themselves from mental slavery – an idea that is indispensable in fulfilling the gains of political independence and civil rights. His words, which were adapted and put to music by Bob Marley, call on us 'to emancipate ourselves from mental slavery, because whilst others might free the body, none but ourselves can free the mind ... The man who is not able to develop and use his mind is bound to be the slave of the other man who uses his mind ... ' (quoted in Hill 1990: 791).

The idea of freedom from racial and colonial subjugation, from ideologies that characterise people of African descent as sub-humans and the vision that we could and should take our place in the modern world and claim the right to self-determination, were central to Garvey's thought.

Garvey's vision of freedom for Africa and African descendents was considered farfetched and unrealistic by many people in the early 20th century. However, by the end of the century the map of the world had been redrawn, through the emergence of dozens of new independent states in Africa and the Caribbean. Through this, millions of African descendents in Latin America, the US and Europe have secured their civil liberties. This process is generally referred to as 'political decolonisation'. Contemporary ideas about the African Renaissance and Pan-Africanism, the African Union's initiative to foster links between Africa and the diaspora, owe much to the legacy of Marcus Garvey and the Garvey movement. With this history of solidarity and political action in mind there must be much more to 21st century politics in the postcolonial and post-apartheid era than the consolidation of neoliberal economics and the enrichment of the new elite.

Notes

1 See United Nations Resolution A/RES/64/169. http://www.un.org/french/documents/view_doc.asp?symbol=A/RES/64/169&TYPE=&referer=http://www.un.org/fr/events/observances/humanrights&Lang=E
2 For a survey of Marcus Garvey's anti-colonialism see Lewis (1988).

3 For latest work on Henry Sylvester Williams, see Sherwood (2010).
4 See Olusanya in Lewis and Warner-Lewis (1994).

References

Baptiste, F. and R. Lewis, eds. 2009. *George Padmore: Pan-African revolutionary*. Kingston: Ian Randle Publishers.

Hill, R., ed. 1983a. *The Marcus Garvey and UNIA papers*, Volume 1: 1826 to August 1919. Los Angeles: UCLA Press.

Hill, R., ed. 1983b. *The Marcus Garvey and UNIA papers*, Volume II: 27 August 1919 to 31 August 1920. Los Angeles: UCLA Press.

Hill, R., ed. 1990. *The Marcus Garvey and UNIA papers*, Volume VII: November 1927 to August 1940. Los Angeles: UCLA Press.

Hill, R., ed. 1995. *The Marcus Garvey and UNIA papers, Africa for the Africans, June 1921–December 1922*, Volume IX. Los Angeles: UCLA Press.

Hill, R., ed. 2006. *The Marcus Garvey and UNIA papers, Africa for the Africans, 1923–1945*, Volume X. Los Angeles: UCLA Press.

Hill, R. and G.A. Pirio. 1987. 'Africa for the Africans': the Garvey movement in South Africa, 1920–1940. The Regents of the University of California. In *The politics of race, class and nationalism in twentieth-century South Africa*, ed. S. Marks and S. Trapido, 209–253. London and New York: Longman.

Hooker, J.R. 1975. *Henry Sylvester Williams: imperial Pan-Africanist*. London: Rex Collings.

Jacques-Garvey, A. 1970. *Garvey and Garveyism*. New York: MacMillan.

Jacques-Garvey, A., ed. 1992. *Philosophy and opinions of Marcus Garvey*. New York: Atheneum.

Kornweibel, T. 1988. *Seeing red: federal campaigns against black militancy, 1919–1925*. Bloomington: Indiana University Press.

Lewis, R. 1988. *Marcus Garvey: anti-colonial champion*. New Jersey: Africa World Press.

Lewis, R. 2006. The significance of the Garvey movement among West Indian builders of the Panama Canal. In *Regional footprints: the travels and travails of early Caribbean migrants*, ed. A. Insanally, M. Clifford and S. Sheriff, 84–91. Kingston: Latin American-Caribbean Centre, UWI and SALISES, UWI.

Lewis, R. and M. Warner-Lewis. 1994. *Garvey, Africa, Europe, the Americas*. New Jersey: Africa World Press.

Magubane, B.M. 1987. *The ties that bind: African-American consciousness of Africa*. New Jersey: Africa World Press.

Mathurin, O.C. 1976. *Henry Sylvester Williams and the origins of the Pan-African movement, 1869–1911*. London: Greenwood Press.

Meli, F. 1988. *A history of the ANC: South Africa belongs to us*. London: James Currey Ltd.

Olusanya, G.O. 1994. Garvey and Nigeria. In *Garvey: Africa, Europe, the Americas*, ed. R. Lewis and M. Warner-Lewis, 121–134. New Jersey: Africa World Press.

Sherwood, M. 2010. *Origins of Pan-Africanism: Henry Sylvester Williams, Africa, and the African Diaspora*. London: Routledge.

Willan, B. 1984. *Sol Plaatje: South African nationalist, 1876–1932*. London: Heinemann.

Whose Diaspora Is This Anyway? Continental Africans Trying on and Troubling Diasporic Identity

Handel Kashope Wright

Introduction: Diaspora and the Complexity of African Identity

Each of the half dozen brief excerpts below could be read as saying something about Africans, either continental or diasporic or both. Read in the sequence in which they appear here, they are a series of statements about African identity and location, each of which serves to endorse, complicate or trouble the others:

> No matter where you come from
> As long as you're a black man
> You're an African.
> (Peter Tosh, "African")

> Since I was born in the Antilles, my observations and my conclusions are valid only for the Antilles--at least concerning the black man at home. Another book could be dedicated to explaining the differences that separate the Negro of the Antilles and the Negro of Africa. Perhaps one day I shall write it. Perhaps too it will no longer be necessary- a fact for which we could only congratulate ourselves.
> (Frantz Fanon, *Black Skin, White Mask*)

> Its not where you're from, its where you're at.
> (Rakim, in Paul Gilroy, *SmallActs*)

> Just because the mangrove tree lives in the middle of a river,
> that does not make it a crocodile.
> (Nigerian proverb, in Ola Rotimi, *The Gods Are Not to Blame*)

> our voices rise,
> angled against the equator;
> we think Kew gardens and
> Browning, even that eve bitter
> so cold, and
> against St. Agnes;
> for, the seasons right, we go
> (one foot raised up
> against the navel)
> on pilgrimages.

for, having believed, then
men love to go on pilgrimages.
(Lemuel Johnson, "A Dance of Pilgrims")

In terms of my cultural and more specifically musical identifications,
I'm as white, queer, English, and black as I am Pakistani.
(Nabeel Zuberi, *Sounds English: Transnational Popular Music*)

The lyrics from Jamaican Peter Tosh's (1976) reggae song, "African" identifies a collective African identity based on blackness as a fundamental unifying characteristic that unites (or ought to unite) all black people, irrespective of current location. The excerpt from Martiniquean Franz Fanon's (1967) *Black Skin, White Masks* portrays identity based on a similar underlying notion of racial unity but it complicates Tosh's portrayal by insisting there are significant differences between continental and diasporic Africans, due in part to their different experiences, which are in turn related to their different locations. The black English hip-hop artist Rakim's (in Paul Gilroy, 1993) postmodern assertion is unabashedly presentist and location centred, insisting that black identity is not about some master narrative of one's history or distant ancestral 'home' (Africa) but is being forged in the here and now (somewhere outside the continent and moment to moment) from the hodgepodge of cultural elements available to one and which one produces. The Nigerian proverb employed in Ola Rotimi's (1971) play goes against Rakim's presentist and hybrid notion of identity by insisting on the discreteness and permanence of identity and on difference as alterity, irrespective of supposedly shared cultural and physical environment. The excerpt from the Sierra Leonean Lemuel Johnson's (1995) poem, "A Dance of Pilgrims" troubles virtually all the previous depictions, going against the grain of both postmodern notions of identity and modernist portrayals of Africa and Africans by portraying continental Africans who refuse to be fixed in an African location and culture, who prefer to both wax nostalgic about the (former) colonizer's home and culture as partly theirs as well and to actually sojourn periodically in pilgrimage from their African margin to the(ir) European mother/promise land. Finally, the quote from Pakistani-English academic Nabeel Zuberi's (2001) book troubles a crucial and taken-for-granted idea underlying all of the previous depictions, namely that African diaspora and black diaspora are synonymous, by introducing a British, more comprehensive notion of blackness (that includes South Asianess), insisting on the importance of a multiplicity of identifications over a singular identity, troubling the heteronormativity of blackness by naming queer blackness, and identifying a reconceptualized blackness as part of the diaspora of the Indian subcontinent rather than Africa.

Considered in juxtaposition with one another, these excerpts could be seen as a bewildering hodgepodge of positions on and depictions of identity and identification. The point, of course, is not to attempt to discern which of these portrayals is 'accurate', nor is it to attempt the even more daunting task of rendering them commensurable. Rather the point of the juxtaposition is to put us in a position to face and even embrace the complexity of identity these depictions collectively convey and the tension and even unease they might evoke. This messy, confusing, uncomfortable beginning is, I would suggest, only fitting for the topic of this editorial and the collection of essays in this special issue of *Critical Arts* specifically and the problematic of continental/diasporic African identity/identification in general.

Introduction to the Issue

This editorial serves as an introduction to the second of two consecutive special issues of *Critical Arts* that have been devoted to the exploration of continental and diasporic Africa(ns) and the problematic of identity. The first (vol. 16, No. 2, 2002) covered the theme 'Continental Africans and the Question of Identity' and this second covers the theme of 'Diasporic Africans and the Question of Identity.' I took an autobiographical approach in writing the editorial for the first issue (Wright, 2002). This approach allowed me to put myself in the text and write from a personal perspective. The editorial engaged the four essays in the collection principally by indicating how they spoke to the central points I was interested in putting forward about the articulation (in both sense of the term) of continental African identity.

I am taking a similar approach in this present editorial and once more the result of this approach fortuitously means going against the grain of the established discourse. Employing an autobiographical approach means much more than forging a link between the two issues and creating a sense of continuity (as important as that is, given that the two issues are conceived of as part of a larger, multivocal project). It also means focusing on an examination of the problematic of diasporic African identity from a personal perspective and from my location in and relationship to the diaspora. In other words, the focus here is not on the peoples and groups traditionally conceived of as being diasporic: black people in the West who can trace their ancestry several generations or even several hundred years in, for example, the United States, Canada, Britain, the Caribbean and South America (Bristow, 1994) and whose ancestry is assumed to be traceable even further back in time and space to continental Africa (Harris, 1982). Rather, the focus is on people like myself, those who have very recently left continental Africa and are located (be it fleetingly, intermittently, temporarily or permanently) in those same countries where black people are conceived of as constituting an African diaspora. I am interested in addressing both what a dislocation from Africa and relocation in the diaspora means for our (continental) African identity and what our relationship is to the diaspora and to diasporic identity.

Much has been written about the histories and past and present formations of the African diaspora and African diasporic identity, from the global dimensions of the African diaspora (Harris, 1982) to comparisons of African diasporic groups (Carby, 1999; Clark Hine & McLeod, 1999), from histories of the diaspora (Conniff & Davis, 1994, Pulis, 1999) to examinations of the relationship of the diaspora and diasporic Africans to the continent (Ackah, 1999), from holistic representations of diasporic identity (Lemelle & Kelley; 1994; Matsuoka, 2001) to examinations of difference in African diasporic identity (Constantine-Simms, 2001; Terborg-Penn & Benton Rushing, 1996). The literature on ostensibly continental Africans living outside of the continent is relatively new and not nearly as extensive. There are some excellent comprehensive treatments of African immigrants living in the West, including the occasional, intriguing examination of relationships between continental Africans living in the diaspora and diasporic Africans and pointers to the ways in which continental Africans in the diaspora are making changes to accommodate to life outside the continent (Stoller, 2002). However, the almost universal premise of works on this population, shared and even taken *for* granted by both the authors and their subjects, is that African émigrés are 'essentially' (in every sense of the term) continental Africans. Their identities are fixed such that Africa serves not only as place of origin but as the location to which they 'naturally belong' and the accommodations they make or fail to make to life and living in the diaspora only serve to emphasize that they are alien and that their new locations are not now nor ever will be their 'natural home'.

Considered collectively, the six essays in this special issue of *Critical Arts* trouble this taken-for-granted premise for examining the identities of visiting, émigré, exile, immigrant and otherwise currently relocated Africans. They present a much more complex picture that ends up troubling not only our fixed notions of African identity but also our albeit complex notions of what constitutes diaspora and diasporic identity. Francis Njubi Nesbitt's article, 'Migration, Identity and The Politics of African Intellectuals in the North' addresses the issue of émigré African intellectuals and the politics of identity they are confronted with upon immigration to the United States. Jacinta Muteshi's 'Constructing Consciousness: Diasporic Remembrances and Imagining Africa in Late Modernity' examines the appropriation of elements of African cultures by African Americans and the utilization of these elements in the forging of African American identity. Awad Ibrahim's 'Marking the Unmarked: Race, Language, Culture, Identity and the African Experience of Becoming Black in North America' examines the processes by which young immigrants from West Africa appropriate African American and African Canadian culture in the attempt to 'become black'. Wendy Walters' 'Postcolonial Archives: V.Y. Mudimbe's *The Rift*' examines the struggles Mudimbe's protagonist has with writer's block, which is in fact a reflection of his underlying struggles with his own identity as a European educated African. Malka Shabtay's "RaGap': Music and Identity Among Young Ethiopians in Israel' addresses the process by which young Ethiopian immigrants are appropriating elements of African American and Jamaican youth culture in the attempt to forge a black identity in Israel. Finally John Nauright and Tara Magdalinski's 'The Western Media and Framing African Through Eric Moussambani's Olympic Swim' deals with the construction of African identity offered by the Western media in its depiction of the 'performance' of a swimmer from Equatorial Guinea at the 2000 Olympics in Australia.

As with the first special issue, I am employing cultural studies as a loose, inter/anti/postdisciplinary framework for exploring the topic at hand. This means, among other things, that a number of disciplines and methodological approaches are represented in the collection, popular culture is taken up as a serious site of struggle for/over identity, and the body, artefacts, performance and style are taken up as integral elements of identity. Thus, for example, literary criticism, psychoanalytic theory and (auto)biography (represented by Walters' essay), sociology, linguistics and ethnography (Ibrahim's essay), anthropology and ethnography (Shabtay), media studies, sport studies, cultural studies and discourse analysis (Nauright and Magdalinski), interdisciplinary African studies (Njubi-Nesbitt) and interdisciplinary African American studies, art criticism and cultural studies (Muteshi) are all juxtaposed in this collection with the intent to make it, collectively, a text which takes a cultural studies approach to exploring the problematic of diasporic African identity. Also in keeping with a cultural studies framework, several of the essays take popular music (rap in Shabtay and Ibrahim, reggae in Shabtay), youth culture (in Shabtay and Ibrahim), style and fashion (in Muteshi, Ibrahim, Shabtay, and Nauright and Magdalinski), the body (especially in Nauright and Magdalinski), artefacts (especially in Muteshi), language (especially in Ibrahim) and performance (in practically all the essays) as integral, even crucial aspects of the articulation of identity.

In the next two sections, I address the ways in which the authors of the essays in this collection and myself are depicting Africans in ways that trouble taken-for-granted conceptions of continental African identity, the diaspora, diasporic African identity and the relationship between continental and diasporic Africans. One of the principal premises of diaspora is the assumption that continental Africa is spiritual homeland for diasporic Africans (while the diaspora itself not considered a potential homeplace for continental Africans). I've titled this editorial 'Whose diaspora is this anyway' (with apologies to Gates, 1990) to signal a troubling of this taken-for-granted premise for constructing continental and diasporic identities.

Will the Real Africans Please Stand Up! Troubling Continental African Identity

The simplest way for me to identify myself is as an African. If I were to acknowledge the fact that I have been living in North America for much of the past 18 years, I might put forward an explanation of my identity through a chronology that states that I was born an African and goes on to narrate how I came to live as an African émigré in the North America. However, both of these statements call for some unpacking even in their utterance. Statements like "1 was born an African" and "I now live in North America as an African émigré" are simple enough but their apparently innocuous simplicity is a mask that conceals the ambiguity and messiness they can be shown to harbour on closer scrutiny. While I strongly and strategically prefer to err on the side of plain prose, I readily admit that to make these statements without deconstructing them would be to merely underscore and illustrate the incisive insightfulness of Gayatri Chakravorty Spivak's (1988) succinct monosyllabic declaration, "we know plain prose cheats" (quoted in Danius & Jonsson, 1993, p. 33). What does it mean to say I am an African? Gripsrud (1994) has observed that it is academics and intellectuals who are given to constructing, discussing and sustaining national identities and that the average person focuses instead on localized and concrete markers of identity. If national identities are overly abstract for most folks, then continental identity is even more so. Sierra Leoneans bear out Gripsrud's assertion since they are concerned primarily with the local and therefore with the specifics of region, gender, ethnicity, age and social class, and much less with continental and (in a country where the number of non-blacks is negligible) racial identity. Given that such local and concrete markers constituted my early experience of self identified and ascribed identity as a Sierra Leonean, how significant, let alone 'true' is it to say that I was born an African? After living some 18 years outside the continent is it not overly simplistic, even problematically 'essentialist' to continue (or rather begin) to think of myself exclusively as a continental African who happens to be living abroad?

To raise such questions is to remove one's finger from the hole in the dyke of essentialism that keeps the identity African comfortable and secure behind the wall of certainty and familiarity of its essential, singular and fixed conception and to allow a trickle of doubt and reconsideration to build to a torrent of hybridity and multiplicity that drowns certainty and sweeps 'African' up through multiple, shifting, hybrid, and contested (re)conceptualisations into a floating signifier. The underlying basic question of whether or not the displacement of individuals from Africa is one mechanism (among many) that renders 'African' a floating signifier or not, is one engaged either directly or indirectly in all of the essays in this collection.

For Nesbitt the African intellectual in the West remains distinctly a continental African. Even factors which would ostensibly be able to fit in are identified as double edged (you may be fluent in English but you speak with a 'strange accent', you may be highly educated and qualify for a position in academia but that only throws you into the pit of turf rivalry). Though he acknowledges that the émigré intellectual was unlikely to have had a comprehensive continental identity and consciousness, he indicates that being located in the West means being assigned a continental rather than national identity and proceeds to discuss what he identifies as the three options open to the émigré intellectual, each starting from the premise of an assigned continental African identity. While the African émigré is always already African, it is also the case that African identity is a newly assigned identity, one that is under threat from the circumstances of exile, even as it is assigned and taken on. Being African and yet living and working outside of Africa poses a threat to the wholeness of one's identity. Faced with this definitive yet definitely fragile identity, the African émigré is thrown into crisis and the attempt to resolve this identity crisis 'produces', Nesbitt asserts, "three 'types' of migrant intellectuals: the comprador intelligentsia, the postcolonial critic and the progressive exile."

Nauright and Magdalinski's depiction is of a single African, namely the 'swimmer' from Equatorial Guinea, Eric Moussambani. Their focus is not on exploring Moussambani's Africanity nor his lack of swimming prowess. Rather, their focus is on levelling a critique against what they describe as the Western "paternalist imperialist Olympic [movement] and media" for their appropriation of Mousambani and his participation in the Sydney Olympics as fodder for "the discourses of colonialism, orientalism and paternalism." Thus the depiction of the African we get from their essay is a concrete and specific example of the West's projection and appropriation. Everything from the invitation to have Mousambani and other Others participate in the Olympics (the white man's burden and the collection and display of the Other), to the eroticisation of Moussambani's body and bemusement at his unfamiliarity with advanced swimwear (noble savage from technologically backward Africa), to the lauding of his woeful performance as indicative of the true spirit of the Olympics (proof of Western superiority, fairness and generosity, even in the emergence of a 'global culture'), serve to reiterate that African identity can be conceptualised not as singular or natural nor even merely as historically and socially construction but as a Western discursive production and even projection employed for specific purposes.

Walters is twice removed from the African who is the focus of her paper, namely Ahmed Nara, the protagonist in V.Y. Mudimbe's novel, *The Rift*. Her's is a discussion of an author's depiction of an African. Nara is a Paris-educated doctoral student who is making little progress with his dissertation as he is suffering from writer's block. While most readings of *The Rift* have seen it as a critique of the colonial archive, Walters produces an alternative reading that focuses on its exploration of identity and sexuality and sees the novel as "an archive of discourse about identity." Nara is positioned between an (unnamed) African country and France, between gay and straight identity, between the coloniser's and local conceptions of his people's past. These multiple binaries and overlapping, opposing and contradictory identifications immobilise Nara, an immobilisation reflected in his writer's block which is in turn a form *of blocage,* "a self-imposed and self-regulated prison." The prison is one of a narrow conception of African identity as decidedly heterosexual, culturally fixed and impervious, and in terms of intellectual tradition, securely and distinctly Afrocentric. Even though he has returned to Africa, therefore, Nara is an African whose holistic identity is threatened, fragmented, even corrupted by his Western education and his past and anticipated future periods in the West.

Muteshi describes herself as "a temporarily transplanted Kenyan" living in New York at the time she undertook some of the research for her paper. In her essay, she concentrates on diasporic Africans (in the United States specifically) and their appropriation of Africa and African culture for the project of constructing diasporic identity. The principal portrayal of Africa in her essay is one she critiques, namely black diasporic subjects' "imaginings of Africa," principally Africa as resource, as place of origin, as history and roots. This conception does not require living Africans for its fulfilment (except perhaps the visiting and/or immigrant African purveyors of artefacts and cloths from the continent at places like the sidewalks of Harlem). Contemporary Africans potentially detract from and trouble African identity in this conception that focuses on the past and on the tropes that Africa is ancestral home to which one can return and that diasporic Africans are descended from kings and queens of ancient African civilisations.

Ibrahim, who originally hails from the Sudan, explores in his essay the ways in which recently immigrated francophone African youth in Canada perform and try on blackness as an identity. While this process of becoming black is the primary focus of the essay, Ibrahim does indicate the youth in his study do retain certain Africanisms. As one of his informants asserts "my culture is something I am proud of. I would like to keep my culture, but at the same time you know I am going to be very close to Canadians and particularly black peoples." Though they retain and selectively utilise on certain occasions Africanisms such as their mother tongues and dress, they appear to avoid the pitfall of romanticising their African identities. What we have in Ibrahim's account are Africans who are developing a hybrid African identity, one that is readily and positively porous, blending selected aspects of continental cultures with North American hip-hop culture.

Shabtay's essay also deals with recent immigrant youth and their appropriation of rap and hip-hop culture (and reggae and Rastafari) in the formation of a new identity. In her case the youth are Ethiopians resettled in Israel. What is particularly fascinating in Shabtay's account is the youth apparently do not subscribe directly to a specific Ethiopian nor more general continental African culture and identity. Facing racism, poverty and a questioning of their Jewishness by some in Israel, these youth turn to the black diaspora for the cultural building blocks of a new identity rather than to Ethiopian culture. As one of them comments, "rap talks about racism and Reggae about Ethiopia, and I am attached to both of them." This mediation of the link to continental African identity is not altogether surprising when one considers that the parents and ancestors of these youth had indeed considered and proclaimed themselves Jews in Ethiopia and it is their Jewishness, their separateness from other Ethiopian groups that is the very basis of their claim to Jewishness and Israel as homeland.

Whose Diaspora Is This, Anyway? Troubling Diasporic African Identity

When I initially sat down to write this essay, I glanced at my bookshelves and my eyes fell first and rested on Kobina Mercer's (1994) *Welcome to the jungle,* a book I first read almost 10 years ago. While I tried to tell myself this was because it was one of the obvious works that would inform my discussion of diasporic African identity, I must admit that I also felt once again the same strong feelings I had in reaction to the book when I first read it: feelings of belonging and not belonging, relating to and yet being apart from the African diaspora that Mercer explores so engagingly in this collection of essays. My reaction was not to Mercer's book specifically or exclusively: I could well have stopped at any of the other works on that same shelf (which happen to be by bell hooks, Paul Gilroy, Marlene Nourbese, Frantz Fanon, Tricia Rose, Molefi Asante, Michelle Wallace, WEB Du Bois, Houston Baker, Patricia Hill Collins, Henry Louis Gates Jr., Michael Eric Dyson, Greg Tate, Angela Davis, Orlando Patterson and ahdri zhina mandiela) and would have had the same reaction. That reaction is my own ambivalence about how I relate to and whether I fit in the African diaspora and can/ ought to claim an African diasporic identity. I have become interested in how I, as a supposedly continental African, who pursued graduate studies in Canada and currently teaches in the American academy, am positioned and position myself in relation to the African diaspora and a diasporic identity. In this section I point to how the authors and/or Africans they depict position themselves and are positioned in relation to the African diaspora and diasporic identity.

Ibrahim tackles this issue squarely, starting with himself as dramatic example. He provides an account of "the day I was officially declared black," a day on which he was stopped by the police in Toronto on suspicion of being the "dark man with a dark bag" who had just robbed someone in a nearby, upscale neighbourhood. The euphemism "dark man" and the officer's studied politeness did not mask the humiliation of the public search and detailed questioning he was subjected to or the fact that all of this was based on his blackness. No nuances here between continental African and black Canadian, no intellectual and existential angst over whether as a Sudanese living and studying in Canada he could or ought to take on diasporic identity. He was assigned blackness as an immediate, singular, fixed and obvious identity, reduced by the police to an essential, potentially dangerous and criminal blackness. While his experience acts as a reminder that identity is in part that which is assigned/ascribed, his African immigrant youth informants illustrate vividly that identity is not so much about being as it is about becoming. They consciously take up the language (black stylised English), and the elements of hip-hop culture in the effort to fit into diasporic African culture and identity. The principal motivation for these youth, as it is for youth everywhere, is to fit in, to belong. Thus they enthusiastically and unabashedly perform and claim diasporic identity for themselves and because they do not completely eschew their African cultures, their new identity is a hybrid (continental/diasporic), which they construct and perform, apparently with confidence and without anxiety or reservation.

Shabtay's informants are also in the process of becoming black (in their case through the appropriation of not only hip-hop but also reggae and the hybrid combination of the two). These youth are in a fascinating position in relation to the notion of diaspora. The taken for granted idea is that continental Africa is the natural home of blacks (and Ethiopia in particular, the spiritual home of diasporic blacks such as Rasta's) and all blacks living outside of Africa are in the diaspora. As Ethiopian Jews, however, these youths families have always considered Israel to be their homeland and Ethiopia a location in the diaspora. Thus, their very identity as Ethiopian Jews turns taken for granted equation of blackness and African diasporic identity on its head. Their appropriation of hip-hop and reggae is a blending of two ostensibly distinct varieties of diasporic culture (reggae is Jamaican while rap is American) that contributes to the hybridisation of diasporic culture (Shabtay points out the little known fact that rap actually started among Jamaican immigrants in New York). By taking this diasporic route to blackness, Ethiopian Jewish youth complicate their identity even further: originally located in Ethiopia as diasporic Jews they now feel alienation as black Jews in Israel and have turned to the African diaspora as a source of racial pride and an albeit mediated relinking with Ethiopia. What we have then are Ethiopian Jews finally coming 'home' to Israel, only to find themselves alienated from Israeli culture, turning for their identity to Jamaicans who are in turn turning to Ethiopia for their identity.

Muteshi's focus on diasporic Africans utilisation of Africa as resource as well as the museumisation and commodification of African artefacts makes for a take on identity that requires a distant, historical and mythical Africa, one preferably that does not have to deal with the complication of the existence of contemporary Africans on the continent. She asserts that even when diasporic artists undertake the all important 'return' to Africa, they do so to (re)discover art and artefacts (principally traditional, from the past). This fixation on the past and the traditional coincides with the problematic American and European museums' decontextualisation and demystification of symbolic and ritualistic art and artefacts. However, in the case of diasporic artists, traditional art is appropriated for the production of not only contemporary, pastiche black art but also as part of the construction of diasporic identity. Interestingly, the fact that first generation immigrants from the continent (whose identities overlap between continental and diasporic) also undertake similar 'returns' to Africa for inspiration and are generating similar works produces a blurring of the boundaries between diasporic and continental art and indeed between continental and diasporic identities. Though she starts from the premise of a neat distinction between continental (herself included) and diasporic Africans, Muteshi ends on a note stressing the importance of elaborating "on the connective tissue between past and the present," an elaboration made all the more possible by artists positioned between continental and diasporic identities and identifications.

Walters' essay does not take up the West as diaspora since the Paris of *The Rift* is distinctly white and Western, with the historical archives the focus of our attention. In terms of diaspora and identity, therefore, what we have is an absence and limit, an absence of community and the limiting of knowledge and being to that which is archived and compartmentalized. Ultimately, we are dealing with an absence of diaspora and a limiting of the possibilities of identity. Nara's double alienation (from both Paris and Western academic tradition on the one hand, and his country and people and traditional gnosis on the other) is indicative of a failure to reconcile these two worlds. Walters reminds us that Nara's *blocage* need not be the 'natural' result of his experiences by pointing to the author himself, Mudimbe, who is successfully engaging and negotiating between African gnosis, orality and worldview and Western philosophy, anthropology and creative writing. Thus while Nara is trapped in *blocage,* his creator, Mudimbe is diasporic, not necessarily in the sense that he belongs to a cultural and literal community but in the sense that as a continental African academic living in the West he is creating a hybrid intellectual world that sometimes holds in productive tension and sometimes blends the West and Africa.

The West in Nauright and Magdalinski's essay is, like Nara's West, not portrayed as an African diaspora. Their subject, Moussambani, is an African who has not made an émigré's journey to the diaspora but a one time, brief sojourn into a distinctly white West. The fact that Australia and the West in general are in fact also part of the African diaspora for some is not raised in Nauright and Magdalinski's depiction. Rather their portrayal is of a distinctly white, imperialist, racist, Eurocentric and paternalistic West and rightly so since this is what is revealed and what comes into play in the Western media's depiction of Moussambani's swim. Thus the combination of the brevity of Moussambani's sojourn and the depiction of him in the Western media and the authors critique of that portrayal all combine to construct a West that is quite distinct from Africa, a West in which Moussambani cannot but be a stranger in a strange land, a West that is not and indeed cannot be conceptualised as part of the African diaspora.

Njubi-Nesbitt, like Muteshi, starts off with a conception of Africans on the continent and in the diaspora as two, very distinct group. Although to a lesser extent than Muteshi, he allows for some interaction between the two groups. Because his principal focus is on the émigré intellectual in the United States as an African stranger in a strange land, there is not much of a sense of overlapping and commingling of these two identities in his paper. What he does allow and work with are similarities and parallels between the two groups. He holds, for example, that DuBois' notion of double consciousness applies equally if not more to the African émigré as it does to African Americans and that (as Ibrahim also points out), the African intellectual in America is also subject to racism faced by African Americans, including black intellectuals ("color...trumps education, erudition and accomplishment"). Both Africans in America and African Americans "see each other, and themselves," he asserts, "through the eyes of others." He makes the important caveat that the identification with each other, which he is not willing to collapse into a unified identity, is not to be seen as being based on race per se. Rather, through a more careful reading of DuBois, he opines that mutual identification is based on an "emphasis ... on socio-historical ties, not 'race' as a biological essence." Thus there are intersections and parallels between the African American and the African in America experience but that does not make the African in America diasporic nor the African American African: the two remain distinct groups

Conclusion

The essays in this collection collectively depict, extend and trouble taken-for-granted conceptualisations of both continental and diasporic African identity. Some diasporic Africans claim and perform African identity as essence (e.g. the black Canadian dub poet ahdri zhina mandiela (1991) asserts "never seen the motherland / still afrikan / our memory/ ourstory / makes me: afrikan / by instinct" (p. 42)). In a similar fashion Africans in the diaspora from Ethiopian Jews in Israel to francophone African youths in Canada are claiming and performing diasporic identity. Others, like Ibrahim are having diasporic black identity thrust upon them. Relocation to the diaspora in the West (which Nauright and Madilinski as well as Walters remind us is in some sense not diasporic at all but simply alien) functions to complicate African identity and this can lead to angst and immobilisation (Nara) or to the formation of a new, more expansive identity (Ibrahim and Shabtay's informants). African identity can be thought of as distinct and discrete (Nauright & Madalinski, Nesbitt) or as porous and pliant (Ibrahim, Shabtay). It could be considered a resource that could be appropriated for either problematic ends such as the promoting of Eurocentrism (Nauright & Madalinski) and the commodification of Africa (Muteshi) or for progressive ends such as forging links between past and present, continent and diaspora, continental Africans and diasporic Africans (Muteshi). African identity must not be straightjacketed as straight, black and continental: it can also be queer, non-black and outercontinental.

Kobina Mercer (1994) asserts that "emerging cultures of hybridity, forged among the overlapping African, Asian and Caribbean diasporas that constitute our common home, must be seen as crucial and vital efforts to answer the "possibility and necessity of creating a new culture: *so that you can live*" (p. 3–4). This sense of urgency and immediacy works strategically to counter the common-sense and taken for granted conceptions of diaspora identity which are based on a version of what Clinton Allison (1995) has referred to as "the resented present versus an idealized past." However, as a result of this sense of urgency and temporal and geographical immediacy, the diasporic culture alone is represented as hybrid. Because contemporary continental Africa is either completely eschewed or not engaged in a sustained fashion in these articulations of diasporic identities, continental African identity is rendered not only an originary space and moment but also by default, homogenous and essentialised. One of the points the essays in this collection bear out is that hybridity and indeterminacy can be characteristics not only of diasporic but also continental African identity (especially for African émigrés in the diaspora). We are not simply Africans living in the West with our supposedly fixed and comfortable identities intact. Rather our African identity is always already complex and our dislocation from Africa and relocation in the West makes for an overlapping of already complex African/ diasporic identities. We also, therefore, are confronted with the challenges of being and becoming. We too are engaged in the possibility and necessity of creating a new culture and identity *so that we can live*.

References

Ackah, W. (1999). *Pan-Africanism: Exploring the contradictions: Politics, identity and development in Africa and the African diaspora*. United Kingdom: Aidershot, Brookfield, VT: Ashgate.

Allison, C. (1995). *Present and past: Essays for teachers in the history of education*. New York: Peter Lang Publishers.

Bristow, P. (1994). *We're rooted here and they can't pull us up: Essays in African Canadian women's history.*. Toronto: University of Toronto Press.

Carby, H. (1999). *Cultures of Babylon: Black Britain and African America*. London & New York: Verso.

Clark-Hine, D. & McLeod,, J. (Eds.). (1999). *Crossing boundaries: Comparative history of black people in the diaspora*. Bloomington: Indiana University Press.

Conniff, M. & Davis, T. (Eds.). (1994). *Africans in the Americas: A history of the black diaspora*. New York: St. Martin's Press.

Constantine-Simms, D. (Ed.). (2001). *The greatest taboo: Homosexuality in black communities*. Los Angeles: Alyson Books.

Fanon, F. (1967). *Black skin, white masks*. (Charles Lam Markmann, Trans.). New York: Grove Weidenfeld.

Gates, H. L. (1990). Whose canon is it anyway? In B. Wallis (Ed.). *Democracy: A project by material discussion in contemporary culture*. Seattle: Bay Press.

Gilroy, P. (1993). It ain't where you're from, it's where you're at: The dialectics of diaspora identification. *Small acts: Thoughts on the politics of black cultures*. London & New York: Serpent's Tail.

Gripsrud, J. (1994). Intellectuals as constructors of cultural identities. *Cultural Studies*, 8 (2), 220–231.

Harris, J. (Ed.). (1982). *Global dimensions of the African diaspora*. Washington, DC: Howard University Press.

Johnson, L. (1995). A Dance of Pilgrims. *Highlife for Caliban*. Trenton, NJ: Africa World Press.

Lemelle, S., & Kelley, R. (Eds.). (1994). *Imagining home: Class, culture, and nationalism in the African diaspora*. London & New York: Verso.

mandiela, ahdri zhina. (1991). 'Afrikan by instinct.' *Dark diaspora in dub*. Toronto: Sister Vision Press.

Matsuoka, A. (2001). *Ghosts and shadows: Construction of identity and community in an African diaspora*. Toronto: University of Toronto Press.

Mercer, Kobina. (1994). *Welcome to the jungle: New positions in black cultural studies*. New York and London: Routledge.

Pulis, J. (Ed.). (1999). *Moving on: Black loyalists in the Afro-Atlantic world*. New York: Garland Publishers.

Rotimi, O. (1971). *The gods are not to blame*. London: Oxford University Press.

Spivak, G. C. (1988). Can the subaltern speak? Speculations on widow sacrifice. In C. Nelson and L. Grossberg (Eds.). *Marxism and interpretation of culture*. London: Macmillan.

Stoller, P. (2002). *Money has no smell: The Africanization of New York City*. Chicago: University of Chicago Press.

Terborg-Penn, R., & Benton Rushing, A. (Eds.). (1996). *Women in Africa and the African diaspora: A reader*. Washington, DC: Howard University Press.

Tosh, P. (1976). African. *Legalize it*. Don Mills, Canada: Columbia Records.

Wright, H. K. (2002). Editorial: Notes on the (im)possibility of articulating continental African identity. *Critical Arts*, 16 (2), 1–18.

Zuberi, N. (2001). *Sounds English: Transnational popular music*. Urbana-Champaign: University of Illinois Press.

Marking the Unmarked: Hip-Hop, the Gaze & the African Body in North America

Awad Ibrahim

ABSTRACT

Based on personal narrative and 'critical ethnographic research,' this paper is about the process of *'becoming black,'* the interrelations between race, culture, and identity, and their impact on what, who and how we as social beings existing within a social space, identify with. It contends that, having arrived in North America, an immigrant and refugee group of continental Francophone African youths attending an urban French-language high school in southwestern Ontario, Canada, enters, so to speak, *a social imaginary*, a discursive space where they are already imagined, constructed, and thus treated as 'blacks' by hegemonic discourses and groups, respectively. This imaginary is directly implicated in who they identify with — black America — which in turn influences what and how they linguistically and culturally learn. They learn, I will show, 'black English as a second language' (BESL) which they access in and through hip-hop culture and rap lyrical/linguistic styles. Translation and negotiation, I will conclude, are significant identity formation processes which in this study produced a hybrid, temporal and ambiguous 'African' identity existent in North America.

Introduction

Recently, continental Africans have been crossing the Atlantic Ocean to North America in a considerable number (Ibrahim, 1998). In a sense, as Molefi K. Asante (1990) has argued, this is a performative act of defiance[1] to the history of colonialism, imperialism and the middle passage. They are joining the African diaspora by becoming part of it. But they have to first confront the history — the history of the present (Foucault, 1980) — where their bodies are already read as 'black.' They have to translate, negotiate and answer two questions. What does being black really mean in North America?; and if one is 'becoming' black, what does this call for, entail, and thus produce? These are the questions I shall endeavor to answer in this paper. At a personal level, I want to ask the following: As a continental African living in North America, am I a black man? Conjugating the verb *to be* in the present tense is central and 1 am using 'blackness' as defined in North America. If the answer is negative, what does it mean *not to be* a black man, while materially possessing the socially defined black male body? That is, how does one translate and negotiate one's own sense of self *vis-à-vis* the already pronounced social order? On the other hand, if *Iam* a black man, when did I become one? Juxtaposing personal narrative with ethnographic research conducted in 1996 (Ibrahim, 1998), I want to argue that if my research participants (who are themselves continental Africans) and I were not 'black' before emigrating to North America, indeed we became black.[2] This paper is hence an exploration of the processes of *becoming black*. That is, the cultural, linguistic, and socio-psychic implications of what it means to possess a black body in North America (and the Western world in general). I do believe that the narrative and the processes of becoming black, are not only applicable to continental Africans, but to most, if not all, émigrés and displaced refugees who move to North America and whose body is read or socially defined as black. This is what I want to term the politics (if not the curse) of visibility. It is when the unmarked is marked and made visible (see also Hall, 1997). This marking takes place in and through language and is felt on the surface of the body. If the 'norm' - whiteness in North America, for example - is made obscure and invisible through processes of normalisation and naturalisation (Fine *et al.*, 1997; Foucault, 1970; 1980; Frankenberg, 1993), and if these processes are embedded in language and work by hailing and pointing towards the Other and away from the Self (Althusser, 1971; Woodward, 1997), furthermore, if the hailer or the speaker possesses the authorised language and the authorised power to speak and be listened to (Bourdieu, 1991), then the hailed Other - blackness, in this case - can only be made ultra-visible. This, I want to contend, is directly implicated in how African youths and I enter this politics of ultra-visibility, how people relate to our bodies, and hence how we experience the processes of becoming black.

I shall, therefore, firstly distinguish between 'being' and 'becoming' and secondly, narrate a significant incident in my journey of becoming black. I then introduce my research and show how a group of continental African youths encountered a particular imaginary which impacted their self-perception, which in turn influenced what and how they learned. Nonetheless, I shall also show in conclusion, that the African youths produced a hybrid and ambivalent identity that was, I contend, a product of translation and negotiation.

Being or becoming

> We were a politicised grouping of student/activists, athletes, those looking for a place to hang/out, street-wise players & partiers, and people who were just dissatisfied with not seeing enough blackness in school and in the society, generally. We *weren't* "Black" where we came from in the west indies, but in toronto we had to confront the fact that we were seen as "Black," and had to check/out for ourselves what this blackness *was*. (Clifton Joseph prefacing Althea Prince's *Being Black*, 2001, pp. 16–17; italics added)

Hamlet once argued, "To be, or not to be - that is the question" (Shakespeare, 1988, p. 89). Or is it? *Being*, it has recently been argued, can never be (in full and in complete), since it is a work-in-progress, a continuous act of becoming (Butler, 1999; Ibrahim, 1999; 2000a; 2000b; 2000c; Kristeva, 1974; Sartre, 1980). In Clifton Joseph's quote, the negation and the past tense in "We weren't 'Black'" assumes that we 'are' now. I therefore distinguish between *being* and *becoming*. The latter, as I already cited, is a continuous act of becoming (Sartre, 1980). It is not a fixed entity; on the contrary, it is a production, a performative category that is never complete. Borrowing from Judith Butler (1999), performativity, which is central to my research, is a concept that does not assume *idées fixes*, quite the opposite, it requires repetitive, parodic and continual acts of becoming. For Butler, there is nothing fixed about, for example, gender or the category of woman (and I would add race). So gender (or race) is for Butler the repeated stylisation of the body, a set of recurrent acts, words, gestures, or what Roland Barthes (1967; 1983) calls complex semiological languages. These are signs that are open for signification and different readings since they cannot produce verbal utterances yet are ready to speak. For Butler, we produce and perform these complex languages on the surface of our bodies: in and through our modes of dress, walk, in our hair, *maquillage,* lip-gloss; also in architecture, photography, and so on. So we perform who we are, our identities, desires, and investments, at least in part, in and through these complex semiological languages: our dress, walk and talk.

Using the analogy of learning a language, *being* can be similar to a mother tongue while *becoming* is to learn a second language. Although no one can fully and completely master one's mother tongue, one is comfortable enough within it to know its nuances and to even know that which is beyond language: the excess. Whereas, in the case of a second language, one enters that language as an outsider; always with the hope that that which is outside will eventually belong to the self, a second will become a first language. In short, *being* is an accumulative memory, an understanding, a conception and an experience upon which individuals interact with the world around them, whereas *becoming* is the process of building this memory, experience. As a continental African, for example, I was not considered 'black' in Africa. However, as a refugee in North America, my perception of self was altered in direct response to the social processes of racism and the historical representation of blackness whereby the antecedent signifiers (*tall, Sudanese, academic, basketball player,* and so on) that used to patch together my identity became secondary to my blackness, and I retranslated my being: I became black. And May 16,1999 was a culminating day in my understanding of what it means to be black in North America, specifically in Canada. It was the day I was hailed as 'black,' by an authorised speaker who possessed an authorised language. The following is an extract from my diary entitled *Being under surveillance: Who controls my black body?* It is cited here to demonstrate how my 'black' body was hailed, on the one hand, and to explore the social context (of everyday racism (Essed & Goldberg, 2002)) where my research participants form, perform and circulate their identities, on the other.

The day I was officially declared black

It was 1:10 p.m. on a sunny and an unexpectedly hot Sunday. I was more in the mood for poetry than for prose; and bicycling on St. George Street had never been as light. However it is frightening how lightness can so easily whirl into an unbearable heaviness, and how heaviness can cause so much pain. It all began when I had just crossed the yellow light of Bloor Street West. I saw a white car curving into the bicycle lane and I heard hereafter a siren coming from it. Since I was bicycling, I was neither able to fully verify the car nor who was driving it nor why it was requesting me to stop. However, when it was fully halted before my bicycle, I realised it was a police car. From it came veering a rangy white man with full gear and a pair of sunglasses, along with a clean and handsome gun. My immediate thought was, it must be the bicycle helmet, since I was not wearing one; and seeing that there will always be a first time for our social experiences, I whispered to myself "Oh God, this is my first ticket of my life." I was deadly mistaken.

He approached my bicycle and said, "Have you ever been in trouble with the law before?" Shocked beyond any imaginable belief, "No", I said, and "Can I know why am I asked the question?" I added. "You fit the description of a man we are looking for, who just snapped a bag from Yorkville, and I just saw you around the Yorkville area," he said. Suddenly, he began a walkie-talkie conversation with a dispatcher; and I realised when he said, "I am talking to him right now," that it was a continuation of a previous dialogue. I was already under surveillance, talked about. Looking sternly into his eyes, 1 repeated, "Can I know why I was stopped?" Squirmingly, his face turned red and he loudly regurgitated "I told YOU, Sir, that you fit the description of a man we are looking for."

Calmly but unaloofly, "And what is that description?" I wondered. "We are looking for a dark man with a dark bag," he said. I looked at my backpack and it occurred to me that my bag was light blue with one very small black (or as he said 'dark') stripe at the edge. More with my eyes than with my voice, I repeated after him "A DARK man?" Self-consciously, but pesteringly, he exclaimed, "A black man with a dark bag!" He insisted on my bag being "dark"; now I was significantly metamorphosed from "dark" into "black." Not that it matters either way, I reflected later, but it seems that some people either cannot see or have a 'colour problem.'

During this conversation, I saw another police car stopping behind the first; and from it came another white policeman. I was then asked for a piece of identification. I gave the first policeman my citizenship card, but when my bag was widely opened for every passerby to see, I decided to use my University of Ottawa professor identification. After writing down my name and date of birth, he then announced to the dispatcher, "All is okay now." With no apologies, I was ordered to collect my affairs and my bag and, as he uttered it, "You are free to go now."

It's all about the gaze

To fall under the eyes of power - the gaze - is to find oneself within *discourses of closure* where the (black) body is already authored, read, and constantly stabilised across time, language, culture and space (see also Hall, 1997; Foucault, 1980). Here 'I' become fixed, known, and already spoken and talked about. When Nietzsche (1977) asked *"Muss es sein?"* - "Must it be?" one is first tempted to wonder if he had witnessed my above incident and then to add: "Must it be (or happen) this way?" As a response, I offer below a theoretical proposition linking my vignette with the research I will soon discuss. It is a framework connected to the gaze: How am I perceived or imagined and what is the impact of this imaginary on how I am gazed at, consumed, and related to? Even if, as Rousseau would have argued, we "live very much in the public gaze" (In Taylor, 1994, p. 86), we must know the nature of this "public gaze" and what impact it has on our identities, identification, investments, and desires? In what follows I discuss first my research, its contentions, propositions, and questions and then secondly, and succinctly, introduce its methodology, site and subject. I then offer examples of African youths' speech to demonstrate the interplay between subject formation, identification and BESL learning. I also offer students' reflections and narratives on the impact of identification and becoming black, and conclude with remarks on the need to deconstruct this panoptic gaze which limits, as we will see, the production of a full-yet-hybrid African subjectivity, a subjectivity which is already always multicultural, multiethnic and multilingual.

Towards a theory of the imaginary: research subjects, site and insights

This paper constitutes part of a body of larger critical ethnographic research[3] I conducted at Marie-Victorin High School[4] (Ibrahim, 1998), between January and June 1996, that made use of *ethnography of performance*[5] as a methodological approach. The research, which took place in an urban French-language high school in southwestern Ontario, Canada, looks at the lives of a group of continental Francophone African youths and the formation of their social identity. Besides their gendered and raced experience, their youth and refugee status was vital in their what I termed elsewhere *moments of identification* (Ibrahim, 2001): Where and how they were interpellated in the mirror of their society (cf. Althusser, 1971; Bhabha, 1994). Put otherwise, once in North America, I contend that these youths were faced with a *social imaginary* (Anderson, 1983), like the one I faced in the above scenario, in which they were already blacks. This social imaginary was directly implicated in how and with whom they identified, which in turn influenced what they learned linguistically and culturally and how they learned it. What they learned, I demonstrate, is 'black stylised English' (BSE), which they accessed in and through black popular culture. They learned by taking up and repositing the rap linguistic and musical genre and, in different ways, acquiring and rearticulating the hip-hop cultural identity.

BSE is a subcategory of 'black English' (BE). BE is what Geneva Smitherman (2000) refers to as 'black talk,' an African American language, which has unique grammar and syntax. BSE, however, refers to ways of speaking that do not depend on a full mastery of the language. It banks more on ritual expressions such as *whassup, whadap, whassup my Nigger,* and *yo, yo homeboy,* which are performed habitually and recurrently in rap. The rituals are more an expression *of* politics, moments of identification and desire than they are of language or of mastering the language *perse*. It is a way of saying, "I too am black," or "I too desire and identify with blackness."

By 'black popular culture' I refer to films, newspapers, magazines, and more importantly music such as rap, reggae, pop, and rhythm and blues (R&B). I use the term hip-hop, more skeletally, to describe a way of dressing, walking, and talking. *The dress* refers to the myriad shades and shapes of the latest *fly gear:* high-top sneakers, bicycle shorts, chunky jewelry, baggy pants, and polka-dotted tops (Rose, 1991, p. 227). The hairstyles, which include high-fade designs, dreadlocks, corkscrews, and braids, are also part of this fashion. *The walk* usually means moving the fingers simultaneously with the head and the rest of the body as one is walking. *The talk* is BSE. Significantly, by patterning these behaviors African youths enter the realm of becoming black. As an identity configuration, the latter is deployed to talk about the *subject-formation project* (i.e., the process and the space within which subjectivity is formed) that is produced in, and simultaneously is produced by, the process of language learning, namely learning BESL. More concretely, becoming black means learning BESL, as I show below, yet the very process of BESL learning produces the epiphenomenon of 'becoming black.'

The central working contention of the research is that, once in North America, continental African youths enter a *social imaginary:* a discursive space or a representation in which they are already constructed, imagined, and positioned, and thus treated by the hegemonic discourses and dominant groups, respectively, as blacks. Hence the discourse of closure is entered. Here I address the white (racist) everyday communicative state of mind: "Oh, they all look like blacks to me!" This positionality, which is offered to continental

African youths through net-like praxis in exceedingly complex, mostly subconscious ways, does not acknowledge the differences in the students' ethnicities, languages, nationalities, and cultural identities. Franz Fanon sums up this net-like praxis brilliantly in writing about himself as a black *Antillais* coming to the metropolis of Paris:

> I am given no chance, I am overdetermined from without. I am the slave not of the "idea" that others have of me but of my own appearance... I *progress* [italics added] by crawling. And *already* [italics added] I am being dissected under white eyes, the only real eyes. I am *fixed*. Having adjusted their microtomes, they objectively cut away slices of my reality. I am laid bare... When people like me, they tell me it is in spite of my color. When they dislike me, they point out that it is not because of my color. Either way, I am locked into the infernal circle (1967, p. 116).

As a result, continental African youths find themselves in a racially conscious society that wittingly or unwittingly, and through fused social mechanisms such as racisms and representations, asks them to fit racially somewhere. To fit somewhere signifies choosing or becoming aware of one's own being, which is partially reflected in one's language practice. (But if one is to apply the above Fanonian framework: Do African youths, myself, and all who embody the black body really have a choice?) *Choosing,* as Butler (1999) argued, is a question of agency which is itself governed and disciplined by social conditions. To be black in a racially conscious society, like the Euro-Canadian and United States societies for example, means that one is expected to be black, act black, and so be the marginalized Other (Hall, 1991; 1990; hooks, 1992). Under such disciplinary social conditions, as will become clear, continental African youths express their moments of identification in relation to African Americans and African American cultures and languages, thus becoming black. That they take up rap and hip-hop and speak BSE is by no means a coincidence. On the contrary, here, culture and language take on a different spin. They are no longer about language and cultureperse, but become markers of desire and investment; an invocation of political, racial, and historical location.

The site for my research was a small French-language high school (Grades seven to 13) in southwestern Ontario, Canada, which I will refer to as Marie-Victorin (MV). MV had a student population of approximately 400 students from various ethnic, racial, cultural, religious, and linguistic backgrounds. Besides French and English, Arabic, Somali, and Farsi were also spoken at the school. I spent over six months attending classes at MV, talking to students, and observing curricular and extracurricular activities two or three times a week. Because of previous involvement in another project in the same school for almost two years, at the time of this research I was well acquainted with MV and its population, especially its African students, with whom I was able to develop a good communicative relationship. My background as a continental African also helped me to decipher their narratives and experiences. Clearly, we shared a *safe space* of comfort that allowed us to open up, speak and engage freely.

At the time of this research, students who were born outside Canada made up 70 percent of the entire school population at MV. Continental Africans constituted the majority of that figure and of MV's population in general. Firstly they varied in their length of stay in Canada (from one to two, to five to six years); secondly, their legal status was varied (some were immigrants, but the majority were refugees); thirdly, they varied in their gender, class, age, and linguistic and national background. They came from places as diverse as Democratic Republic of Congo (formerly Zaire), Djibouti, Gabon, Senegal, Somalia, South Africa, and Togo. With no exception, all of the African students at MV were at least tri lingual, speaking

English, French, and an African language, a mother tongue. Given their postcolonial educational history, it is significant that most African youths in fact come to Franco-Ontarian schools already possessing a highly valued symbolic capital: *le français parisien* (Parisian French).

My research participants were part of the growing continental Francophone African population in Franco-Ontarian schools. I chose 10 boys and six girls for extensive ethnographic observation inside and outside the classroom and inside and outside the school, and interviewed all 16. Of the 10 boys, six were Somali speakers (from Somalia and Djibouti), one was Ethiopian, two were Senegalese, and one was from Togo. Their ages ranged from 16–20 years. The six girls were all Somali speakers (also from Somalia and Djibouti), aged 14–18 years. Because the majority of interviews were conducted in French I translated them all into English.

Exploring the different sites/sides of BESL learning

Since these youths find themselves in a context where English is the medium of everyday interaction, this inescapability translates into a will to learn English rapidly. Elsewhere (Ibrahim, 1999), I offered popular culture, especially television, friendship and peer pressure as three mechanisms that hasten the speed of learning. I asked students in all of the interviews "Où *est-ce que vous avez appris votre anglais?*" (Where did you learn English?). "*Télévision,*" they all responded. However, within this *télévision* a particular representation - black popular culture – seems to *interpellate*[6] (Althusser, 1971) African youths' identity and identification. Because African youths have few African American friends, and have limited daily contact with them, they access black cultural identities and black linguistic practice in and through black popular culture, especially rap music videos, television programme, and black cinematic representations. The following is a response to my query about recent movies seen by the interviewee, cited by Najat(14, F, Djibouti)[7]:

NAJAT: I don't know, I saw *Waiting to Exhale* and I saw, what else I saw, I saw *Swimmer,* and I saw *Eumanji;* so wicked, all the movies. I went to *Waiting to Exhale* wid my boyfriend and I was like, "Men are rude" [laughs].
AWAD: Oh believe me I know I know.
NAJAT: And den he [her boyfriend] was like, "No, women are rude." I was like, we're like, fighting you know, and joking around. I was like, and de whole time like, [laughs], and den when de woman burns the car, I was like, "Go girl!" You know, and all the women are like "Go girl!" You know? And den de men like "khhh. " I'm like, "I'm gonna go get me a pop corn" [laughs]. (Individual interview conducted in English.)

The influence of black English is clearly manifested in the use of *de, den, dat,* and *wicked* as opposed to, respectively, *the, then, that,* and *really really good.* Another example (a videotaped moment) in a different context, demonstrates the impact of black popular culture on African students' lives and identities. It occurred just before the focus-group interview with the boys. Picture this: *Electric Circus,* a local television music and dance program that plays mostly black music (rap/hip-hop, reggae, soul and R&B) began. "Silence!" one boy requested in French. The boys started to listen attentively to the music and watch the different fashions of the young people on the programme. After the show, the boys code-switched among French, English, and Somali as they exchanged observations on the best music, the best dance, and the cutest girl. Rap and hip-hop music and the corresponding dress were obviously at the top of the list.

The moments of identification in the above examples are significant in that they point to the process of identity formation which is implicated in turn in the linguistic norm to be learned. The western hegemonic representations of blackness, as shown by Stuart Hall (1990), are negative and tend to work alongside historical and subconscious memories that facilitate interpretation by members of the dominant groups. Once African youths encounter these negative representations, they look for black cultural and representational forms as sites for positive identity formation and identification (Kelly, 1998). An important aspect of identification is that it works over a period of time and at a subconscious level. In the following excerpt, Omer (18, M, Ethiopia) addresses the myriad ways in which African youths are influenced by black representations:

> Black Canadian youths are influenced by the Afro-Americans. You watch for hours, you listen to black music, you watch black comedy, *Mr. T.*,[8] the *Rap City*, there you will see singers who dress in particular ways. You see, so. (Individual interview conducted in French.)

Mukhi (19, M, Djiboutian) explored the contention of identification by arguing that:

> We identify ourselves more with the blacks of America. But this is normal, this is genetic. We can't, since we live in Canada, we can't identify ourselves with whites or country music, you know [laughs]. We are going to identify ourselves on the contrary with people of our color, who have our lifestyle, you know. (Group interview conducted in French.)

Mukhi evokes biology and genetic connection as a way of relating to black America, and his identification with it is clearly stated. For Mukhi and all the students I spoke to, this identification is certainly connected to their inability to relate to dominant groups, the public spaces they occupy, and their cultural forms and norms. Alternatively, black popular culture emerged as a site not only for identification, but also as a space for language learning.

"A'ait, Q7 in the house!"

Rap, for African students living in Canada, is an influential site for language learning. However, since rap was more prevalent in the boys' narratives than in the girls', this raises the question of the role of gender in the process of identification and learning.

On many occasions, the boys employed typical gangster rap language and style, using linguistic as well as bodily performance, including name-calling. What follows are just two of the many occasions on which students articulated their identification with black America through the re/citation of rap linguistic styles.[9]

SAM: One two, one two, mic check. A'ait [aayet, or 'alright'], a'ait, a'ait.
JUMA: This is the rapper, you know wha'm meaning? You know wha'm saying?
SAM: Mic mic mic; mic check. A'ait you wonna test it? Ah, I've the microphone you know; a'ait.
SAM: [laughs] I don't rap man, c'mon give me a break, [laughs] Yo! A'ait a'ait you know, we just about to finish de tape and all dat. Respect to my main man [pointing to me]. So, you know, you know wha'm mean, 'm just represen'in Q7. One love to Q7 you know wha'm mean and all my friends back to Q7... Stop the tapin boy!

JAMAL: Kim Juma, live! Put the lights on. Wordup. [Studentstalking in Somali] Peace out, wadup, where de book. Jamal 'am outa here.

SHAPIR: Yo, this is Shapir. I am trying to say peace to all my niggers, all my bitches from a background that everybody in the house. So, yo, chill out and this is how we gonna kick it. Bye and with that pie. All right, peace yo.

SAM: A'ait this is Sam represen'in AQA [...] where it's born, represen'in you know wha'm mean? I wonna say whassup to all my Niggers, you know, peace and one love. You know wha'm mean, Q7 represen'in for ever. Peace! [Rap music]

JAMAL: [as a DJ] Crank it man, coming up. [Rap music] (Group interview conducted in English)

Of interest in these excerpts is the use of black stylised English, particularly the language of rap: "Respect for my main man," "Represen'in Q7," "Kick the free style," "Peace out, wadup," "'Am outa here," "I am trying to say peace to all my niggers, all my bitches," "So, yo, chill out and this is how we gonna kick it," "I wonna say whassup to all my niggers," "Peace and one love". On the other hand, when Shapir offers "Peace to all" his "niggers," all his "bitches," he is firstly re-/appropriating the word *nigger* as an appellation which is common in rap/hip-hop culture. That is, although no consensus, friends, especially young people, commonly call a black friend *nigger* without its traditional racist connotation. Secondly, however, Shapir is using the sexist language that might exist in rap (Rose, 1991). These forms of sexism have been challenged by female rappers like Miss Elliot and Lil' Kim and were critiqued by female and male students. For example, in my interview with the girls, Samira (16, F, Djiboutian) expressed her dismay at the sexist language found in some rap circles:

> OK, hip-hop, yes I know that everyone likes hip-hop. They dress in a certain way, no? The songs go well. But, they are really, really, they have expressions like fuck, bitches etc. Sorry, but there is representation. (Group interview conducted in French.)

Here, Samira is addressing the impact that these expressions might have on the way society at large relates to and perceives the black female body, which in turn influences how it is represented both inside and outside, rap/ hip-hop culture. Hassan (17, M, Djiboutian) also expressed his disapproval of this abusive language: "Occasionally, rap has an inappropriate language for the life in which we live, a world of violence and all that." (Individual interview conducted in French.)

The boys were obviously influenced by rap lyrics, syntax and morphology (in their broader semiological sense), especially by gangster rap. Depending on their age, the girls had an ambivalent relationship to rap. For the most part, the older females (16–18 years old) tended to be more eclectic in how they related to hip-hop and rap. Their eclecticism was evident in how they dressed and in what language they learned. Their dress was either elegant middle class, partially hip-hop, or traditional, and their learned language was what Nourbese Philip (1991) calls plain Canadian English. The younger females (12–14 years) like the boys, dressed in hip-hop style and performed BSE.

Epilogue: Enacting a hybrid African identity[10]

However, African youths' investment in black (and other North American) cultural norms was not in opposition to their own cultural heritage. By cultural heritage, I refer to the embodied everyday material, cultural, religious and linguistic, students bring with them from their homelands. Indeed, in the case of African students, they produced their 'own culture' where continental African memory and experience were amalgamated and mixed with North American cultural and linguistic experience. For theoretical reasons I will to refer to The African experience as *first space,* and North American experience as *second space.* The first and second spaces are as much about language as they are about cultural values, including religion and tradition. In the case of African students, for example, first and second space are simultaneously pronounced in the same sentence and ethnographically performed in the different garments students put on (see also Ibrahim, 1998). The product of this amalgamation and mixture of first and second spaces, is a unique hybrid *third space* (for a different use of this term, see Bhabha, 1990).

This is a space where Africa is not seen in opposition to North America, but as an indispensable memory and experiential site from which to *translate* and hence *negotiate* the new geo-cultural-and-linguistic space. Once in North America, I want to argue, like all displaced subjects, African students become ethnographers. They observe, take note of and live through and experience North American everyday life. They translate what it means to be a North American, more specifically, the state of being black. Translation here refers to the cultural understanding of daily nuances that are expressed in the current and recurrent language. They ask how and why people dress, eat, walk, and talk the way they do? Significantly, these questions are not posed consciously; they pose themselves. They pose themselves as one is walking in the street, eating in a restaurant, or watching television or a movie. Hence, they are asked unconsciously, and their answers come about not only unconsciously, but also gradually. In what follows, I give three examples illustrating, and in many ways performing, the third space. The following excerpt is from my group interview with the boys.

> Sam [19, M, Djiboutian] :*Je reviens* man, you know. It's from Mecca, yo, e represen'in, you know, Mecca a'ait [laughs]. (Somali). *Wallahi bellahi,*[11] ei ei, (Somali) a'ait a'ait. You know wha a mean? Represen'in Q7 you know, you know wha a mean?

Sam's example is one among many others. Purposeful or not, Sam has always been quite playful with language. He could not only very easily code-switch from French to (black stylised) English to Somali, but he could also rap in all three languages. Code-switching here, however, should not be read at the prescriptive – good/correct vs. bad/incorrect – language production, since this would do injustice to the complexity of 'interlanguage' (Rampton, 1995). It should be analysed as a manifestation of the state of being in-between languages. The following two examples, taken from my ethnographic notes, show the complicated nature/phenomenon of identity formation of, particularly young, displaced people.

1. February 12, 1996. It was during lunchtime that I was sitting in the foyer of the school, just under the best students recognised by the school. Najat [14, F, Djiboutian] and a group of black girls were holding a tape recorder which they brought with them. They stopped in the middle of the foyer on their way from the gym to the library; two girls were *hijabed* – veiled. "School sucks," Najat said to me in English. At the beginning of her second sentence, one of the girls with her plugged in the tape recorder: It was Cool J [an African American rapper] rapping. Najat turned around and spoke to one girl in

Somali and hereafter everyone joined in the dance. Hands were moving, bodies were swinging and the girls were talking in Somali, French, and English. Two girls were putting on Islamic *hi/ab*, others were in the Somali national dress of Boubou – a piece of cloth put around the waist, others were dressed in baggy hip hop dress.

2. April 4, 1996. Picture this: it was lunchtime. Amani, Aziza, Ossi, Asma, Samira[12], and five African boys were sitting on the ground of the second floor revising for a test. The girls were dressed very elegantly and *à la mode:* tight jeans with wide bottoms, white and coloured blouses with long or short sleeves, black and white sweaters, and two had Victorian hats. The hair was a fashion show: braids, ponytails, dyed short hair with a long braid descending by the side, and corkscrew style. Their faces were beautifully done with soft make up. The boys, on the other hand, dressed either in the hip-hop style with baggy clothes, topped with sports sweaters or basketball T-shirts or in traditional African dress. Interestingly, the two boys who wore traditional African dress also dyed their hair blond and brown like the girls. Boys as well as girls were code-switching primarily in English and Somali but also in French whenever they were talking academically. They were discussing 19th European literary trends, among them humanism. Michael Jackson was playing in Aziza's tape recorder, and some were dancing to his music.

Clearly, the code-switching in these excerpts is no longer just linguistic, that is from English to French or Somali for example; it is also cultural. Africa, Islam, black popular culture, including Cool J are all to be found in the same space; in it, the new mixes with the old in ways that do not polarize or oppose the other. These non-oppositional performances and mixings can only be a product of 'inbetweenness'. A third space is thus created. To be in this space, for African youths, is to become; and yet to become a double-edged product, an ambivalent one. It is also clear that boys as well as girls entered this space of inbetweenness; although girls entered it with considerable difficulties, reservation, and restriction. This is because male and female bodies are prescribed differently in religious and social texts and traditions. Yet, importantly, the translating and negotiating of the Canadian and North American context in general was highly influenced by racial apparatus. Mukhi [19, M, Djiboutian] expresses this very eloquently:

> My culture is something I am proud of. I would like to keep my culture, but at the same time, you know, I am going to be very close to Canadians and particularly black peoples. I am going to even be friend with them, you know, but also hold on to my culture. (Group interview conducted in French.)

What Mukhi expresses as an on-going negotiation between his and the North American black/Canadian culture is something African youths are quite cognisant of. In my interview with the boys, this is how they conceptualise (the inevitable state of?) inbetweenness:

MUSA [19, M, DJIBOUTIAN]: Here, we live in Canada, you see. We are going to keep our culture, but at the same time there is the new technologies, the new musics. There is also glamour and modernisation of the cities and towns.

MUKHI: The way we dress, the way we talk; we are in Canada. It is like we can't dress in like Raphar or our Galdoté, *you know.*

SAM: *Tight jeans you know.*

MUKHI: The small Angoloté you know, the small cloth we put around [the waist], it's like the way we dress back home. We need to mix in different genres of dress here. The way I am dressing now [hip-hop style] is because I am influenced, you see, and that is why I dress the way I do. Back home, for example, we put on Boubou and all that. But I don't find it embarrassing to go out like that. But I feel more comfortable with clothes like the ones I have on, you see!

The need to "mix in different genres of dress," language, and cultural norms is what I term negotiation. But this need, I want to argue, does not come to be by an act of conscious. Indeed, a considerable portion of our negotiation with what surrounds us takes place unconsciously. In the case of African students, the 'new' is not a path we open and simply slip into, nor is the 'old' a dormant and secure place resting in peace. On the contrary, negotiation requires arduous tasks and difficult choices. Amani expresses this:

> You know in any culture, there are advantages and disadvantages, strong points and weak points. I will keep the strong points and leave the rest. There are points we love about our culture and others we don't like. So, it's about making choices; do you accept the weak points [of your cultural heritage], or don't you? But that doesn't mean I am rejecting my culture when I choose a new one, I keep what's valuable in my culture. (Individual interview conducted in French.)

In conclusion, knowing what we do about the politics and identity formation in the third space, how do we then engage these identities pedagogically? To say that this is a difficult question is to state the obvious, yet I would like to venture and propose a few ideas to address. First, we need to acknowledge the complexity and the difficulty of displaced identity formation processes. By displaced identity, I am referring to immigrants, refugees and others who move from one geo-cultural-and-linguistic space to another, for any reason. As we have seen, to be a Somali in Canada is undoubtedly to be in the middle, in between. Here, the cultural heritage one brings with him or her cannot escape the bumpy road of (re)translation and negotiation.

Second, we need to appreciate the multifaceted and multi-layered nature of culture and cultural heritage. In a classroom situation, do we as educators engage the Somali culture as exists in Somalia and thus in its static notion: "This is what Somalis do"? Or do we engage Amani's retranslation of her Somali culture as exists in Canada? I am obviously arguing for the latter, since the static notion of culture can only perpetuate a colonial hegemonic mentality. This brings me to my last point.

We need to urgently decolonise the public space and public imaginary, which sees in African youths and myself only blackness. Indeed, the purpose of my dealing with the hybrid African identity is to show its complexity; its on-going production which is yet to be completed. Fanon's intention in *Black skin/white masks* (1967) is to show how white people assume, act, relate to and behave as if they know him only by looking at him. They see through him. He becomes a tableau to be drawn and redrawn and a canvas to be read unidimensionally, and not necessarily to be dialectically engaged with. Being locked into that infernal circle where one is a slave of one's own appearance is indeed my notion of social imaginary. We have seen how painful it is, or it can be, when it is put to task. My incident with the police, and African youths integration into the Canadian society, are two significant examples calling for a deconstruction of this symbolic, yet materially felt social imaginary. Oneway of doing so is by addressing and redressing Africanness and blackness in its ontological essence. That is, Africanness and blackness are not interchangable entities; on the contrary, they are, to the knower, inherently multiethnic, multilingual and multicultural.

Notes

1. Thanks, in part, to the discourse of Afrocentrism and diasporic/African studies departments, there is a new dialogue created between Africans and diasporic Africans (see also Gilroy, 1993). And part of this dialogue is enhanced by, ironically, tourism and immigration (as well as involuntary displacement). In defiance of history, diasporic Africans in North America, for example, are making the journey back to Africa and continental Africans are making it to North America.
2. Against the legacy of apartheid in South Africa, my statement needs to be qualified. It is not accurate for the whole continent, since it does not hold ground in the latter context where blacks indeed 'became blacks.' However, aside from South Africa, there is hardly any overt African context where someone's skin colour has ever been a social concern. As one reviewer of my article put it, "An African (in the general sense of the term) does not "become black" in an African country where there is no history of racial discrimination."
3. For Roger Simon and Dan Dippo (1986, p. 195), *critical ethnographic research* is a set of activities situated within a project that seeks and works its way towards social transformation. This project is political as well as pedagogical, and who the researcher is and what his or her racial, gender, and class embodiments are, necessarily govern the research questions and findings. The project, then, according to Simon and Dippo, is "An activity determined both by real and present conditions, *and certain conditions still to come which it is trying to bring into being*" (p. 196). The assumption underpinning my project was based on the assertion that Canadian society is "Inequitably structured and dominated by a hegemonic culture that suppresses a consideration and understanding of why things are the way they are and what must be done for things to be otherwise" (ibid).
4. All names are pseudonyms.
5. As a research methodology, ethnography of performance argues that ethnographers' best access to the research subjects' inner-selves is the latter's verbal and non-verbal performance. Put otherwise, the juxtaposition of what people actually and materially perform on and through their bodies on the one hand, and what they say and think about those performances on the other, give ethnographers the least distorted picture of their research subjects and their identities.
6. The subconscious ways in which individuals, given their genealogical history and memory, identify with particular discursive spaces and representations and the way this identification participates hereafter in the social formation of the subject (identity).
7. Each student name is followed by age, gender (F=female, M=Male), and country of origin; and each extract is followed by the type of interview (individual or group) and the language in which it was conducted. The following transcription conventions are used: **underlined text** = English spoken within French speech or French spoken within English speech. [] = Explanation or description of speaker's actions. […] = Text omitted
8. Mr. T. is an M.C. of a local Canadian rap music TV programme called *Rap City*, which airs mostly American rap lyrics.
9. The names cited in the extracts are Sam (19, M, Djibouti), Juma (19, M, Senegal), Jamal (18, M, Djibouti), and Shapir (17, M, Somalia).
10. For a full analysis of the theory of hybridity, third space and further examples, see Ibrahim, 2000c.
11. This is an Arabic expression used by Muslims meaning, "If Allah wishes and in Allah's name."
12. All five girls are of Somali origin and members of my research subjects. Amani is 17 years old, Aziza 18, Ossi 17, Asma 16 and Samira 16. Asma and Ossi are sisters.

References

Althusser, L. (1971). *Lenin and philosophy*. London: New Left Books.
Anderson, B. (1983). *Imagined communities: reflections on the origin and spread of nationalism*. London: Verso.

Asante, M. K. (1990). Afrocentricity and culture. In Molefi Kete Asante & Karimu Walsh-Asante (Eds.), *African culture: the rhythms of unity* pp. 3–12. Trenton, NJ: Africa World.

Barthes, R. (1983). *Elements of semiology*. (Original work published 1967.) New York: Hill and Wang.

Bhabha, H. (1990). The third space: Interview with Homi Bhabha. In J. Rutherford (Ed.), *Identity community, culture, difference* (pp. 26–33). London: Lawrence & Wishart.

Bhabha, H. (1994). *The location of culture*. London and New York: Routledge.

Bourdieu, P. (1991). *Language and symbolic power*. (G. Raymond and M. Adamson, Trans.). London: Polity Press.

Butler, J. (1999). *Cender trouble: Feminism and the subversion of identity*. (Original work published 1990.) New York: Routledge.

Essed, P. & Goldberg, D. T. (Eds.). (2002). *Race critical theory*. Malden, Mass: Blackwell Publishers Inc.

Fanon, F. (1967). *Black skin /white mask*. New York: Grove Weidenfeld.

Foucault, M. (1970). *The order of things*. London: Tavistock.

Foucault, M. (1980). *Power/knowledge: Selected interviews and other writings*. New York: Pantheon.

Fine, M., Powell, L., Weiss, L., & Wong, L. M. (Eds.). (1997). *Off white: Readings on race, power and society*. New York: Routledge.

Frankenberg, R. (1993). *White women, race Matters: The social construction of whiteness*. Minneapolis: University of Minnesota Press.

Gilroy, P. (1993). *The black Atlantic: Modernity and double consciousness*. London & New York: Routledge.

Hall, S. (1990). Cultural identity and diaspora. In J. Rutherford (Ed.), *Identity, community, culture, difference* (pp. 222–237). London: Lawrence & Wishart.

Hall, S. (1991). Ethnicity: identity and difference. *Radical America, 13* (4), 9–20.

Hall, S. (1996). Introduction: Who needs 'Identity'? In Hall, S. & du Gay, P. (Eds.), *Questions of cultural identity* (pp. 1–17). London: Sage Publication Ltd.

Hall, S. (Ed.). (1997). *Representation: Cultural representations and signifying practices*. London: The Open University.

Heller, M. (1992). The politics of codeswitching and language choice, *Journal of Multilingual and Multicultural Development, 13:* 1&2: 123–142.

Heller, M. (1994). *Crosswords: Language, education and ethnicity in French Ontario*. Berlin and NY: Mouton de Gruyter.

hooks, b. (1992). *Black looks*. Boston, MA: South End Press.

Ibrahim, A. (1998). *'Hey, whassup homeboy?' Becoming black: race, language, culture, and the politics of identity. African students in a Franco-Ontarian high school*. Unpublished doctoral dissertation, OISE: University of Toronto.

Ibrahim, A. (1999). Becoming black: rap and hip-hop, race, gender, identity, and the politics of ESL learning. *TESOL Quarterly, 33,* (3), 349–369.

Ibrahim, A. (2000a). "Hey, ain't I black too?" The politics of becoming black. In R. Walcott (Ed.), *Rude: contemporary black Canadian cultural criticism* (pp. 109136). Toronto: Insomniac Press.

Ibrahim, A. (2000b). "Whassup Homeboy?" Black/popular culture and the politics of "curriculum studies": Devising an anti-racism perspective. In G. J. S. Dei & A. Cai liste (Eds.), *Power, knowledge and anti-racism education: a critical reader* (pp. 57–72). Halifax: Feronwood Books Ltd.

Ibrahim, A. (2000c). Trans-framing identity: race, language, culture, and the politics of translation, *trans/forms: Insurgent Voices in Education, 5,* (2), 120–135.

Ibrahim, A. (2001). "Hey, whadap homeboy?" Identification, desire, and consumption: hip-hop, performativity, and the politics of becoming black. *Taboo, 5,* (2), 85102.

Kelly, J. (1998). *Under the gaze: Learning to be black in white society*. Halifax: Fernwood Publishing.

Kristeva, J. (1974). *La révolution du langage poétique* [Revolution in Poetic Language] Paris: Lautréament et Mallarmé.

Nietzsche, F. (1977). *A Nietzsche reader*. New York: Penguin Classics.

Philip, M. N. (1991). *Harriet's daughter*. Toronto: The Women's Press.

Prince, A. (2001). *Being black*. Toronto: Insomniac Press

Rose, T. (1991). "Fear of a black planet": Rap music and black cultural politics in the 1990s. *Journal of Negro Education, 60,* (3), 276–290.

Sartre, J-P. (1980). *Being and nothingness: A phenomenological essay on ontology.* (Hazel E. Barnes, Trans.). New York: Pocket Books.

Simon, R. I., & Dippo, D. (1986). On critical ethnography work. *Anthropology & Education Quarterly, 17,* 195–202.

Smitherman, G. (1994). *Black talk: Words and phrases from the hood to the Amen Corner.* Boston: Houghton Mifflin.

Taylor, C. (1994). The politics of recognition. In D. T. Goldberg (Ed.), *Multiculturalism: a critical reader.* Oxford: Blackwell.

Walcott, R. (1995). *Performing the postmodern: black Atlantic rap and identity in North America.* Unpublished doctoral dissertation, OISE: University of Toronto.

Woodward, K. (Ed.). (1997). *Identity and difference.* London: The Open University.

Constructing Consciousness: Diasporic Remembrances and Imagining Africa in Late Modernity

Jacinta K. Muteshi

ABSTRACT

Several simultaneous aesthetic movements have emerged in the African Diaspora that critically explore and reference Africa to address the questions of 'history, migrations and trans-national practices'. This paper critically examines some of these recent processes of deploying and displaying particular African aesthetic forms in North American museums to raise questions about the re-telling of Africa's past in the Western museum.

The paper also seeks to explore the new deployments that diasporic blacks, who are revisiting, exploring and evoking Africa, are evolving in the process of making art. Art that nourishes the act of becoming, articulating new identities and forging new meanings of existence that extends the meanings and identities of the black self even as they speak from a particular place, history, and experience.

A preamble

It is mid-summer and like many previous summers, I walk along West 125th street in Harlem, New York City. I stroll here because as a temporarily transplanted Kenyan there is a familiarity in what seems to be a veritable African market place and I am in search of a decorated calabash. The very idea of a market is a compelling metaphor here as illustrated by the Yoruba proverb *'Aya loja orun nile'*(the world in which we live is no more than a journey to the market place-at some point we return home).[1] To walk into Harlem is to encounter a world of things African in light of the commodification of African artefacts and "African inspired products" that are "being shaped by a deepening and expanding African Diasporic identity, as well as capital's willingness to derive profits" (Byfield, 2000, p. 7).

Thus the producers and consumers of Africa are here on the street. There is an explosion of cultural and material exchanges; there is a strong sense of temporality and fluidity, and all is negotiable, as is suggested by a market place that operates off folding tables and the pavement. Accessible in this American city are African cultural artefacts of weaved and dyed cloths, basketry, beadwork, sculpture, ritual artefacts, music and other artistic works. The products on sale here are representative of a powerful African aesthetic or symbolism for the originating African groups. Thus the Kente cloth, an emblem of Ghanaian traditional wealth and status is conspicuous, popular and lucrative here. Indeed, there also seems to be a celebration of the mythic and heroic and a "re-Africanisation of the Americas" (Lao-Montes, 2000, p. 59). Thus cloths such as Kente and Kuba have become not only signifiers of identity but also possible referents of self-determination.

There are also simultaneously aesthetic movements that have emerged to critically explore and reference Africa in order to address questions of 'history, migrations and transnational practices'. These questions are being addressed by looking back through artistic productions to extend the meaning of .the African self and understand the process of making art as an act of becoming, articulating new identities and forging new meanings of existence. Richard Powell (2002, p. 151) notes that:

> The period of the 1970s and early 1980s that saw the institutionalisation of black art through the acquisitions of work by black artists by mainstream institutions and the "plethora of new 'black art'" publications signalled a dramatic shift in the mainstream art world. This change in perception acknowledged not only individual black talent, but the idea of a collective artistic genius based on race, history, and a creative drive whose source was a spirituality that, in turn, sprang from the phenomena of cultural connections through out the African diaspora.

Of interest to me are the processes of deploying particular African forms by diasporic blacks. I revisit and explore certain artistic positionings at the crossroads of different African cultures that evoke Africa and are articulated at specific sites and in art works of the late 1990s by black diaspora artists, particularly those resident in America but with an example also from the United Kingdom. People who live in the diaspora and "people who cross boundaries are subject to multiple identities" (Lutzeler, 1995, p. 453). Through an examination of the display of works from continental Africa and the works of certain diasporic artists, I aim to show that multiple identities are available to the diaspora. Such Africa-based identities are produced in part by diasporic artists who, acting as ethnographers, have access to different cultural objects and spaces to enable new identities. The artistic works that emerge then function to assign positive conceptions of cultural identity and what the black female artist Lubaina Himid (cited in De Souza, 2001, p. 101) claims is also "a recognition that we speak from a particular place, out of a particular history, out of a particular experience, a particular culture without being contained by that position".

Diaspora as discursive practice

The presence of African populations in the Americas, as a result of "historical movements - forced, chosen, necessary or desired" (Grossberg, 1998, p. 92) produced shared stories of dislocation, domination, violence, and struggle with cultural identity. More recently, post-colonial democratic struggles and unstable economies on the continent have set into motion a new migration of Africans to the Americas that further unsettles identifications, attenuates differences and creates a new dynamism, further mediated by class, gender and race stratification among African diasporic communities in the West.

The idea of an African diaspora and the development of that diaspora stems from traditions that construct and articulate a consciousness and identity that recalls Africa as home among people of African descent living in the West. "The constituent elements of such a consciousness," notes Tiffany Patterson and Robin Kelley (2000, p. 15), citing William Safran (1991), "include dispersal from a homeland, often by violent forces, the making of a memory and a vision of that homeland, marginalisation in the new location, a commitment to the maintenance/restoration of the homeland, desire for return, and a continuing relationship and identity with the homeland that shapes the consciousness and solidarity of the group". In addition to this, Judith Byfield's (2000, p. 2) mapping of the complexities of the diasporic consciousness further points out that "the notion of an African diaspora for which Africa was the homeland was not a natural development. It had to be socially and historically constituted, reconstituted and reproduced."

These shared experiences of displacement, loss and resistance have not, however, resulted in a universally shared construction of blackness (Butler, 1998). Instead, as K. Butler goes on to argue, struggles over selfhood, race and the meaning of community emerge and collide as multiple identities of blackness continue to be constructed within and in response to the specific economic, cultural, social and political settings in which dispersed black populations have found themselves. These complexities and differences in the African-Diaspora are further highlighted by the multiple positionings of the black self that V.Y. Mudimbe (1998, pp. 84–7) represents 'as a being *for* others'; 'as a being *with* others'; and 'as a being *for* me'. Such (re)positionings have been compelling. Located in 'an imagined community' and 'an imaginary Africa' has provided the meanings and symbols for identifications (Hall, 1995) and a consciousness.

Imaginings of Africa: What is Africa to the contemporary black diasporic subject?

> In art as in politics, religion and so forth, all manner of traditions are contemporary with each other, co-existing, often mutually reflexive, each with its particular temporal status and functional locus, (cited by Victoria Rovine, *Africa Arts* Summer 1996, p. 19)

To what purposes are Africa's cultural products and Africa inspired products being put in contemporary North America by African-Americans? Africa is a geographical place, a trope, and even an unmediated sign in the work of many diasporic Africans. However, the idea of Africa has not been static. Rather, a history of cultural imagining and productions show that it transverses idealised, romantic, heroic, mythic, pristine associations; from the exotic stereotypical images of primitive Africa, to perceptions of the revolutionary Africa of Pan-Africanism and finally to the dream of Africa undergoing reculturation or redefinition that is not yet complete.

At first look, given the images of the afore mentioned marketplace, it seems that there has been an emphasis on the mythic and the transcendent to counter demeaning discourses of what it means to be civilized. African textiles, especially their presence in the contemporary market place, elucidate for me more then any other African artistic productions not only the receptivity and thus persistence of particular African aesthetic forms; such as the ubiquitous Kente and Kuba cloths, but also diasporic responses to African visual art through iconic textiles and textiles as forms for imagining the new to displace what has been historically signified.

Thus specific and the most resonant icons of African textiles can be seen as selectively filtered through numerous creative adaptations, manufactured using new Western technologies and factories, and expensively exchanged through new international marketing networks and a global market for completely new uses, thus bringing new displacements upon artistic debates and practices. 'Africa' serves as a 'resource' and to be reduced to a resource requires imbuing certain meanings upon the 'colonised' subject, in order to satisfy the discursive systems of imperialism, colonialism and now globalisation. Indeed these current employments of Africa by the diaspora are not outside of dominant discourses of Africa that focus on traditions, a certain primitivism, exoticism, and the commodity value of Africa.

Africa as a resource had and has symbolic value for African-Americans as well as commodity value for African-American and Anglo-American cultures. For both, Africa has also increasingly come to fulfil the function of being the embodiment of the exotic - be it its nature (wildlife) or its culture (as decoration and fashion), inviting interest, curiosity, and penetration in the desire to fulfil fantasies. Nevertheless, it has also always been possible to strongly discern the risks taken in emphasising the political and personal histories of African-Americans as constituted in difference, signalled by the use of 'Africa' as sign. Difference that is a result of initial and continuing inequities in the relationship between African-Americans and Anglo-Americans. Thus the struggles for political and social equality makes demands upon identity formation challenging how the black subject might negotiate a common identity, a multiplicity of identities and the memory of origins especially given forced migrations.

Imaginative rediscovery: Places the black subject can find their way to.

If Africa figures in the background of the black diasporic imagination, how do artists interrogate its memory? How do diasporic subjects begin to examine and reflect on where they can and cannot proceed with projects of finding 'home'? The original 'Africa' wrote Stuart Hall (1995) no longer exists, history has intervened, and he cautions that "we can't literally go home again", indeed that would not be possible if the desire is to return to an "unchanging past". Instead Hall suggests the possibilities of "symbolic returns ...by another route [to] what Africa has become in the New World" (p. 399). That there may be several ways to return, is brought to the fore by Moya Okediji (2000) who posits "philosophical-intellectual returns, mythopoeic returns, psychic returns, and direct physical returns" (p. 34). 'Return' and 'journeys' are powerful tropes especially when we recall the legendary 'Door of no return' on Goree Island, Senegal, the beginning point of forced transportation into slavery. For African-Americans to therefore return to this African shore has had significance for a people seeking not only to establish a claim to a historical heritage, but also to return to themselves. For more recently migrating continental Africans fleeing into forced exile to the West as a consequence of 'post'-colonial political, social and economic upheavals, repressions and violence; 'returns' to Africa are made in order to negotiate and forge cultural identities out of multiple geographic spaces. Marjorie Salvodon (1999, p. 91) argues that 'exilic' conditions that may or may not be temporary:

> Demand a perpetual *errance*, a condition that continually subverts any singular position, choice, or fixed meaning. When staking one's territory in multiple geographical spaces which are not rigid and absolute, one necessarily engages in a constant play of exchanges among differing meanings and positions.

The journey of return be it imaginary or physical, are often circulatory journeys to the African continent that allows for a cultural reclamation of what may have been left behind before once again returning to the Americas. Diasporic African women and men embark on these journeys to Africa with quests that are similar because they seek self-understanding given colonial and postcolonial subjects multicultural contexts. These journeys are also gendered, with women articulating their journeys within the specificity of their concerns as women within the practices of everyday life, opening up the sexual differences that inflect artistic culture and using the artistic cultural space to explore and reconstruct the multiple intersecting identities of women thus providing a new if challenging appreciation of what racialised and gendered identities might artistically imagine and the nature of their engagement with artistic media from a space called woman.

I am particularly interested in expressive culture or art for its role as a vehicle for such 'returns'; and also for the opportunities it offers to dialogue with African-diasporic artistic forms and as a space that throws into relief the wider dimensions of political critique. And the American museum is the terrain where these journeys home through art can be tracked.

First stop: The Museum for African Art

> The past continues to speak to us. But it no longer addresses us as a simple factual past, since our relation to it, like the child's relation to the mother, is always-already 'after the break'. It is always constructed through memory, fantasy, narrative and myth. Cultural identities are the points of identification or suture, which are made within the discourses of history and the culture. Not an essence but a positioning. (Hall, 1990, p. 226)

In 1993, in New York City, the Museum for African Art assembled a show that I went to see out of curiosity about the African secrets that were about to be revealed. The exhibition reflected sacred and magical African cultural products that was titled "Secrecy: African art that reveals and conceals". On view were ancient traditional objects of divination, tools for healers, and the figures and insignias that have ceremonial, magical and sacred significance for particular rituals. Healers and diviners using these objects on behalf of their clients mediated between the gods, spirits and ancestors and the human community through a variety of processes that included the divination process.

On display were wooden boards that appeared tray or plate like and that were often used during divination ceremonies either spread with soil or dust and upon which signs are traced and 'read' for meanings. These boards varied in the intricacies of their carved motifs that were reflective of the values and visual traditions of their original communities. Tappers, stick like forms used for tapping the boards and made of materials similar to the boards, were also plain, textured or finely carved objects. Other items on display fashioned of wooden and fibrous type materials included small figurines, cup like vessels, small gourds, bowls and calabashes, all of which had served as containers of divination objects and of the medicines that were primarily gathered from the forest. Masks, also on display, afforded communication with the spirit world when used in rituals of masquerades or ritual performances enabling the honouring of ancestors from whom help was often sought. The masks on show were made of organic materials. There were also everyday functional objects such as pottery, stools and shields that were part of the paraphernalia of healing and divination.

The mystical objects on display created in various media, the names of their creators unknown to us now, had been employed in celebration and helping in community communication with the spirit world, the ancestral world. These ritual objects, some of which were sculptural given the embedded decorative or ornamental carved figures - human, animal or abstract - were intended to evoke particular local values.

We learned from the museum display that divination was used to solve problems, diagnose and heal, expose wrongdoing and offer protection from adversity and help achieve community or personal intentions and harmony. We were informed that these objects are made magical, ceremonial and embedded with power through secret rituals undertaken by the diviners.

Conversely, we receive silence on the circumstances that brought these items to the West in the form of art. This exhibition, as many of its time, never politically engages or renders visible the illegal historical appropriation and circulation of these objects from their sources to their display in Western museums. Nor was the question raised of the new entry of African-Americans into the displaying of "the spoils of modernism" to borrow Marlene Nourbese Phillip's (1992, p. 93) term, in museum space now given to recognising the African-American presence and the connection to Africa. Phillip (1992) also goes on to posit that the logic of European colonial power identified Africa and Oceania as "possessable and certifiable an approach that worked with the appropriations of early cultures to enable a double erasure,... erasure of the context within which these objects existed, and the erasure of the circumstances of removal from the places they belonged" (p. 96). Furthermore, missionaries often forbade the use of ritual objects given their transgressive nature with regards to Christianity and the result was not only the local destruction of these objects but the subsequent removal of these objects to become part of Western colonial collections.

The objects included in this show were displayed to have both ethnographic and aesthetic purposes. Ethnographic practices with regards to Africa were invoked by the contradictory nature of the naming of the exhibition as 'Secrecy: African art that reveals and conceals'. This contradiction continues through the processes of identifying, writing descriptions, and cataloguing these objects which in turn informs public consumption of the ritual knowledge of Africa by its being displayed in a museum that is normally the purview of only a few, thus erasing its ritual function by revealing it secrets. Naming these ritual objects as art is a Western construct for purposes of appropriating them as museum displays, for distancing them, and for surviving what was becoming increasing onslaughts on American museums on what is to constitute or be named art and by whom.

On viewing this show I could not help but think about who will be looking and who is being addressed by this exhibition. The primary audience is racialised America. The gaze of the visitor to this display is guided towards the iconic weight of a singular African past, by the silences and therefore exclusions of any African present in the structuring of this exhibition.

It struck me that these objects from the past, removed/displaced from their customary and authentic settings were no longer carriers of their cultural meanings. How then were these ancient forms on show at the Museum of African Art to be accessed and experienced by the Diaspora?

The items on display enabled traditional practitioners of sacred and magical rituals to be the link and the moral balance between the visible and invisible world by allowing access to transcendent knowledge; but now given an aesthetic value and becoming art in an American museum. Who participated in controlling this naming? Was this occurrence of naming pursued to ensure 'ontological closure' as suggested by this Foucauldian term?

Presented as art in this relocation, African aesthetics and creativity is fore-grounded, but only of that which was created long ago, in its glorious past. One can understand the excavation of history in this way for a diasporic people scripted out of history and now seeking to remind that they already have a viable and sustaining culture. However, in my mind such a showing has failed to pay sufficient attention to the fact that this ceremonial and magical past had in its origins been assembled, organised and given value by European anthropology and more frequently then not for European consumption. Ultimately there seems to be a refusal to move through history given what has become of contemporary Africa.

Utilising the tropes of Africa's past as the 'Secrecy' exhibition does requires questioning how such encounters with the past in the present allows us to unravel where we are now, the transformative power of such symbols for the present and its possibility for enabling collective agency that will define social change. Such transformative moves are suggested by the transatlantic artistic dialogue that emerged within another American museum space.

Second stop: The National Museum of African Art

This space, part of the Smithsonian Institutions in Washington DC, houses permanent collections of the visual culture from Africa. The majority and dominant exhibitions here have concentrated on works with historical status and by far its last displayed collections are what it calls tradition-based. Recent exhibition examples have included: 'The Ancient Nubian City of Kerma', 'The Ancient West African City of Benin', 'The Art of the Personal Object', and 'Images of Power and Identity'. Even temporary exhibitions like 'The Artistry of African Currency' and 'Wrapped in Pride: Ghanaian Kente and African American Identity' have depended far more on cultural products from the African past then the present. Contemporary works of African art form much smaller collections. Thus a recent exhibition in keeping with the metaphors and practices of 'return' 'journeys' and entitled 'Transatlantic dialogue: Contemporary art in and out of Africa' is particularly remarkable and exciting in this particular museum space. This show brought together seven African-American and seven African artists living in the West into dialogue with one another about the way one is and becomes a black diasporic subject. Both groups would encounter in each other's artistic works cultural elements that were a consequence of their sought migrations/ journeys to each other's shores on both sides of the Atlantic in exploration of their identities. This composition of artists speaks of the recognition of the meaning of diaspora.

I have selected to focus on four of the artists featured at this transatlantic exhibition. John Bigger, a male African-American painter; Yvonne Edwards- Tucker and Curtis Tucker, an African-American married couple working in ceramics; and Moyo Okediji, a male African painter, all of whom reside in the United States, and Sokari Douglas-Camp, an African woman sculptor living in London and whose work was also on show with the above named artists. I select only one example each of their work from the exhibition to allow me to easily and readily explore the transatlantic returns and departures that inform their art and enables social and political projects through their chosen mediums.

On view at the National Museum of African Art were many works ranging from paintings to collages to mixed media, ceramics, sculpture and earthenware, and to installations termed 'returnee' art (Okediji, 1999). This artwork was produced by diaspora artists who journeyed to Africa and then returned to the West to produce art informed by these visits. These journeys were physical, philosophical, and circular and the vehicle for doing so was art. Indeed much of the work on display self-consciously explores the recovery of place and memory. Illuminating the nature of the statements made by these visual artists about the world they perceive, Jeff Donaldson, one of the artists, speaks of how "our generation, several generations later want to recapture whatever it was we had in Africa, because we can show how important a role it played for us over there, and how it can play the same kind of role here. It helps to establish who we are, why we are, and why we should continue to exist" (cited by Okediji, 1999, p. 41).

African diaspora artists from the Americas have a long tradition of journeying to Africa since the late 1920s and 1930s. However it is during the 1960s that we see "a more aggressive exploration of African art and culture by young African-American artists, writers and intellectuals" (Visona, M.B., R. Poyer. H.M. Cole and M. D. Harris, 2000, p. 514). For many this would mean actual physical travel to Africa at a time of "Black nationalism, Black arts movement, the revitalisation of Pan-Africanism and the increasing number of African nations throwing off the yoke of colonialism" (Visona et al, 2000, p. 514).

Among returning/journeying artists, John Biggers is often recognised as the most well known and notable African-American painter to have gone to Ghana in the late 1950s. His return to Africa led to a reconceptualisation of his thinking; painting the black body in ways that Jeff Donaldson, another African-American painter of renown, saw as the recognition of "our people at the height of their glory. At the height of their humanity" (cited in Okediji, 1999, p. 37), Biggers thereby established "an aesthetic orientation grounded in a transatlantic dialogue while maintaining American and modernist location" (Okediji, 1999, p. 36).

Painter Biggers' piece shown is 'Drummers of Ede' (1959), which I found powerful in its absence of colour and its monochromatic use of shades of black, grey and white, illuminates his encounter with African music. The picture focuses on three Yoruba musicians dressed in traditional Yoruba hand-woven garments and playing percussion instruments. The exhibition catalogue (Okediji, 1999, p. 39) notes that this painting was a result of Biggers visit to Ede, a Yoruba town in Ghana. During that visit the King, Timi Laoye, who was himself a musician of distinction, invited Biggers to a royal session of drumming by him and his local master musicians. Biggers was to paint a section of this ensemble of drummers.

The Diaspora artists in this exhibition draw frequently on musically or rhythmic themes as seen in the painting of Yoruba drummers ('Drummers of Ede', by John Bigger), mixed-media installations that allude to jazz sounds ('Riff for John Coltrane', by Al Smith), ceramic pottery expressing the music culture of American blues ('Homage to B.B King', by Yvonne Edwards-Tucker and Curtis Tucker) and the movement of the dancing sculpture of the masquerade ('Women With Palm-Leaf Skirt', by Sokari Douglas Camp). This referencing of music by diasporic blacks has been the key to diasporic connections. Writing about the multitudes of diasporic black artists present in Nigeria in 1977 for the second African Festival of Arts and Culture (FESTAC), Powell, (2002, pp. 157–8) noted that:

> Although FESTAC presented visual arts, theatrical performances, and literary readings by black artists from all over the world, music drew the Festival's disparate black peoples together more than any other art forms... That the world's various black music's had an allure that crossed boundaries of culture, nationality and racial identity was something that many visual artists knew and attempted to recreate.

In many parts of Africa, there is a clear separation of female and male creative and artistic expressions. For example potters are usually women and metal-smiths are often men. However some of women artists in this show have interrupted this order of things. I was intrigued by the transformations done to pottery by the collaborative work of the African American wife and husband artist team of Yvonne Edwards-Tucker and Curtis Tucker, for this is a primary medium for African women's creative and expressive expressions. As a couple they provide a counterpoint to the gendered image of the pottery maker, as returning ceramist artists they rework and remould the traditional meanings that attach to African pots as they contemplate and reclaim that past heritage. For example, the Tuckers' collaborative creative dialogue with Africa seeks to exemplify the multiple sources of identities that exist for African-Americans by means of a pottery piece whose design, shape, decorative patterns, colour, pottery making technique and the image of B.B King integrates African, Asian and European underpinnings.

Thus the pottery titled 'Homage to B.B. King' (1991), has a body that seems distinctly divided into four parts and is incised with various figures and patterns that recall African pottery decorations and textures that occupy the wide lip, neck, and narrow base of the pot and are dark coloured. The middle cylindrical part of the pot, coloured black and white displays a distorted human figure with a cropped brow, partly enclosed with lines that form curving swelling rhythmic shapes. Okediji (1999, p. 41) notes in the exhibition catalogue that the lip of the Tucker pot has the "sensuous lip of Eshu, (the god of crossroads) a type of wide and generous lip that is frequently found in many pots in West Africa" he goes on to also observe that the body of the pot resembles Greco-Roman vases especially the squat *lekythos*.

The Tuckers, through creative and intentional selection, seek to recall through the materials and techniques of pot making that they employed, the legacy of diverse ancestors, identities, races and continents that link diasporic blacks. Yvonne first travelled to Nigeria in 1975 to learn more about pottery making, having already mastered and favoured Japanese raku techniques of pottery making. Her journey to Africa created an opportunity to bring together both the raku forms and hand building pottery forms of a Nigeria potter called Ladi Kwali inspiring Yvonne to create more sculptural ceramics. The Tuckers approach ceramics as art rather then craft, and clearly the "Homage to B.B. King" shows no elements of utilitarian use. Instead this pot reveals the dialogue of a multiple past and present blending seamlessly in the curves of a modern pot. Theirs was a modern form that was beginning to inform the future, for pottery making which has traditionally been the work of women in Africa is now through the collaborative work of the Tuckers expressing a gender inclusive form.

The work of Sokari Douglas Camp a sculptor, a Kalahari woman originally from the Delta region of the lower Niger and now living in London; her 'returns' to Africa are to the dance and performances of her Kalahari people that she grew up watching. That she works with steel to create sculpture is a break with the common traditions of her people where only men work with metal, create sculptures, make masks for masquerades, and only men stage the performances of those masquerades. She therefore radically questions the image of the African woman artist. Michael Harris (1999, p. 24) reviewing her work in the exhibition writes "it is rare in Western art traditions to find women artists, rarer to find women sculptors and terribly rare to find a woman working in welded steel". I might also add even more rare to find the female figure cast in steel.

One of Sokari Camp's steel sculptures on display is labelled 'Woman With Palm-Leaf Skirt' (1986). We are told it forms part of a masquerade ensemble. Given its multi-dimensional aspects it shows a woman, with her arms raised as if in exhilaration, the middle part of her body wrapped in a spectacular steel open-work skirt that suggests beautiful patterns of leaves and is billowing open behind her. Utilising crayon and paint the steel 'clothing' that covers the figure's upper body is painted white while the steel 'wrapper' on her lower body is reddish maroon. Camp's remembering of her Kalahari roots brings attention to the detail of clothing that conveys her recognition of the long standing traditional role among West African women in the display, exchange and discourses of extraordinary cloths, fashion and appearance especially for a woman's entry into public spaces. As part of other sculptures called 'audience ensemble' not shown at this exhibition, this particular piece of 'Woman With Palm-Leaf Skirt', expresses Camp's personal history of growing up watching rather then participating in the dramas of such masquerades. Camp's sculptures re-make these traditional masquerades manipulating steel to create group or individual sculptures of the maskers to the masquerade and giving them relevance for gender politics by creating masquerade sculptures that are both male and female forms. Her steel sculptures appear weightless given their openwork and state of movement or performance.

Camp's artistic work therefore, has not simply re-staged those traditional masquerades of her Kalahari community. Instead all of her works seem "transnational, industrial, and postmodern" (Powell, 2002, p. 200), given the choice of modern media: steel, the non-traditional image: female, and the always animated quality of the figures: dynamism. Yet the works always return to Africa for inspiration. The ritual of the masquerade dance reminds us, as noted earlier, "all manner of traditions are contemporary with each other, co-existing, often mutually reflexive" (Picton cited by Rovine, *Africa Arts 1996*, p. 19). Camp's work thus brings attention to art as movement, the range of responses and demands upon art by the diaspora artist, and their creative engagements in the post-colonial period of traditions in response to changing social environment and locations.

Moyo Okediji is a Yoruba painter now living in the United States since the early 1990s. His painting framed the entrance to this exhibition. The work titled 'The Dutchman' (1995), was very clearly informed by the tropes of journeys, returns, and the Atlantic. Okediji credits his early political awareness and the appreciation of his Yoruba heritage to African-American woman artist Winnie Owens-Hart, who had journeyed to Nigeria to teach at the University of Ife where he was a student.

Okediji's painting 'The Dutchman', notes Harris (1999, p. 18), "was inspired by Robert Hayden's poem, *Middle Passage*". In Okediji's visualisation of the middle passage that was the transatlantic slave trade, the most dominant colours in the painting are varying but intense shades of blue, shot through with strong earthy tones of reddish brown, black and different tints of purple. It is a very large canvas that helps create compelling suggestions of light, darkness and powerful turmoil. The painting is full of swirling, mingling shapes of fragmented human figures as well as sharks that seem caught in the middle of nowhere - the middle passage of the transatlantic slave trade. Okediji's journey to that painful watery space that separated diasporic blacks may be understood as an attempt at resurrecting this often submerged history for continental Africans. It may also be seen as a "psychic reconnection" (Harris, 1999, p. 18) for a modern continental African with his ancestors on both sides of the Atlantic but also other modern day diasporic blacks.

Journeying and returning artists have been concerned with making connections with the places to which they returned. The images and mediums they selected have been oriented towards recollections of the *what had been;* therefore more often then not their selected vehicle for artistic dialogue has harked back to the traditional African past. Importantly however, these contemporary artistic memories have also been inventive and transformative of the materials and traditions they were working with; such that these

African-American artists have extended and enriched the landscape of contemporary art, addressing modernist questions of history, migrations, and transnational cultural practices. Their acts of artistic productions carried out using media/mediums of the West, while at the same time shaping it to introduce memories of Africa enriches the complexity of these artists various strategies at reclaiming multiple identities.

For the four artists engaged consciously in transatlantic dialogue their first departures, whether a consequence of forced historical migration or recent migrations away from Africa created a necessity to 'return' to Africa and thereby return to the self. A self now informed by a new consciousness of what it means to be a diasporic African woman and man, has then produced artistic works informed by new perspectives made possible by what we carry with us when we leave 'home'.

In juxtaposing the two very different exhibitions at the New York and Washington DC museums, I have sought to expand the meanings of African art for diasporic Africans. One museum exhibited the secret products of Africa's ritual past as art and that art remains static given its ethnography and non-engagement with history. For example, the masks and headpieces on display remain still and silent objects, their very powerful ritual authority incomprehensible to those who gaze upon them in a Western museum space. Yet these ritual pieces in reality would have been continually evolving creations for the healer or diviner.

On the other hand, at the second museum space, sculptor Sokari Douglas Camp's interpretations of maskers (those who don the masks) is very concerned with movement, motion inspires her work and viewing her works in this Western museum one senses most unmistakably that the sculptured figure is partaking in a live performance. The second museum's exhibition thus pays homage to a long history of dynamism, continuity and receptivity in African art, while interrogating the false assumptions that separate the traditional/past from the modern/present.

If at both museums the artistic cultural productions have been about counter-remembrance, that is, the calling into question the silences and absences and the re-inscription of a people into history, then we already see the imperative for art to establish practices of counter-memory that yield multiple, being black in the world, voices. The ongoing critical need is to address the diversity of desires that are within the self and in the collectivity of the Diaspora.

I have therefore also sought to elaborate on the connective tissue between the past and the present to move beyond the notion of the traditional as frozen, as seems encapsulated by the constant harking back to Africa's material culture of the pastas the dominant artistic productions of Africans. Age-old practices and traditions can be shown to have continuity with the present. For the ancestral, when remembered, is always with us, alive and well and informing the present.

Note

1 Exploring transatlantic arrivals and departures among diasporic Africans, Okediji cites this Yoruba proverb in speaking of the African-American visual artist's return to Africa to sample of Yoruba forms. Moyo Okediji, 1999. "Returnee Collections: Transatlantic Transformations," In *Transatlantic Dialogue: Contemporary art in and out of Africa*, ed. Michael Harris. North Carolina: Auckland Art Museum, The University of North Caroline at Chapel Hill, 38.

References

Butler, K. (1998). *Freedoms given, freedoms won: Afro-Brazilians in post-abolition Sao Paulo and Salvador.* New Brunswick, New Jersey: Reuters University Press.

Byfield, J. (2000). Introduction: Rethinking the African diaspora. *African Studies Review, 43* (1), 1–9.

De Souza, P. (2001). Multicultural discourses. In F. Carson & C. Pajaczkowska (Eds.), *Feminist visual culture* (pp. 89–103). New York: Routledge.

Grossberg, L. (1998). Identity and cultural studies - is that all there is? In S. Hall & P. du Guy (Eds.), *Questions of cultural identity* (pp. 87–107). London: Sage Publications, Ltd.

Hall, S. (1990). *Identity: Community, culture difference.* London: Lawrence & Wishart.

Hall, S. (1995). Cultural identity and diaspora. In P. Williams and L. Chrisman (Eds.), *Colonial discourse and post-colonial theory* (pp. 392–403). New York: Columbia University Press.

Harris, M. D. (1999). *Transatlantic dialogue: contemporary art in and out of Africa.* North Carolina: Auckland Art Museum, University of North Carolina at Chapel Hill.

Lao-Montes, A. (2000). Unfinished migrations: Commentary and response. *African Studies Review, 43* (1), 54–60.

Lutzeler, P. M. (1995). Multiculturalism in contemporary German literature. *World Literature Today, 69* (3), 453–457.

Mudimbe, V. Y. (1998). On diversity and meeting worlds. In R. Lavrijsen (Ed.), *Global encounters in the world of art: Collisions of tradition and modernity,* (pp. 79–88). The Netherlands: Royal Tropical Institute.

Okediji, M. (1999). Returnee Collections: Transatlantic Transformations. In M. Harris (Ed.). *Transatlantic dialogue: Contemporary art in and out of Africa* (pp. 32–51). North Carolina: Auckland Art Museum, The University of North Carolina at Chapel Hill.

Patterson, T.R. & Kelley, R. (2000). Unfinished migrations: Reflections on the African diaspora and the making of the modern world. *African Studies Review, 43* (1), pp. 11–45.

Phillip, M.N, (1992). Social barbarism and the spoils of modernism. *Frontiers: Essays and writings on Racism and Culture 1984–1992.* Mercury Press, Canada . pp. 94102.

Powell, R. (2002). *Black art: A cultural history.* London: Thames and Hudson Ltd.

Rovine, V.L. (1996). The art of African textiles: Technology, tradition and lurex. J. Picton (Ed.). Review, *African Arts, xxix* (3), pp. 19, 89–90.

Visona, M.B., R. Poyer. H. M. Cole and M. D. Harris. (2000). *The history of art in Africa.* United Kingdom: Thames and Hudson.

Part V
Methodology and African Cultural Studies

Cultural Studies as 'Psycho-babble'

Keyan G. Tomaselli

ABSTRACT
Methodology, policy and the turn to post-LitCrit, are both strengths and weaknesses in cultural studies. As strengths, they have freed the field from the tyranny of quantitative methods and a deterministic positivism; but they are simultaneously weaknesses, in that cultural studies now exhibits an ambiguous relation to the 'material' – to contexts. Texts are disarticulated from contexts in the post-LitCrit 'tradition'. The consequences of inapplicable appropriations of cultural studies are now seen in regressive applications supposedly couched within the democratising imperative that was once the raison d'etre of the field. This study examines the consequences of the loss of the 'material' from certain inflections of cultural studies. Reports of the South African Human Rights Commission into Racism and the Media constitutes my case study. Using the concept of dynamic justice, I propose a return to context based on evaluative criteria rooted in the human condition. Instead of 'Texts', or even 'class consciousness', I argue that the principal contextual criteria for cultural studies research could be based on the socio-political value ideas of Freedom and Life Chances.

[T]ensions and contradictions abound: sophistry has replaced rigour in many an instance and dilettantism parades as expertise and informed judgement.

John Williams (1999) on intellectuals in the 'new' South Africa.

I'm not racist, I only hate whites, not blacks

> Ma Maloi, rejecting her daughter-in-law's allegations about her racism against their white neighbours. Going Up, sitcom, Episode 24, South African Broadcasting Corporation.

Though cultural studies emerged from an impeccable lineage of both theoretical critique and empirical immersion, some post-1990 variants reflect an ambiguous relationship with empirical methodology, factual accuracy and the material. Media studies exhibits an often strained relationship with content analysis and numerical methods (Ruddock 1998). Cultural policy studies tend to forget the dialectic which keeps critique alive in its delicate relationship with state and funding agencies (Tomaselli and Shepperson 1996). Originally concerned with the study of power relations and démocratisation, cultural studies has been on occasion over the past decade definitionally reduced merely to a form of 'writerly expression' (Willoughby 1991). Conversely, it has been accused of becoming a discourse of pseudo-liberation McChesney 1996), and, during the struggle against apartheid, of being the vanguard of new fascisms (Edgecomb 1984). For some, cultural studies is the central disorganising principal in journalism education (Windschuttle 1998). The relationship between cultural studies, which emphasises the 'popular', and the propositions of human rights movements, is also unclear.

Paradigm Affiliations: State and Opposition Before 1990

The state's research bodies had during apartheid adopted an administrative research paradigm with a heavy reliance on statistical and quantitative methods. In effect, the oppressor would 'do it with numbers' to justify its policy to supporters, and to defend itself against criticism. A cadre of state policy researchers thus emerged who tried to entrench a positivist view of social issues as matters that could be settled by measurement.[1]

In contrast to the quantitative approach, opposition from the left used qualitative analysis to refute 'apolitical' numerical reductionism. By 'doing it with rhetoric', they stressed the incapacity of the state's research to capture the effects of its apartheid policies in terms of the masses' lived experience. Thus, a cohort of quantitatively-oriented and politically conservative scholars tended to associate qualitative methods, even when rigorously applied, with Marxism. This judgement 'proved' that any research predicated on these methods was based on subjective and, therefore, unscientific premises.[2] The lack of epistemological debate within these disciplines resulted in a general research community that was – no matter the claimed paradigm or ideological position – conceptually ill-equipped to deal with the fundamental socio-political shift that it now faced (cf De Beer and Tomaselli 2000; Tomaselli and Louw 1993). This was particularly so with regard to policy work in all sectors of state and society (Williams 1996).

The 1990s in South Africa brought a sea-change with regard to cultural studies paradigms, the relationships between them, and the nature of their articulations and re-articulations. A variety of policy-related publications, stemming from the late 1980s emerged in quick succession (Collins 1992; Louw 1993; Mpofu et al 1996; Thorne and Sorensen 1996).[3] This was a period in which sections of the left shifted their rhetoric from neo-Stalinist conceptions of media and culture to the principle of plurality (Teer-Tomaselli 1993; Louw 1993). Although pluralism was increasingly being articulated as a social value, media monitoring projects within civil society continued to implement narrow and conceptually flawed 'methods'.[4]

Replicable methods, or unambiguous applications, were not then high on the leftwing's agenda. Research for this constituency primarily was a means of proving what it already 'knew'. Academics had warned as early as 1991 that clear distinctions needed to be made between 'proving a point' and 'justifying a line'. They cautioned that epistemological differences existed between rhetoric and analysis, and ideology and theory, and that *a priori* assumptions and 'scientific findings' are not commensurable. They warned that the 'problem with ... monitors is that they tend to become self-styled censors, replacing precisely the state agencies and censorious practices they have committed themselves to eradicating' (Tomaselli *et ai* 1994:87). These cautions went unheeded. Ten years later, at the turn of the millennium, the same group of monitors and the South African Human Rights Commission were still perpetuating similar epistemological mistakes.

Transporting Method: A Post-Colonial Viewpoint

Given the skewed allocation of resources fostered under apartheid, a pressing need was for monitoring to develop new sensitivities toward previously excluded constituencies. Monitoring research, argued Themba Masilela (1997), needs to be linked to the emergent democratic process, public participation, participation in the electoral process, and the concept of communication as a right.

Masilela's warning[5] anticipated the sandwiching of the general public between constituency and class-led political struggles. The elimination of public voices and different interpretations permits new politically correct grand narratives to be nurtured and protected. A solely text-based emphasis of monitoring researchers is thus anti-democratic as it silences the encounters which different constituencies have with the media. Two key research components with regard to monitoring research were specified by Masilela (1997:18):

(a) social researchers need to be responsive, *participatory and consultative both with those who want the research done and those that are the subjects of research inquires* (sic) (emphasis in original).[6]
(b) Every research institution's selection and promotion of research, administrative and support staff, should be made on the basis of equal opportunity employment.

Masilela (1997) identified the 1993/4 voter education campaign of the Independent Electoral Commission and monitoring of the SABC by the Campaign for Open Media during 1993/4 as especially prone to analysis of 'textual signification' - a phrase which was later to appear often in the South African Human Rights Commission (SAHRC) *Interim Report of the Inquiry into Racism in the Media* (1999).[7] The problem, concludes Masilela, is that textual emphasis ignores the context of reception and alternative readings. Masilela (1997:30) then asks three fundamental questions:

(a) How are media-based textual significations mediated by discourses, sentiments and predispositions (knowledge, impatience, frustration, fear, apathy and high expectations) among the audience? In other words, how is citizenship articulated in practices of media consumption? (Ang and Hermes 1991);
(b) Which perspective on the reception process (the humanistic cultural studies tradition, or cognitive psychologically oriented studies) has the higher heuristic and practical value, and what theoretical and methodological considerations have to be taken into account in conducting such studies? (Hoijer 1990);
(c) What lessons can be learned from other public knowledge projects in the country, for instance, those studying the use of the electronic media and newspapers for educational purposes (Naidoo 1993; Burton *et al* 1993)?[8]

Masilela (1997) might have added that monitoring projects which conduct themselves in total ignorance of the above discussion are themselves imposing yet another grand narrative, a singular textual hegemony, against which all receivers shall be evaluated – no matter their actual contexts, frames of reference, interpretations, or differing professional practices and experiences.[9] This is a return to a crude 'scientific' positivism, no matter how many times the great First World gurus of cultural and media studies and discourse analysis are cited by monitoring projects.

Negotiating Method: The South African Human Rights Commission (Sahrc)

The SAHRC's Inquiry comprised the following sections:

i   background to and announcement of the Inquiry, stemming from general complaints about racist reports in the media from the Black Lawyers and Black Accountants Associations respectively;
ii the media reaction to the SAHRC announcement, which was largely dismissive;
iii terms of reference and procedure. These were to: (a) investigate the handling of race and possible incidence of racism in the media, and whether such racism as may be manifested in these products constitutes a violation of fundamental human rights as set out in the Constitution; and (b) to establish the underlying causes of racism and examine the impact on society as manifested in the product of the media;
iv summary of submission;
v   the Braude (1999) and MMP (1999a) reports.

The academy's failure to address issues of methodology in the early 1990s came back to haunt media monitoring projects soon after the 1998 general election. The flashpoint occurred in early 2000, over the SAHRC's (1999) *Interim Report*. The vagueness of the SAHRC's terms of reference relating to causes' and 'products' – and its exclusion of study of the organisational dynamics and personnel practices of the very media institutions under scrutiny, resulted in flawed research approaches which failed entirely to understand the nature of the media, how news is made, or how theory is applied.[10] The result, as Guy Berger (2000a) commented, was that one of the SAHRC's consultants, Claudia Braude (1999), 'went in search of racism in the media - and found it everywhere, much like the apartheid regime used to discover reds under every bed and behind every bush'. If Berger's (2000a) characterisation of Braude's (lack of?) method is accurate, then this self-proclaimed cultural studies scholar is herself functioning within ideology rather than engaging it. Althusser's (1971) theory of ideology may still have some serious explanatory power after all! Both SAHRC reports, therefore, are stark reminders that serious unfinished business remains within the broader left's anti-apartheid agenda. This relates to questions of, and struggles over, media freedom and media policy: media monitoring, content and reception analysis; and associated methodologies (Louw 1991; Louw 1993; Teer-Tomaselli 1995; Tomaselli and Shepperson 1996; Tomaselli et al 1994; Tomaselli 2000; Van Zyl and Kantor 1994; Botha 1996; Conradie 1994; Masilela 1997; Malan 1995; Stewart 1999a; Berger 2000a, Steenveld 2000).

Particularly noticeable in the lead-up to the SAHRC Inquiry was the way in which struggles over monitoring and media policy were subsequently articulated in the media industry's submissions to the Truth and Reconciliation Commission (TRC – Skjerdal 1998), and the Arts and Culture Task Group (Tomaselli and Shepperson 1996;1999; Botha 1997; Williams 1996). In submissions to the TRC (1995–1998), Afrikaans journalists and editors had clashed over the journalism values which had driven their respective professional relationships with the apartheid regime. This split in the ranks of media professionals, in conjunction with responses to the SAHRC, opened up a much wider popular debate on definitions of racism.

As the Australian experience over the 1990s revealed, policy research (as a dimension of cultural studies) can be conceived as a form of critical practice. However, during apartheid the South African anti-apartheid left lacked an epistemological basis for such practice. Indeed, before 1990 there had been no *ethical* basis for discussion on it either: no cooperation could occur with an illegitimate state. Thus, for all the differences between there and here, the Australian 'cultural policy moment' provided at least a starting point for analysis of the South African case.[11]

For all this, however, the South African experience confirms Edward Said's (1983) observation that as theories and paradigms travel they mimic Western metropolitan assumptions, reconstitute initial emphases, and even forget their origins. After apartheid, new discursive positivisms claiming cultural studies lineages, of which Braude's (1999) is one example, the final SAHRC Report (2000) is another, simply replaced earlier state-aligned trajectories: calls for censorship, regulation, monitoring and shielding continued apace. The SAHRC *interim Report*, for example, was accused by editors of the libertarian persuasion of infringing freedom of the press via McCarthy-like tactics.[12] Every product identified, whether white- or black-targeted, owned, or managed, or written, fell foui of the SAHRC's *a priori* judgements. Indeed, the final SAHRC Report (2000) itself failed to respond coherently to press criticism,[13] describing the media response as that of 'mocking commentaries, outrage and ridicule' (p 48). Parody was met with parody. The press's response was not only symptomatic of this institution's insecurity relating to freedom of the press and perceived threats of regulation and possibly censorship, but it was also possibly indicative of a lack of understanding of journalism, media and communication studies theories and methodologies amongst both the media and the SAHRC's supposedly 'independent' researchers. The Commission did, however, try to engage the academic responses more coherently (SAHRC 2000:48–65 - see below).

As Berger (2000b) argues with regard to Braude (1999) and MMP's (1999a) reports to the SAHRC: 'Bad research can backfire disastrously. Their studies gave a lot of people an excuse to avoid dealing with the real issue of racism, and discredited the SAHRC inquiry severely.' All these debates, however, entirely failed to address the underlying philosophical issue: the actual role of the concept of Justice as a criterion of evaluation in the field of media criticism and socio-cultural theory. In the following section, I will motivate the concept of Dynamic Justice as: (i) a context within which to analyze the relevance of existing monitoring and critical research; and (ii) to suggest how cultural studies can incorporate human rights, while maintaining its emphasis on 'the popular' and its allegiance to the notion of 'difference'.

Media Criticism and The Concept of Dynamic Justice[14]

The concept of Dynamic Justice emerged in response to the fragmentation and sectarianism inherent in the cultural relativism paradigm (Heller 1987). If there is no way to rank or judge cultural norms and values, then any human social group adhering to the extreme relativist paradigm must necessarily claim *'one more* true opinion and right norm than all other cultures' (Heller 1987:42. Emphasis in original). Principally, however, the concept of dynamic (or radical) justice depends on the view that - from the 'viewpoint of values' – the bewildering plurality of humankind is in itself the interpretation of an empirical fact. It thus becomes possible to view this plurality as itself embedding some form of value.

Dynamic Justice, therefore, seeks value ideas that are applicable to human beings irrespective of their social and/or cultural group affiliations or attachments. Where classical societies operated with ethical systems of justice, either philosophical as in classical Athens, or religious as in Jerusalem, these were essentially *complete* in the sense that they assumed a perfected political order. In modernity, these *complete ethico-political* concepts stumbled on the paradoxes of reason or faith respectively (Heller 1987:55–73). Thus the idea of the *socio-political concept of justice* emerged as the dynamics of modernity began to rationalize the relationships and orders of power (Heller, 1987:153–4). Instead of basing justice in 'eternal' universals, as early human rights movements tended to do, the dynamic nature of the socio-political concept of justice reduces the discussion to the 'dissection' of *themes* of justice rooted the 'dissection of the socio-political body' (Heller 1987:55–73). Examples of these include the institutionalization of retributive justice (Heller 1987:156–79); systems of distributive justice (180–204); and the 'just war' theme (205–19).

The main problem with the socio-political concept of justice, however, is that it relies on precisely the 'models of Man' that are implied in the construction of the models of society that define the political forms taken on under modernity. These range from the 'state of Nature' constructs inherited from Hobbes (conflictual Man) and Rousseau (co-operative Man), to the Marxist-Keynesian models of 'economic Man'. Each model entails an 'original position' at some Time One, in the development from which 'Man' is either alienated (Rousseau/Marx), or into which 'Man' becomes more advanced as in the theories of Jeremy Bentham, J S Mill, or John Rawls (Heller 1987:203–5; 248–56). These theories, however, fail to provide a *goal* for the just person or the just society: every Time One condition in socio-political theories of justice places 'the sum total of human beings who inhabit our globe' in the position of not being able to question the goals of society. People thus live in a world where these goals are *already present,* and beyond their power to change (Heller 1987:248–9).

Dynamic justice incorporates the minimum general value ideas that can be interpreted from the factual claims that arise from the conditions of those who constitute the sum total of humanity present on the globe. The two value ideas common to all constituencies are Freedom and Life Chances (Heller 1987:305–10). The former is defined in terms of the Kantian Practical Imperative: *people must always be recognized as ends in themselves and never as mere means.* Life Chances arises from the demand that *social arrangements should promote the potential for all people to develop their endowments into talents* (Heller 1987:191–2).

Dynamic Justice and Socio-Political Transformation

Time One occurs when discourses about justice are officially and constitutionally initiated, as in South Africa in February 1990. In the context of dynamic justice, however, this period is *always present* because humankind is concerned about justice in many places in a plurality of contexts (Heller 1987:250). Thus people anywhere can now question the justice of their conditions. They do this by *both* acting to maximise Freedom by reducing conditions of tutelage under which they or others are mere means, *and* by entrenching Life Chances by enhancing choice and access to scarce social resources. Basically, the goal of dynamic justice is the radical utopia: the making of the *best possible* socio-political world (Heller 1987:240–56: 271: 323–7).

South Africa's social and cultural pluralities are only now, *after* apartheid, beginning to explore long repressed voices and expressions. This is a direct consequence of the stasis entailed in apartheid's contradictory attempt to merge two historically antithetical trends. On the one hand, the early apartheid state attempted to retain the static conception of justice rooted in the permanent apartheid division of people into racial categories. On the other, the state was trying to regulate the necessary dynamism, or inherent challenges to static norms, which it had accepted when it took upon itself the country's transition from an agrarian to an industrial economy after 1948. The essentially static (or cyclic, but logically these two qualifiers are indistinguishable) worldview associated with the agrarian *Boer* republics resonated with the anthropological categories applied to presumably premodern African societies. Hence tradition and custom remained part of the discourse of justifying the separations of apartheid and, indeed, this dynamic continued into the post-apartheid transition.[15]

However, the essentially *mobile* nature of industrial modernity demanded an adaptability in the categories and concepts of Justice. The need for this adaptability arguably underpinned the logic of the anti-apartheid struggle. Dynamic Justice accommodated the new emphasis on human rights, in that it stresses interpretations of simple value ideas. The concept provides a means of contextualising these rights within the human rights agenda regarding communication and media studies (see, eg Van Zyl 1994; Tomaselli and Gerbner 1996; Hamelink 1997; see also Sarkin 1998).

Method and Value in Media Research

Using the value ideas of Freedom and Life Chances discourages romantic notions of democracy and of the benignity of the political terrain. Dynamic justice is precisely the procedure of questioning generally-accepted norms and rules (Heller 1987:127). As intellectual professionals, it is ethically incumbent on media and policy researchers to monitor both the procedural validity *and* the value-consistency of those who would assume the business of legislating the transition to, and entrenchment of, a more just national dispensation.

The contemporary research environment tends to ignore the full implications of dynamic justice in a context of constitutional rights-based representative government. Awareness of these implications is notably absent in both the interpretation of terms of reference in the SAHRC project, and in the reactionary potential of MMP's (1999a) definition of racism. Braude and MMP researchers, in writing up their separate sections, inexorably found racism, even in black-produced reports, by imposing a deterministic form of media theory, which they term 'Textual Analysis', via 'cultural studies', without examining the contexts from which that reporting was produced. MMP provided the 'discourse analysis' supported by an incomprehensible numerical analysis to give scientific validity to Braude's rhetoric.

No matter how much Braude dressed up her cultural-studies jargon (referred to as 'psycho-babble' by the press), her main accomplishment was to recover the oft misapplied transmission model of communication from the mothballs to which cultural studies had consigned it in the early 1980s. Braude's analysis, and the monitoring data supposedly providing the 'scientific' findings underlying it,[16] further relies on unreconstituted and largely misunderstood theory imported from the West. Stuart Hall, Michael Gurevitch, Jean Baudrillard, Oscar Gandy etc, would be astonished, I think, to be associated with the extraordinarily muddled argument by assertion which characterises Braude's (1999) Report.

The lack of understanding of cultural and media studies is a necessary consequence given MMP's definition of racism as: 'A complex societal system in which peoples of European origin dominate peoples of other origins, especially in Europe, North America, South Africa, Australia and New Zealand' (Van Dijk 1991:24; MMP 1999a:6). This definition, which is offered without qualification, was possibly borrowed for its allegedly 'neutral' content, rather than using one arising directly out of the South African experience.[17] The attraction of Van Dijk is due to the researchers' own academic backgrounds in comparative literature, literary studies and drama. However, the problem with Van Dijk's definition as interpreted by MMP is that it explicitly assigns to racism a blanket origin in a specific place among specific peoples. It effectively homogenizes *all* people of one continent and essentially one skin pigmentation in ideological terms, thereby forcing individuals and racially defined communities to find other definitions for race-based oppression or violence elsewhere. This definition cannot, thus, label the outright genocide occurring in Central Africa as 'racist' because the perpetrators are not 'peoples of European origin' (MMP 1999a:6).

Had the SAHRC's consultants cited Van Dijk's definition completely, and taken further account of his subsequent discussion of ethnicism (Van Dijk 1991:26–7), then their judgements would have been far less clear-cut. To complete the definition from where the MMP report leaves off, Van Dijk continues: 'This relation of dominance may take many forms of economic, social, cultural, and/or political hegemony, legitimated in terms of, usually negatively valued, different characteristics ascribed to the dominated people(s)' (Van Dijk 1991:24).

By further excluding Van Dijk's (1991:26) subsequent discussion of the emergence of 'ethnicism' as 'the modern variant of racial differentiations of earlier western ideologies', the MMP report neatly deludes its readers into the conclusion that such 'discourse' cannot be appropriated by others. MMP's partial appropriation of Van Dijk's definition 'because it recognises racism at the group ... level' (MMP 1999a:6), renders the term 'racism' meaningless. Further, by asserting that racism is an ethnically-defined character, MMP means that the accused simply cannot mount a defence.[18] It is not surprising, therefore, that MMP and Braude 'found' racism even before searching for it and that the SAHRC's final report (2000) was therefore able to exhonerate these research consultants and offer a conclusion based merely on the bald assertion that racism exists in the media. Consequently, methodology is not necessary, for equating MMP's 'findings' with pre-determined outcomes satisfies the respective objectives of both MMP and the SAHRC.[19]

Claims to be using cultural studies and discourse analysis, therefore, provide little more than *a priori* justification of the popular myth as is comedically articulated by Ma Maloi in the *Going Up* sitcom, quoted at the start of this article. However, at the societal level, the universal and official justification of MMP's definition of racism resulted in a moral panic communicated via the SAHRC hearings (and the Commission's Conference On Racism held in early September 2000). The SAHRC's Commissioners (incuding some whites) assumed that 'only whites are racist'. The kinds of discursive exclusions, elisions and decontextualizations evidenced in the Inquiry reduced the entire exercise to what can be only called 'sham enquiry'. Thus, what the SAHRC researchers delivered at taxpayers' expense is a pseudo-inquiry aimed at making a case for a predetermined conclusion immovably believed in advance of the inquiry itself (Peirce 1905). More to the point, the Report's assumption of a partial definition of racism 'at the level of the group' (MMP 1999a:6) amounts to what Susan Haack (1997) calls 'preposterism' (following Jacques Barzun (1968), an 'atmosphere of puffery'. Having first embedded racism as an ethnic sociobiological character, the MMP Report then blazes away with sham inquiry claiming to provide 'radically new' conclusions!

Rephrased in Heller's terms, the Braude and MMP Reports set out to quantify the extent to which media discourse affects the political value of citizens' Freedom on the basis of their racial origins. But this is hampered by the definition which associates racism with racially-defined factions, irrespective of the actual historical development of racial discourses. The point here is simple: **there is a fundamental difference between racism and ubidiscourses about race** (Arendt 1951), which is implied in another (mis)quote offered by MMP (1999a:6) sourced to Fair and Astroff (1991:72). Here, MMP conflates its discussion of 'racist ideologies' with 'racialisation'. The former is a (negative) value held by an individual; the latter is a form of societal organisation embedded in processes and policy such as affirmative action. In ignoring, or in fact being ignorant of this distinction, the research reports additionally reveal their authors' lack of engagement with prevailing discussions on method. Their one-sided definition of racism forced them into a position where they necessarily contradicted Masilela's (1997:18) first criterion for monitoring research. The SAHRCs consultant researchers were confrontational from the start of their inquiry; they failed to interview journalists; they sometimes misinterpreted the articles and pictures under scrutiny, and then when the SAHRC subpoenaed editors to explain themselves, they dissociated themselves from this action. Editors consequently found themselves responding to *a priori* propositions abstractly generated by discourse analysis rather than reports which they had actually published.

General discourse about race cannot be *purely* an ideology. If it were, the potential for opinions associated with the topic could not be corrected by the broader range of experiences brought by participants to the liberal public forum. Aside from its methodological flaws, the research reports also betray their authors' denial of further need for dynamic justice in contexts of transformation. By restricting racism, an ideology, to people of a single geographical origin, the reports assign to these discursive targets ends that they themselves do not necessarily choose. This contradicts the idea of Freedom, which enjoins us *always* to consider people as ends in themselves. That is, the Report assigns *a priori* 'one more value' to *every* ethnic or racial grouping. They do this in the sense that a predetermined 'value' of racial superiority necessarily defines the European ethnic community of racism. The final report suggests that its Inquiry started from the domain of 'experience' - that racism experienced by blacks from whites. If this refers to the experience of communities of readers, like the Black Accountants and Black Lawyers' Associations, who first made representations to the SAHRC, then focus groups needed to have been conducted with these and other communities of readers to ascertain how they came to their perception that the media (or reports they objected to) is or is not racist. But the Commission claims that such research is not necessary!

The MMP (1999a) report also contradicts the value of Life Chances. If people are to be encouraged to develop their endowments into talents consistent with the need for others to remain ends in themselves, then MMP's ascriptive definition of racism denies the possibility that members of any group associated with any ideology can come to conduct themselves differently.

MM P's definition of racism *identifies* ideology with race, instead of *distinguishing* racist ideology from public discourse within a forum where racial divisions (or their cultural consequences) are an issue that concerns free people. This confusion is continued in the final report. The distinctions between 'race' and 'racialism' are imprecise and confusing. Concepts and policies resulting from them cannot be neutral, as is argued. Race is a socially constructed category, and racialism is a way of ordering and differentiating a society in terms of race. Institutions or reporting that is not 'racially proportionate' seems to be the new common sense understanding of non-racialism, or democracy. The exclusionary racialism of apartheid is thus being discursively substituted with a new kind of demographically/racially validated form of social, workplace and institutional racialisation. These terms cannot, then, be neutral as is stated in the Report.

In effect, this also clashes with Masilela's second monitoring method criterion – that of equal opportunity employment. One of the complaints from those black journalists and editors who supported the SAHRCs intervention (if not its research) was that all the SAHRC's consultants were white, and therefore could not themselves have experienced racism, and/or therefore identify it let alone write about it.

Psycho-Babble and Spin Doctoring: 'Doing it with Rhetoric'

If the events of 1990 initiated an attitude-change among previously positivist scientifically-oriented South African scholars, the SAHRC episode clarifies a comparably opportunistic shift on the Left. The Braude and MMP contributions to the SAHRC *Interim Report,* and the final report's exoneration of their so-called studies as merely a record of 'an accumulation of research commissioned' (SAHRC 2000:10) demonstrates how natural-scientific positivist discourses still jostled uncomfortably alongside media studies of both the early Birmingham and post-disciplinary, post-LitCrit kinds. Although this contestation and ambivalence was not in itself a bad thing at the start of the political transition, there is some difficulty with these researchers' inability to separate *a priori* left-wing rhetoric masquerading as Marxist (or qualitative) analysis on the one hand, from rigorous critique and paradigmatic logic on the other (Williams 1999).

What perusal of the SAHRC *Interim Report* confirms, is that state-sponsored research and researchers have simply traded in their old quantitative statistical model 'administrative numbers' paradigms for the latest bells-and-whistles qualitative 'administrative rhetoric' models. Where in the past 'doing it with numbers'[20] was considered 'scientific' in the context of administrative and policy research, now 'doing it with rhetoric' indicates a positive and appropriate response to the new post-apartheid context. The irony of this situation is not that state-sponsored inquiry has shifted to its near-polar methodological opposite; instead, it seems that both state and critical research are contesting the qualitative high ground for the most radical-sounding rhetoric.[21] This led to the abandonment of methodical rigour in favour of an eclectic combination of expressive and theoretical legerdemain. Shifting to this advocacy-driven position has, to a very alarming extent, relegated the logic of inquiry to that of digging up the dirt on rival theorists or parties. In short, research has begun to take on the hue of spin-doctoring.

I now confront the question: why and how certain inflections of self-proclaimed cultural studies have fallen prey to sham reasoning in both SAHRC reports.

Media Monitoring and Discourse Analysis: 'Doing it with numbers'

A common claim in the monitoring projects is to be 'doing discourse analysis'. This is the 'missing [conceptual] link' which supposedly connects Braude's cultural studies with the MMP's quantitative monitoring machinations. It also appears as justification for an equally muddled economistic report on advertising for the Commission on Gender Equity (CGE 1999). In effect, all three projects used very different 'methods'. They nonetheless claim to be analysing the same manifestation in 'media products' - that of 'discourse'.

Van Dijk's work is a recurring citation in the reports discussed by supportive black press commentators. Yet his structuralist rigour is nowhere evident in any of these studies or commentaries. None engage Van Dijk's discussion of racism and ethnicity. As noted earlier, the recourse to other sources does not serve to ground inquiry, but to bolster presupposed conclusions.

The appearance of the term 'Discourse analysis' – along with the manipulation of numbers applied in meaningless frameworks - provides 'scientific' affirmation for what is already known. All three reports are thus characterised by teleologically-driven, aprioristic arguments, stated in simplistic categorical terms, and expediently assembled and presented under the rubric of cultural studies/science. As Johan Casti (1990:13) remarks, '[T]here is no such thing as an "empirical" observation or fact, we always see by interpretation, and the interpretation we use is given by the prevailing paradigm of the moment'. In this context, then, the way that discourse analysis is used very conveniently legitimised:

(a) *a priori* interpretations. The extremely vague – though adamantly articulated – misgivings by the Associations of Black Lawyers and Black Accountants about the 'subliminal racism' they claimed to have found in press cuttings submitted to the Commission was taken as the researchers' point of departure;[22]
(b) numbers which provide the data in which the 'proof of frequency' of racism and/or sexism is already inscribed in discourse (MMP 1999a; MMP Women's Media Watch 1999b; CGE 2000);
(c) an overarching framework within which to merge dated, synchronic and deterministic cultural studies with numbers and a statistically incoherent form of content analysis.[23] And, therefore,
(d) myth masquerading as method. Myth is required to 'find' what is already known, prior to doing any research, while claiming paradoxically that this is not the case (MMP 1999a:6–7). MMP's (1999a:7–8) 'Propositions'-driven method and its tautologous definition of racism, totally negates their own self-claimed cautions about not confirming their *a priori* assumptions (MRP 1999:6).

What this boils down to is that the change in the socio-political context has led policy and monitoring researchers into the position where any analysis that is couched in terms that come across as *anti-positivist* is acceptable. Where the apartheid state used numbers to blind the masses with science, the new dispensation claims that using rhetoric *necessarily* achieves Enlightenment. A new grand narrative emerges: only *one* outcome is anticipated no matter the method, theory or approach (cf Jacobs and Masuku 2000 who seem to share this modernist perspective).[24] Different methods are required because reality presents facets, each facet becoming more defined as the relevant disciplines' inquiry polishes it. It is, in the pragmatic terms of CS Peirce, the *evolving* reality of these facets that transdisciplinarity brings to the fore: indeed, every such finding has the potential to *add new facets* to an ever-evolving postmodern reality.

Seeing and Believing/Believing and Seeing

The flaw in the 'textual signification' thesis relates to the denial of aberrant, discrepant, negotiated, rejected, disarticulated and rearticulated decodings. Braude (1999) was adamant that 'her' interpretation of media is the only 'true' one - that the media attack on her Report was nothing less than a racist media conspiracy to discredit her. She justified not consulting journalists on the stories identified as 'racist' because she was 'discouraged' from doing so by the SAHRC. The narrow Terms of Reference the SAHRC set for itself considerably limited the approaches that could be taken by its researchers.

The realisation that texts can obscure, and that textual signification is the literary equivalent of endistancing, is subtly reflected on by literary scholar, Charles Malan, of the Human Sciences Research Council's Cultural Reconstruction and Research Programme (CURED). Offering a revealing anecdote on one of his personally conducted projects in the black working class township of Mamelodi near Pretoria, he self-reflexively critiques the opacity of the literary academic enterprise and its endistancing from real people and real problems:

> As a willing servant of the RDP [Reconstruction and Development Programme] he (the 'white Afrikaner male') is no longer protected by rows and rows of texts about texts, that he in his study of literature and 'culture' has over years intersected between himself and 'them' - that is the others whose subjectivity has been dispersed amongst the same texts to such an extent that they have remained, often conveniently, a faceless mass. It is only by literally facing them that he realizes how they have become the real victims of the post-modernist condition, how their subjectivity has been unfocused, the subject fragmented in an endless field of discursivity (Malan 1995:20).

The Mamelodi respondents had asked some [im]pertinent questions: who defines meaning, and what benefit is there for them, the 'subjects' of Malan's research? Malan found himself flung into the field, into the messy and demanding empirical world of real, alienated and angry people, and into the harsh material realities being addressed by the Reconstruction and Development Programme in the early 1990s.

The discursive borders between 'texts' and 'contexts' had been demolished in Malan's need to 'meet' the other on 'their' terms in the spaces into which 'they' had been ruthlessly confined by apartheid. Malan (1995) suggests that the 'politics of the popular' offers a motor for 'reconstruction' of formerly white, high culture, literature departments.[25]

Malan therefore argues that cultural studies offers a route towards reconstruction of the literary enterprise, offering the scholar a methodological reconnection with the realities that literary theory has excluded from the academy. This is quite the opposite of the way that the 'popular' or Post-LitCrit strand of discourse analysis has sometimes been applied in South African media studies, achieving a decontextualising and a further endistancing mechanism. The supposed 'dialogue' in approaches to knowledge becomes again the sectional purview of powerful rhetorical constituencies aligned with the new state and the new petty bourgeois class emerging within it.

Faultlines: a Comment on the Final Report

It is most pleasing that the SAHRC, various Cabinet ministries and some state departments are increasingly mobilising media and cultural studies in grappling with pressing social problems. However, the ever-present dangers of superficial disciplinary and paradigmatic understandings, questionable methodological applications, *a priori* assumptions and essentialistic thinking, are very clear with regard to the contemporary discursive terrain in South Africa. The final report is entitled *Faultlines,* because the SAHRC sincerely believes 'that racism marks a volcanic fault-line in our body politic'. There is no quibble here.

Simply asserting, however, that 'racism exists in the media' (SAHRC 2000:86) has neither theoretical nor empirical validity. The provision of clear evidence, and a systematic explanation of how that evidence was found, corroborated and interpreted, is what was required but not provided. The final report largely ignores the methodological issues raised here with regard to discourse analysis and numerical methods. Rather, they introduce two new theorists to the mix: Paul Gilroy and David T Goldberg. The Commissioners' heavy reliance on Goldberg (1993), in particular, commits them to the latter's somewhat restricted conception of modernity. Modernity's origins are considerably more complex than Goldberg's sociology of knowledge permits (Shepperson 2000). Indeed, the sociology of knowledge's generally unrecognized Nietzschean grounding places the analysis of research data somewhat at odds with the premises of the theory used. Thus do the flawed premises of the *Interim Report* now reemerge under a different guise in the final report.

The SAHRC's final report appears to be written on the basis that the only way people can rank or prioritise that which is right or wrong, is necessarily a question of Authority. Steenveld, for example, is 'correct' in her definition of racism (SAHRC 2000:52–5); Van Zyl and Patel 'do not understand racism or they are simply wishing it away' (p 52), while for 'the likes of Berger and Tomaselli, nothing really turns on whether or not the research was empirically or statisticlly based'. Thus are the arguments of all these commentators relexified into Imputation by Faith. If practitioners and scholars cannot know about racism, whether they are black or white, then there is nothing to be done. The principle of Dynamic Justice fails as a new 'true opinion' dislodges the old one in a reranked hierarchy.

Summary: Making Methodology Meaningless

The monitoring work done in South Africa on racism and gender is characterised by the following methodological flaws:

(a) **transmission and media effects models** are assumed.
(b) **Anticipating results.** MMP commits the logical error of *petitio principii* (or 'begging the question') in settling on a definition of racism in which racist ideology is associated purely with one race – itself a social and discursive construct. In effect, this means that MMP has by means of this definition already included its conclusions in the premises of its logic.
(c) **Ahistorical analysis vis-a-vis the structure of the media industry is unable to account for, let alone identify, shifts in, and of, content over time.** Van Dijk's discourse analysis, even if applied properly, is synchronic.

(d) **An overemphasis on imported Western cultural and media studies theories without any attempt at reconstitution in the local context.** MMP and CGE are guilty of an extremely crude semiotics, often recuperating a highly dated, early structuralist version, of theories of ideology and society offered by Althusser (1971), into which the much more sophisticated subtle postulates of Gramsci (1971) and Stuart Hall have been sandwiched without any consideration of their differences, nuances or contexts.[26]

(e) **A visual imperialist thesis**, which disempowers audiences and readers from any response other than that 'found' (ie imposed) by the researcher. In all the reports cited here, the researchers project their intentions and the readers' interpretations, irrespective of the readings that receivers themselves might make of the messages being analyzed (see Sless 1986).

(f) **No research was done inside the media industry;** and no research was done on journalist, editorial or gatekeeping practices. In responding to my suggestion that it examine 'products' in relation to both news production and reception, the Commissioners claimed that to 'have delved into the details of the news industry, ownership, race and gender representation would have been a mammoth task ... there was concern that the commission would be going about snooping into newsrooms ...'. Obtaining such information does not require 'snooping', least of all by the SAHRC and/or its 'independent researchers' (SAHRC 2000:49). The information was already available in peer-reviewed and published form (Goga 2000; Tomaselli 1997; Berger 1999, and in computerised data bases managed by McGregor's *Who Owns Who* and Businessmap). Goga's information on gender, race, income and status was obtained with the cooperation of the media industry in general, and was actually submitted to the Commission and even acknowleged (Braude 1999:147).

(g) Extreme violence is done to cultural studies by forcing a **functionalist and conspiratorial framework** onto this approach. The researchers in each case failed to problématisé their own contradictory subjectivities within their respective research projects and definition of racism. This definition, as the Black Editors' Forum reminded MMP, is one in which they fundamentally implicate themselves within racism as a discursive practice. How, therefore, can the self-acknowledged *de facto* discursive racists in MMP identify racism? Similarly, if European racism is sociobiologically embedded in that region's historical discursive encounter with Africa, the use by Braude and MMP of European theories to discover such racism is tautologous. These paradoxes are never addressed in either of the two SAHRC Reports.

(h) All three studies assume that a **homogeneous readership/audience** exists, which clearly is not the case in South Africa – if anywhere. This is clear from their over-reliance on Stuart Hall and other first world theorists' generalised discussions relating to media in Western societies. This also reproduces the notion that audiences are passive, without agency and cannot themselves fill in contexts not supplied by the stories being read and viewed.

(i) **Far too much power is assigned the media by all the studies cited.** Literary notions of the 'reality effect' (SAHRC 1999; CGE) suggest audiences have no way of telling fact from fiction, or the relevance of messages to their own conditions of existence, values or culture.[27]

(j) Braude uses **exceptional particulars to confirm a general rule,** when basing her research on self-acknowledged small right-wing extremist media (Radio Pretoria and *Die Afrikaner*). The bulk of Braude's harangue deals with these two minority outlets; but it was the corporate press and public broadcaster which bore the brunt of the SAHRC's public questioning and allegations of racism.

(k) Braude (1999:57) **reduces the endless contradictions in reporting into a 'single over-arching text'.** Has this 'text' no contradictions, fissures or fractures? Is it really so functionistly conspiratorial? Is it really so timeless and all-encompassing?

(l) **None of the reports provides information on news item selection.**

(m) **The MMP Women's Media Watch report focuses purely on the representation of women.** This emphasis ignores the whole point of gender rights and relations. Men and women are gendered solely in association to the social relation between them. Thus, the 'emphasised femininity' needs to be understood in relation to 'hegemonic masculinity'. Consequently, the report says absolutely nothing about how these relations are being normalized under the ideals of non-sexism.

(n) **The reports are couched in the discourse of myth** (HRC 2000:58). Utterances exist; they exist without individual utterers (ie journalists). Propositions exist; they are pre-structured in language; Propositions apparently do not exist in African languages or black or the 'other's' discourses about whites or Europeans, or their descendants. In terms of MMP's definition of racism, therefore, a particular group of utterers (ie [white] editors) becomes separated from all other groups of utterers in the media, and saddled with collective responsibility (in abstract inherited discourse) for the sins enshrined in the prior definitions. Myth is related to the notion of 'dogma' as articulated by CGE:

(o) **CGE (2000:7–8) works on advertisers' unsubstantiated claims that they reflect reality.** CGE then proceeds to argue that because advertising is purely a representation in a context where there is no single thing called reality, it is therefore also true that women are marginalised and/or subordinate in product media representations. However, if they are assuming that one cannot utter anything true or false about reality how can we then accept CGE's conclusions about women in the media as either true or false? Effectively, CGE must have to admit that they are telling us nothing! This, then, destroys any possibility of action or dynamic justice.

(p) **An assumption that stereotypes can only be negative.** Stereotypes can also be positive and 'laudatory' (Holt 2000), and provide short-hand metaphors for positive role models, and be recognised as such by role players being interpellated via the screen (CGE, MMP 1999b).[28] Such signs provide an affirming shorthand depiction of much loved characters like King Shaka (as employed by the KwaZulu-Natal Tourist Authority, and Nelson Mandela, as imaged by the media in general, on T-shirts, in advertising, and so on. The imaging of women as 'mothers' (CGE) is not an *a priori* negative stereotype. If this imaging is a negative stereotype, then all depictions of anyone in any social role is necessarily stereotypical. *Ergo,* all depictions of social roles are stereotypical. If the SAHRC wants to use cultural studies then it cannot bolt from this paradigm when it suits it (SAHRC 2000:79–80) and give us the *Concise Oxford Dictionary* definition. Such definitions relate to common sense, rather than theoretical use.

Conclusion

The kind of monitoring 'research' discussed above is an indication of the sorry state of affairs that certain NGO-led, and media, cultural and gender studies, achieved in South Africa in the 1990s. The irony, of course, is that many of us were making exactly the same criticisms during the 1980s against those positivists whose conventionalist work was so effectively mobilised by the apartheid regime (Le Grange 1981; De Koning 1979).

It was not long after Mandela's release in February 1990 that the romantic grand narrative of 'the Left' (Louw 1992) began to fade and left-wing constituency struggles were fought out at every conceivable site of the state and civil society. Coming into sustained engagement with the global literature for the first time and seeing how it was being appropriated for sectoral interest by scholars who fail to understand the sophistication of the cultural studies project as a strategy to bring about democratic change woke us up to the dangers of deterministic rearticulation of the field of cultural studies. As Berger (2000b) observes, one:

> effect of the HRC research ... was to discredit the rote of academics as contributors to contemporary issues, it would be hard to find many journalists (or media studies academics) –of whatever race – who would feel respect for the work that was done by Braude and the MMP. To undo this damage, academics need to take extra special care to produce quality research.

The SAHRC's project is not in dispute here. What is in dispute is that the methodology used *obscures* rather than contributes to clarity. The real issue is to find out how the concept of 'racism' is articulated and 'discovered' in everyday life – as was achieved by Goga (2000) in her analysis of experiences of employees within large media organisations. It is necessary for all parties involved in the debate to discuss issues in terms of: (a) how subjects are taught at tertiary institutions; (b) how they impact the media industry specifically in terms of gender and racial sensitivity; (c) reporting genres, language choice and practices; (d) and in terms of how readers and audiences decode media messages in relation to their own social practices, racial and cultural perceptions and experiences, and in terms of their specific frames of reference. The SAHRC too, needs to engage these theories and debates more directly, especially as it, like the independent researchers it commissioned, draws on specific overseas cultural and media theorists like Paul Gilroy (1997) who is not referenced) and David Goldberg (whose chapter in Harris 1999 is cited), who themselves are writing from very specific historical contexts, experiences and theoretical paradigms. Focusing only on the Text forgets the contexts – the terrain of discursive production, the sociological structure of life and language.

Social problems ignore disciplinary fences; therefore, solutions should traverse disciplinary boundaries. Approached in this manner and appreciated in terms of the dialetic between social change and cultural continuity (Williams 1973) as being the only constant, interdisciplinary inquiry [variously termed as cross-/multi-/post- etc] should be a *sine qua non* to grasp the multi-dimensionality of the human condition. This both retains the focus of disciplinary rigour and opens the boundaries of disciplines. Transdisciplinarity acknowledges the specific insights of particular disciplines with the view to establishing their dialectical relations across specific social issues in an attempt to obtain a more integrated understanding of the human context in its multiple forms and dimensions.

A focus on research and inquiry prevents opportunistic appropriations of terms such as 'interdisciplinary', 'post-disciplinary', 'transdisciplinary' and 'cross-disciplinary' as convenient cover for essentialistically reactionary, conservative, and even left-wing agendas/

discourses.[29] My evolving focus on the twin interrelated value ideas of dynamic justice serves as a counterweight to the abstracted universalising of human rights discourses, which are equally readily appropriated by reactionary factions.

In trying to find a positive note on which to end this analysis, a properly applied cultural studies could have provided the basis for a policy-oriented analysis, which could have made a significant difference. But, as John Williams (1999), whose quote starts this paper states, sophistry is prevailing in all aspects of South African intellectual life. Clearly, there is a lot of methodological reconstruction to be done if we are to properly address racism and sexism at the fundamental levels of social process and structure, language and discourse, and in media institutions and content. The task is both and intra- and intergenerational one, and cannot be resolved in the short term.

Notes

1. The upshot of this reductionism is the privileging of numbers [of instances/observations] at the expense of people in their contextually diverse circumstances where particularized notions and experiences of Freedom and Life Chances obtain. This disregard for the human condition in its manifold forms and multiplicity of meanings is technism at its most vulgar, as humans and their associated social problems/concerns/aspirations are reduced to disembodied numbers manipulated at the whims and caprices of technical and methodological experts in the employ of a plethora of think-tanks, research institutes, policy centres, consultancies, expert groups and so forth (John Williams, e-mail, 7 June 2000).
2. This is not to suggest that quantitative methods are inherently flawed. As Williams points out, it is the injudicious uncoupling of the quantitative from the qualitative that results in all manner of crude applications and flawed findings (E-mail, 7 June 2000).
3. Some of these coalesced around Viljoen (1991). See also Viljoen and Cronje (1993); Louw 1993:276–293.
4. Discussions on monitoring involving the Campaign for Open Media (COM) and academic institutions occurred between 1991 and 1993. See Van Zyl (1994) for a description of COM and other liberal and left-wing media NGOs operating during the transition between 1990 and 1994.
5. Masilela's paper was first delivered at a media conference in Harare, Zimbabwe, in August 1993, nine months before South Africa's first democratic elections in April 1994.
6. Studies which were participatory include Goga (2000) and Conradie (1994), and an appeal for someting similar is made by Jacobs and Masuku (2000)
7. For much more nuanced experiential analyses see Teer-Tomaselli (1995, 1996); and Conradie (1994).
8. Stefan Sonderling (1994) provided a reconstitution of discourse analysis in which the emphasis is moved from the study of the formal structure of language delinked from social context to an approach which studies the discursive character of human practice. This approach to some extent broadens discourse analysis in terms of formal linguistics. But it too has been ignored by South African monitoring projects.
9. Gavin Stewart (1999a:7), an academic turned newspaper editor, predicted with regard to the HRC *Interim Report*, especially the sections written by Braude, 'Other ways of examining content – such as the methods of critical studies, semiotic and structural analysis – encounter similar problems. The insights they provide are often dazzling, but they are very largely in the eye of the believer.'
10. The Final Report counter-argues, fairly, that the objective was to analyze 'products', that the academics did not contest this objective when first published. However, the discourse analyst, Teun van Dijk (1991), (mis)applied by MMP argues quite clearly that his method cannot be adequately applied without: (i) understanding media theories of how news is made; and (ii) doing reception analysis on minorities within majorities. MMP thus applied an inappropriate methodology in terms of the aims of the Inquiry.

11 Australian sources were used by the Department of Arts and Culture, Science and Technology, in cultural, film, heritage and video policy (ACTAG 1995). The Human Sciences Research Council's Cultural Reconstruction and Research Programme also connected with Australian scholars. Tony Bennett of the Griffith Centre for Cultural Policy Studies and Tom O'Regan of Murdoch University's Centre for Research in Culture and Media were keynote speakers at conferences organised by the HSRC in conjunction with UNESCO, UNISA and CCMS (Natal) held in Pretoria in 1996 and 1997 respectively. See O'Regan (1998) and Tomaselli and Kasongo (1997).

12 Two externally contracted monitors pointed out that the SAHRC's hearings 'seemed to be a mixture of a discussion session, a trial and an inquiry' (Jacobs and Masuku 2000).

13 The press, with some exceptions, did tend to read the *Interim Report* selectively, highlighting what to them read as bizarre and sensational, and thereby fastening upon a few factual inaccuracies. They made fun of the quotations they did not understand in terms of broader contexts and work. However, a sustained intellectual debate did occur via Howard Barren's commentaries and submission as reported in *The Mail and Guardian* during early 2000.

14 I am indebted to Arnold Shepperson for his assistance on this section.

15 For example, in KwaZulu-Natal traditional leaders accused the African National Congress-led government in early 2000 of severely compromising their ancestral and traditional rights to govern areas via a restructuring of municipal boundaries.

16 In responding to the SAHRC's announcement of its investigation, Gavin Stewart (1999a) warned that there is no 'prospect of arriving at a generally acceptable measure of the "impact" or "effects" of media content'. He added that the relationship between monitoring, content analysis and policy-making is a very insecure base for policy-making.

17 The SAHRC's monitors also argued that the Commission failed to adopt a functional definition of racism of relevance to the South African experience (Jacobs and Masuku 2000).

18 Van Dijk (1991:26–7) continues: '… when we speak of "racism" in this book we refer to the type of racism or ethnicism prevalent in western countries, both against "black" groups, including peoples of African origin and those of (South) Asian origin, as well as against specific, such as Mediterranean or Arabic, peoples or immigrants from the "borders" of Europe, or against Hispanics in the US.'

19 This kind of theoreticism has become hegemonic in state policy. President T Mbeki, for example, refused to admit a link between the HIV virus and AIDS, and has embraced 'dissidents' whose arguments are of a dated theoretical nature in defiance of empirical work proving the link.

20 With apologies to Ruddock (1998) who is trying to examine the commonalities between media studies and cultural indicator research.

21 MMP distanced itself from the coercive practices used by the HRC to ensure attendance by editors. But the damage had been done.

22 Jacobs and Masuku (2000) observe that the HRC's inquiry was 'built on two specific complaints against an individual newspaper, where the bases of these claims were not even well articulated themselves'.

23 MMP's content analysis offers merely the frequency with which certain items appear in the media. The Project's reports consider 'discourse analysis' to be simply a list of keywords which indicate whether some report or source constitutes or represents one of a restricted list of interest groups. Reports are thus 'biased', 'fair' or 'balanced' – concepts that have little purchase in cultural studies. Publicising what is effectively multiple-choice frequency monitoring as 'discourse analysis' appears to cover the prior decision to classify any ideology, rhetorical manoeuvre, or policy statement as 'discourse'.

24 They state that 'As we understand, Professor Guy Berger's main attack was that the methodology used by Braude was flawed, but that the same conclusions arrived at by Braude could be reached by a different methodology'. Berger did not say or intend this. Jacobs and Musuku's (2000) assumption here is positivist, and spuriously assumes that only one outcome is possible no matter the method applied.

25 This debate is also found in journalism studies – see Windschuttle (1998; Tomaselli and Shepperson 1999) and Windschuttle's many post-LitCrit detractors.

26. Lest I am accused of overstating my case, let me run through some of the problems on pp 8–9 of the CGE document. Its authors claim, without page citation, that Gramcsi (1971) understands ideology as a 'relatively fixed system of representation originating in a social class, most importantly the dominant class'; and that his 'real world' 'resided in the economic level'. Nowhere does Gramsci state this. Althusser is claimed to have 'divided society into … the ideological … the political and legal; and the economic'. Nowhere does he do this. 'Determining' is confused with 'determination', for example, 'More recent theories have dispensed with the notion of the final determination of the economic'. Who are these authors, and in what context are they writing? Indeed, what does this sentence mean? CGE claims that Althusser offered a 'model'. Theory, not a model, is offered by Althusser. '[G]ender ideology', we are told, is a 'social group'. 'False consciousness', is 'connotation'. Foucault, as interpreted by a secondary source, is thrown into the mix on discourse analysis. Discourse avoids the 'weaknesses of ideology as well as economic determinism'. Method (the verb) is confused with a noun and analysis with ideology itself. And, if we are not convinced by this pseudo-theoretical drivel, the early Stuart Hall is clawed in for ultimate legitimation. All this occurs in the space of three paragraphs. Hall, Foucault and Van Dijk are all assumed to have the same understanding of 'discourse' and history.

    The discussion on advertising is even worse. On p 12 we are told about 'gender branding' which, lest the reader is unaware, is 'achieved … largely on the perception of gender roles in a particular society'. There is a difference between 'gendered products' and 'gender branding'. Branding relates to the identity of the product not the social role. The role may be 'gendered' but this does not make it a 'brand'. The feminist theory used is of the 1970s and is not updated or problematised in terms of the South African experience.

27. No distinction is made between concepts of 'reality', 'reality effect' (SAHRC), 'reflecting reality' (CGE), and realism, the 'impression of reality' on a screen (Metz 1971). The result is the short-circuiting of the signifier and signified to mean exactly what the researchers intend these terms to mean (with apologies to *Alice in Wonderland*).

28. *The Peoples Communication Charter* also identifies stereotypes as a problem. However, the Charter is a dynamic document, and is offered merely as a point of departure for further debate (Hamelink 1997). The final report admits to a more open ended view of stereotypes following Goldberg, and accrept that they are not necessarily irrational nor unscientific (p 50).

29. Williams points out that 'In like manner, in recent years, the historical materialist concept, "civil society", has been largely stripped of its etymological, change-inducing/empowering potential/ substance to operate merely as convenient, floating signifier in the service of highly dubious, and largely *status quo* oriented policy frameworks' (E-mail, 7 June 2000).

References

ACTAG. Arts and Culture Task Group. 1995. Pretoria: Ministry of Arts, Culture, Science and Technology.
Althusser, A 1971. *For Marx*. London: Verso.
Ang, I & Hermes, J 1991. 'Gender & Media Consumption'. In Curran, J & Gurevitsch, M (eds) *Mass media and Society*. London: edward arnold, 307–28.
Arendt, H 1951. *The Burdon of our Time*. CUP: Chicago.
Barzun, J 1968. *The American University*. New York: Harper and Row.
Berger, G 2000a. Submission for HRC Investigation into Racism and the Media. Mimeo.
Berger, G 2000b. 'Reinventing Research: Industry-Academic Relations', *Greyville* Gazette (forthcoming).
Berger, G 1999. 'Towards an analysis of the South African Media in Transformation, 1994–99', *Transformation*, 38: 84–116.
Botha, M 1997. 'My Involvement in the Process which led to the White Paper on South African Cinema', *South African Theatre Journal* 11/1&2, 269–285.
Braude, C 1999. Cultural Bloodstain: Towards Understanding the legacy of Apartheid and the Perpetuation of racial Stereotypes in the Contemporary South African Media. Research report commissioned by the South African Human Rights Commission. 171 pages. Published in HRC report.

Burton, S, Marcus, T, Draper, M & James, A 1993. Bushwacking the Locals: A Preliminary Assessment of the Impact of Rural Television Network in Natal. Paper presented at the Making Media Work for Southern Africa's Development Conference, Rhodes University, Grahamstown, 27–29 April, 193.
Casti, J L 1990. *Paradigms Lost: Images of Man in the mirror of Science.* London: Abacus.
Collins, R 1992. 'Broadcasting Policy for a Post Apartheid South Africa: Some Preliminary Proposals', *Critical Arts,* 6(1):26–52.
CGE. Commission on Gender Equality. 1999. Mimeo. 63 pp. (No title).
Conradie, P 1994. 'Independent Media Commission: Report on Audience research – Election 1994', *Communicatio,* 20(2):71–83.
Conradie, P 1994. 'Independent Media Commission: report on Audience Research – Election 1994', *Communicatio,* 20(2):71–83.
De Beer, A S & Tomaselli, K G 2000. 'South Afrian Journalism and Mass Communication Scholarship: negotiating ideological schisms', *Jouralism Studies,* 1 (10):9–34.
De Koning, T L 1979. 'Quantitative Analyses of Activist Newspapers', *Communicatio,* 5:3–21. (In Afrikaans.)
Edgecomb, R 1984. 'English Studies: Two Reviews', *Social Dynamics,* 10(1):97–99.
Fair, E J & Astroff, R J 1991. Constructing Race and Violence: US News Coverage and the Signifying Practices of Apartheid, *Journal of Communication,* 41 (4). (As cited in the MMP 1999 report.)
Goga, F 2000. *Towards Affirmative Action: Issues of Pace and Gender in Media Organisations.* Durban: UNESCO and Graduate Programme in Cultural and Media Studies.
Goldberg, D T in Harris, L (ed) 1999. *Racism.* New York: Humanity Books.
Gramsci, A 1971. *Prison Notebooks.* London: Lawrence and Wishart.
Haack, S 1997. 'Science, Scientism, and Anti-Science in the Age of Preposterism.' *The Skeptical Inquirer* Nov/Dec. http://www.csicop.org/si/9711 /preposterism.html
Hamelink, C 1997. 'People's Communication Charter: An International Covenant of Standards and Rights', *Culture/Ink,* 19:171–175.
Heller, A 1987. *Beyond Justice.* Oxford: Basil Blackwell.
Hoijer, B 1990. 'Studying Viewers' Reception of Television Programmes: Theoretical and Methodological Considerations', *European Journal of Communication,* 5:25–56.
Holt, A 1998. An Analysis of Racial Stereotyping in SABC-TV Commercials in the Context of Reform. Ph.D Thesis, University of Natal.
HRC 1999. *Interim Report of the Inquiry into Racism and the Media.* Human Rights Commission, Johannesburg.
Hunter, I 1993/4. 'Bureaucrat, Critic, Citizen: On Some Styles of Ethical Life', *Arena,* 2:72–102.
Jabulani! Freedom of the Airwaves: Towards Democratic Broadcasting in South Africa. 1991. African-European Institute: Amsterdam.
Jacobs, S & Masuku, T 2000. 'Opinion on the Human Rights Commission's Hearings into Racism in the Media'. May 4:2000. Mimeo.
Le Grange, L 1981. 'Responsibility of the Press Seen from the Position of the Government', *Ecquid Novi,* 1 (2):139–149. (In Afrikaans.)
Louw, P E 1992. 'Rethinking the Leftist Struggle in South Africa', *Critical Arts,* 6(1):1–25.
Louw, P E 1991. 'Obstacles to Digging Out the Dirt: frustrations in researching Broadcast Policy in the New South Africa', *Critical Arts,* 6(2):68–78.
Louw, P E 1993. *South African Media Policy: Debates of the 1990s.* Johannesburg: Anthropos.
Malan, C 1995. The Politics of Self and Other in Literary and Cultural Studies: The South African Dilemma', *Journal of Literary Studies,* 11(2):16–28.
Masilela, T 1997. 'Towards an Agenda on Media and Democracy in South Africa'. In Zhuwarara, R, Gecau, K and Drag, M (eds) *Media, Democratization and Identity.* Harare: Department of English, University of Zimbabwe, 16–33.
McChesney, R 1996. 'Is There Any Hope for Cultural Studies?' *The Democratic Communique,* 14(2):12–16.
MMP. Media Monitoring Project. (October 1999a) The News in Black and White: An Investigation into Racial Stereotyping in the Media. Mimeo: printed in the HRC Report, November 2000. 61pp.

MMP. Media Monitoring Project (December 1999b). A Snapshot Survey of Women's Representation in the South African Media at the End of the Millennium. Mimeo: Commissioned by Women's Media Watch, 33pp.

Metz, C 1971. *The Language of Film*. The Hague: Mouton.

Mpofu, A, Manhando, S & Tomaselli, K G (eds) 1996. *Public Service Broadcasting in South Africa*. Anthropos: Belville.

Naidoo, K 1993. Prospects for the use of Media for Educational Development in Southern Africa. Paper presented at the 'Making media Work for Southern Africa's Development' Conference, Rhodes University, Grahamstown, 27–29 April.

O'Regan, T 1998. Policy, Governance and Culture. *Critical Arts* theme issue, 12(1/2).

Peirce, C S 1905. *Collected Papers*. In Hartshorne, C, Weiss, P & Burks, A (eds). Cambridge: Harvard University Press, 1931–58, 5.520 (c 1905).

Rorty, R 1980. *Philosophy and the Mirror of Nature*, Oxford.*

Ruddock, A 1998. 'Doing It by Numbers', *Critical Arts*, 12(1/2):115–137.

SAHRC 2000. Faultlines: Inquiry into Racism in tbe Media. Johannesburg: SA Human Rights Commission. Mimeo.

SAHRC 1999. *Interim Report of the Inquiry into Racism and the Media*. Johannesburg: SA Human Rights Commission. Mimeo.

Said, E W 1983. *The World, the Text and the Critic*. London: Faber and Faber.

Sarkin, J 1998. The development of a Human Rights Culture in South Africa', *Human Rights Quarterly*, 20:628–665.

Shepperson, A 2000. 'Understanding the "Africa" in South Africa: Race and Theory in the SAHRC Report on Racism in the Media.' Mimeo.

Skjerdal, T 1998. Mapping the Gap: South African Journalists in Disagreement over the Truth and Reconciliation Commission Media Hearings. Mimeo.

Sless, D 1986. *In Search of Semiotics*. London: Croom Helm.

Sonderling, S 1994. 'An Exploration of Poststructuralist Discursive Critique and its Implication for the Study of Communication', *Communicatio*, 20(2):9–24.

Steenveld, L 2000. Theoretical Considerations in the Study of Racism in the Media. Submission to HRC. Mimeo.

Stewart, G 1999a. The HRC Investigation: How do we Avoid Racism in a Time of Ubiquitous Racism?' *Rhodes Journalism Review*, 17:7.

Stewart, G 1999b. Discussion Paper. Delivered at the SA National Editors' Forum, November. Mimeo.

Teer-Tomaselli, R E 1995. 'Moving Towards Democracy: The South African Broadcasting Corporation and the 1994 Election', *Media, Culture and Society*, 17(4):577–602.

Teer-Tomaselli, R E 1993. 'Militancy and Pragmaticism: the Genesis of the ANC's Media policy'. In Louw 1993:227–240.

Thorne, K and Sorensen, S 1996. *Voice and Visions: Audio-Visual Media in the New South Africa*. Copenhagen: ZEBRA.

Tomaselli, K G 2000. 'Faulting Faultlines: Racism in the Media,' *Ecquid Novi*, 21(2):7–27.

Tomaselli, K G 1997. 'Ownership and Control in the South African Print Media: black empowerment after apartheid, 1990–1997', *Ecquid Novi*, 18(1):21–88.

Tomaselli, KG & Gerbner, G 1996. 'The Viewers' Declaration of Independence: A Manifesto of the Cultural Environment Movement. A Commentary', *Communicatio*, 23(1):73–78.

Tomaselli, K G, Mpofu, A, Skinner, K, Manhando, S eta\ 1994. 'Media Monitoring and Methodology', *Communicatio*, 20(2):84–87.

Tomaselli, K G & Louw, P E 1993. 'Shifts Within Communication Studies: From Idealism and Functionalism to Praxis – South Africa in the 1980s'. In Dervin, B and Hariharan, U (eds) *Progress in Communication Sciences, Vol XI*. New Jersey: Ablex.

Tomaselli, K G & Shepperson, A 1999. The Poverty of Journalism: Media Studies and "Science" ', *Continuum: Journal of Media and Cultural Studies*, 13(2):237–253.

Tomaselli, KG & Kasongo, E (eds) 1997. Culture and Communiation. *Africa Media Review* Theme issue, 11 (1).

Tomaselli, K G & Shepperson, A 1996. 'Misreading Theory, Sloganizing Analysis: The Development of South African Media and Film Policy', *South African Theatre Journal,* 10(2):161–175.

Van Dijk, T A 1991. *Racism and the Press.* London: Routledge.

Van Zyl, J & Kantor, L 1994. 'Monitoring the Media: A Shift from Vertical to Horizontal Monitoring', *Communicare,* 13(2):23–43.

Van Zyl, J 1994. 'Civil Society and Broadcasting in South Africa: Protecting the Right to Communicate', *Communicatio,* 20(2):62–70.

Viljoen, C 1991. *Report of the Task Group on Broadcasting in South Africa.* Pretoria: Government Printer.

Viljoen, C & Cronje, P 1993. 'Report of the task group in Broadcasting: a Personal Perspective', In Louw, 27–39.

Williams, J 1999. 'Cultural Studies and Development Trends in the "New South Africa": Some Critical Perspectives', *Critical Arts,* 13(1):102–120.

Williams, J 1996. 'Critique of the report of the Arts and Culture Task Group Presented to the Minister of Arts and Culture, Science and Technology, June 1995', *Critical Arts,* 10(1):107–122.

Williams, R 1973. *The Country and the City.* London: chatto and Windus.

Willoughby, G 1991. 'Keyan Tomaselli and the Task of Cultural Criticism', *Journal of Literary Studies,* 7(1):64–75.

Windschuttle, K 1998. The Poverty of Media Theory. *Quadrant* (March):11–18.

South Africa in the Global Neighbourhood: Towards a Method of Cultural Analysis

Michael Chapman

I wish to explore a method of cultural analysis that might be appropriate to the mid–1990s. In looking at South Africa in the global neighbourhood what, as we rejoin the world, can we offer that is distinctly our own? What, at the same time, can we take from the world that is particularly valuable? My argument is that, as a starting point, a comparative method should modify the modes of analysis that were generally employed in the 1970s and 1980s according to which Africa and the West were regarded, conveniently, as self-contained entities in colonial/anti-colonial antagonisms. But is South Africa, Africa? Is the United States or Western Europe, the West? These are the initial questions that a comparative, as opposed to a binary, analysis should pose. To complicate the concept the West, Europe tends to seek its identity in the past, the United States in the present, while Japan from the East is a major Western power which embraces a future consciousness that is simultaneously a traditional consciousness: Western technology is experienced not as the decisive 'modern' factor splitting science from religion, but as a special contextual extension of spirit, a means of solving practical problems in an integration of the spiritual and the pragmatic that is, interestingly, closer to traditional African belief systems than to Western Protestantism. Turning to South Africa we find a country of huge disparities in which a high-tech first-world sector has closer links to the United States or at least to Latin America and the Indian Ocean rim than, say, to Zambia or Namibia while subsistence traders or survivors — the wretched of the earth who fall outside socialist class analysis — have parallels in Africa, Asia, South America and, in significant pockets, in Eastern Europe and even on heated sidewalk grates in New York's ghettos. In short, what comparison should reveal is a complication of the old binaries, Africa and the West, a complication even of the more recent binaries, the poor South and the rich North.

Comparative questions, of course, can amount to little more than common sense: an inevitable stage in observing cultural products, or just the world. Yet comparative studies have a contested history that coincides with concerns of national identity and pride.[1] In seeking instead a method of understanding that is non-nationalistic and reasonably democratic, we may heed Foucault's distinction between a comparison of measurement — that is, a comparison of equality and inequality — and a comparison of order, the latter of which establishes the simplest elements and arranges differences (1970). What is required is a shift of emphasis from measurement — the earlier assumption of comparative studies — to a more recent concern with non-hierarchical mapping. Such a shift, however, can almost render the term comparative studies redundant at least in its literary-cultural attachment to ahistorical formalism according to which the high-art of Europe and, more recently, the United States are taken together to constitute the apex of Western civilization. Analogies of the metropole and the colony — the centre and the periphery — are similarly evident in comparatistics' deep-rooted attach merit to ideas concerning the fidelity of source texts in contrast to the derivativeness of target texts; non-hierarchical mapping, however, severely qualifies the assumptions of the 'source' and the 'target' while recognizing the activity of translation as cultural interchange: the interpenetration and transformation of the source by the target, and vice versa, so that doubts are cast on the continued usefulness of the binary method. Interestingly, Bassnett concludes her study, *Comparative Literature* (1993), with the observation that cross-cultural work should insist on translation studies as the principal discipline, with comparative literature as a valued but subsidiary subject.

Certainly, the recognition of equality in difference is a key to what is termed the postcolonial approach: an approach — based inescapably on comparison and translation — which rejects the 'great books', or great civilizations, assumption of old-style comparative studies while emphasizing the political objectives of its pursuit. The move from an idealist to a materialist view is summarized by Said in his own major intervention in comparative study, *Culture and Imperialism* (1993),[2] in which it is recognised that the world, in an elaboration of power, has always had overlapping territories and intertwined histories. Postcolonialism, as understood in the academy, does not imply studies after colonialism: we are all expected to know that colonialism in forms of global capitalism and US electronic media continues to ensure the economic and cultural domination of the North over the South. Rather, 'post' means as a consequence of colonialism with the result that geographical entities and time scales shift, and postcolonial investigations range from Shakespeare's *The Tempest* — as Césaire, Lamming and others have reminded us, the play could not have been conceived 'pre' Renaissance voyages of discovery to Rushdie's *Imaginary Homelands* (1991), and beyond. The empire not only writes back to the metropole, but displaces the very categories, thus invigorating with creolised speech and hybrid experiences the decay of the old world's drawing-rooms.

From the vantage point of the rim, postcolonialism, accordingly, opens up the question of what constitutes one's own culture; themes of exile, belonging and non-belonging are common preoccupations; the problematics of language and identity — the colonial language in the indigenous terrain raise issues about English as the lingua franca, or the language of state; the significance of oral cultures and the status of indigenous languages in conditions of modernity are central concerns; questions about periodisation (what are the implications in Africa of Western schemas?) provoke new investigations of particular forms — the epic, the novel — as the products of particular histories. As we attempt to encompass these issues in a conceptual frame, the multiple perspectives of the postcolonial approach to comparative understanding forces upon us — as I suggested earlier on — reconsiderations of the great generalized categories, Africa and the West. None of the topics mentioned here, for instance, should be the sole concern of the rim. If South Africa is multilingual, has grinding poverty amid affluence, is a violent society, and experiences the stresses of migrant populations, so does the United States where any comprehensive cultural history would need to begin with Native American folklore and, alongside the great tradition of Whitman, Melville and the rest, include studies of Hollywood as well as the recognition of a growing Chicano voice. Instead of African area studies, the US in an attempt to overcome its particular obsessions might consider Mexican or, more daringly, Cuban area studies.

To look southwards, categories too should be regarded as far from secure: culture in South Africa has since 1652 reflected a to-and-fro between Africa and the West, and even our records of Bushman oral expression come to us in severely mediated form, having been recollected by respondents in colonial times and recorded by Victorian linguists and missionaries. Our contemporary popular culture cannot escape the long reach of North American predominance, while our transition from apartheid to democracy upset the stereotypes about the rational West and the intuitive Africa: white and black alike displayed a range of modem intelligence. Were the arduous deliberations that avoided the predicted violence, for example, a Western inheritance of constitutional negotiation or an African inheritance of consensual indaba? We might remind ourselves here of another inheritance — *satyagraha* which was given to us in the early years of this century by the young Gandhi while he was in South Africa and adopted as both principle and strategy in the 1950s ANC — led Defiance Campaign. The point is not the impossibility of Africanizing the so-called Gandhian yogi tradition because — as Mazrui thinks — it is difficult to persuade Africans to fast to death or to lie across railway lines (1990: 211). Rather, it is to remember that Gandhi's soul power was forged in resistance politics and had to consider ethical discipline in conditions pertaining to any particular campaign. South Africa is multifaceted: the comparative method — or should the term yield to the postcolonial method" — offers us the possibility of new insights and understandings in unexpected connections.

Despite several advantages in substituting the term 'postcolonial' for that of 'comparative', however, there remains a danger of superficiality in certain applications of the postcolonial method: a celebratory attachment to the aesthetics of representation which can end up ignoring material conditions and endorsing as imaginative brilliance conglomerates of style that, dubbed postmodern, might actually be impoverishing to the imagination. This is the simulacrum — the form with no content — of first-world commodity and consumer culture. When postcolonial comparisons are described breathlessly as heterogeneous, syncretic and inter-textual, it is worth recollecting the warnings of Appiah who, in questioning the universal applicability of matters 'postcolonial', points to what should be a key African consideration: ethical humanism. For Africanicity is not about alterity, but about suffering. Postcoloniality, Appiah continues, is the condition of a relatively small, Western-style, Western-trained group of writers and thinkers, who are usually 'diasporic' in their location and inclination. Whereas all aspects of contemporary African cultural life have been influenced by the transition of African societies through colonialism, such societies are not in any relevant sense postcolonial (1992: 221–58). Where the West and Africa enrich and contaminate each other are at levels more profound than styles of aesthetic representation. Rather, it is that the challenges and problems of modern life require common solutions beyond the cold war of ideas. A humanism that is historically contingent — whether the perspective is West or East, North or South — should presumably find reasonable commonality in the core values of respect for life, liberty justice, caring and integrity.

Such values can of course remain merely fine-sounding words which, as several critics suspect, are endorsed by the United Nations Commission on Global Governance in order to justify the management of the post-Cold War world by globalizing elites in ways that ignore the everyday problems and struggles of people who live in real neighbourhoods.[3] As South Africa prepares to re-enter the world, it faces a context of culture which is being pulled simultaneously by unprecedented global unity and unprecedented local fragmentation. As the conference "Appropriations: New Directions in African Cultural Studies"

(Centre for African Studies, UCT, 1993)[4] concluded, South Africa's 'new nation' is having to be imagined in the context of world-wide tensions between the potential of homogeneous and heterogeneous responses. At a time defined by physical and mental boundary transgressions, Bertelsen is correct to regard cultural analysis in South Africa as faced with a dilemma (1996: 87–106). Does one — she asks — continue in the pre-1990 mode by attacking the apparatus of the capitalist state? Do we instead throw weight, uncritically, behind the Reconstruction and Development Programme? Or do we fashion a postmodern resistance to commodity domination in the precocious display of urban/cash styles and choices where the shopping mall becomes the guerrilla playground of game wars? The fact that all of these directions, as well as others, are discernible in South Africa underscores the point that — since the unbannings of 1990 — the identity of both white and black people has been assaulted by an array of new local and global discourses, programmes, modes of thought, accents and subjectivities. Whereas pre-global times were characterized by oppositions, global times are about proliferations; instead of unitary systems we have diverse modalities and rapid mobilities.

We may recognize all this but end up — as in pre-global times — continuing largely in South Africa to imitate themes, practices and methodologies which have travelled to us from Western European or United States institutions. While class recognitions in South African cultural analysis of the late 1970s and early 1980s provided a necessary check on an earlier liberalism's racial explanations, for example, the materialist analyst tended to locate the key alternatives on the scene as capitalist or socialist. With capital employed usually as a synonym for white liberal, and socialist as a synonym for black worker, the brutal centrality of apartheid's psychology — its manipulation of the ethnic factor — was too often marginalized. Yet South Africa — unlike Western Europe — had only a ragged class consciousness while it had an obsessive, even a paranoid ethnic consciousness. The unbundling not only of Eastern Europe but of this country was predicated — we now see — on complicated intersections of economic politics and identity politics, in which forms of liberalism have proved to be more protean than were permitted in the caricatural depictions favoured by the previous decade's materialist critic. It is possible to concur, in retrospect, that cultural and social developments have generated a need in global times for bold and imaginative rephrasings of the older binaries: rephrasings that — to quote from the summarizing remarks at the conference "Appropriations..." — can account for "different angles, which converge as difference and as similarity" (Cooper and Steyn: 197–207).

The trouble is that — at the periphery — one can too easily experience the postcolonial method as an intrusion: a kind of careerist invasion by the Western academy. To be less cynical it may not be the appropriate condition of the unitary society to be preoccupied with the splitting of identities and the unmasking of hegemonies. The traumatised, divided society may need instead to accentuate the rehabilitation of identities and the reconstitution of civil structures. As the activity of translation has always played a major role when societies or cultures have perceived themselves to be marginal or have experienced crises or dramatic turning points, the term 'cultural translation' may be permitted to qualify the assumptions not only of comparative but also postcolonial methodologies. The qualification is particularly apt in the South African situation in which recognition of dissimilarities should find symbiosis with the need for greater cultural relationship. A South-North focus would wish to avoid parochialism while attempting to effect the conceptual leaps necessary to its own particular circumstance. To return to my earlier question — what can we offer the world that is distinctly our own? — I would suggest the unique experience of our ongoing transition from an oppressive to a non-oppressive society. For what such a consideration of change demands is the investigation of complex, unexpected possibilities of human and cultural integration: possibilities that — as we try to live together harmoniously in the shadow of a divisive history — call for and test to the limits the necessity of generosity tempered with critical acumen. We should not, for example, be talking separately of sceptical analysis and the desire for reconstitution. No intellectual, clearly, should support RDP — speak so blindly as to encourage the new government to posit itself above public account. At the same time, the bona fides of the new government should be granted as the critical role is re-assessed in the current condition. In short, the government inherited a mess: it is of limited use, therefore, simply following the example of the mainstream press and mouthing phrases of independent opposition borrowed without appropriate modification from the mature Western democracies. Should cabinet ministers whose idealism leads to a waste of taxpayers' money automatically resign? Liberalism — usually affluent and white — says, unequivocally, yes! Africanism — speaking for the 'majority' — is uncomfortable about hints of white supremacy: are blacks incompetent to run a modern state?

To turn more specifically to cultural issues, should we be suspicious of grand narratives while seeking, instead, wisdom in innumerable local knowledges? This poststructuralist preoccupation seems to have been a recurrent concern at the conference to which I referred above. We should be suspicious, certainly, of any forms of nationalism in a country which for forty years suffered the ravages of Afrikaner sectional domination and which remains susceptible to a volatile Zuluness. Simultaneously, however, we need to distinguish between the sectarian imperative and the imperative to create a single, functioning society. (I avoid deliberately the originary and mythical insinuations of nation-building in favour of the prosaic technicalities of country-wide institutions and constitutions). In turning to local knowledges we may recognize, here too, our peculiar ambiguities, in which a neglect of the local can result and has resulted — particularly in academe — in derivative import rhetoric masquerading as universal truth. But before we settle, in neat contrast, into small, usually un-middle class communities — academics gazing at pot-makers and basket-weavers — it is worth recollecting Pechey's valid point that nowhere may modernity's project of emancipation be more justified than in South Africa (Pechey, 1993). Having experienced under apartheid the worst of ethnic particularisms, black South Africans especially might very well be prepared to risk whatever dangers are supposed to accompany the 'plot' of universal humanism. In the local context, therefore, postmodernist critiques of totality could seem to be a metropolitan irrelevance (1993: 11).

Or, as Nixon observes in contrasting 'multiculturalism' in the United States and South Africa, the language of multiplicity has in South Africa been the language of false endings: "Apartheid is an old hand at presiding over and surviving its own burial by clothing itself in a winding sheet embroidered from a patchwork of differences" (1994: 208).

In pursuing connections and disconnections — in establishing the simplest elements while arranging the differences — have we any commonalities of substance? I want to return here to the point I made earlier on: in avoiding violence through negotiation, was our tradition that of Western constitutionalism or African indaba? To be consistent with my own argument, the answer need not be either/or. South Africa's long history of involvement with the West permits the answer, both/and. Our differentiated modernity, our hybrid condition, should ensure that we resist splitting our story into that of Africa and the West.

Because of our fractured history we are under an obligation — as the West no longer thinks it is — to identify the potential of shared storytelling, in which the compelling power of the story defines us as human beings. Whereas popular folk traditions — are these local or grand narratives? — have largely been forgotten in the literary histories of Western countries, it is important that and we begin a study of our literature with a study of our rich oral tradition. What such a retrieval should teach us, of course, is that ancient expression emerged in real conditions: that the Bushmen and early Bantu-speaking Africans were neither others nor essences, but people whose stories about human sense-making in early times deserve consideration along with any of the great mythologies of the world. What our oral expression can remind us, too, is that oral man is both traditional and modem, both communally oriented and individualistically inspired in that the patterns of folk tale show necessary ambition tested and returned to community accountability.

In Bunyan's *The Pilgrim's Progress* — the book used by nineteenth-century missionaries in South Africa to bridge the gap between the indigenous 'heathen' and Christian salvation — we recognize Bunyan's debt to vernacular tradition at the same time as we recognize the 'modem' Calvinist conscience that sends Pilgrim on the road of trials and tribulations towards rewards or punishments in the life hereafter. The African folk tale, in contrast, has the pilgrim return, after trials and tribulations, to the family-centred village, for the traditional African religious view is closely tied to earthly matters. The protagonist is not judged by the Supreme God, but by fellow human beings according to norms of social behaviour. Is this an essentially African view, however, or an orientation similar to that which we are likely to find in any pre-modern tale? Whatever the response, the model provides a useful variation on that of Western individualism. In the life-world of the village the hero's determination — the 'warrior' ethic in times of war — has to be qualified for the sake of communal co-operation by *ubuntu*: our capacity for sharing, understanding and empathy. The *ubuntu* is not nativist. ethnic or millenarian but entirely rational in that versions of the truth are held up for assessment. The *ubuntu* is social not socialist in that the character of the folk hero changes in its relations with others. The character is also generational in that as it rows older in relational understanding it becomes more of a personality, more itself. The greater the sharing of humanity the greater our *isithunzi, or seriti*: our aura or prestige. Thus the dichotomy of the individual and the society is rendered invalid in the formulation that involvement in community with others permits one's self-actualisation as a distinctive person.

Let us not be uncritical. To venerate the hero has its dangers. But let us identify the embodiment of the human character I have just sketched in the figure Mandela. I say this deliberately to elicit a reaction from the ever-sceptical intellectual: the intellectual who having lived through the interregnum of the 1970s and 1980s — the time when the old order was dying and the new struggling to be born — can see in the dynamic instability of transition only narratives of suspicion, and not narratives of reconstitution. A key aspect of Mandela's African integrity is that it refuses to be embraced by Western internationalism without calling for remembrance of apartheid and commitment to its utter demise. The point is however that the categories 'African integrity' and 'Western internationalism' continually escape the limitations of binary analysis. Whether in the guise of the folk-tale hero or the modern leader, the character portrayed here need not be regarded as peculiarly African. *Ubuntu* as a social, cultural and philosophical contribution to human thought and conduct requires that Africa and the West be set not in contrast, but in comparison.

Antithesis anticipates synthesis, and the synthesis will have to engage in a fresh — post-apartheid, post-Cold War — dialectic of the local and the universal. Such a dialectic, which globalises the village while localising the globe, is neither a melting pot nor the end of history. It is an extended act of translation, though, which in respecting cultural difference seeks intercultural exchange. To accept a negotiating position somewhere between comparatistics and postcolonialism — some-where between the mimetic entity and the simulacrum — is perhaps an apt metaphor for a process of transition. In any analysis of the world of the 1990s the dialectic recognizes, also, the need for both generosity and equity. Whether all of this could be considered a contribution of the South to cultural debate I leave as an open question.

Notes

1 For concise overviews of comparative studies including translation and post-colonial theory. See, respectively, Bassnett (1993) and Ashcroft el. al. (1987).
2 For Said's comments on comparative studies see Said (1993): 50–72.
3 See *Our Global Neighbourhood* (1995') and Berger's (1996) cynical response.
4 Papers published in Cooper & Steyn (1996).

References

Ashcroft, B., Griffiths, G.. & Tiffin, H. (1987). *The empire writes back. Theory and practice in post-colonial literatures.* London: Routledge.
Appiah, K. A. (1992). *In my father's house: Africa in the philosophy of culture.* London: Methuen.
Auerbach, E. (1946, 1953). *Miinesis: The representation of reality in western literature.* Princeton: University Press.
Bassnett, S. (1993). *Comparative literature: a critical introduction.* Oxford: Blackwell.
Berger, M. (1996). The new millennium and the mirage of global modernity: the United Nations, the Commission on Global Governance and the New World Disorder. *Critical Arts,* 10(2): 171–184.
Bertelsen, E. (1996). Post mod-cons: Consumerism and cultural studies. *Critical Arts.* 10(1): 87–106.
Bloom, A. (1987). *The closing of the American mind.* New York: Simon and Shuster.
Cooper. B., & Steyn, A. (Eds.). (1996). *Transgressing boundaries: New directions in the study of culture in Africa.* Cape Town and Athens: UCT Press and Ohio University Press.
Cooper, B. (1996). Cultural identity, cultural studies in Africa and the representation of the middle passage. In B. Cooper & A. Steyn (Eds.), *Transgressing boundaries. New directions in the study of culture in Africa* (pp. 164–183). Cape Town and Athens: UCT Press and Ohio University Press.
De Lomnitz, H. M. (1877, 1973). Present tasks of comparative literature. In H. J. Schultz & P. H. Rhein (Eds.). *Comparative literature: The early years* (pp. 53–62). Chapel Hill: The University of North Carolina Press.
Foucault. M. (1970). *The order of things.* London: Tavistock.
Fukuyama, F. (1992). *The end of history and the last man.* New York: Maxwell Macmillan International.
Hall, S. (1992). The question of cultural identity. In S. Hall, D. Held & T. McGrew (Eds.), *Modernity and its futures* (pp. 274–316). Cambridge: Polity in association with Open University.
Mandela, N. (1994). *Long walk to freedom: The autobiography of Nelson Mandela.* Johannesburg: Macdonald Purnell.
Mazrui, A. A. (1990). *Cultural forces in world politics.* London and Nairobi: James Currey and Heinemann.
Minkley, G., & Steyn. A. (1996). South African cultural studies in the moment of the 1990s: "Dominant voices" and trends in theory. In B. Cooper & A. Steyn (Eds.). *Transgressing boundaries: New directions in the study of culture in Africa* (pp. 196207). Cape Town and Athens: UCT Press and Ohio University Press.

Nixon, R. (1994). *Homelands, Harlem and Hollywood: South African culture and the world beyond.* London and New York: Routledge.

Our global neighbourhood: The report of the Commission on Global Governance. Oxford: OUP. 1995.

Pechey. G. (1993). Post-apartheid narratives. In F. Barker et. al. (Eds.). *Colonial discourse, post-colonial theory* (pp. 1–11). New York: Manchester University Press.

Rushdie, S. (1996, September). The novel's not yet dead ... it's just buried. Review of Books, *Mail & Guardian.* Johannesburg.

Said., E. W. (1993). *Culture and imperialism.* London: Chatto and Windus.

Cultural Studies as Praxis: (Making) an Autobiographical Case

Handel Kashope Wright

ABSTRACT

This autobiographical essay 'takes cultural studies personally', drawing on experience, identity and the personal to indicate how and why the author is proponent of and is working on developing a model of cultural studies as social justice praxis despite the constraints academia in general and of the university as an institution in particular. The paper travels roughly from the author's student and teacher days in Sierra Leone through his graduate student days in Canada to his current role as university teacher in the USA. He selectively concentrates on his experience as a teacher of literature (and African multi-role utilitarianism), education and cultural studies (using one of his cultural studies courses and students' questions about the utility of cultural studies as example), his shifting and overlapping racial/ethnic identities (African/black) and the politics of identity, and his thoughts on the place of theory in cultural studies and a black approach to theory (black ambivalent elaboration) as contributory factors. While this account acts in its own way as an argument for conceptualizing cultural studies as praxis, the primary focus is more modestly on my own autobiographical account as a specific case. In fact, an autobiographical approach is employed precisely to be specific and in the attempt to avoid the pitfalls of over-generalization and the authority of authenticity.

Introduction: the road not taken

When Daniel Mato invited me to contribute a paper to a session he was organizing on 'Intellectual Practices in Culture and Power: Transnational Dialogues' for the Fourth Crossroads in Cultural Studies Conference (June/July 2002, Tampere, Finland), I readily agreed. After all, one of my graduate level cultural studies courses, 'Issues in Cultural Studies', reflected a concrete attempt to address such issues as theoreticism in cultural studies and the conceptualization of cultural studies as a form of social justice praxis (inextricably linking theory and practice, exploring issues of power, blurring the boundaries between the academy and the community, and working for equity and social justice). Cultural studies for me is not merely a body of knowledge nor simply an inter/anti/post/disciplinary approach to the study of culture: it is also, and more importantly, an intervention in institutional, sociopolitical and cultural arrangements, events and directions. My conception is reflective of and informed by Meaghan Morris (1997) attempt to turn our attention from the passive, albeit important question, 'what is cultural studies' (Johnson, 1986/7; Storey, 1996), to the more active, even potentially activist question, 'what does cultural studies do?'

I understood from some of my e-mail exchanges with Daniel that these were issues he was also interested in addressing and that I could discuss the course I had developed as a minor example of the kind of work Daniel was interested in having the panel put forward and discuss (i.e. work that went beyond the university and academic writing, which was interdisciplinary and critiqued the division of labour between the academy and the community). In short, the topic was of considerable interest and I had some thoughts on and a concrete example to discuss.

I therefore proposed a paper that was to make a case for cultural studies as social justice praxis, mention a number of projects from around the world that could be readily identified as involving cultural studies as praxis and discussing my course as an example of local work on cultural studies as praxis. The paper was to be built on two related premises: cultural studies as praxis work and cultural studies as praxis is endangered by theoreticism. I was going to point to both the proper place and role of theory in cultural studies and identify various projects representative of cultural studies praxis around the world. Then I was going to focus on a graduate course I teach at the University of Tennessee that brings together theory and international and regional examples of cultural studies work, empirical research and service learning as an example of a model that constructs and promotes cultural studies as social justice praxis work.

However, I quickly became uncomfortable about several aspects of the proposed paper, from how readily I was taking and inviting others to take for granted the danger of theoreticism and the notion that cultural studies is a form of praxis and should explicitly address social justice issues to the presumption that there is a definitive proper place and role for theory in cultural studies and that I could pinpoint that place and role, from the *ad hoc* identification of a few projects from around the world as examples of cultural studies as praxis to the awkward and potentially immodest juxtaposition of that international set of models with my own individual course as a model in and of itself. Compounding these problems was the fact that some of the central aspects of this project involved mere reiterations (for example, the conception of cultural studies as praxis is well established and the danger of theoreticism has become a perennial problem in cultural studies, one Stuart Hall (1992a) had been cognizant of as long ago as the 1970s and warned of the dangers of in the early 1990s).

Seeking a path less travelled

No longer comfortable undertaking the project in the form I had initially proposed, I nevertheless was and continue to be quite passionate about every element of it. I do believe that cultural studies ought to be a form of social justice praxis work, and that this conception is perennially under threat because academic work in general and, ironically, critical discourses in particular tend to sway us toward theory and theorizing as privileged and prestigious ends in and of themselves. Quite aware that these are not novel arguments, I nevertheless believe strongly that the need for cultural studies praxis and the endangerment of cultural studies as praxis means they can bear reiteration. I also believe it is important to point to concrete examples of cultural studies as praxis, not only because this grounds and substantiates an otherwise ethereal argument for praxis but also these examples can inform future cultural studies as praxis work. Finally, while it may have originated with one course, the idea of articulating theory, empirical research, and service learning as interrelated elements of cultural studies work my students undertake is coalescing for me as a viable model of cultural studies as social justice praxis.

In terms of the panel and this special issue of *Cultural Studies*, a discussion of cultural studies as social justice praxis work in general and the course and evolving model in particular offer an opportunity to point to ways in which the rigid dichotomies between the academy and the community, academic and non-academic work, theory and practice, text and lived cultures, etc., can be breached. What is emerging for me as a viable means of bridging these dichotomies is an approach that juxtaposes cultural studies, empirical research and service learning.

What was my motivation for initially proposing a paper that one the one hand undertook a potentially 'ho-hum' reiteration of cultural studies positions and on the other presumed to outline a singular 'correct' approach to cultural studies? Why am I interested in presenting and promoting cultural studies as social justice praxis, even in the face of these potential pitfalls? What role has experience and my identity played in my passion for this conception of cultural studies? How was I to discuss such personal issues, my course and the model of cultural studies praxis I have been developing, all of which I am passionate about, without slipping into issuing imperatives and making exaggerated claims?

As I reflected on these questions, it became clear that using the third person and employing the (dis)stance and language of the disembodied subject would be particularly inappropriate for this paper. As is evident by now, I decided to speak personally, autobiographically, not only at the conference presentation but in this paper. Initially frowned upon by early cultural studies figures such as Richard Hoggart, autobiography is becoming increasingly prominent in progressive academic work, from the reflexive turn and the rise of autoethnography in research to feminist assertions of women's ways of knowing and articulating knowledge and is even being utilized and theorized in cultural studies work (Hall, 1992a; Probyn, 1993).

This change in presentation strategy is accompanied by a change in the substance of the essay. Instead of an in-depth discussion of what constitutes cultural studies as praxis, international versions of cultural studies as praxis and of the model of cultural studies as social justice praxis I see evolving at my institution, I concentrate here on a much more modest examination of what leads me to advocate and promote cultural studies as praxis. This personal, autobiographical account works in its own way to advocate cultural studies praxis but operates primarily as a case study primarily concerned with explicating how one individual has come to prefer and advocate cultural studies as social justice praxis.

Part of what I am interested in addressing, in this paper, though not directly, is the split between the university and academic work on the one hand and political, activist and performative work in the community and society on the other. In an earlier paper (Wright, 1998), I stressed the need for cultural studies to revive the praxis conceptualization and pointed out that even the early CCCS work was limited in terms of undertaking such work and that non-academic work, including 'cultural studies in the streets', ought to be more readily acknowledged and taken up as cultural studies work. In her response to my paper, Maureen McNeil (1998) rightly pointed to the constraints we operate under in the academy and how being subjects of the university as an institution limited CCCS work and continues to limit university-based cultural studies' ability to undertake the kind of praxis work I was advocating. Part of what I am interested in here is to indicate that while the university does constrain what can be done as praxis work, some of the work we undertake in the academy can serve to bridge the gap between university and community and academic and intellectual work. In addition, I want to reiterate that the university itself must not be overlooked as a site of praxis, a site where issues of difference, representation and social justice, and even what constitutes legitimate academic work are being contested.

Taking cultural studies personally

Part of my rationale for making the shift in emphasis from the larger picture of an international scope of cultural studies as praxis to my own individual case as proponent of cultural studies as praxis is the realization that with the original project I might well be preaching to the choir of those who readily acknowledge that cultural studies is or ought to be a form of praxis on the one hand and presenting an argument to the deaf ears of those who prefer not to conceptualize cultural studies as praxis on the other. Rather than simply make generalized recommendations of and exhortations about cultural studies as praxis, my amended project is a more personal exploration of the source and rationale for my recommendations, the role experience and identity have played in my attraction to, relationship with and conception of cultural studies, as well as how I position myself and am positioned as a teacher, especially a postcolonial African migrant teacher of cultural studies in the USA. In sum what I am interested in here, following Gregory Jay's (1995) idea and strategy of 'taking multiculturalism personally', is taking cultural studies personally. In part, the essay addresses what brings me to cultural studies, what I ask of cultural studies and the ways in which cultural studies responds (sometimes adequately, sometimes inadequately) to my expectations and what all of this means for how strongly I feel about and advocate cultural studies as praxis. Essentially, I am attempting to undertake work here based on the feminist maxim that the personal is political without being essentialist, which means taking seriously Grossberg's (1992a) caveat that the political cannot be reduced to the personal.

Questions of experience, identity and representation and the autobiographical are central in this text and it is important to point out at the outset that for me these are not given, fixed notions nor sources of authenticity but rather constructed, procedural, multiple, overlapping, contradictory and performative. Ann Gray (2003) sums up the conception of the relationship between experience and identity I am working with rather well when she explains that 'experience can be understood as a discursive "site of articulation" upon and through which subjectivities and identities are shaped and constructed.' (2003: 25). Even as I personalize this discussion of cultural studies as praxis and speak autobiographically, I do so with a conception of the personal and my identity as cultural studies teacher not as authentic and authoritative but as a performance, even, following Jane Gallop (1995), as an impersonation.

Furthermore, I speak autobiographically and to my experience, not in an attempt to claim the authority of authenticity – precisely the opposite. In the introduction to his autobigraphical essay, Stuart Hall asserts that 'autobiography is usually thought of as seizing the authority of authenticity. But in order not to be authoritative, I've got to speak autobiographically' (Hall, 1992a: 277). Following Hall (1992a), I speak autobiographically here in an effort to avoid the pitfalls of overgeneralization, assumed authenticity and authority and the various burdens of representation in cultural studies. In my case, given that both my collective identity and the areas of cultural studies I work on are distinctly underrepresented (in both senses of the word), there is the danger that my account may be taken up variously as the authentic and authoritative representation of blacks, Africans, black cultural studies, African cultural studies or cultural studies in education.

Identity, experience and cultural studies

The elements I believe are important to explore here are my own identity and multiple, shifting and contradictory identifications in relation to cultural studies, including how I position myself and am positioned in the North American academy. (I'm working here with a conception of identity, not as given, stable, singular and essentialist category, but as a number of 'identifications come to light' (Fuss, 1995), as a concept which though 'under erasure' can be usefully deployed strategically (Hall, 1996a) with the caveat that any declaration of identity be recognized as positional, selective, and provisional.) Put more specifically: factors that have influenced my interest in cultural studies as social justice praxis include the primacy of the performative in African literature and the concept of African multi-role utilitarianism; my identification as African and transition from Africanness to blackness (and overlapping of the two); being located in the contradictory space of the third world in the first world that is the Appalachian region of the USA; being located in the centre that is the US academy but undertaking work at the dual margins of cultural studies that are African cultural studies and cultural studies in education, and the standpoint and approach to theory that I am calling black ambivalent elaboration.

Since my days as both a student and high school teacher of literature in Sierra Leone, I have been fascinated by the dichotomy between the Anglocentric, predominantly aesthetic-based conception of literature and the image of lonely writer in the attic on the one hand and the African-centred, predominantly utilitarian conception of literature and the image of the writer as politicized communualist on the other. I not only favour the African multi-task utilitarianism (the utilitarian conceptions of the author and literature), but readily embrace Anthony Easthope's (1991) exhortation, 'literary into cultural studies'. In my doctoral and subsequent work, I have utilized this conception in making a case for a transition from a literary studies to a cultural studies approach to literature studies in Africa (e.g. Wright, 1996a, 1996b, 2000, 2004). My arguments included the need to acknowledge and incorporate traditional African orature, new media and popular culture texts, the expertise of non-academic teachers (e.g. traditional *griots*), an emphasis on performance and the utilization of literature in African development. The result is a discourse and praxis that obfuscates borders between text and lived culture, the academy and the community, the canonical and the popular, the literary and the socioeconomic, electronic and traditional texts.

African multi-role utilitarianism is the term I use to indicate that most African writers have eschewed singular identities and roles and have instead routinely taken on multiple simultaneous roles (e.g. Nigeria's Wole Soyinka as poet, dramatist, literary critic and political activist; Ghana's Ama Ata Aidoo as dramatist, literary critic and politician, and Kenya's Ngugi wa Thiong'o as novelist, community activist, theatre developer, literary critic, university professor). Underscoring this conception of author as someone necessarily involved in multiple roles has been the fact that a majority of African literary critics (Izevbaye, 1971; Ngugi, 1981,

1988; Irele, 1990; James, 1990; Soyinka, 1993) and certain Africanist (Gugelberger, 1985) critics are in agreement that African literature and literary criticism are driven by utilitarianism as much as, if not more than by aesthetics. This is not to suggest that African writers and critics eschew aesthetics completely. Rather, it is the art-for-art's-sake conception of aesthetics that is eschewed in favour of a utilitarian and highly politicized conception that Udenta Udenta (1993) has described as African 'revolutionary aesthetics'. Literature and orature are taken up primarily as 'texts' for performance (often with an assumption of active audience participation).

Jostein Gripsrud (1994) has rightly pointed out that, 'the construction of cultural identity is always an intellectual enterprise. Ordinary folks normally don't care very much. [In fact] Intellectuals as a rule have a hard time convincing people about the relevance of these identity constructions' (1994: 220). Continental identities are even more esoteric: like most Africans, I had not strongly nor even consciously identified as African while living in Sierra Leone (gender, ethnic and territorial identities and identifications were much more meaningful and important in that context). Interestingly, in the move from Sierra Leone to Canada and then the USA, I have been assigned and have taken up not only African identity but also 'black' identity.

The complexity of identity means that rather than being singular or merely replacing one form of identity with another (e.g. ceasing to be Krio and becoming 'black') identity is a series of complimentary and contradictory identifications operating simultaneously, with some coming to the fore or receding depending on context. I live and work in the USA but am not an American citizen; I am 'black' but not African American; I am simultaneously a continental and a diasporic African.

Issues of identity and identification and considerations of the complexities of essentialist, anti-essentialist, and anti-anti-essentialist conceptualizations have made identity a central problematic for me. I have therefore always considered the exploration of identity and the politics of identity an integral, even pivotal aspect of cultural studies work (Wright, 2002). Rather than seeing postmodernist and poststructuralist critiques of essentialist identity politics as reasons to consider identity passé, if not dangerously limited and limiting, I view them as providing caveats that press us to articulate more nuanced conceptualizations of identity and emphasize its strategic deployment (e.g. Gayatri Spivak's (1990) notion of strategic essentialism, Stuart Hall's (1996a) assertion that identity is still useful if deployed strategically, and David Blades (2000) nautical strategy of tacking back and forth between the modernist/humanist and the postmodernist).

While cultural studies is a useful discourse for exploring issues of identity and the politics of difference as important political issues in and of themselves, it is also the case that identity can in turn be used as an incisive tool to critique and contribute to the development of cultural studies. The feminist and black interventions in general at the CCCS (Women's Studies Group, 1978; CCCS, 1982) and the work of Paul Gilroy (1991, 1993) in particular, especially his *There Ain't No Black in the Union Jack* served as both early examples and inspiration for me for undertaking work that utilized identity to both critique the status quo of cultural studies for its failure to represent and include certain marginalized groups and to begin to indicate what cultural studies might look like if it did include those voices and perspectives. Thus, part of the answer to Morris' (1997) question, 'what does cultural studies do', is that it enables the exploration of identity and the politics and significance of socio-cultural difference while incorporating identity and the politics of difference to enrich and expand its own discourse.

Trajectories of cultural studies and the migrant academic

My move from Sierra Leone to North America is, in academic and postcolonial terms, a move from the margin to the centre, from the underdeveloped world to the overdeveloped world. The transition, however, is not a definitive one that automatically brings with it all the privileges (some of them rather dubious) of being located at the centre. Spivak captures the positioning of migrant postcolonial academics well when she describes herself, not as firmly located in the centre but rather as 'still scratching at the rift between global postcoloniality and metropolitan migrancy' (1999: 375). What does this mean for how we are positioned in the western academy? Spivak explains it thus:

> Strictly speaking, we have left the problems of post-coloniality, located in the former colony (now a 'developing nation' trying to survive the ravages of neo-colonialism and globalization) *only* to discover that the white supremacist culture wants to claim the entire agency of capitalism – recoded as the rule of law within a democratic heritage – *only* for itself; to find that the only entry is through a forgetfulness, or a museumization of national origin in the interest of class mobility; or yet coding this move as 'resistance!'
>
> (Spivak, 1999: 398)

In terms of international academic work in general and conferences in particular, she rightly observes that 'the privileged inhabitant of neo-colonial space is often bestowed a subject-position as geo-political other by the dominant radical (one is most struck by this when planning or attending international conferences)' (Spivak, 1999: 339). In sum then, as a migrant postcolonial academic my position is one that is always already politicized. Not surprisingly, therefore, a substantial aspect of the attraction of cultural studies holds for me is that it is explicitly politicized academic work concerned with representing the marginalized other and working for social justice. While it is true that in the USA, cultural studies politics (especially its neo-Marxist underpinnings and its explicit social justice agenda – O'Connor, 1989; Pfister, 1996) has been considerably downplayed in many circles, there are some of us for whom the politics of difference is virtually unavoidable and for us, therefore, cultural studies remains, as Stuart Hall has cogently described it, 'politics by other means'.

Through its own success and institutionalization in the academy around the world cultural studies has evolved from being not only interdisciplinary but also distinctly anti-disciplinary to becoming, in Tony Bennett's words, a 'reluctant discipline'. As it has gone global, a little-discussed hierarchy of regions has emerged, with British (especially English) cultural studies and American versions apparently battling for peak position (British cultural studies can claim originary status while American cultural studies, through the size of its academy and greater financial resources, can claim current prominence) and Australian and Canadian cultural studies attempting to articulate distinct national/regional versions of cultural studies in the shadow of the very dominant British and American versions respectively. Cultural studies is also spreading in Europe, Asia and Africa, though these regional versions remain distinctly marginal.

Arguably, African cultural studies is the most limited in terms of resources and presence, institutionalized substantially only in South Africa (e.g. the Centre for Media and Cultural

Studies in Durban, the journal *Critical Arts* and the work of figures such as Keyan Tomaselli (1998a, 1998b,2001)). Thus, to work on African cultural studies as I do is to work on the margins of a once globally marginal discourse and to contribute to the attempt to move African cultural studies 'from margin to centre' (hooks, 1984) of international/transnational cultural studies. Holding cultural studies to its much vaunted openness, what is at stake in this project is not only the trajectories and the evolution of international/transnational cultural studies but also its history and narratives of origin (Wright, 1995, 1996, 1998). Because of the African emphasis on utilitarianism, African cultural studies tends to emphasize praxis (Tomaselli, 1998b) and thus contribute to the evolution and promotion of transnational cultural studies as praxis.

Black ambivalent elaboration

There are at least two principal sources of the threat of theoreticism in cultural studies. First, there is a general academic valorization of theory, especially high theory, as privileged, prestigious and an end in itself, and hence understandably insular (divorced from practice and politics) and self-referential. Academic cultural studies is not immune to this conception and there is a constant danger that students (and faculty) and the discourse of cultural studies itself will be engulfed by the attractions of 'facility' with theory (with specific difficult concepts, bodies of theory, the work of specific theorists) and with armchair theorizing as an end in and of itself. Second, the western, especially US, turn to the right in terms of popular culture and politics (Grossberg, 1992b) has resulted in the left's retreat from politics proper to cultural politics (Rorty, 1998), and to theory for its own sake via arcane language, the apolitical discourses of postmodernism and poststructuralism and the discursive turn (McChesney, 1996). While there is no denying the centrality of theory and theorizing in cultural studies work, the simultaneously modest and expansive approach recommended by Hall (e.g. the image of reading theory being like 'wrestling with angels', his suspicion of facility with theory and the decidedly functionalist role he sees for theory) remain good guides against theoreticism

As I have worked on how to take up theory in my own work, I have identified and utilize a phenomenon and approach I label 'black ambivalent elaboration'. Both a standpoint and a reading strategy, black ambivalent elaboration articulates Homi Bhabha's 'ambivalence', Gramsci's *elabore*, and a healthy dose of 'critical scepticism'. This is an international phenomenon that ought to give progressive postie theorists considerable pause since it is not based on ideological differences and in fact originates from presumed allies. Black cultural studies figures such as Stuart Hall (Hall, 1992a, b, 1996; Drew, 1999), Manthia Diawara (1996) and Paul Gilroy (1993) have put forward black suspicion of cutting edge theory very directly. Hall asserts that '[The] theoretical encounter between black cultural politics and the discourses of Eurocentric, largely white, critical cultural theory which in recent years, has focussed so much analysis of the politics of representation . . . is always an extremely difficult, if not dangerous encounter. (I think particularly of black people encountering the discourses of post-structuralism, postmodernism, psychoanalysis and feminism)' (Hall, 1996a: 443). In a similar vein, Diawara has asserted that 'many black thinkers have a suspicious attitude toward poststructuralism and postmodernism in part because they interpret the emphasis that these theoretical projects put on decentring the subject politically-as a means to once again undermine the black subject' (1996: 306). Paul Gilroy is decidedly wary of blacks catching what he describes as 'the postmodernism fever' (1993: 107) and considers the application of postmodernism to the appreciation of black art a rush to 'premature black postmodernism' (1993: 127).

Examples of black ambivalence about theory in general and the posties in particular include Barbara Christian's (1990) dismissive assertion that many academics are involved in 'a race for theory'; Wole Soyinka's (1976) assertion that African Marxist literary critics interested in high theory constitute a 'Leftocracy'. Michael Eric Dyson has asserted that we need to 'dirty language, to dirty theory, to make more gritty the realities that so smoothly travel from European culture to American theory, especially as they are applied to African-American culture' (in Dobrin, 1999: 92). Then there is Stuart Hall's ambivalence about postmodernism's ambivalent fascination with difference and his declaration that 'there's nothing that global postmodernism loves better than a certain kind of difference: a touch of ethnicity, a taste of the exotic, as we say in England, "a bit of the other"' (Hall, 1992b: 23). Finally, there are Gayatri Spivak's assertions that 'deconstruction cannot found a political programme of any kind.' (Spivak, 1990: 104), and that we, Third World people, have been called to speak by postmodernism.

The other side of this position is that having expressed these reservations, Soyinka has himself been accused of using such esoteric language in both his creative work and his criticism that he cannot be understood by the majority of Africans for whom he claims to write. Spivak not only utilizes deconstruction extensively in her work but is also widely regarded as a leading deconstructionist. Dyson insists on the importance and applicability of the work theorists like Foucault and Derrida, and Hall selectively employs aspects of the discourses of these theories in his work (e.g. his insistence that race be conceptualized not only as a discourse but more specifically as a floating signifier (Hall, 1996c). What we have in these examples then is an ambivalent, wary use of theory in general and 'the posties' in particular. It is both a suspicion of and yet a wary willingness to elaborate these theoretical frameworks to apply to black subjectivity and issues of concern to blacks. I subscribe to this simultaneous suspicion and wary utilization and black elaboration of theory in general and postmodernism and post-structuralism in particular as both a black standpoint and strategy in what I am calling black ambivalent elaboration. It is black ambivalent elaboration as a standpoint and strategy that I utilize in my own approach to theory in undertaking cultural studies work.

Cultural studies and education

I was introduced to cultural studies as a doctoral student at the University of Toronto's Ontario Institute for Studies in Education. With a continuing interest in both literature and education, the intersection of cultural studies with both literature studies and education became a dual focus of mine and the following are a few reflections on the latter area.

In historicizing cultural studies, the dominant narrative has referred to a series of crises in the humanities and social sciences as the context and impetus for the emergence of the discourse (e.g. Bratlinger, 1990, Gray and McGuigan, 1993). Raymond Williams' (1989) much more specific assertion is that cultural studies emerged from within the field of adult education. This more specific narrative has been eschewed in favour of the more expansive narrative of the crises, the latter being more attractive undoubtedly because it involves several and more prestigious disciplines.

Though education was an integral aspect of the concerns of the CCCS (e.g. Willis, 1977; CCCS Education Group, 1981; Education Group 2, 1991), the field of education has been marginalized in the process of the globalization of cultural studies and education now appears to have become cultural studies old aunt in the attic. Probably seen as overly practical and pedantically pedagogical, education is the close relative that cultural studies is embarrassed to acknowledge, especially when good company like postmodernist, post-structuralist and psychoanalytic theory come calling. Education, equally uncomfortable, appears to see cultural studies as a snobbish young upstart given over to theoreticism and of rather limited relevance to educational issues. Even critical educational theorists have mixed feelings about cultural studies: Shirley Steinberg and Joe Kincheloe (1997), for example, declare: 'We are enthused by the benefits of cultural studies of childhood yet critical of expressions of elitism within the discourse of cultural studies itself- a recognition made more disturbing by the field's claim to the moral high ground of a politics of inclusivity' (1997: 6).

The consequence of these perceptions cultural studies and the field of education have of each other has been a mutual wariness which Henry Giroux has described thus: 'educational theorists demonstrate as little interest in cultural studies as cultural studies scholars do in the critical theories of schooling and pedagogy.' (1994: 279). It is hardly surprising then, that when disciplines and fields that have and continue to contribute to cultural studies work are discussed, education is often ignored in edited collections that undertake to indicate cultural studies wide disciplinary roots and connections (e.g. Nelson and Gaonkar, 1996) and underrepresented at conferences with the broadest sweep of topics (Maton and Wright, 2002). To work on the intersection of cultural studies and education as I do, is to work at the margins of cultural studies. However, because education work tends to emphasize practice, especially pedagogy, my work on the intersection of cultural studies and education means undertaking cultural studies as praxis, especially in relation to taking pedagogy seriously.

Strategies for engendering cultural studies praxis

There are at least three principal strategies for engendering cultural studies as praxis, namely engagement with policy, performative acts and empirical research. In terms of policy, Tony Bennett's (1992) advocacy of 'putting policy into cultural studies' is particularly significant as it involves not only incorporating policy issues as part of cultural studies work but the transformation of cultural studies into a form of cultural policy studies. Examples of performative acts include the work of figures such as Trinh Minh-Ha (1989, 1991, 1992) and Isaac Julien (1992), both of whom have not only written theoretical essays about identity but have made films that depict, trouble and theorize about identity, research and, indeed what forms theory can take. To such figures I would add the work of Ngugi wa Thiong'o (1981, 1986), who has not worked as a novelist and literary critic but was a political activist (jailed for his activism) and was involved in the building of a community theatre and the writing and staging of a play. Finally, empirical research has been a principal means of grounding cultural studies work since the days of the CCCS and the work of a figure such as Paul Willis who produced one of the earliest and most influential cultural studies ethnographies (Willis, 1977) and continues to conduct and theorize about ethnography (Willis, 2000) exemplifies research based cultural studies praxis. Although cultural studies is 'theoretically' very open in terms of methodology (Nelson et al., 1992), it is obvious that qualitative approaches and ethnography in particular have been favoured since the days of the CCCS. Ann Gray's (2003) most recent book underscores this point and in making explicit links between ethnography and cultural studies and identifying ethnographic research as an approach to 'doing' cultural studies serves to endorse empirical research as a means of engendering cultural studies as praxis.

Conclusion: issues in cultural studies and the unexpected pedagogue

My work on the relationship between cultural studies and education in general and my experience with designing and teaching the course 'Issues in Cultural Studies' lead me to propose two additional strategies for engendering cultural studies as praxis, namely pedagogy and service learning. Although it is part of the work of academic cultural studies, pedagogy is, for the most part, not only taken-for-granted but also overlooked as a strategy for engendering cultural studies praxis. In fact, outside of the field of education, most academics including those in cultural studies (with Larry Grossberg (1994) being a notable exception) would rather not openly discuss let alone theorize about pedagogy. As Jane Tompkins once put it, pedagogy is 'exactly like sex', 'something you weren't supposed to talk about or focus on' (1990: 655).

If cultural studies were to seriously engage education and pedagogy, it would mean acknowledging that cultural studies emerged in fact not only from the field of adult education but also more specifically from the pedagogical encounters between Williams and his students. It was their questions about the relevance and appropriateness of the texts and approaches being employed in his extra- mural classes that led Williams to begin to develop what we now acknowledge as early cultural studies work. In short, taking education and pedagogy seriously in cultural studies means acknowledging that cultural studies originated as praxis.

Service learning is, at first blush, a rather unusual suggestion for engendering cultural studies praxis, especially since it is supposedly a decidedly liberal and undertheorized discourse and practice (Carver, 1997; Hepburn, 1997) principally concerned with fostering civic participation by having students volunteer with corporations and community groups and reflect on their service in a classroom setting. However, at the University of Tennessee, a Community Partnership Center was established by two progressive faculty, John Gaventa (sociology) and Fran Ansley (law), which forged links between the university and progressive community groups and promoted a decidedly radical form of service learning labelled 'service learning for social justice' (Fisher, 1997). It is service learning for social justice, with a strong component of fostering town-gown relationships, that I blend with cultural studies and empirical research in the model of cultural studies as social justice praxis I am developing (Wright, 2001/2002).

My recent (re)engagements with Dorothy Smith's (1987, 1990a, 1990b) sociology for women in general and her institutional ethnography (IE) and the derivative political activist ethnography (PAE) in particular (G. Smith, 1990) – as well as with academics and activists undertaking IE and PAE work – have led me away from my initial tendency to collapse service learning and empirical research into a version of activist cultural studies or cultural studies praxis (Wright, 2001/2002). I am now more inclined to believe cultural studies works best as praxis when it is juxtaposed and thus held in productive tension with service learning and ethnography in general or institutional ethnography in particular.

As an African and even as a black person teaching at a decidedly white institution, I am the unexpected colleague and teacher. The cultural studies in education programme in which I teach utilizes cultural studies as an umbrella discourse for undertaking a critical approach to graduate studies of both sport and education (social foundations of sport and sport psychology and social foundations of education) and also involves cultural studies as an area of specialization. Cultural studies is still a rather novel approach to education in the USA and even more so to sport studies. Many students have no previous conception of cultural studies. (I think of myself, therefore, as the unexpected pedagogue teaching the unexpected discipline). The silver lining to this situation is that students in general and those with a strong practice orientation in particular (e.g. those interested in teacher education and in sport psychology) consistently ask such questions as 'what is the relevance of cultural studies to my field?' 'How can I utilize cultural studies in my practice?' 'Where are the examples of local and regional cultural studies work?' 'How can we do cultural studies and yet find opportunities to work with athletes/teachers and the community?' Apart from my own interest, it is these questions and probings from practice-oriented students that has kept my focus on the development of courses like 'Issues in Cultural Studies' and a model of cultural studies as social justice praxis.

References

Bennett, T. (1992) 'Putting policy into cultural studies'. In Lawrence Grossberg, Cary Nelson and Paula Treichler (eds) *Cultural Studies*. London: Routledge.
Blades, D. (2000) 'Coming about: reason, rebellion and responsibility in postmodern curriculum theorizing'. Paper presented at the American Educational Research Association conference, Montreal.
Brantlinger, P. (1990) *Crusoe's footprints: Cultural Studies in Britain and America*. New York: Routledge.
Carver, R. (1997) 'Theoretical underpinnings of service learning'. *Theory Into Practice*, 36(3): 143–9.
CCCS Education Group (1981) *Unpopular education: Schooling and social democracy in England since 1944*. London: Hutchinson.
——— (1982) *The Empire Strikes Back. Race and Racism in 70s Britain*. London: Hutchinson.
Christian, B. (1990) 'The race for theory'. In A. JanMohamed and D. Lloyd (eds) *The nature and Context of Minority Discourse*. Oxford: Oxford University Press.
Diawara, M. (1996) 'Black studies, cultural studies: performance acts'. In John Storey (ed.) *What is Cultural Studies: A Reader*. London: Arnold.
Dobrin, S. (1999) 'Race and the public intellectual: a conversation with Michael Eric Dyson'. In Gary Olson and Lynn Worsham (eds) *Race, rhetoric, and the post-colonial*. Albany, NY: SUNY Press.
Drew, J. (1999) 'Cultural composition: Stuart Hall on ethnicity and the discursive turn'. In Gary Olson and Lynn Worsham (eds) *Race, Rhetoric, and the Postcolonial*. New York: SUNY Press.
Easthope, A. (1991) *Literary into Cultural Studies*. New York: Routledge.
Education Group 11 (Dept of Cultural Studies, University of Birmingham) (1991) *Education Limited: Schooling, Training and the New Right in England since 1979*. London: Unwin Hyman.
Fisher, Steve (1997) 'Service learning for social justice workshop: Opening remarks'. Unpublished paper.
Fuss, D. (1995) *Identification Papers*. New York: Routledge.
Gallop, J. (ed.) (1995) *Pedagogy: The question of impersonation*. Bloomington & Indianapolis, IN: Indiana University Press.
Gilroy, P. (1991) *'There ain't no black in the Union Jack': The cultural politics of race and nation*. Chicago: University of Chicago Press.
——— (1993) *Small acts: Thoughts on the politics of black cultures*. London: Serpent's Tail.

Giroux, H. (1994) 'Doing cultural studies: Youth and the challenge of pedagogy'. *Harvard Educational Review*, 64(3): 278–308.
Gray, A. (2003) *Research Practice for Cultural Studies*. London: Sage.
—— and McGuigan, J. (eds) (1993) *Studying Culture:An Introductory Reader*. London: Arnold.
Gripsrud, J. (1994) 'Intellectuals as constructors of cultural identities'. *Cultural Studies*, 8(2): 220–31.
Grossberg, L. (1992a) '"You can't always get what you want": The struggle over the left'. *We gotta get out of this place: Popular conservatism and postmodern culture*. New York and London: Routledge.
—— (1992b)*We gotta get out of this place: Popular conservatism and postmodern culture*. New York and London: Routledge.
—— (1994) 'Introduction. Bringing it all back home: Pedagogy and cultural studies'. In Henry Giroux and Peter McLaren (eds) *Between Borders: Pedagogy and the Politics of Cultural Studies*. London & New York: Routledge.
Gugelberger, G. M. (ed.) (1985) *Marxism and African Literature*. Trenton, NJ: Africa World Press.
Hall, S. (1992a) 'Cultural studies and its theoretical legacies'. In Lawrence Gross-berg, Cary Nelson and Paula Treichler (eds) *Cultural Studies*. New York & London: Routledge.
—— (1992b) 'What is this 'black' in black popular culture?' In Gina Dent (ed.) *Black Popular Culture*. Seattle: Bay Press.
—— (1996a) 'Introduction: Who needs identity?' In Stuart Hall and Paul du Gay (eds) *Questions of Cultural Identity*. London: Sage.
—— (1996b) 'New ethnicities'. In David Morley and Kuan-Hsing Chen (eds) *Stuart Hall: Critical Dialogues in Cultural Studies*. New York: Routledge.
—— (1996c) *Race, the Floating Signifier. Classroom Edition* [Filmed lecture]. Media Education Foundation.
Hepburn, M. (1997) 'Service learning in civic education; a concept with a long, sturdy roots'. *Theory Into Practice*, 36(3): 136–42.
hooks, b. (1984) *Feminist theory: From margin to center*. Boston: South End Press.
Irele, A. (1990) *The African experience in literature and ideology*. Bloomington and Indianapolis, IN: Indiana University Press.
Izevbaye, D. S. (1971) 'Criticism and literature in Africa'. In C. Heywood (ed.) *Perspectives on African literature*. London: Heinemann.
James, A. (1990) *In their own voices: African women writers talk*. Nairobi: Heinemann.
Jay, G. (1995) 'Taking multiculturalism personally: ethnos and ethos in the classroom'. In Jane Gallop (ed.) *Pedagogy: The question of impersonation*. Bloomington & Indianapolis, IN: Indiana University Press.
Johnson, R. (1986-7) 'What is cultural studies anyway?' *Social Text*, 16: 38–80.
Julien, I. (1992) '"Black is, black ain't": Notes on de-essentializing black identities'. In Gina Dent (ed.) *Black Popular Culture*. Seattle: Bay Press.
Maton, K. and Wright, H. K. (2002) 'Editorial: returning cultural studies to education'. *International Journal of Cultural Studies*, 5(4): 379–92.
McChesney, R. (1996) 'Is there hope for cultural studies?' *Review of the Month*, 47(10): 1–18.
McNeil, M. (1998) 'De-centring or re-focussing cultural studies: a response to Handel K. Wright'. *European Journal of Cultural Studies*, 1(1): 57–64.
Morris, M. (1997) 'A question of cultural studies'. In Angela McRobbie (ed.) *Back to Reality? Social Experience and Cultural Studies*. Manchester: Manchester University Press.
Nelson, C. and Gaonkar, D. P. (eds) (1996) *Disciplinarity and Dissent in Cultural Studies*. New York: Routledge.
——, Treichler, P. and Grossberg, L. (1992) 'Cultural studies: An introduction'. In Lawrence Grossberg, Cary Nelson and Paula Treichler (eds) *Cultural Studies*. London & New York: Routledge.
Ngugi wa Thiong'o (1981) *Detained: A Writer's Prison Diary*. London: Heinemann Books.
—— (1986) *Decolorizing the Mind: The Politics of Language in African Literature*. London: James Currey.
—— (1988) *Penpoints, Gunpoints, and Dreams: Towards a critical theory of the arts and the state in Africa*. Oxford: Clarendon Press.
O'Connor, A. (1989) 'The problem of American cultural studies'. *Critical Studies in Mass Communication*, 6: 405–13.

Pfister, J. (1996) 'The Americanization of cultural studies'. In John Storey (ed.)*What is Cultural Studies? A Reader*. London: Arnold.

Probyn, E. (1993) 'True voices and real people: the "problem" of the auto-biographical in cultural studies'. In Valda Blundell, John Shapherd and Ian Taylor (eds) *Relocating Cultural Studies: Developments in Theory and Research*. London & New York: Routledge.

Rorty, R. (1998) *Achieving our country: Leftist thought in Twentieth-Century America*. Cambridge, MA: Harvard University Press

Smith, D. (1987) *The everyday world as problematic:A feminist sociology*.Toronto: Univer- sity of Toronto Press.

—— (1990a) *Conceptual Practices of Power: A Feminist Sociology of Knowledge*. Toronto: University of Toronto Press.

—— (1990b) *Texts, Facts and Femininity: Exploring the Relations of Ruling*. London: Routledge.

Smith, G. (1990) 'Political activist as ethnographer'. *Social Problems*, 37(4): 629–48.

Soyinka, W. (1976) *Myth, Literature and the African World*. Cambridge: Cambridge University Press.

—— (1993) *Art, Dialogue and Outrage: Essays on Literature and Culture*. London: Methuen.

Spivak, G. C. (1990) 'Practical politics of the open end'. In Sarah Harasym (ed.) *The Post-Colonial Critic: Interviews, Strategies, Dialogues* . New York: Routledge.

—— (1999) *A Critique of Postcolonial Reason:Toward a History of the Vanishing Present*. Cambridge, MA: Harvard University Press.

Steinberg, S. and Kincheloe, J. (eds) (1997) *Kinderculture: The corporate construction of childhood*. Boulder: Westview Press.

Storey, J. (ed.). (1996)*What is Cultural Studies: A Reader*. London: Arnold.

Tomaselli, K. G. (1998a) 'African cultural studies: excavating for the future'. *Inter- national Journal of Cultural Studies,* 1(1), 143–53.

—— (1998b) 'Recovering praxis: cultural studies in Africa'. *European Journal of Cultural Studies*, 1(3): 387–402.

—— (2001) 'Blue is hot, red is cold: doing reverse cultural studies in Africa'. *Cultural Studies < – > Critical Methodologies*, 1(3): 283–318.

Tompkins, J. (1990) 'The pedagogy of the distressed'. *College English*, 52, 653–60.

Trinh, Minh-Ha (1989) *Surname Viet Given Name Nam* [Ethnographic film]. B & W Film.

—— (1991) *When the moon waxes red: Representation, gender and cultural politics*. London & New York: Routledge.

—— (1992) *Framer Framed*. London & New York: Routledge.

Udenta, U. (1993) *Revolutionary Aesthetics and the African Literary Process*. Enugu: Fourth Dimension Publishing.

Williams, R. (1989)*The Politics of Modernism:Against the New Conformists*. London:Verso.

Willis. P. (1977) *Learning to Labour: How Working-Class Kids Get Working-Class Jobs*. Aldershot: Saxon House.

—— (2000) *The Ethnographic Imagination*. Cambridge: Polity.

Women's Studies Group, CCCS (1978)*Women Take Issue: Aspects of Women's Subordination*. London: Hutchinson.

Wright, H. K. (1995) 'Would we recognize African cultural studies if we saw it? A review essay of Ngugi's Moving the centre: The Struggle For Cultural Freedom'. *Journal of Education/Pedagogy/Cultural Studies*, 17(2): 157–65.

Wright, H. K. (1996a) 'In defense of transitions from literary to cultural studies'. *Taboo*, 2(1): 87–110.

—— (1996b) 'Take Birmingham to the curb, here comes African cultural studies: an exercise in Revisionist Historiography'. *University of Toronto Quarterly*, 65(2): 355–65.

—— (1996c) 'E-mail in African studies'. *Convergence*, 2(1): 19–29.

—— (1998) 'Dare we de-centre Birmingham? Troubling the origin and trajectories of cultural studies'. *European Journal of Cultural Studies*, 1(1): 33–56.

—— (2000) 'Not so strange bedfellows: Indigenous knowledge, literature studies, and African devel- opment'. In George Dei, Budd Hall and Dorothy Rosenberg (eds) *Indigenous Knowledge In Global Contexts: Multiple Readings of Our World*. Toronto: University of Toronto Press.

—— (2001/2002) 'Editorial: cultural studies and service learning for social justice'. *Tennessee Education*, 31/32(1, 2): 11–16.

—— (2002) 'Editorial: Notes on the (im)possibility of articulating continental African identity'. *Critical Arts*, 16(2): 1–18.

—— (2003) 'Editorial: Whose diaspora is this anyway? Continental Africans trying on and troubling diasporic identity. *Critical Arts*, 17(1+2): 1–16.

—— (2004) *A Prescience of African Cultural Studies: The Future of Literature in Africa is not what it was.* New York: Peter Lang.

Navigating the African Archive – A Conversation between Tamar Garb and Hlonipha Mokoena

Tamar Garb and Hlonipha Mokoena

ABSTRACT

As curators, museums, galleries and collectors grapple with the meaning of 'African Art', and as a younger generation of African artists produce an ever more complex expression of what it means to be African, Tamar Garb and Hlonipha Mokoena set out some of the ways in which they have participated in projects that trouble and extend the meaning of the African archive. Ranging in scope from photography to style to dress and to the problem of fakes, the conversation does not assume that the keywords and concepts currently used to write and think about the African archive have been exhausted. Instead, the starting point is that our vocabulary for naming and labelling African photographs should necessarily expand in preparation for the images that are yet to be produced or yet to be found. Without limiting themselves to just the ethnographic and historical photographs, the interlocutors venture into the world of contemporary African photography and the ways in which even contemporary photographers are appropriating the past in order to think through their practice in the present.

This text represents an edited excerpt from the full transcript of an 'In Conversation' round table discussion that took place at the conference 'Curatorial Care: Humanising Practices, Past Presences as Present Encounters' (University of Johannesburg, 11–13 April 2018), which provided a space to reflect, in retrospect, on the exhibition and edited volume, *Distance and Desire: Encounters with the African Archive*, Walther Collection 2013–2014, curated/edited by Tamar Garb with contributions by Cheryl Finley and Hlonipha Mokoena, amongst other writers.

This panel discussion will address the vexed question of the "African" archive. In particular, we want to explore how we can engage with it critically, dialogically and creatively while honouring the specificities that anthropological, ethnographic and portrait photographs possess. We are excited by the challenge of curating this contested archive responsibly and with due "care". How do we interpret and account for the artifices and conventions of the studio, the album and honorific portraiture, all so central to the African archive? And what about the delimiting protocols of mug shots and anthropometric images used to contain, classify and control African subjects? And to whom does the archive belong? These are some of the questions that we would like to engage with at the same time as unravelling the contradictions and complexities out of which this archive is made.

Tamar Garb (TG): Let's start with talking a bit about the Walther Collection, which itself raises all sorts of questions in that it is a European collection of African photographs. Already, in its formation, there are issues to be considered. Where is the collection made? Where does it reside, to whom does it address itself, what is the audience that it imagines? How might it be received in Africa? It's also crucial to understand that the Walther Collection is not only a repository of archival images and historical documents. It's also an ongoing collection that seeks to juxtapose an historical archive of nineteenth- and early-twentieth-century photographs (in albums, prints and books) with contemporary practices. One of the important considerations of the curation of *Distance and Desire* was the decision to use contemporary practices as the filter through which to think about historical questions of representation and the formation of modes, genres, conventions and habits of depiction, mediation and portrayal. This was so crucial for us because we could take our cue from contemporary African artists whose engagement with the archive is so alive and dialogical that it helped us to navigate its sometimes painful and derogatory materials. And the writers and critics that we brought into the project helped us to understand and decode the signification and rhetorical gestures of the imagery. Hlonipha, you were one of those.

Hlonipha Mokoena (HM): My own interest in historical photographs from Southern Africa stemmed from my time at Columbia University when I worked alongside Tina Campt. At that point I was interested in Zulu masculinity and particularly in how Zulu men have been presented in photographs, especially those of African men in the military and in the colonial policing services. It's a strange archive because it doesn't actually exist in any one place. So one of the things that I am interested in is what happens when you don't have a physical archive, and you have to create your own archive, by going to different places and putting together a narrative, sometimes based on stories that seem to have very little to do with each other. Another thing that interests me is the way that the archive *fakes*. Quite a lot of the photographs to be found in the African archives are fake. They are often the product of photographers' fantasies. Take for example the image of Cetshwayo. The majority of the photographs of the last Zulu king show him undressed. He was cajoled and forced to appear in a particular way for the photographs. In fact, many of the subjects that we deal with were asked to dress in a specific way, usually to present a particular ethnicity. In this case it was to present Zuluness in a recognisable way. When you read the biography of the photographer or narratives of the photographic encounter you often read of the refusal of the subject to be an *ethnic other*. So, there are accounts of the Zulu king saying that he didn't want to be photographed like this, or at all. Yet again, there's a constant struggle between an ethnic exoticism and then the refusal of being that ethnic other.

TG: I think that we see this a lot in the photographs that we are dealing with. It's fascinating to explore how people negotiate their subjectivities in multiple, subtle and complex ways through photography, sometime rebelling against clichés and conventions, sometimes mimicking and masquerading in their terms. Being positioned as an African photographic subject required complex performances of identity within the photographic studio.

It's interesting to think about the photograph we used for the poster image of the show in these terms, and also in relation to the idea of care. Here you have two young African girls involved in an act of grooming and quiet intimacy. They project so much more than a superficial portrayal of "African" beauty or exotic display. For their lively expressions and address to the camera is offset by the tactile care that is exchanged between them—the trust, the intimacy, the caress of hand on hair: all of these exceed any exoticising or spectacularising forms of portrayal.

HM: Although, as a poster, when it is enlarged and rendered into a huge public image, something changes. Scale is so important and the small gestures of the everyday become monumental. The poster mediates the photograph and alters it. But that's true too of the objects in the photograph which are so often taken out of their original context. So while care may be thematised here, this may indeed be symptomatic of an act of carelessness. For example when you go to museums, African combs, like the one that you see in this picture, are so often separated from their actual site or function. In my own research I look at this often in relation to African sticks and weapons which were designed to be used or held in a certain way but get distorted and misused in photographs where they serve as ethnic signifiers designed to stand for a generic Africanness without due care to context, authenticity or truth.

TG: They function as props used to furnish a costume drama designed for the studio or photographic sitting. It's interesting to think about the notion of care in relation to things and images and how they circulate. I like to think of care as a mode of attention. To care for is to attend to, to pay attention to the specificity of something or someone. It can never be generic. This means reading clues and signs attentively so as not to misrepresent or misconstrue something or someone. This kind of attention to detail is what we learn from art history—a kind of careful looking and scrutinising of visual signs and clues. This is not only important for understanding what we are looking at, it also provides protection against weaponising images or objects, making them serve our own political or ideological agendas.

There's also a lot of care entailed in making selections and in using images responsibly. This was a real issue with the Walther Collection where we had to make certain difficult choices. I was absolutely determined that we would have a range of representations of Africa and Africans and that we would show the diversity and richness of photographic image making, beyond the stereotypical, for example of the stick wielding Zulu warrior or the Zulu mother with her baby strapped to her back, each of which became a representational trope that was endlessly repeated in colonial times. Of course, we included images of this type and these recycled tropes appeared in multiple images and repeated and reproduced standard representations of Africans. But it was important to look for ways of complicating or undermining them, and of drawing on contemporary art that exposed and deflated their assumptions.

One of the challenging and fascinating bits of the collection are those images produced by Alfred Martin Duggan-Cronin, who was a Kimberley-based Irish photographer, who worked for de Beers but devoted decades to documenting what he saw as the vanishing "Bantu tribes" of South Africa. Duggan-Cronin was an expert at props and accessories and he had his own travelling costume box that he would take with him on his travels when he was looking for "authentic" subjects to photograph. During a time of rapid modernisation and urbanisation, Duggan-Cronin feared that a truly African way of life was disappearing, but at the same time he manufactured his notion of pure, timeless Africanness through the objects that he used to compose his shots and the costumes that he used to guarantee the "authenticity" of his figures: skins, sticks, beads, clay pots and baskets abound in his images, his figural groups often composed against vast vistas of open landscape, occasionally dotted with huts and traditional structures. There is no sign of modernisation or urbanisation in his pictures or of the complicated and multiple identities that people inhabit in transforming times. It's easy now to unpack these romantic and idealised images and to see them as packaging a nostalgic fantasy of a receding past. But at the same time, for many contemporary African viewers they do affirm something noble and strong. One of their most passionate admirers for example was Nelson Mandela who went to the Duggan-Cronin Museum in Kimberley and defended them strongly as icons of a proud African subjectivity.

It's important as curators to take care to honour the complexity of different responses, to ask questions rather than to tell people how or what to think. Rather than write didactic and censorious captions at the Walther Collection, we wanted to open up various possibilities for thinking with the images. This involved showing them in many juxtapositions and iterations: as vintage prints framed on the wall, as pages from the books in which they originally appeared under the title *The Bantu Tribes of South Africa* and as "illustrations", wrapped in ethnographic commentary and anthropological verbiage. All of this provides context for shifting and contingent meaning. Photographs are so malleable and changeable—they are made to be reproduced and reprinted and each time you do this, their meanings can change in subtle and interesting ways.

HM: Yes, but it's interesting too to think about how Duggan-Cronin engaged in his own kind of insidious intrusion and invasion of space because when you look through his thousands of images you see that he wasn't a perfect photographer. There are some photographs, for example, where you see his shadow in the image, lurking and intruding into the space. He was also very keen to enhance his own profile and one of the things that he did was to send his printed volumes to different universities. So nearly every university in South Africa that is over a hundred years old has a Duggan-Cronin original copy of one or more of his 11 volumes somewhere in their archive. But the tragic thing is that our archives are in such a mess that many of these universities don't actually know where the Duggan-Cronin volumes are. At some point someone may have taken them off the shelves and left them in a cupboard somewhere and then they disappeared from sight. It's so ironic. African photographs have achieved a certain market value internationally. The Duggan-Cronin volumes are now collectors' items in Europe and North America but when they are here on the African continent many of these photographs tend to meet some kind of tragic end and disappear without trace. We have to care for our things more diligently.

TG: That's true. The photographs and the volumes allow us to tell complex stories about the past. You see this too from understanding the circumstances in which the pictures were taken. Duggan-Cronin of course employed his own assistant, who functioned as his "native informant". This was a man called Richard Madela who spoke local languages and could communicate with the sitters. He was also a photographer and he travelled with Duggan-Cronin and helped dress people up in "authentic" costume which came out of the dressing-up box that they took with them on the road. There are some fantastic photographs that show Duggan-Cronin and Madela in the rural areas alongside their portrait subjects dressed in all manner of costume combinations, amalgamating modern, traditional and hybrid forms. But the photographers set out to "re-Africanise" them and "re-authenticate" them as typical representatives of the specific tribal groups that feature in *The Bantu Tribes of South Africa*. But in the Duggan-Cronin Museum in Kimberley there are also many, many photographs that didn't make it into the edited volumes. Amongst these are the "failures", the ones where Duggan-Cronin's own shadow intrudes, or where Madela is shown to be mediating the shot, or where the integrity of the "tribal" illusion breaks down through the incursions of modernity: the presence of a car, the visibility of the camera, the lack of coherence in costume, the curiosity of onlookers etc.

HM: I also want to mention the photography of children in this context. One of Madela's jobs was to distract the children while Duggan-Cronin tried to get a good shot. So there is a photograph of one of the Batswana Chiefs when he was a small child and Duggan-Cronin relates that this photograph would not have been taken if he had not had the child being distracted by the assistant. I think that, the photographing of children used to present a particular problem/challenge in the colonial archive. How do you get children to sit still and embody an ethnic or tribal identity or type? The photographs present them as coherent entities, distillations of an essence or ethnicity. But of course, we know how artificial this is since in reality there must have been a lot of motion and disruption going on in the space while the photographs were taken. We see this from some of the pictures of "Zulu mothers" whose bodies served a whole series of cultural projections but whose role also stretched to keeping the children in tow so that they could pose and perform for the camera.

TG: All of these things were in our minds when we were thinking about how best to show the Duggan-Cronin photographs. We were determined to both show the quality of the photographs (and the vintage prints are so exquisite and refined) but also the way they are mediated and transformed alongside print and captions. It's easy just to think of them as compromised by the colonial narrative, but when you look at the images as portraits, in many of them you also get a sense of the sentience and inner life of the subjects, something that anthropological classification is not concerned with. So they do also exceed that instrumentalised mobilisation and we wanted to show that. What helped us to bring out the complexity of our relationship to this archive was through the lens of contemporary practice.

From the start we thought about setting up a dialogue between the Duggan-Cronin images and Santu Mofokeng's *Black Photo Album*. This happened in the installation so that while you were looking at the Duggan-Cronins you could always, out of the corner of your eye, see the Mofokeng project, and vice versa. Mofokeng's "album" is made up of different components: a slide show of re-photographed vintage prints, digital prints shown on the walls of the original photographs he has collected, and the old photographs themselves that form the basis of his collection and its offshoots. In the 1990s, Mofokeng started to collect photographs that appear as a corrective to the images that present Africans as part of the "flora and fauna" of the land. Instead Mofokeng amassed images of Africans dressed in their Sunday best for the portrait studio. Such items are stored and kept by families throughout the world, and Africans, like everyone else in the modern, industrialised world where cameras exist and makeshift studios appear, had themselves photographed for posterity. So, instead of a long piece of text on the wall explaining all of this, we took care to design the installation so that the Mofokeng collection provides a visual challenge to the Duggan-Cronins, opening up their underlying principles and assumptions to question. We also managed to make a showcase in which we included Mofokeng's notes that make allusion to Duggan-Cronin and his way of photographing Africans, showing these alongside the salvaged vintage prints kept by families.

So there is an actual dialogue that is going on between contemporary practice and the anthropological archive in order to mediate it and in order to offer a rejoinder to it by showing a different side of popular image making.

One of the important points we wanted to communicate is that at the very same moment that Africans were being frozen in time in their fabricated "traditional" costumes, many of them were also wanting to be seen in their Edwardian or Victorian attire. Mofokeng's whole project is about looking at the ways in which urban, and aspirant families across socio-economic groups and amongst upwardly mobile families across South Africa, many of whom were Christianised, used the studio as an arena through which to perform different notions of the self so that one could be more than one thing at once. Photography allows this of course. Anything is possible in the studio. In fact what you, Hlonipha, pointed out to me when we were standing together in the exhibition some years ago, is that these could be the very same people who appear in one instance in "tribal" regalia, and in another in Western glad-rags. Skins and spears were no more authentic than hats and gloves. You talked about the fluidity with which people can mobilise different kinds of sartorial signifier and the many different personae that people could project through costume, demeanour and gesture.

HM: Absolutely. I think this relates to what I call, the "black stylistic" which has to do with the way in which black people choose to style themselves for the photographer as well as for themselves. For example, the archives contain many stories about Zulu weddings, including details of what people wore, how many pearls they had on etc.—so how do you square that with the pressure to speak to a particular ethnic or cultural identity, when really it's about you having the joyous experience of being photographed or dressing up..? We no longer talk about the concept of "Sunday best", but this was something very valuable to our grandparents and our great grandparents. You know that there are certain clothes that you don't wear when you want to present a particular kind of image—projecting respectability and upward mobility was so important to them. Also, it's so important to remember that there are different kinds of families. People don't all have to be related to each other to be a family. This is one of the things we often have a difficulty with. In my own family, we have a family photograph in which half of the people in it aren't blood relatives, but they are in the picture because they grew up with us and so on … I'm interested in the affective bonds that glue people together in photographs and so often this is symbolised by how people dress, whether it manifests anxiety or joy or both.

TG: I think it's interesting to think about these things in relation to the notion of care. We have already hinted at the issue of embodiment and pleasure and the kind of knowledge of self and other that comes from intimate exchange and communities of proximity, of touching, of shared costume and custom. The abstract Cartesian models of knowledge production and exchange really downplay the bodily. It's all in the mind and what gets lost is that so much of our knowledge of being and belonging in the world is gained through our bodies, through gesture and expressions that are pre-linguistic and visceral—laughter, tears, facial expressions—alongside all the symbolisation and sophisticated language that we learn. The photographic studio is a place where all of this can come into play. It's a place for the projection of a configured self, but it's also a space in which that can break down and different kinds of embodied knowledge can be conveyed through touch and gesture and expression. You see this in so many of the pictures that Mofokeng salvaged and reproduced. He frames his scanned slides with all sorts of metatextual questions about the gaze and colonial power relations, but built into the pictures themselves are already questions and conundrums about the performance of self, power and proximity.

HM: Yes, it's important to take on board how complex and contradictory these historical photographs are. For example, in one of the images, a man appears to be wearing riding breeches thus prompting people to wonder if Africans actually rode horses. That leaves one reeling. Why should you assume they didn't is what I think? You know if there were horses available then obviously Africans rode, just like anyone else. Sandra Klopper has written a fascinating article about these photographs. Mangosuthu Buthelezi, for example, was quite an avid horse rider when he was a young man. I think several Zulu Kings have been photographed in their riding breeches and yet people assume that Zulus don't or can't ride. So some of these photographs actually show people as they were really dressed, and not in some kind of fantasy dress up scenario. And Zulu horsemen is one such a possibility that we see here.

TG: So Hlonipha, you have written a lot and thought a lot about the way in which the Zulu king Cetshwayo is depicted in photographs. In some of the albums that Arthur Walther collected, which we displayed opened up so that you could see them page by page, you see him on a boat, semi-naked; behind him is a tyre. Can you explain a bit about how this came to be?

HM: Yes, he's posed in front of a rescue buoy with the words "SS Natal" printed on it. This is the name of the ship that transported him from the southeast coast of South Africa to his exile in Cape Town. When the Zulus fought the British in 1879 and defeated them there was a rush for Zulu photos or photographs of Zulu people. Because all of a sudden there was a need for the British to understand who these people who had defeated them were. There is even an interesting case that implicates the London Stereoscopic Company in all of this—coincidently the same agency associated with a majority of the Victorian photographs unearthed by Autograph—including those of 'The African Choir'—during 'The Missing Chapter' archive research programme and displayed in 'Black Chronicles II and IV' curated by Renée Mussai. In this case, the Lord Mayor of London issued an order of cease and desist against a shopkeeper who displayed photographs of Zulus in his window and the case brought out the whole photographic community of London. When the order was issued, the Lord Mayor imagined it would be just him and the shopkeeper standing accused of violating London's by-laws by displaying pornography on the windows. On the day of the hearing, the Lord Mayor was surprised to walk into a court room filled with photographers and photographic companies, who all appeared as "friends of the court". In defence of the shopkeeper, they insisted that the images were not pornographic at all and that they represented the Zulus in their "natural state". It was a test case for ethnographic photography since those who had a vested interest in the business presented evidence to support their claims that the pictures displayed in the shop window presented the quintessence of being Africans. All sorts of colonial adventurers and journalists were called to testify to the fact that this is how Africans actually dress and that therefore the "nudity" in the photographs is justifiable. The "friends of the court" went so far as to state that if the photographs had been of English people, instead of Zulus in South Africa, then of course they would be pornographic. The entire transcript of the trial was printed in *The British Journal of Photography* and it was also in the same journal that the editors exuberantly welcomed the publication of photographs of Cetshwayo. Up until that point, the only images of the Zulu monarch that the British public had seen were the efforts of illustrators to capture his appearance. In the editors' exultant notice, photography is praised for making available the true countenance of the Zulu king. On the other hand, if you then read the account of the photographer who took Cetshwayo's photographs, it's a totally different story. The photographer reveals the tricks he had to perform to persuade the king to undress. The final photographs, which received so much praise for *The British Journal of Photography* are therefore not what Cetshwayo wanted. He was not happy to be photographed semi-naked. And he additionally didn't want to be photographed with his wives. The funny part is that even though it was pre-Photoshop days, Cetshwayo actually told the photographer that he would not sit with his wives and instructed him to combine the two separate images, the group photo of his wives and his own image. Problem solved. So Cetshwayo was anticipating the emergence of Photoshop by saying "just photoshop me into the photo" and thereby refusing to play the part of the polygamous Zulu patriarch. As a consequence there are only photographs of his wives or of the king, never both. It's actually because he purposefully refused his photograph to be taken with his wives; and this is despite all the trying and bribing by the photographers. Yet Cetshwayo would receive the photographers' gifts and give them to his wives. In one of the accounts Cetshwayo's wives are given an accordion which they play the whole night thus keeping him awake. In the morning, he was so annoyed he pretty much told the photographer to "take the damn photograph".

TG: These photographs of the semi-naked King are so different from the ones that he had taken in London when he went on his deputation to see Queen Victoria as an attempt to demand that the British return the Zulu Kingdom to the Zulus. This failed but it did produce some fascinating images.

HG: I have a funny anecdote about this picture. When I was young my grandparents used to make a joke about what would happen to us if we didn't wear shoes. They said we'd be like Cetshwayo! Apparently when they travelled to England they couldn't find a shoe size big enough for the King so even though he is wearing his suit he's actually probably barefoot! As I said, I know about this because it was a joke amongst our grandparents that if you don't wear your shoes then your feet would expand and there wouldn't be a shoe size for you.

TG: It's interesting to think of this alongside the images of the Zulu mother, another recurring trope of the African archive. We showed different versions of this in *Distance and Desire* and had about 10 variations of one photo sitting showing Zulu women with their babies strapped to their backs. Chris Geary wrote a wonderful essay about these for our catalogue. It was important to show these as bits of material culture, cards intact with stamps and inscriptions, sometimes commenting on the images in objectionable and demeaning ways, sometimes just inserting a personal greeting over the card. This was such an important instance of the way that textual accompaniment mediates how images are read, as do their supports and physical or material properties. So these are not only interesting as icons that produce certain recurring features (the "natural" mother, the impoverished child, the "primitive pair", for example); they are also things that have a life in the world as tokens of exchange or gifts or mementos. And having so many of them in all their variations (of colouring, tone, inscription) helped us to make a point about replication, recycling and repetition. But some clever detective work done by Chris Geary also uncovered some related images (photographs?) of the children alone, which we were able to use as a space of speculation about the role of the mothers as carers and participants in the curation of their own image, not only as passive cyphers for the projections of others.

HM: Yes, it's also important to see the African archive as a site of experimentation, technically and formally as well as performatively. Editing and re-editing was such a crucial part of the picture (the picture-taking process?). There were no digital images so African subjects become edited over and over again. Another instance of this is the photograph of the "Zulu Dandy" who appears in East and West Africa as well.

TG: And the captions have lives of their own. They are appended in sometimes arbitrary ways. For example, you could just get an image of a standing man and the caption would read, "Zulu Dandy" or a reclining female figure who would be labelled "African Cleopatra" or a woman with a baby who is called "Zulu Mother" irrespective of what community or ethnicity they actually represent. And who knows if they are mothers at all, or carers of another kind. The fact is that this is how they come to signify in the African Archive. I wrote a lot about this in the catalogue in relation to the incredible collection of *cartes-de-visite* that we showed. On close scrutiny of the cards and their inscriptions on the backs, I saw that the same models were labelled as representatives of completely different ethnic groups and that familiar categories (Hottentot Venus or Zulu Warrior, for example) were used by the card's early collectors to describe predicable figural groupings. Zanele Muholi brilliantly addresses some of the pictorial conventions of "Zuluness" and particularly the gendered assumptions that underpin them in their figure studies. These wilfully undermine the stereotypes that the archival images convey. Showing them alongside the archival images exposed their mythic and recycled assumptions. In *Distance and Desire*, the contemporary work functioned as a series of propositions about how one can interpret this archive and live with it, acknowledging its problems but without being oppressed and silenced by it. Carrie May Weems superimposed her own texts on anthropometric shots taken from the archives of slavery in order to overwrite them with questions. In the installation of the exhibition at the Walther Collection headquarters in Ulm, they confronted the viewer as one entered the contemporary space, creating a kind of filter through which to look at the historical work. You didn't need long wall texts and didactic or prescriptive instructions. The contemporary art showed the way of living with vexed and compromised archives in dialogical and subversive ways. Another work that did this so beautifully was Berni Searle's *Snow White*, a video work in which the artist herself seems to suggest the way that brown female bodies carry the weight of domestic and allegorical labour—Searle is seen crouching and kneading dough, while a cascade of white flower and then trickles of water descend onto her naked skin, invoking both the baking and breaking of bread as well as representational conventions and norms. Another artist who deals with the inter-weaving of past and present is Sabelo Mlangeni and we showed his documentary photo essay on young women who return to the rural areas for annual initiation and coming of age ceremonies, donning "traditional" dress but still bearing the imprint on their bodies (through tan stripes, jewellery, and hair dos) that register their simultaneous urban and metropolitan lives. Mlangeni's images have all sorts of formal synergies with Duggan-Cronin's but instead of censoring out the signs of the modern, they embrace them as charged references to the multiple and contradictory lives of the contemporary.

HM: I think the complexity of these photographs is really important. We cannot shy away from that. Firstly, our visual past needs rescuing. As curators we salvage the remnants of the past, but then also, we are called in to interpret things and to excavate histories and narratives. Our job is to offer commentary on how historical images may be read, both in the past and in the present, and so curating from my perspective is really about a long engagement, a kind of attention to the ways in which you can pull an object or a photograph apart and offer multiple and competing interpretations—that you need to justify and defend. What I've learnt from working in the first place with the Walther Collection, and then on other exhibitions with some of the same artists (for example Sabelo Mlangeni and Zanele Muholi) is that attentiveness to the connectivities that underpin the African archive doesn't make us better curators necessarily, but it does make us better and more nuanced thinkers. We deal with the remnants of the past but we also have to engage with the photographs that have not yet been found, the contested traces of the past that might be hidden or destroyed. So, the work that you do with the photographs that are in front of you is partly a preparation for the photographs you haven't seen. For what's to come. Care in curating might just be about being prepared for an imagined future through searching the archives of the past (Figures 1 and 2).

Disclosure statement

No potential conflict of interest was reported by the authors.

ORCID

Hlonipha Mokoena http://orcid.org/0000-0002-1359-9345

Index

Note: Tables are indicated by **bold**. Endnotes are indicated by the page number followed by 'n' and the endnote number e.g., 20n1 refers to endnote 1 on page 20.

Acholonlu, C. 3
Africa's state-centric development approach 92
African archive: anthropometric images 274; black stylistic 279; complexities 275–6; historical photographs 280; images 276; passive cyphers 282; photographer 281; photographs 275, 277–8, 281, 283; poster mediates 276; traditional costumes 279; Walther Collection 276, 277
African diaspora: cultural identity/cultural diversity 169; democratisation/media 170–1; globalisation 167, 172–4; identities 174–7; model of analysis 168; twenty-first century technology 178
African feminist theorisation: conceptualisation and target 52–3; cultural imperialism 47; inclusion vs. exclusion 49–52; indigenous feminist models 48; Nigerian feminisms 48, 49; resolutions 54–5; social cohesion 48; womanism 48
African Global South: activist cultural studies 22–5, 29; African variants 22; area studies 21; cryptocurrencies 28; electronic gaming environment 27; encoding/decoding model 26; ISIS's one-dimensional ideology 29; materialities 25, 26, 28; North–South linear dichotomy 22; stock exchanges 28
African-centred methodology 4
Africanfuturism comics: African languages/ metonymic gap 155–6; Afrofuturism 152–4; Black diaspora 151; Egungun 158–60; global Blackness 150; intertextuality 156–7; Shuri 154–5, 161
Afrocentrism 4
Afrofuturistic theory, Wakandan: African utopia 132; antagonism 147; Black Panther 133; Dora Milaje 138–40; empowering epistemology 135; European anthropological scholarship 145; gender roles 146; methodology 136–7; post-human world 135; queen mother 141–2; results 137; technological division 140–1; technological inventions 144; tribal council positions 137–8; war dog, Nakia 142–4; Womanism 133–5
Afrofuturuism 3
Afropessimism: Aristide 91; British justifications 89; continent 88, 90; Critical Arts 87, 93; dark continent 96; democracy 92, 93; development/socio-cultural analysis 87; forms of discourse 94; HIV/AIDS 95; language 89; perspectives **88**; political/economical system 90; social capital 93; triple articulation 95
Agbaje, F. I. 145
Ahmed, S. 14
Allison, C. 198
Althusser, A. 232, 242
Amadiume, I. 145, 148
Amin, S. 40
Anim-Addo, J. 70
Arseneault, J. 11
Asante, M. 34
Astroff, R. J. 237

Bakhtin, M. 60
Barthes, R. 201
Barthes, R. 71, 78, 81n4
Bassil, N. R. 96
Bauman, Z. 40
Bennett, T. 5, 268
Berger, G. 232, 233, 244
Bernabé, J. 77, 81
Bhabha, H. K. 78, 82n12
black English as a second language (BESL): rap linguistic styles 207–8; sites/sides 206–7
black stylised English (BSE) 204
Boyce-Davies, C. 70
Brah, A. 18
Brathwaite, E. K. 71–3, 81
Brathwaite, K. 69
Braude, C. 232, 243
Breward, C. 78
Brown Givens, S. M. 135
Burke, E. 106

Butler, J. 201, 205
Byfield, J. 216

carnivalising theory 71
Casti, J. 239
centre for communication media and society (CCMS) 24
centre for contemporary cultural studies (CCCS) 35
Chadya, J. 67
Chapman, M. 251
Checinska, C. 69
Chenoune, F. 78
Chitando, E. 59
Chitauro, M. 58, 59
Christian, B. 267
Connor, S. 35
contemporary cultural studies (CCCS) 4
contemporary orientations: Afrofuturism 14, 17; Afropessimism 15; Afropolitanism 16; born free generation of South Africa 13; cultural forms and genres 12; face work 17; floating signifier 16; genealogies 11, 18; intra-and inter-continental movements 14; knowledge capitalism 15; planetary electronic commons 16; postcolonial and globalisation studies 13; precolonial art 13; race talk 17; signalling 12; snapshot 12; tradition and modernity 13
Cooper. B. 257n4
Copeland, T. T. 132
Cornut-Gentille D'arcy, C. 39
Craik, J. 82n14
creolised African Caribbean self-fashioning: better cloaths 74; Caribbean language 73; creolisation 72; cultural expressions 72; fashioning and refashioning identities 81; French Revolution 80; Haitian Revolution 77–80; Nation Language 73, 75; plantations 77; regional aesthetics 75; spiritual powers 76; uneven power dynamic 71
cultural analysis method: colonial/anti-colonial antagonisms 251; constitutional negotiation 253; cultural translation 254; ever-sceptical intellectual 256; modem Calvinist 256; post-Cold War 253, 257; post-colonial approach 252, 253; poststructuralist preoccupation 255; pre-global times 254; socialist class analysis 251
Curtin, P. D. 108

D'Adamo, S.
dark continent: Africa ancient attitudes 98–100; Black Africa/Britain, European expansion 103–5; black Africans 98; British discourse 110; colonialism 96, 97; European exploration, black Africa 100–2; racism 96, 107–9; slavery/abolitionism 105–7; trans-Atlantic slave 96

Davis, D. B. 107
de B'béri, B. E. 87
de la Beche, H. 76
Dery, M. 3
diaspora identity, African: complexity 188–9, 198; continental African identity 192–4; émigré intellectual 197; Ethiopia 196, 197; issues 190–2
diasporic blacks: aesthetic movements 216; artists 216; cultural imagining/productions 217–18; historical movements 216; imaginative rediscovery 218–19; museum for African art 219–21; national museum, African art 222–5; producers/consumers 215
Diawara, M. 266
Dijk, V. 236, 246n18
Dippo, D. 212n3
Drake, St. C.
Drescher, S. 107
Dube, C. 58, 59

Ede, A. 16
Equiano, O. 75
Evans, M. 112
Ezeigbo, A. 52

Fair, E. J. 237
Fall, N. 62
Fanon, F. 189
Farmer, P. 91
female body, audio-visual propaganda: choir 59; cultural nationalism 59; jingles/choir/mothering, Zimbabwean nation 61; male-dominated national liberation movement 67; masculinist nationalist project 60; motherhood, ambivalences 66–7; objectification/metaphorisation 61–3; political music 58; propagandistic jingles/carnivalesque 65–6; women as symbolic reproducers 63–5
floating signifier: autobiographical approach 32, 33; issues 39–40, 41; national/regional/transnational forms 37–9; origin(s)/global spread of cultural studies 35–6; politics 41; unpacking and multiplying studies 33–5; utilitarian approach 39–40
Flugel, J. C. 78
Foucault, M. 32, 41

Gallop, J. 262
Garb, T. 274
Garvey movement: colonialism 181; degradation 180; impact 186; imperial remapping 179; Pan-Africanism 181–4; philosophy and praxis 184–5; solidarity 179; UN resolution 180
Gilroy, P. 244, 264, 266
Glissant, E. 71, 72, 81
Goldberg, D. T. 241, 244
Gramsci, A. 242

Gray, A. 262
Gripsrud, J. 192, 264
Grossberg, L. 262
Gunner, L. 58, 59

Haack, S. 237
Hall, S. 4, 33, 36, 65, 167, 218, 260, 266
Harris, A. 132
Harris, M. 223
Hartley, J. 39
Hassim, S. 63
Herr, R. S. 61, 67
Hodappm, J. 150
Hudson-Weems, C. 51

Ibrahim, A. 49, 200
institutional ethnography (IE) 269
Islamic State of Iraq and the Levant (ISIL) 39

Jacobs, S 246n22
Jaffer, F. 42n10
Jay, G. 262, 269
Johnson, L. 189
Johnson, R. 5
Julien, I. 268

Kincheloe, J. 268
Kittay, E. 63
Kolawole, M. 50

Laclau, E. 33
lesbian, gay, bisexual, transgender and intersex (LGBTI) women 54
Levi-Strauss, C. 33
Lewis, B. 96
Lewis, R. 179
Long, E. 76
Lorimer, D. A. 107, 109
Louw, P. E. 87

Majors, R. 76
Malan, C. 240
Mancini Billson, J. 76
Mashigo, M. 3
Masilela, T. 230, 231
mass democratic movement (MDM) 23
Masuku, T. 246n22
Maxwell, R. 36
Mbembe, A. 61, 66
Mboti, N. 5
McClintock, A. 59, 67
McWatt, M. 81n1
Mercer, K. 198
Minh-Ha, T. 268
Mokoena, H. 274
Monahan, J. L. 135
Morris, M. 5, 35, 259, 264
Moten, F. 15
Moyo, D. 93

Mudimbe, V. Y. 217
Murray, S. 3
Mutekwa, A. 58
Muteshi, J. K. 215

Ngoshi, H. T. 58
Ngugi's Marxism 38
Nietzsche, F. 203
Nkealah, N. 47
Nnaemeka, O. 52
North America, African body: act of being and becoming 201, 202; blackness 200; gaze 203; hybrid African identity **208–12**; normalisation/naturalisation 201; officially declared black 202–3; research 204–6
North–South linear dichotomy 22
Nuttall, S. 16

O'Connor, A. 42n3
Ogundipe-Leslie, M. 50
Ogunyemi, C. 51
Okediji, M. 218, 223
Okorafor, N. 3
Oyewumi, O. 145

Pachmanová, M. 62
Pakenham, T. 109
Phillip, N. 220
political activist ethnography (PAE) 269
Powell, R. 216, 222
psycho-babble: cultural policy 229; dynamic justice 233–5; faultlines 241; media monitoring/discourse analysis 239–40; media research 235–8; policy-oriented analysis 245; racism and gender, methodologies 241–3; SAHRC's 232–3, 244; socio-political transformation 234–5; spin doctoring 238; state's research 230; textual signification 240; transporting method 230–1
Roscoe, W. 3
Rotimi, O. 189

Safran, W. 216
Said, E. 32
Salvodon, M. 218
Sere, S. 132
Simon, R. 212n3
Smith, D. 269
Smith, M. 42n10
social justice praxis: academic work 265–6; black ambivalent elaboration 266–7; cultural studies 262–3, 269; cultural studies/education 267–8, 270; engendering cultural studies 268–9; identity/experience/cultural studies 263–5; inter/anti/post/disciplinary approach 259; path less travelled, seeking 260–2; service learning 269
Sofola, Z. 133

South African Afropessimism online: commentators 118; controversial site 118; *Death of Johannesburg* 121, 122; farm attacks 120; farm murder 115, 116; forums 113; HIV/AIDS 116, 117; homecoming revolution 124–6; homesick remedies 121–4; Internet 119, 127; marginalisation 120; new media technologies 115; news networks 112; online expatriate responses 114; social crises 113; social networking sites 114, 115; YouTube polices 117
South African Human Rights Commission (Sahrc) 232
South African Police Service (SAPS) 116, 117
Soyinka, W. 34
Spencer, R. C. 133
Spies, D. 118
Spivak, G. C. 33
Steinberg, S. 268
Stewart, G. 245n9
Steyn, A. 257n4

Strauss, H. 1
Stuart Hall's encoding/decoding model 21
stylin: carnivalising theory 70–1; great masculine enunciation 70; transformative act 69

Tomaselli, K. G. 1, 21, 229
Tosh, P. 189
transnational theory 21
transvaal agricultural union (TAU) 116
Turley, D. 107

Wark, M. 38
(West) African feminisms *see* African feminist theorisation
Williams, J. 245
Williams, R. 267
Wright, H. K. 1, 5, 11, 19, 32, 188, 259

Zimbabwe African National Union-Patriotic Front (ZANU-PF) 59
Zuberi, N. 189

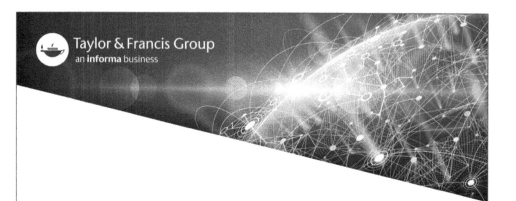

Taylor & Francis eBooks

www.taylorfrancis.com

A single destination for eBooks from Taylor & Francis with increased functionality and an improved user experience to meet the needs of our customers.

90,000+ eBooks of award-winning academic content in Humanities, Social Science, Science, Technology, Engineering, and Medical written by a global network of editors and authors.

TAYLOR & FRANCIS EBOOKS OFFERS:

- A streamlined experience for our library customers
- A single point of discovery for all of our eBook content
- Improved search and discovery of content at both book and chapter level

REQUEST A FREE TRIAL
support@taylorfrancis.com

www.ingramcontent.com/pod-product-compliance
Ingram Content Group UK Ltd.
Pitfield, Milton Keynes, MK11 3LW, UK
UKHW050606020125
452764UK00024BA/90